COMPOSITIONS *in*
ARCHITECTURE

COMPOSITIONS *in* ARCHITECTURE

Don Hanlon

John Wiley & Sons, Inc.

For Michelle

Published by John Wiley & Sons, Inc., Hoboken, New Jersey

Published simultaneously in Canada

For general information about our other products and services, please contact our Customer Care Department within the United States at (800) 762-2974, outside the United States at (317) 572-3993 or fax (317) 572-4002.

Wiley also publishes its books in a variety of electronic formats. Some content that appears in print may not be available in electronic books. For more information about Wiley products, visit our web site at www.wiley.com.

Library of Congress Cataloging-in-Publication Data:

Hanlon, Donald Livingston.
    Compositions in architecture / by Don Hanlon.
        p. cm.
    Includes bibliographical references.
    ISBN 978-0-470-05364-5 (pbk.)
1. Architectural design. 2. Architecture--Composition, proportion, etc. I. Title.
    NA2750.H28 2009
    720--dc22

                                        2008039321

Printed in the United States of America

10 9 8 7 6 5 4 3 2 1

CONTENTS

PREFACE   vii

INTRODUCTION   1

CHAPTER ONE
FIVE FORMAL PROPERTIES
OF A COMPOSITION   3

CHAPTER TWO
NOTES ON THE PLAN   21

CHAPTER THREE
TYPE   29

CHAPTER FOUR
THE SQUARE   53

CHAPTER FIVE
LAYERING   79

CHAPTER SIX
LINEAR FORMS   110

CHAPTER SEVEN
CORE AND SHELL   141

CHAPTER EIGHT
FRAME AND OBJECT   157

CHAPTER NINE
CLUSTERS 178

CHAPTER TEN
SUBTRACTIVE SPACES
AND THE DEEP WALL 242

CHAPTER ELEVEN
ARTICULATED SKIN 258

CHAPTER TWELVE
METAMORPHOSIS 280

CHAPTER THIRTEEN
DEFORMATION 291

CONCLUSION 318

GLOSSARY 319

BIBLIOGRAPHY 321

INDEX OF BUILDINGS 325

PREFACE

This book has emerged from a method I have used to help students clarify and focus
their work in design. Underlying all of my analyses of architectural precedents is a
search for relationships among them, patterns of composition. While I am interested in the unique qualities of an architectural work, I am also interested in how
designers share, borrow, and interpret architectural ideas. Sometimes this is overt,
one design clearly derived from another. However, what is more interesting is how
designers produce similar solutions without an obvious historical or cultural connection between them. This suggests an underlying logic of form that architects
discover through the act of design.

The projects in this book are a collection of my work over many years, a com-
pendium of analytical problems. I have maintained a freehand style of drawing
because it places an interesting constraint on how I shape and convey information.
Due to its rough character, freehand drawing encourages simplicity and directness,
and it maintains a personal, intimate relation with the subject. I have learned that
the act of drawing by hand is a way of thinking; it is not merely representation.

Though not ideological, the work presented here suggests a particular analytical
approach to design. Since my interest in architecture is broadly inclusive, I am providing a variety of points of view in the book without a strong theoretical bias. This,
I hope, will make it a practical resource that students can use to find their own way
in design.

INTRODUCTION

THIS IS A WORK OF INTERPRETATION. IT IS A COLLECTION OF ARCHITEC-
tural compositions that I have found interesting and useful. I do not
claim that this is a comprehensive view of composition in architecture; it
is, in fact, selective. I am interested in describing the characteristics of composition
rather than defining types of composition, so the book is not meant to be a taxonomy of building types or an architectural encyclopedia; it identifies tendencies, not
categories, of composition. As a guide for general compositional techniques in architecture, I hope it becomes a useful resource for instructors and architectural design
students at any level, in studios and in seminars devoted to theories of form. It
demonstrates how the analysis of precedents, whether ancient or contemporary, provides basic organizational strategies for design, and it illustrates a research method
that can reveal these strategies.

The book also illustrates the power and universality of simple ideas. Contemporary students of architecture tend to assume that the dramatic technological
advances of the recent past and the present place them in an entirely different world
of ideas than the one of their predecessors. I would argue that despite differences in
appearance and in methods of construction, at the conceptual level of composition
little has changed over thousands of years of formal exploration.

Since the book is nonlinear, the reader is free to read it in any order or simply to use
it as a reference. One can read it graphically or read the captions of the illustrations as a
kind of open-ended narrative. The analytical diagrams and their captions reveal underlying patterns of organization that may not be readily discernable in the building as a
whole or even in its plan. These studies also reveal surprising relations between disparate
examples, illustrating how architects separated by geographical, historical, and cultural
distance nevertheless solve similar problems in similar ways. Whereas the drawings and
their captions concentrate on specific subjects, the introductory text for each section is
comparative and explores various ways a compositional method may be used.

Being of an eclectic nature, I have collected examples from a wide range of
sources. Subjects for analysis include designs from diverse cultures and historical
periods without prejudice. My principal motivation in choosing these particular
subjects—some famous, many not well known, some even obscure—is to demonstrate different interpretations of similar ideas. My premise is that meanings in
architecture and urban design are both global and local, that they combine universal compositional strategies with the particular physical and cultural conditions of
the moment. Though each example has a unique meaning, it is their collective
meanings, the ways in which they relate to patterns that cut across the boundaries of
history and geography, that fascinate me.

For most of human civilization, architecture has been the preeminent feature of material culture; so much of the meaning that architectural or urban composition conveys is specific to its time and place. However, the more we study the forms created by diverse cultures, the clearer it is that despite variations in meaning they share underlying patterns of organization, that there are relatively few basic compositional strategies, and what initially appears to be new is actually a variant of a widely utilized theme. Often these themes are not readily apparent and require analysis to reveal them. I use two techniques in my analyses. The first is to discern common patterns among numerous examples. The second is to investigate a single example in greater depth to reveal the various patterns nested within it.

I admit to a bias for the plan. It is usually the key diagram, because it establishes the underlying logic for a building and reveals much of how the architect was thinking through the process of design. Buildings are extremely complex phenomena, and there are certainly many other ways to explore the meanings of the projects included in this book. However, the use of the plan as the primary analytical tool produces a relatively accessible study that is useful for designers in many ways. I consider the result descriptive, not prescriptive. Since the general headings I use are merely for convenience, the reader could study many of the examples under several of the headings for a variety of reasons. I leave it to the reader to discover these relationships through an exploration of the book as a whole.

Underlying my view of architectural composition is a lifelong fascination with forms found in nature. I don't mean an organic theory, but rather an interest in the patterns we find in the organization of energy, manifested in matter, as we observe it in nature, and what this can suggest to us for another kind of design—our own. The patterns of order in nature follow a rule of theme and variation. There appear to be relatively few fundamental compositional themes in nature, such as linear, segmental, or clustered strategies. These comprise a limited or closed system of possibilities. However, the infinity of variations on these themes (including hybrids and deformations) comprises an unlimited or open system of possibilities. The relation of these two systems of order guarantees a rich diversity, which is of course the key to survival in the natural world. I do not propose a direct correlation between the systems of composition found in nature and those found in architecture, though I suggest that the general pattern of theme and variation can help us understand relations among architectural compositions, and it helps to subvert facile assumptions of uniqueness, novelty, or style as well.

Remember that all of the drawings are in one way or another abstract; they are not realistic representations of buildings or cities. Generally the orientation of drawings is with north toward the top of the page, but by largely ignoring orientation as well as scale I hope to focus readers on the character of the drawings instead, dissociating them momentarily from their contexts so as to see them primarily as patterns. The purpose of abstraction is not reductive: abstraction should not reduce complex compositions to lifeless diagrams. Analysis is devoted to simplifying and clarifying composition without losing the rich polyvalent meanings we find in sophisticated design. I am aware of the limitations of the technique I use and do not claim it is a comprehensive approach to understanding architectural form. However, I have found that since the act of drawing requires a high degree of graphic editing, each drawing emphasizes a particular quality of composition. Therefore, the information in each drawing is highly selective, even in what appears to be a conventional plan. That is what I mean by a work of interpretation.

CHAPTER ONE

FIVE FORMAL PROPERTIES OF A COMPOSITION

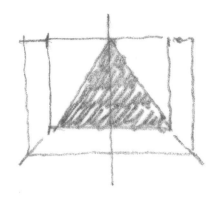

ARCHITECTURAL DESIGN IS ESSENTIALLY PATTERN MAKING. The composition of a building is a set of patterns of various complexities organized one within another, like nested Russian wooden dolls. Ideally, every aspect of a building—from the plan in its most abstract sense to the smallest physical detail—appears in a pattern, and all of the patterns relate to one another dimensionally to create a seamless continuum of scale and complexity. This is what we observe in the organic compositions of the natural world—compositions that have five related formal properties: **number, geometry, proportion, hierarchy,** and **orientation.** They produce patterns at all scales of the natural world, from the scale of the cosmos to that of the atom.

Number is the fundamental property. The two dominant theories of the physical world—general relativity at the macro scale and quantum mechanics at the scale of subatomic particles—both rely on a mathematical language, that is, they assume that all physical phenomena are in essence numerical. Between these extremes of scale, nature is composed of numerical structures. Some structures are relatively easy to discern whereas others, such as the chaotic structures of weather systems, are extremely complex. Likewise, any analysis of formal order in architectural composition must begin with numerical relationships. Common features of space and time as we ordinarily experience them in architecture, such as rhythm and cadence, are numerical progressions.

Geometry is the shape of number. Like numbers, geometries in nature vary widely in complexity. Geometry is an underlying ordering mechanism that establishes a consistent language of form for a given phenomenon. For example, a crystalline pattern may assume a hexagonal geometry (based on the number six), whereas many plant forms depend on a pentagonal geometry (based on the number five). Each geometric figure has intrinsic qualities. The square, for example, is defined by its four equal sides and right angles. In architectural design, the relation of geometric figures is a visual language that is central to our reading of pattern. In many of the plans of Frank Lloyd Wright's houses, for example, spaces vary in size and other attributes, but they are geometrically consistent. Though their relations are complex, their geometrical similarity is critical to producing a sense of unity and continuity.

Proportion is the ratio of numbers within a geometric figure or among parts of a larger composition. For example, triangles of varying proportion are constructed from three points on a plane. The ratios of the distances between the vertices may be equal, producing an equilateral triangle, or they may have some other ratio, such as the series 3:4:5. Proportion also establishes the relative sizes and positions of the parts of a composition and is therefore essential to their functional relationships. It operates in the natural world, within some parameters of variation, as a means to produce consistency. For example, the human face has a proportional organization such that its features appear more or less in predictable places in relation to one another; extremely subtle variations in proportion are essential to producing individual identity and expression. Proportion also governs scale in architecture. Externally, it relates a building to the scale of its physical setting (landscape or other buildings) and to the scale of people. Internally, proportion controls the relative sizes of the parts of the architectural composition.

Hierarchy indicates the relative importance of the parts of a composition and is dependent on number, geometry, and proportion, since each of these contributes to the identity of each part and its position relative to others. Nature avoids uniformity because forms in nature respond directly to the distribution and collection of energy. Since sources of energy are concentrated or intermittent, not uniform, forms must organize themselves hierarchically to produce structures that mediate between places of high concentrations of energy and those of low concentrations. Analogously, in architectural patterns, not all parts are of the same significance. We can consider them in respect to energy as well—literally in respect to natural light, but also figuratively in respect to their visual, emotional, or spiritual energy.

Orientation operates in two ways in patterns: externally and internally. All natural phenomena are oriented in space in some way, in response to forces around them, such as sunlight or a magnetic field. They may be oriented externally toward patterns outside themselves, such as the sun or a direction of movement. They are also oriented internally by virtue of an organization of their parts (e.g., the axis of symmetry that controls the position of the head, thorax, and abdomen of a beetle and indicates its direction of movement). Likewise, in architectural design, we find buildings oriented externally toward distant objects, such as the Kaaba in Mecca for mosques or the polestar for some Anasazi kivas. Internally, orientation may take the form of an axis of symmetry, but there also may be a series of changing orientations in a choreographed movement though linked segments of space.

A Maple Leaf

A maple leaf is a simple example of how these five formal properties produce a pattern in nature. It is composed of five lobes, three large and two small (1.1). Geometrically, the lobes are within a 180° arc in four 45° sections (1.2). Proportionally, the leaf fits within a rectangle that inscribes an equilateral triangle, a rectangle therefore with the proportion of 2:√3 (1.3). Since the function of the leaf's structure is to collect and distribute energy, it is hierarchical by means of primary, secondary, and tertiary veins (1.4). Finally, its orientation is symmetrical about a vertical centerline rising from a horizontal baseline (1.5). What is most fascinating about this rigorous system is that among the countless maple leaves nature has produced, no two leaves are ever exactly alike. The underlying rules of a maple leaf pattern (number, geometry, proportion, hierarchy, and orientation) ensure consistency without uniformity.

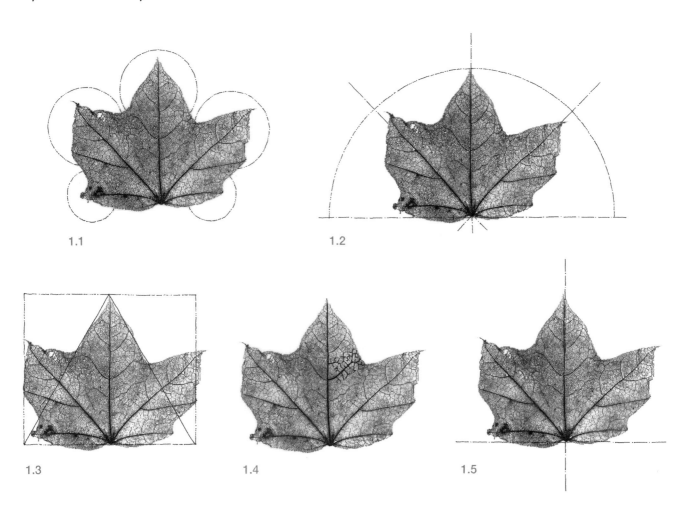

1.1

1.2

1.3

1.4

1.5

1.1
Number: three major and two minor lobes.

1.2
Geometry: division by 45°.

1.3
Proportion: the 2:√3 rectangle.

1.4
Hierarchy: primary, secondary, and tertiary veins.

1.5
Orientation: horizontal and vertical axes.

Architectural Examples

Though all buildings have all five of these properties, we will focus on each one of them in separate examples to understand them better. The courtyard elevation of the house of Rondane Bey in Tunis (1.6, 1.7) demonstrates how number is fundamental to organizing elements of an architectural composition and establishes repetition and rhythm. Geometry operates at many levels of composition but in some cases it is strikingly evident in the forms of masses and voids, such as in the Church of Saint Michael in Hildesheim, Germany (1.8). A close analysis of even complex designs, such as the Schröder House by Gerrit Rietveld (1.9) reveals an underlying proportional system; in this case, the golden mean operates in plan and section. Hierarchy may manifest itself in buildings in various ways; one way is in the massing of forms, such as in the case of the Süleymaniye Mosque in Istanbul (1.10). An example of external orientation, that is, the orientation of a building to something outside of itself, is the position of the main prayer hall of a typical mosque that, like the three examples in Tripoli (1.11), directs the users of the building toward the Kaaba in Mecca for prayer.

Number, geometry, proportion, hierarchy, and orientation operate at all scales of architectural design. For example, a door in the house of Ibn Arafa in Tunis (1.12) is an elegant composition, balanced and varied in its forms and materials. Underlying its appearance, however, we find the five basic properties at work. It has three major parts nested one within the other (1.13), a geometry limited to related circles and rectangles (1.14), a proportional system based on the equilateral triangle (1.15), a hierarchy of forms from the center outward (1.16), and an orientation based on a centerline of symmetry as well as an indication of front and back (1.17).

Two building plans illustrate how architects have used the five properties to order their compositions. The 14th-century Certosa del Galluzzo (1.18) is divided into two major parts, each with subsidiary numerical organizations (1.19); it adheres to an orthogonal arrangement of similar rectangles (1.20) within a generalized proportional system based on equilateral triangles (1.21); a strict hierarchy governs the relations of its parts in respect to both masses and voids (1.22). And each of the two major parts of the plan has a distinct method of orientation; the one for the monks is based on the centerline of the cloister and meeting room, while the one for lay people is a series of orientations that control a processional (1.23). The proposal for a courtyard house by Ludwig Mies van der Rohe is equally rigorous compositionally (1.24). Numerically, it is two figures, one superimposed upon the other, that produce three zones (1.25). Geometrically, it is restricted to relations between circles and rectangles (1.26). The rectangles emerge from the superimposition of squares and rectangles produced by equilateral triangles, that is, in the proportion of $2:\sqrt{3}$ (1.27). Hierarchically, Mies made a clear distinction between the formal courtyard, as it relates to an interior space, and the service courtyard (1.28). Finally, the system of orientation is a series of carefully controlled segments of a processional from the exterior through the interior (1.29).

Use of the five properties of composition as the foundation of a design method does not constrain creativity; it liberates creativity from arbitrariness by providing a realistic and systematic basis for decision making at an early stage in the design process. A successful design is going to rely on these properties anyway; all of the projects in this book have these properties, whether they are by famous architects or by vernacular designers. It is therefore best to be conscious of them from the outset and use them proactively, because the first decisions made are the most critical to a design's logic.

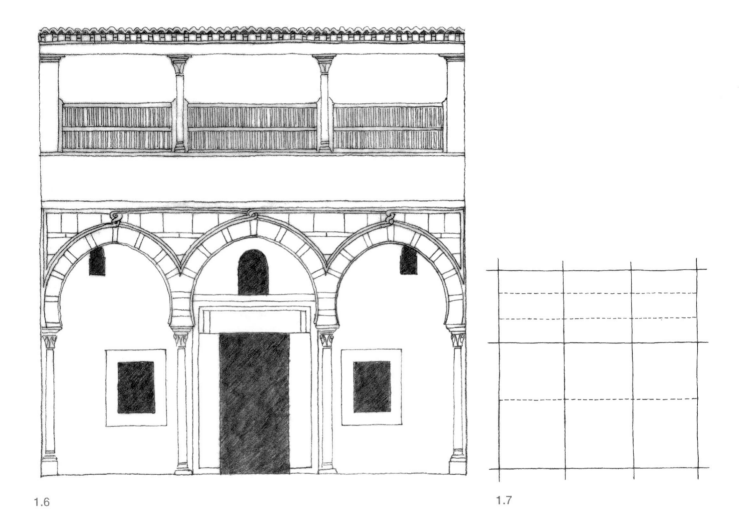

1.6

1.7

1.6

Number: House of Rondane Bey, Tunis. Courtyard. Elevation.

Number plays two roles in architectural composition. First, the designer arranges parts of a composition in some way—sequentially or repetitively—producing rhythm. Rhythm, which is the relation of similar and dissimilar parts, is in essence an arrangement of numbers. The second role of number is symbolic. For example, numbers connote unity, a duality, a triumvirate, or in the case of the four-quartered square, an ideal form of the terrestrial world.

1.7

House of Rondane Bey. Diagram.

In this example, the composition has three parts, left to right, subtly indicating two similar bays flanking one central bay. The architect divided the composition vertically into two zones, the top one, in turn, into three and the lower one into two. Despite the simplicity of this arrangement, the rhythm appears complex when scanned both vertically and horizontally.

1.8

Geometry: Church of Saint Michael, Hildesheim, Germany, 1010–33. View.

In this example of early Romanesque church architecture, the geometric conception dominates the form. The plan is a basilica with two choirs (one at each end), two crossings, and two pairs of transepts. The crossings are square in plan; the dimensions of this square produced the planning module for the entire church. With clean, crisp edges, minimal apertures, and unadorned wall surfaces, it is a tour de force of elemental three-dimensional forms: cubes, cylinders, pyramids, and cones. Destroyed in World War II and rebuilt in the 1950s, the church is now a United Nations Educational, Scientific and Cultural Organization (UNESCO) World Cultural Heritage site.

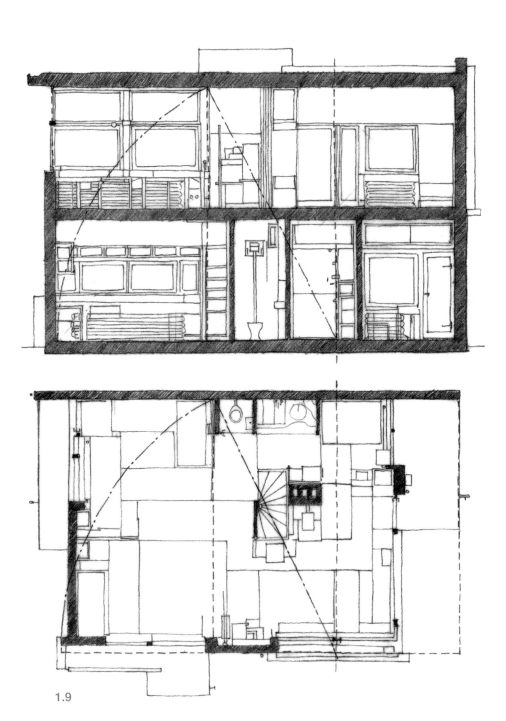

1.9

Proportion: Schröder House, Utrecht, Netherlands, 1924.
Gerrit Rietveld. Plan and section.

Despite the complexity of the design, Rietveld relied on a traditional proportion for the building as a whole: the golden section is the basis for both the plan and the section. (Note that these two drawings are at different scales.) The rationale for the use of an abstract ratio such as the golden section has two theoretical bases. First, since much of the natural world appears to be ordered by the golden section (including our own bodies), humans are presumably predisposed to find it aesthetically pleasing. The second theory is that because it can be subdivided systematically to produce identical ratios at different scales, its use achieves a harmonic relation among the parts of a composition.

1.10

Hierarchy: Süleymaniye Mosque, Istanbul, 16th century. Mimar Sinan. View.

The center of this large complex of buildings is a mosque. Sinan perfected a compositional system, derived from Byzantine precedents, by which relatively small domes, half domes, monumental arches, and buttresses supported a gigantic central dome. The result is a powerfully hierarchical composition that produces a cascade of volumes from the center to the periphery. In its entirety, the composition harks back to an ancient Asiatic metaphor of the cosmic mountain that connects the terrestrial world with the cosmos.

1.11

Formal Orientation: Three mosques in Tripoli, Libya. Plans.

A formal orientation of a building, as distinct from a processional orientation, fixes internal elements of a plan to an external phenomenon—for example, a cardinal direction, another building, or a view. As with all mosques, in this case it is a distant referent, the Kaaba in Mecca. Left to right: Ahmed Pasha Karamanli, Carruba, Gurgi.

1.10

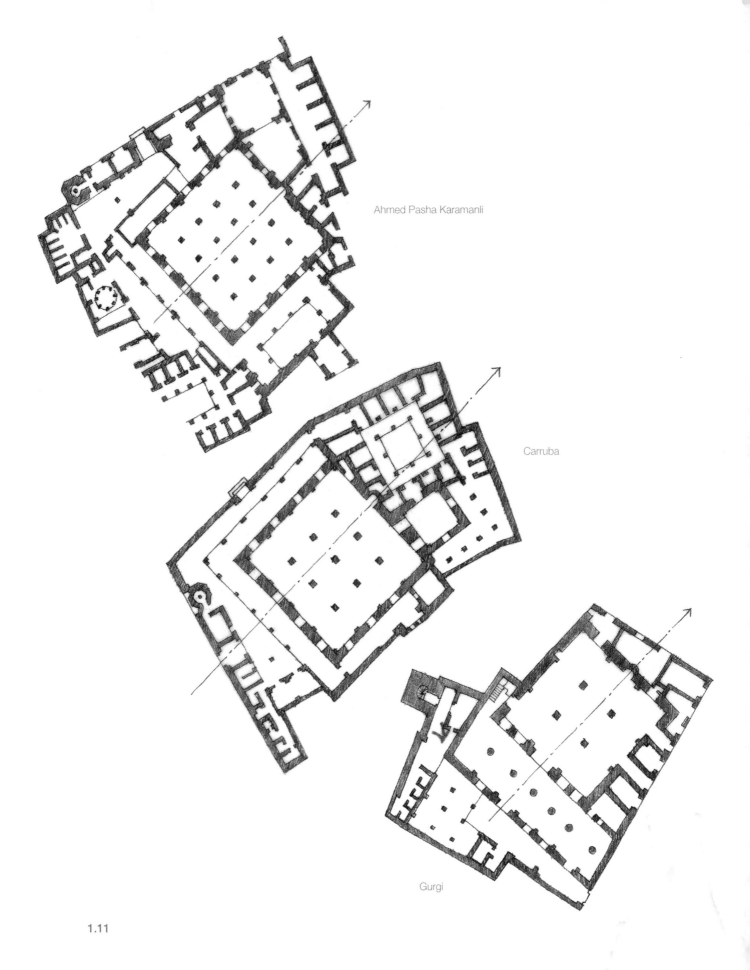

Ahmed Pasha Karamanli

Carruba

Gurgi

1.11

1.12

1.13

1.12
Door: House of Ibn Arafa, Tunis, 19th century. Elevation.
The door is of bronze and copper within a finely detailed limestone portal that is, in turn, within a rougher limestone panel of the facade.

1.13
Door. Number.
The composition consists of three portals descending in scale, one within another.

1.14
Door. Geometry.
The geometry relies on the relation between a set of similar rectangles and a set of circles.

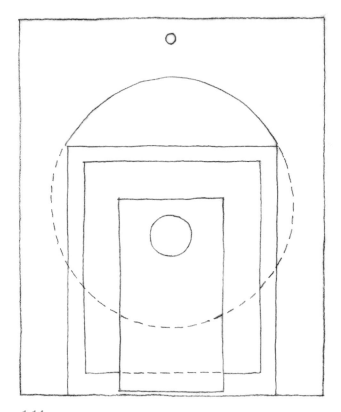

1.14

1.15
Door. Proportion.
The circle that forms the arch is the key to the proportional system. It is replicated twice, with the circumference of each of the new circles above and below it passing through its center, producing two vesicas and a matrix of equilateral triangles. This order establishes the positions of all major features of the composition.

1.16
Door. Hierarchy.
The bronze door is the primary figure, the surrounding arched portal is the secondary figure, and the rough limestone portal is the tertiary figure. A constellation of minor objects, such as decorative plaques, apertures, and door handles, surround the major elements of the composition.

1.17
Door. Orientation.
A central axis of symmetry organizes all elements of the composition monumentally and implies a formal order beyond.

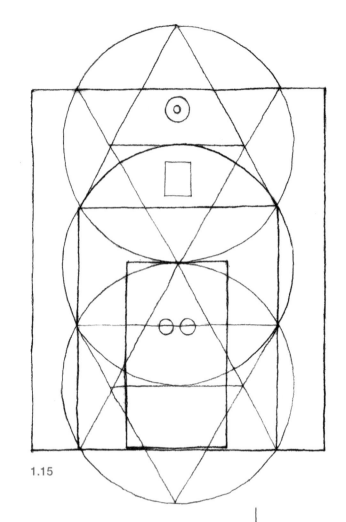

1.15

1.16

1.17

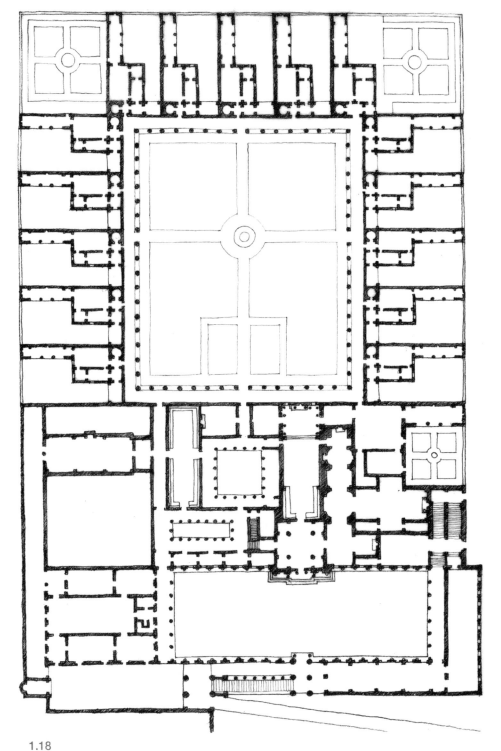

1.18

Certosa del Galluzzo, near Florence, Italy, mid-14th century. Plan.

Niccolò Acciaiuoli, the scion of a prominent Florentine banking family, founded the large complex of buildings in 1341. Through later additions and modifications, it became an important example of late Italian Renaissance architecture and art. Pontormo contributed paintings and frescoes for the cloisters when he took refuge there from the plague in 1523–25. The plan follows the austere prescription for the Carthusian order, with each monk living in a small L-shaped house with a garden, a rationalist approach to domestic life that influenced Le Corbusier's design for the Unité d'Habitation projects in Marseilles and Berlin.

1.18

1.19
Certosa del Galluzzo. Number.

A continuous transverse wall divides the complex into two parts, each one focused on a courtyard. To the south are all of the buildings associated with the lay brothers and secular visitors, including the church, while to the north of the wall is a large courtyard with an arcade on four sides that exclusively served the resident monks.

1.20
Certosa del Galluzzo. Geometry.

Despite a great variety of building types and functions, the entire plan is composed of rectangles that do not intersect but are adjacent to one another.

1.21
Certosa del Galluzzo. Proportion.

The predominant proportional feature of the composition is a rectangle with the ratio of $2:\sqrt{3}$. The ratio also determines the positions of the two entrances—one at the top of the approach ramp, the other opposite the church entry.

1.22
Certosa del Galluzzo. Hierarchy.

The church and the courtyard dominate the great variety of buildings and spaces in the south half of the plan. To the north, hierarchy is less obvious; from the courtyard, all of the monks' residences appear equal, though the ones at the northwest and northeast corners enjoy larger gardens and the interior of the northeast residence is slightly larger as well. With this apparently uniform boundary, the focus of the courtyard is the small rectangular cemetery on the south side.

1.23
Certosa del Galluzzo. Orientation.

The two halves of the composition have different types of orientations. An axis of symmetry that passes from the courtyard into a small cloister organizes the northern half; from the small cloister, monks could access the chapter house to the west and the choir of the church to the east. Orientation in the southern half is not axial, but rather processional, that is, a series of segments of movement from the exterior into the church.

1.19

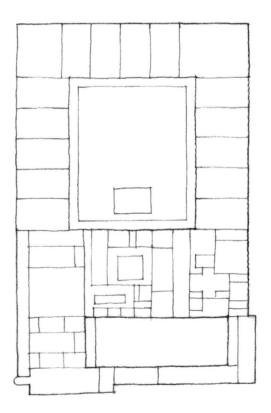

1.20

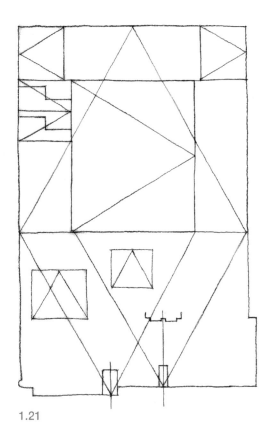

1.21

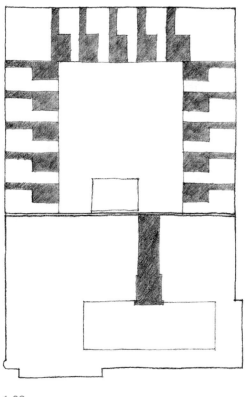

1.22

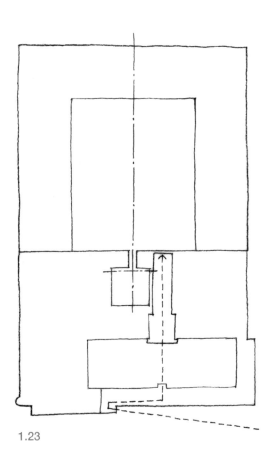

1.23

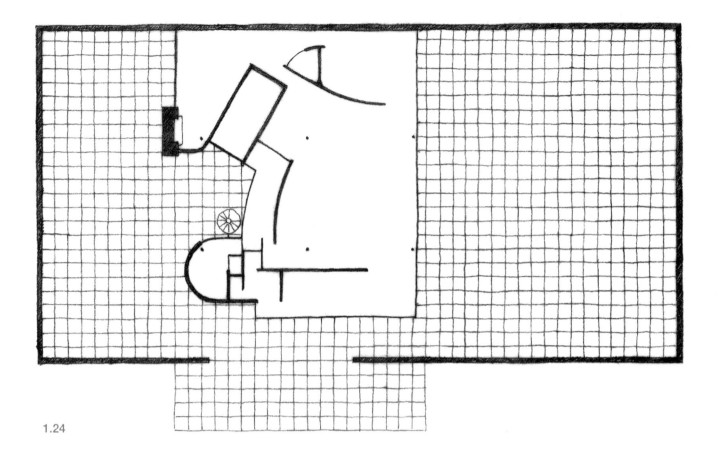

1.24

1.24
Brick Courtyard House Proposal, 1934. Mies van der Rohe. Plan.

The house, one of several hypothetical designs by Mies from the 1930s, is a composition of glass planes and thin nonbearing brick partitions beneath a flat roof supported by six slender steel columns. It occupies part of a paved space enclosed by a brick wall in which a single opening serves as the pedestrian entry as well as a driveway. The position of the house divides the enclosed space into two courts: a service court to the left and the formal court associated with the house's interior to the right. An exterior circular stair in the service court leads to the roof. In the interior, an arc of service spaces—including the garage, kitchen, and bath—separates two leisure spaces: a formal one defined by four columns facing the formal court, and a more intimate space centered on a hearth at the rear of the house.

1.25
Brick Courtyard House Proposal. Number.

In this composition, number can be interpreted two ways. On the one hand, Mies divided the rectangular enclosure into three zones: service court, house, and formal court. On the other hand, the composition implies that the house is an autonomous form applied to a single preexisting tiled enclosure, thus creating a dialogue between only two elements.

1.26
Brick Courtyard House Proposal. Geometry.

The plan is an abstract composition of circles and rectangles similar to contemporary Neoplasticist paintings by Piet Mondrian and Theo van Doesburg, as well as to the Constructivist compositions of Kasimir Malevich and Alexander Rodchenko.

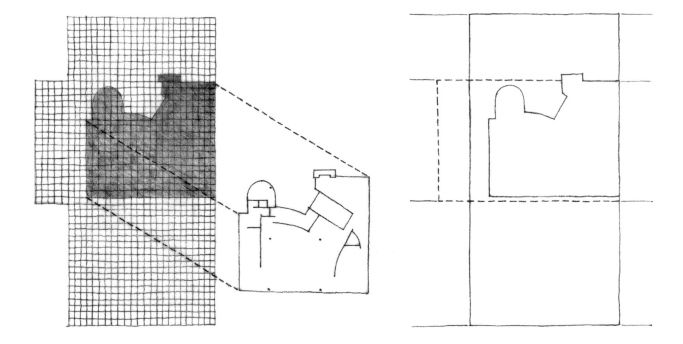

1.25

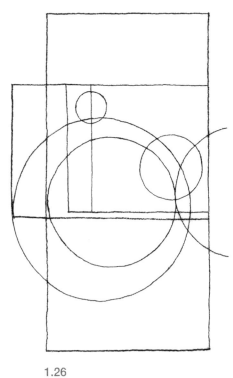

1.26

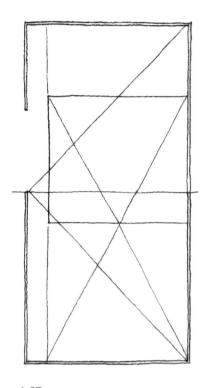

1.27

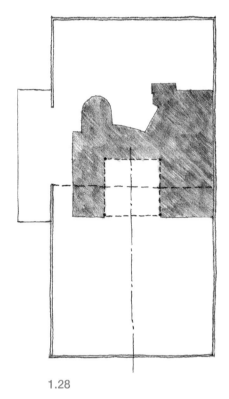

1.28

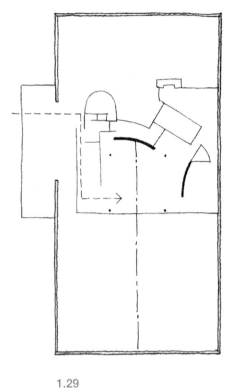

1.29

1.27

**Brick Courtyard House Proposal.
Proportion.**

There are two geometries working in tandem.
The entire enclosure is in the proportion of 1:2,
that is, two squares, whereas the house and
the formal court are each 2:√3 rectangles. The
difference between, or the remainder of, these
two systems determines the width of the service court.

1.28

**Brick Courtyard House Proposal.
Hierarchy.**

Mies denotes the primary hierarchical position
of the main interior leisure space by defining its
four corners with four steel columns. It is directly, that is axially, related to the exterior formal court. The two interlocked squares establish the hierarchy of the entire composition: the
served and service spaces.

1.29

**Brick Courtyard House Proposal.
Orientation.**

There are two types of orientation operating in
this composition: formal and processional. A
concave partition terminates an axis that establishes a formal orientation through the main
living space and its court. The processional orientation consists of three segments of movement: the approach to a gap in the street facade, a right turn into the house, then a left
between the end of a reception space and a
column and into the main interior leisure
space. A convex partition terminates this sequence of movements.

CHAPTER TWO

NOTES ON THE PLAN

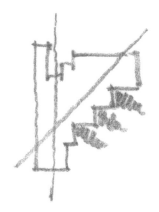

MOST OF THE DRAWINGS IN THIS BOOK ARE PLANS OF ONE KIND OR another. This is not to suggest that an analysis of a building relies solely on its plan. Many important features of a building and the ideas that lie behind them do not appear in a plan. However, in most cases the plan conveys the central organizing strategy of a building. It is full of clues as to the designer's values and attitudes toward the landscape, theories of order, methods of construction, and the control of social relations, to name just a few of many concerns. A plan is so powerful as a means of uniting diverse interests that architects cannot be blamed if they sometimes equate the plan with the physical building. This is because a plan is not just a set of data: it is iconic—it constrains and directs the way we think. It reveals a set of values, ideas, analogies, and metaphors that have shaped information in a particular way.

Though plans purport to be factual, none are entirely so because each emphasizes certain kinds of information at the expense of others. Plans are therefore interpretive. Facts such as dimensions, orientations, and relations among parts reside in a symbolic logic that is always abstract and far removed from the form of the building to which they refer. Every plan exists within a spectrum of abstraction, from those that are to a scale proportional to the actual building to those that are an impressionistic gesture. So all plans employ graphic editing because they cannot include all of the information known about the building for which they stand. Given this limitation, what a plan implies is usually more interesting and even more useful than what it explicitly states.

I edit the drawings I use intensively. Due to the medium I employ and the content I am trying to convey, I leave out some information in order to emphasize certain ideas of concern to the designers or ideas derived from the plan that may be useful elsewhere. My drawings are therefore hypotheses, since the plans I produce derive from "readings" of other plans. The process of graphic editing is not merely one of simplification but rather an attempt to reveal an underlying conceptual order. In this respect, the act of drawing is an essential means of analysis in its own right, not merely a mode of representation. In my work, the ideas embedded in the plan are not preconceived; the act of drawing reveals them as I produce each graphic edit of the plan.

Different kinds of plans provide different kinds of information. Sometimes a highly abstracted plan shorn of detail can reveal ideas not readily evident in highly detailed plans. Even a plan reduced to little more than a gesture devoid of specifics such as dimensions can be more compelling iconographically than its more technically correct antecedent. In the series of plans of the town hall at Saynatsalo, Finland, for example, each plan is a valid abstraction of the building insofar as each conveys a particular set of ideas.

The first drawing is similar to the most widely published plan of Aalto's building. Close to the representational end of the spectrum, the plan provides information about structure, scale, and movement, and the inclusion of furniture indicates the organization of the interior and the functions of spaces. The second drawing is a figure/ground diagram, a kind of plan that is concerned with the silhouette of the building on its site, or its footprint. The figural quality of the courtyard and the gaps between the two buildings take on greater significance in this version. The third drawing abandons scale, detail, and the normal qualities of a plan altogether and reduces the plan to a gesture. Note that the graphic style of the drawing emphasizes the central importance of the courtyard. It is, in its own way, as valuable as its two antecedents because it conveys a strategic concept economically—as an ideogram. A critical skill in one's own design process, as in the analysis of the designs of others, is the ability to explore ideas through varying degrees of graphic abstraction.

2.1

Town Hall, Saynatsalo, Finland, 1950–52. Alvar Aalto. Three plans.

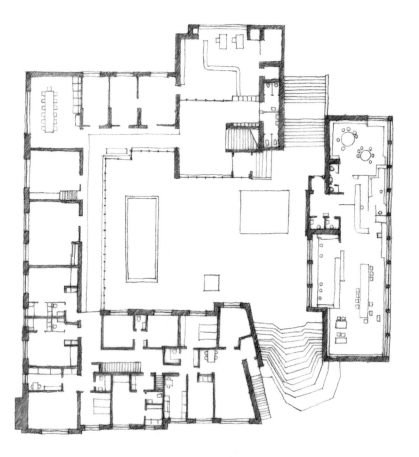

2.1

Drawing plans, especially freehand, immerses the design researcher in the process of editing for the sake of revealing the ideas embedded and sometimes hidden in the plan. Stripping away detail may enhance certain characteristics of an architect's thinking and reveal ideas that can be useful in one's own work. This is the purpose of precedent analysis. Furthermore, the process of simplification in analysis can reveal similarities among buildings that would not be evident if one were to accept plans at face value. In the following example, I compare two buildings from vastly different cultures that nevertheless have some compelling similarities: the 17th-century Shoiken Teahouse within the compound of the Katsura Imperial Villa in Kyoto, Japan (2.2), and the 20th-century Josef Esters House in Krefeld, Germany (2.3), designed by Mies van der Rohe.

There is circumstantial evidence to suggest that Mies was at least aware of, and perhaps influenced by, the plan of this Japanese teahouse. In the early 1930s when Mies was designing the Esters House, his colleague Bruno Taut was sending descriptions and drawings of the Katsura buildings back to other architects Germany. The modernity of the villa excited Taut, Mies, Le Corbusier, and Walter Gropius (2.4). They saw clear parallels between their own work and the functionalist, modular, austere but spatially rich design of the Katsura. However, the similarity of these two buildings would be just as useful if there were no direct historical connection between them.

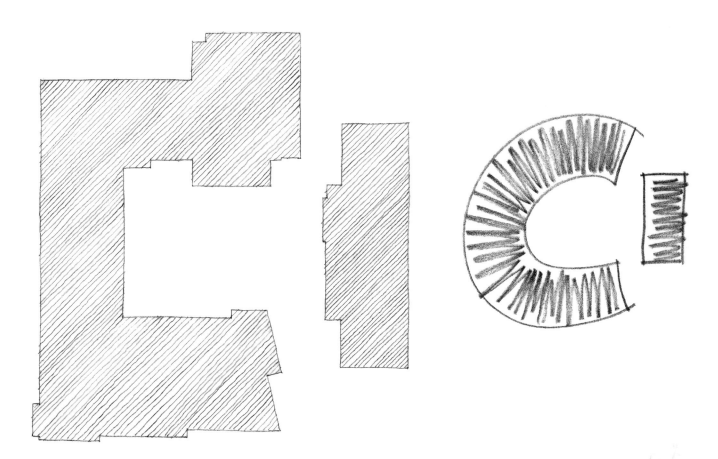

What I find interesting are the similarities of abstract order translated into a specific method of shaping architectural space. The buildings are different in some respects; for example, the Esters House is a two-story brick structure, while the teahouse is a single-story wood frame. Their plans, though, have striking formal similarities. Their partis are virtually identical: compactly organized service spaces are to the left of the entrance, with formal spaces cascading to the right to provide views of the landscape beyond (2.5). Their entries follow the boundary between the service and served spaces, and the general order of interior spaces forms diagonals through the buildings (2.6, 2.7). A rigorous module controls the shaping of interior spaces, the ken in the teahouse, and a square grid in the Esters House (2.8). These modules form larger units of space that have similar proportions in plan and interpenetrate in similar ways as well (2.9, 2.10). This minimalist approach to the design of interior spaces created diagonal relationships and multiple readings of spaces orthogonally. Finally, both buildings employ a set of peripheral spaces that are extensions into the landscape but maintain the orthogonal order of their interiors. In the Japanese tradition, this is *en,* or the "in-between." The verandas of the teahouse and the Esters House establish spaces that blur boundaries between the interior and the exterior; they are both of the interior and of the exterior simultaneously (2.12).

A plan drawing is an economical and compelling graphic device for conveying essential ideas about order in a building. Creative designers train themselves to use the plan, as well as other kinds of drawings, in various degrees of abstraction, not just to explore the organization of a building but also to discern its meanings. We generally assume the purpose of a drawing we produce is to convey information to other people, but throughout the design process, the true purpose of our drawings is to more accurately understand that information ourselves so we can be conscious of our decisions and be self-critical. Information about a building has many layers of complexity, so as we design we must be adept at using the type of drawing appropriate to the layer of complexity we are investigating.

2.2

Shoiken Teahouse, Katsura Imperial Villa, Kyoto, Japan, ca. 1645. Plan.

2.3

Josef Esters House, Krefeld, Germany, 1930–32. Mies van der Rohe. Plan.

2.4

Shoiken Teahouse. Interior view.
Typical of classical Japanese interiors, an orthogonally framed succession of spaces flows through a series of sliding shoji screens to produce a double reading, that is, of both individual spaces and a single space that leads one's gaze toward an undisclosed destination.

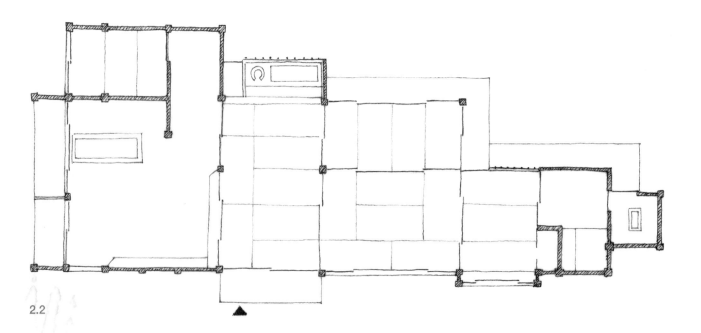

2.2

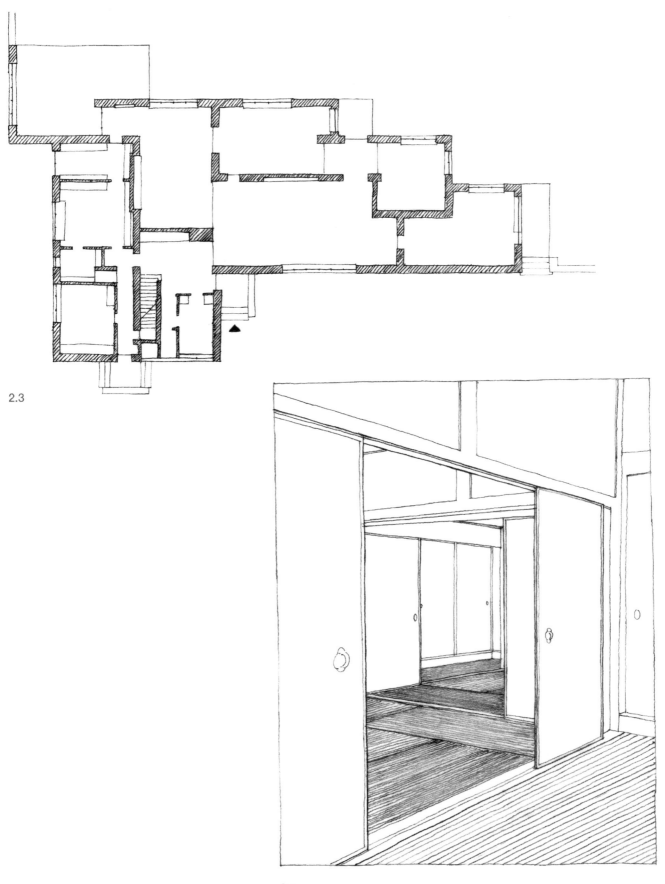

2.3

2.4

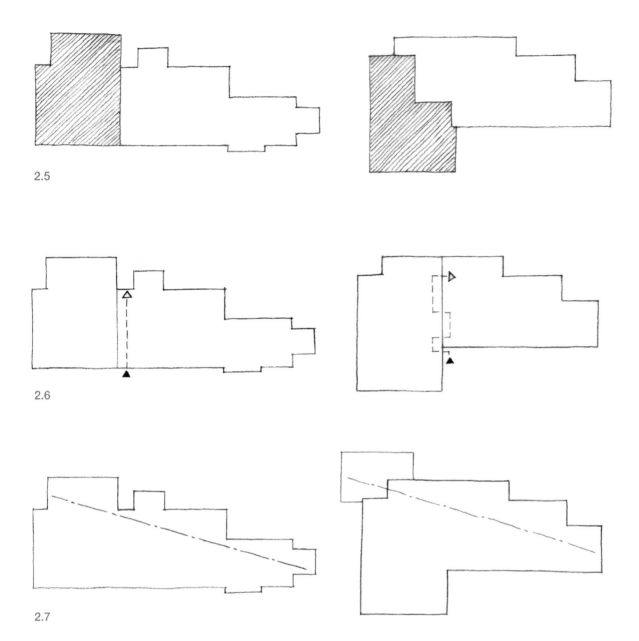

2.5

2.6

2.7

2.5
Parti.

The parti of both plans makes an unambiguous distinction between service and served spaces. Service spaces are compact and static, while served spaces open to the landscape through a series of steps or serrations in the plan that produce shifting volumes affording both longitudinal and lateral views outward from the interior.

2.6
Entrance.

In both plans the entrance is at right angles to the major axis of the plan and at the seam between service spaces (to the left) and served spaces (to the right). The seam is a continuous lateral datum line. In the Esters House one moves back and forth across this line, whereas in the teahouse one moves consistently along its right side toward a tokonoma in the far elevation.

2.7
The Diagonal.

Both plans indicate that the intended spatial experience is a diagonal relation among the primary living spaces controlled internally with staggered connections between spaces and externally with the stepped plan form. The interior perspective of the Shoiken Teahouse illustrates the spatial quality this method produces, one of receding planes seen through offset apertures.

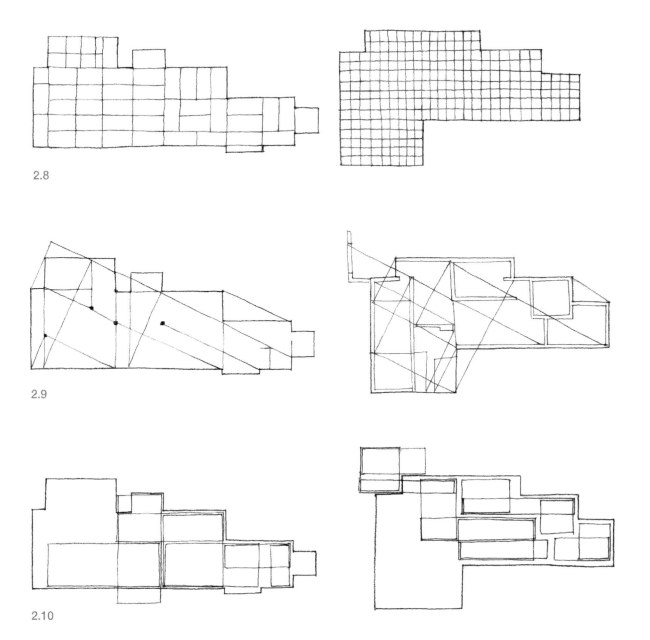

2.8

2.9

2.10

2.8
Module.

Both plans rely on a module. In the Shoiken Teahouse, the module is the ken, as measured by the tatami mat that has a proportion of 1:2. Traditionally, the number of tatami mats within a room identified it as a type (e.g., a six-mat room). Mies, characteristically, organized his building with a grid of square modules.

2.9
Proportion.

Adherence to a modular system allowed both architects to coordinate the proportions of rooms in plan. In the Esters House, we find a set of complementary rectangles determining the position of interior boundaries for identifiable rooms. In the Shoiken Teahouse, the regulating lines, tied to the columns, pass through a fluid space that uses implied boundaries to a greater degree, thus creating a more subtle proportional relation between spaces.

2.10
Interlocking spaces.

Mies was working in the Western tradition of bourgeois houses, which required interiors to have distinctly enclosed rooms, like little boxes within a big box. He subverted this notion to some degree in the Esters House by opening rooms to one another more than was customary to imply the sharing of space by adjacent rooms. In contrast, the Japanese were unencumbered by the idea of discreet rooms. The *fusuma,* or system of sliding shoji screens, allowed interior spaces to interpenetrate in a variety of ways.

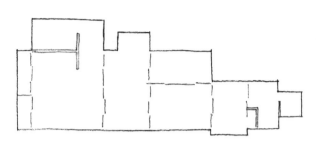

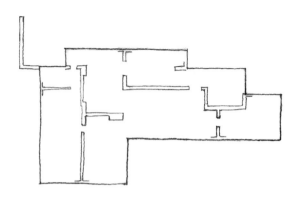

2.11

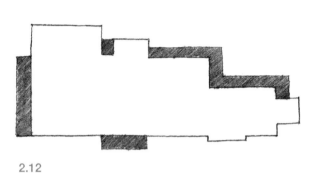

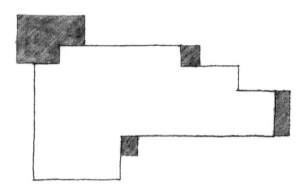

2.12

2.11

Orthogonal space.

Systems of overlapping vertical planes related to one another orthogonally yet dynamically organize the interiors of both the Josef Esters House and the Shoiken Teahouse. In the Esters House, the planes are opaque, stationary, and merely imply movement, while in the Shoiken Teahouse the planes are translucent and movable, thus providing opportunities for variable interior spatial patterns.

2.12

En.

All of the Japanese arts, including music and literature, relied on the concept of *en,* or the in-between. Its architectural interpretation was the veranda, or *engawa,* beneath a low over-hanging eave that, in partnership with layers of different materials, produced a space that was of the interior and of the exterior simultane-ously, an in-between space that mediated be-tween architecture and the landscape. Mies used a similar device in the Eskers house. The four porches all have corresponding roof over-hangs associated with apertures in the enclos-ing wall that allow interior spaces to fuse with exterior spaces.

CHAPTER THREE
TYPE

O NE OF THE TENETS OF MODERNIST ARCHITECTURE WAS THE proposition that the form of each building should emerge spontaneously from the specifics of its program and its site in a process analogous to scientific analysis and without reference to precedents or norms, which many Modernists considered little more than habits and prejudices. The premise of this theory is that modern culture is fundamentally different from previous cultures, that the Cartesian method of analysis liberates us from habitual thought and allows us to approach each problem without any preconceptions or preconditions whatsoever—that is, unencumbered by history and tradition. In extreme cases, knowledge of the past was a handicap.

In practice, few architects were ever able to approach the state of total cultural amnesia this theory required. Despite superficial differences in appearance, many of the Modernist projects that were ostensibly entirely analytical and objective nevertheless adhered to basic, traditional organizational strategies for two good reasons: there are not that many strategies available, and the traditional methods of design—whether of high art or the vernacular—were at their core just as rational as the new, purportedly scientific method. Vernacular, in particular, requires a profound understanding of the physical, social, and psychological conditions that architecture must accommodate. It requires careful, incremental experimentation that often achieves the optimal balance among the various forces at play in design.

The reaction against mainstream Modernism in the late 20th century questioned the existence of pure reason and whether architecture was merely a utilitarian device, and it reasserted the role of architecture as a means to understand the human condition in all its complexity. Many architects realized that basic to a person's relation to his or her environment is a sense of recognition—that the new is understood in relation to forms that resonate deeply in individual and collective memories. Far from being a hindrance to creativity, historical precedents, understood as underlying design strategies, carry an enormous amount of valuable information, information that establishes the intellectual context for new ideas. Precedents may also provide the emotional context for creativity, since design that refers to a well-known pattern often stimulates our imaginations to search for a new interpretation of a familiar form. The seduction of familiarity is an effective means to introduce new ideas and move people to question their preconceptions. To paraphrase Pablo Picasso, who despite his reputation as a revolutionary was a master of traditional forms: art makes the familiar strange and the strange familiar.

Consistent with a gradual rejection of the ideology of uniqueness of every design problem (much of which led, paradoxically, to stultifying uniformity) was a growing interest in the type. Type is a model, a standard of reference that exemplifies qualities found in forms that are more complex. In architecture, a type prefigures basic characteristics of a design and places that design within a family of similar ideas, all of which share an underlying order. Architects use types in two ways: in respect to similarities and in respect to differences, or variations.

Similarity

The study of typology in design reveals similarities of architectural forms that cut across cultural, social, historical, and geographic boundaries—we find people solving similar problems in similar conditions by similar means. Two examples of house types serve to illustrate this phenomenon. The first is a core and colonnade type that nests a long, narrow masonry core within a peripheral colonnade beneath a low overhanging roof (3.1). Numerous openings in the core—tall, narrow doors—allow air to circulate freely through the interior spaces, while the surrounding veranda within the colonnade shields the interior from the sun. Interestingly, this building type can be found in a virtually identical form on the Argentine pampas and on the plains of New South Wales, Australia, not because someone transplanted the design from one place to another but because vernacular designers, thinking logically, solve similar problems similarly. The use of type, therefore, is not habitual; it is rational.

The second example is also a house, the block with ramada type (3.2). Its thick earthen walls support a flat roof structure of peeled tree trunk timbers that in turn support a woven mesh of smaller wood members, woven rush matting, and layers of clay. It has an entry porch, the ramada, consisting of four columns of peeled tree trunks supporting heavy wood capitals and a single beam. We find identical specimens of this house type in the southwestern United States and in equally arid areas of Iran and Afghanistan. In these cases, the architectural type is consistent even though the cultural circumstances differ considerably.

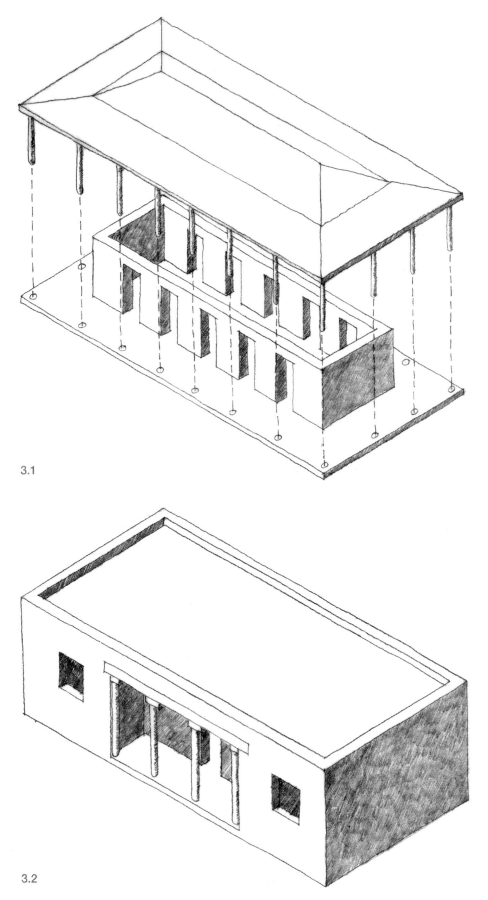

3.1

Core and Colonnade Type.
Schematic axonometric.

The core and colonnade type appears throughout the world because it is useful in a variety of climates, whether hot and dry or wet. Similar to a Greek peristyle temple, the building is essentially two separate buildings: a solid core with apertures on a platform, and a lightweight colonnaded porch supporting a low roof that acts as an umbrella for the core. When properly oriented, its narrow form allows prevailing breezes to ventilate the interior volume thoroughly. Interior partitions are usually minimized to avoid disrupting airflow. The deep, low overhanging roof prevents direct sunlight from entering the tall, narrow openings of the core. The thermal inertia of the thick masonry core allows it to moderate the temperature of the interior because it heats up and cools down slowly.

3.2

Block with Ramada Type.
Schematic axonometric.

A common freestanding house type in hot, dry climates where wood is scarce, the block with ramada house type is inexpensive to build and has a simple, functional plan. In the American Southwest as well as in Iran (among many other locations), the walls are usually of earth, either rammed or adobe blocks. In addition to being readily available and inexpensive, earth has a high degree of thermal inertia that tempers the interior in severe climates. The use of timber is equally simple and straightforward. Peeled tree trunks serve as the principal beams to support a lattice of small branches, often woven into a herringbone pattern for strength and topped with a reed matting and mud plaster. This drawing illustrates the basic unit, but more complex houses follow the same general design approach to create L-shaped, U-shaped, or courtyard plans.

3.2

Variation

Whereas these two examples illustrate virtually identical solutions to different problems, the use of type more often results in diverse forms that, though similar in basic configuration, relate differently to unique circumstances. A type does not impose uniformity but rather provides a theme from which a designer may derive variations. Theme and variation is a primary lesson of biological morphology. The spectacular invention of forms in nature is entirely dependent on a process of variations on compositional themes, or types. For example, a series of sketches of bird skulls reveals that they are variations on a single formal structure: a spherical brain case, a beak, and a bony armature that connects the two to accommodate nasal cavities and eye sockets (3.3). This standard organizational strategy is a general design constraint that solves a structural problem that all birds share, but it permits an unlimited number of permutations in response to the specific needs of individual species. Vernacular designers tend to respond to natural constraints in a similar way, searching for an efficient formal structure based on an economical use of available material and a direct, low-energy response to their environment. Similar to the study of bird skulls, the structures from two Micronesian cultures—the Yap Islands and Tinian—are each based on an underlying structural type that allows for the invention of forms that satisfy a variety of functions (3.4, 3.5).

A ubiquitous type throughout the world is the courtyard house (3.6). The reason it is so common is that in hot, dry climates it responds economically to several needs of its inhabitants. It provides private, secure outdoor space in an exposed location or in a crowded urban environment. The courtyard produces a central communal room, the ceiling of which is the sky, to which all other rooms in the house can refer. It can also control the relation between private spaces of the family and the need to welcome outsiders into the center of the house. Lastly, it serves to control light, air, and heat passively within the core of the house through diurnal and seasonal cycles. The schematic sketch shown here provides only the general idea of a thick protective mass surrounding a soft, private courtyard. From Morocco to central Asia and northern India, one finds innumerable variations on this type. Constructed in dense patterns within villages, towns, and cities, these houses are efficient responses to the natural environment as well as to the social structures of their communities, providing each family with a design specific to its needs and physical constraints yet also providing the primary physical manifestation of culture. One variant, an example from 18th-century Cairo, has all of the features of the typical Cairene house, particularly the crooked entry into one corner of the courtyard and the relation of the principal living room on the second floor open to the courtyard below (3.7).

The courtyard plan belongs to the general category of the atrium type, in which a building mass surrounds and encloses a central space with an abrupt transition between the two parts of the composition, generally just the inner wall surface of the building mass. Two similar types are the *cortile* and the cloister (3.8). In the *cortile*, a colonnade or arcade articulates the inner surface of the enclosing mass, giving the enclosing wall a partially open character so the central space can then penetrate into the surrounding mass. In the cloister, a colonnade or arcade pulls away from the building mass toward the center to create an intermediate space between the mass and the central void, a space that has a dual identity—both of the mass and of the void. Used in their purest forms, these types can produce a serene architecture that aims at perfection, as in the cloister of a Cistercian abbey. Architects can also combine or distort these forms to create compositions of complexity and ambiguity, as in the town hall of Saynatsalo, Finland, by Alvar Aalto.

The use of a type allows people to recognize a familiar form that conveys important ideas about their culture. However, varying a type also allows for individuality and invention. A set of plans for a 16th-century palazzo in Genoa serves to illustrate this point (3.9). The optimal arrangement of spaces appropriate for a palazzo derived from an implicit agreement among the members of a particular social class in that place at that time; this constituted the type. It was an abstract order, or formal structure, and while no palazzo ever adhered to it literally, all palazzi were variations of it. The type established a series of spatial layers on the ground floor that proceeded from the main entrance on the street through a loggia (a vestibule flanked by stairs), to a second loggia, to a rear *cortile* or a garden, all flanked by salons. The six examples shown here were among a large number of palazzi constructed within a few years on a new street devoted to a cohesive social class of wealthy Genoese merchants. Though each plan satisfied the personal tastes and aspirations of a particular client, all of the plans were variations on an underlying plan type (3.10).

Similarly, when the Spanish invaded and colonized the upper Rio Grande valley in what is now New Mexico, the Franciscan friars charged with the task of constructing mission churches in the indigenous pueblos and villages imposed an architectural type derived from the design of small parochial churches in Spain (3.11). The plan was a simple rectangular box, and in its early stage of development, the facade required only an entrance and a belfry; a courtyard to one side served the friar's residence. The interior of the church had a choir loft above the entrance, and later versions of the church added a small door at the upper level so the clergy could preach to people gathered in front of the church. This evolved into a porch that was at first a cantilevered platform from the facade and later became an elaborate indentation in the facade to allow the friar to celebrate mass and to conduct large-scale baptisms outdoors. In the case of the church at Santa Fe, the elaboration of the central porch split the belfry into two flanking towers. Despite changes in complexity and scale, the preservation of the underlying type was critical to keeping the entire development of the Spanish mission church within a single architectural tradition.

Early American baseball parks were also variations on a theme (3.12). By the beginning of the 20th century, there was agreement about the general form and dimensions—that is, the type—of a baseball park. However, since the largest of them had to accommodate existing patterns of streets and buildings in cities, they could only be rough approximations of that type, and baseball players had to adjust their play to the idiosyncrasies of each park, which added a dimension to the game. Starting in the 1960s, new baseball parks became just one function within multifunctional structures built on open land either in the suburbs or in vast areas of cleared urban land surrounded by parking lots. As parks were standardized in respect to the type, many of the idiosyncrasies of the game were lost.

The plans of three small houses provide an example of how variations on a type may be designed not in reaction to existing conditions but in a conscious effort to provide variety within a cohesive group. The type consists of a spine, which is a datum wall with service functions to which are attached several kinds of interior living spaces and exterior courtyards (3.13, 3.14).

Variations also occur over time. The type provides a baseline from which to gauge these changes, giving us a form to which we can compare all subsequent changes so that no matter how elaborate a composition may become, there is still a primal referent form. For example, in a study of the morphology of Texas vernacular architecture, a former student produced a series of possible permutations of a basic frontier house type as its inhabitants might have adapted it over time to their changing needs and fortunes (3.15).

There are three ways to consider the variation of a type as a design method. The first is to understand it as an ad hoc process, as the example of the Texas vernacular suggests. More abstractly, a second interpretation is to design a building based on a durably recognizable type in anticipation of change over time so its core form persists despite radical deformations. A third, even more abstract approach is to design a building as a complete composition that implies that it has already deformed from its original condition. The design of the 11th-century Monastery of Saint Martin du Canigou in the French Pyrenees illustrates the third condition. It is a descendant of the Benedictine formula for the planning of a monastery. Saint Benedict and later Saint Bernard of the Cistercians established a strictly utilitarian plan type for their monasteries by placing all functions of monastic life in modular buildings surrounding and attached to a central, square cloister (3.16). The Abbey of Royaumont came closest to an architectural plan derived from this abstract type, largely because the complex of buildings occupied an optimal site (3.17). The Abbey of Saint Martin, on the other hand, sits precariously on a rugged, rocky ridge in the mountains. As a variation of the type, it deviates considerably from the orthogonal relation of parts (3.18, 3.19). Though individual buildings are rectangular in plan, their connections are eccentric due to the irregular terrain. However, despite the irregularity of the plan, a strong desire to adhere to the type is still discernable: the challenging topography has not broken the spell of the type. Parts of the building program are still in the general locations specified for them, and we can imagine the form of Saint Martin as having originated in a plan much like that of Royaumont's.

Sometimes, permutations on one type may not be able to solve all of the problems confronting a designer. When conditions of a site or program differ so greatly, they may require the use of a combination of types. The forms of villages, towns, and cities serve to illustrate this point. There are two major types of city plans: geomorphic and geometric. Geomorphic plans tend to conform to the landscape, their streets following the topography in lines of least resistance; such towns may also take advantage of a geological condition for defensive purposes. Geometric plans tend to ignore topography and follow a rigid, preconceived design—generally an orthogonal or radial grid—without regard to features of the landscape. Changing circumstances of their inhabitants, however, have resulted in many variations of these two major types.

Barcelona is an interesting example in which a geometric Renaissance grid of broad avenues (called *ramblas*) surrounds the original geomorphic medieval core. However, as the city grew farther outward into more rugged topography, the pattern reverted to a geomorphic type to accommodate steep hillsides. The medieval European plans illustrated here show the three common types of that era (3.20). The first is a linear market town based on the central road through it, the second is a town that grew in concentric layers around a central point (in this case an abbey), and the third is a plan that was an orthogonal grid—a *bastide*. The *bastide* plan was useful for the rapid development of small towns in southern France depopulated by war (3.21). In the unusual case of Carcassonne, in southern France, we find the two types—geomorphic and geometric—adjacent to one another (3.22). The original town was geomorphic, having grown around an ancient hilltop citadel. When it surrendered to Simon de Montfort in 1209, he forced the surviving inhabitants to construct and inhabit a new geometric—and indefensible—town in the valley below under the strict supervision of its new ruler. Thus we find that beyond their day-to-day use, types of urban patterns can have underlying political significance.

Throughout the history of architecture, types have emerged for good reasons. They represent the distillation of knowledge about the functions of buildings and their relation to their physical and human context. Functions may be practical and utilitarian, or they may be metaphorical and symbolic; both are important in establishing the meaning of a design. As these examples demonstrate, the use of a type as the basis or starting point for design does not constrain or limit creativity. To the contrary, it allows the designer to establish at the outset an important quality of architectural form—familiarity. From there the designer can introduce new, innovative ideas.

3.3

Skulls of Four Bird Species.

1. Common snipe
2. Barn owl
3. California thrasher
4. Horned puffin
5. Schematic of the type

Each of these bird skulls has three parts: a roughly spherical brain case, a beak, and a bony armature that unites the two. All bird skulls are variations on this type. The specifics of the variation depend on behavior, diet, and environment.

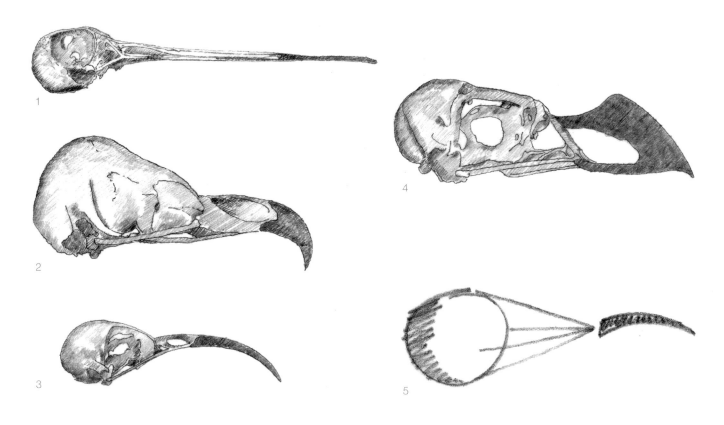

3.3

3.4

**Variations of a House Type, Yap
Islands, Micronesia. Elevations
and section. (After W. N. Morgan,
Prehistoric Architecture in Micronesia.)**

Top to bottom:

Daughter's house

Cook house

Copra drying house

Boat house

The four buildings are variations upon a structural type. The model requires two center posts to support a ridge beam. Short peripheral posts rest on an elevated platform of either timber or stone, its roof framing consists of lightweight lateral rafters and longitudinal purlins, and cladding varies according to the need for light, air, and privacy. The copra drying house and the boat house illustrate how the basic building shape can be deformed.

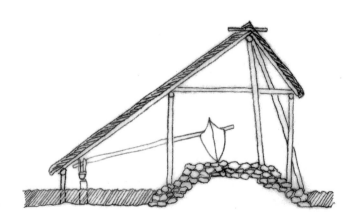

3.4

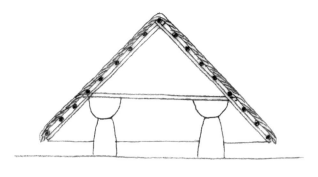

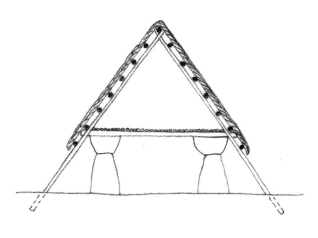

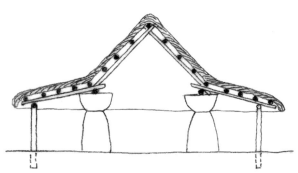

3.5

Superstructures of "Latte" Houses, Tinian, Micronesia. Sections. (After W. N. Morgan, *Prehistoric Architecture of Micronesia*.)

The timber superstructures of the houses built by the original inhabitants of Tinian no longer exist. However, the "latte" stones, which were colossal columns of volcanic rock, persist. These four designs were proposed by archaeologists as possible variants of the superstructure based on the standard scale and plan of the latte stones.

3.5

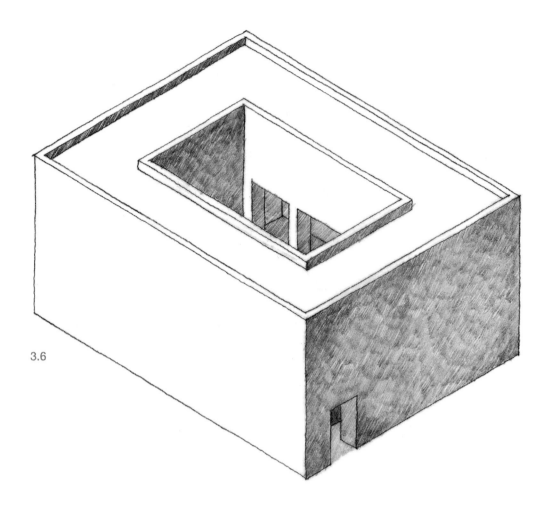

3.6

3.6
Courtyard House Type. Schematic axonometric.

The courtyard type can be found throughout the world, particularly in regions that are hot and dry. As a strategic idea it has several important advantages. The courtyard is the principal living space of the house. Protected from the sun, wind, and dust, it is a room whose ceiling is the sky. It acts as the lungs of the house, buffering the extremes of a climate in which days can be extremely hot and nights are cold. At night the courtyard allows the accumulated warm air in the house to escape from surrounding spaces into the night sky. The cool, moist air that settles into the courtyard at night is heavier than the day's warm, dry air and remains contained within the volume of the courtyard, gradually seeping into the house's interior the following day. The courtyard serves a critical social function as well by providing a private outdoor space that can be occupied or enjoyed from adjacent interior spaces, a particularly important asset in urban situations where buildings are densely packed, and for cultures in which the privacy of family life and the control of social relations are paramount.

3.7
Courtyard House, Cairo, Egypt, 18th century. Plans.

This plan demonstrates several typical features of a traditional Cairene courtyard house. The courtyard is offset, rather than in the center, to allow for the compact planning of interior spaces. Entry requires two turns through a vestibule and an alcove to ensure the courtyard's privacy even when the door is open to the street, and one's first view of the courtyard is on the diagonal, the largest dimension of the space. The connection of the courtyard with the building interior also requires two turns through a vestibule and an alcove. The principal relation of the interior with the courtyard is a second-floor living space that connects with the interior on three sides but is open to and overlooking the courtyard on one side. This space usually faces north to capture prevailing breezes and to keep the summer sun to its back. The principal interior living room on the lower level is a three-part space with a fountain at its center. It is usually a double-height, top-lit space so women in the harem on the second floor can discreetly watch the men below. Plan drawings such as these that reduce the design to two or three floors are somewhat misleading since architects did not design the interiors of Cairene houses with respect to continuous floor levels. Instead, they designed each room volumetrically, with attention to proportions, light, and air; they then arranged stairs and passages to serve these spaces whose floors are at various elevations above ground level. The figure/ground illustrates the simple planning concept of the building as a whole.

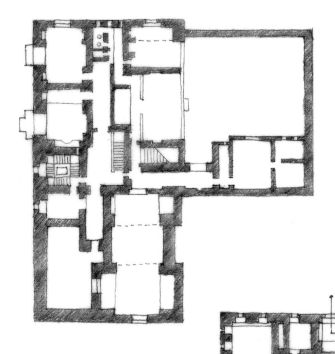

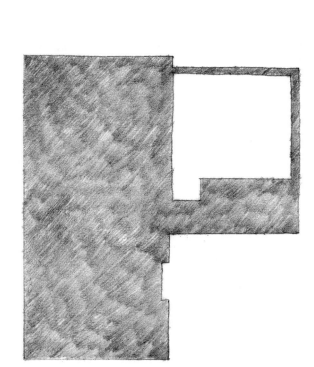

3.7

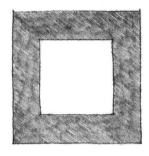

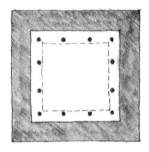

3.8

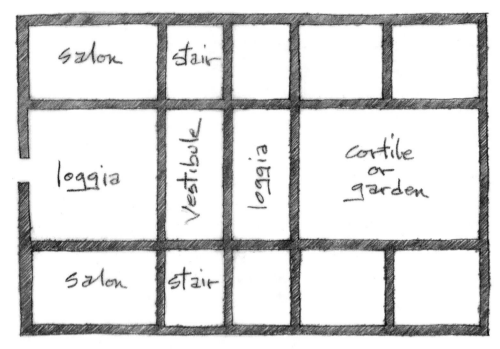

3.9

3.8

Atrium, *Cortile*, and Cloister. Schematic plans.

In the European architectural tradition, the courtyard type—an outdoor room that serves as the focus of a building form—has three variants, or subtypes, depending on the articulation of the wall that surrounded the central space. An atrium consists of a solid wall with doors and windows opening into it, much as if it were an exterior wall; in many cases, the structure of the wall is, in fact, visible. A *cortile* has visible structure that is part of the enclosing wall (e.g., arches and columns), often with a passageway behind it within the mass of the building. A cloister relies on a structure of arches or columns with its own roof that is separate from the enclosing wall of the central space. This structure stands within the central space for the sole purpose of providing a covered passage around it.

3.9

Palazzi of Strada Nuova, Genoa, 1450. Plan type.

The intention of the Strada Nuova—the earliest example of Renaissance urban design of its kind—was to create a predetermined form of urban space with a composition of buildings. The street consisted entirely of palazzi for the wealthy merchant class. Though each palazzo satisfied the specific taste and requirements of its owner, they were all variants of a type that had emerged within the previous fifty years. The model was a rectangular enclosure, approximately in the proportion of 1:1.5, with an entrance facade directly on the street boundary. At ground level, the rectangle had three lateral zones that allowed salons and circulation to flank central formal spaces. Longitudinally, the plan had four zones from front to back devoted to a vestibule, loggia, stairs, and a *cortile*.

3.10

Palazzi of Strada Nuova. Plans.

These six plans represent variations on the type for the palazzo along the street: 1. Palazzo di Baldassarre, 2. Palazzo di Luca Grimaldi, 3. Palazzo Rosso, 4. Palazzo di Tobia Pallavicino, 5. Palazzo di Giambattista Spinola, 6. Palazzo di Agostino Pallavicino.

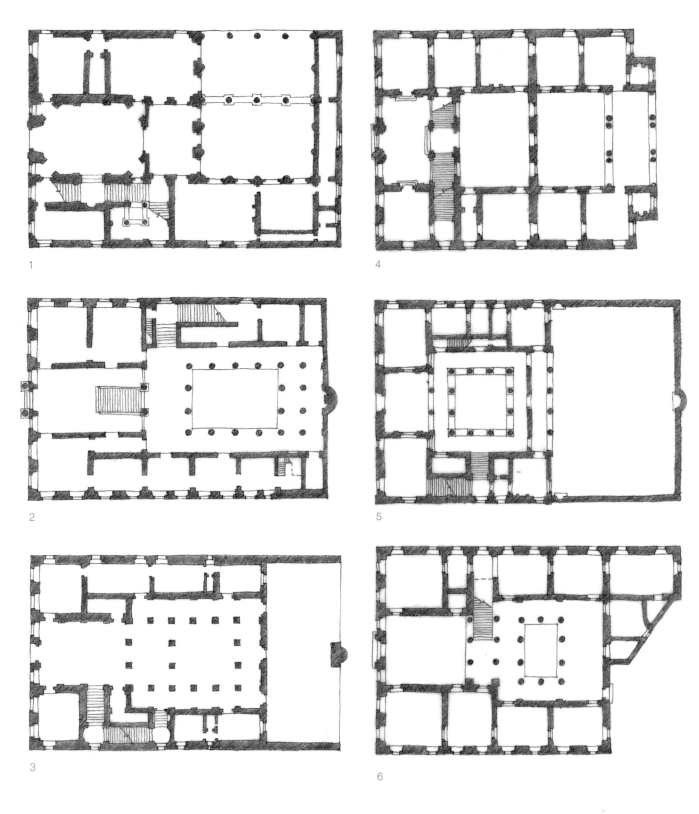

1

2

3

4

5

6

3.10

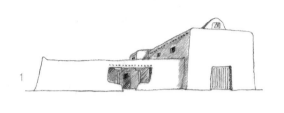

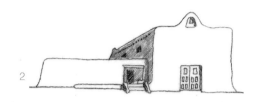

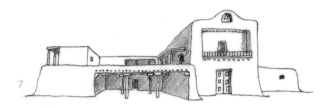

3.11

3.11

Spanish Mission Churches of the Upper Rio Grande, New Mexico, 16th to 19th centuries. Views.

1. Santa Clara, 2. Cochiti, 3. Zia, 4. Jemez, 5. San Juan, 6. Nambe, 7. San Ildefonso, 8. Santo Domingo, 9. Santa Fe. Indigenous Pueblo Indians built village churches under the direction of Spanish friars according to a model that was alien in form and scale to that of their villages and pueblos. The type was a simple rectangular adobe box with a flat roof of peeled tree trunks for beams (*vigas*), lightweight purlins often in a herringbone pattern (*lattias*), and covered with a rush matting and mud. The exterior walls had a mud plaster finish, renewed annually. The morphology of the facade is particularly interesting. In the simplest structures (e.g., Cochiti), the belfry was no more than a slight deformation of the wall, whereas in later, more elaborate examples (e.g., Santa Fe), the facade split into towers, each with a belfry. Similarly, the small door above the main entrance (e.g., Zia) that allowed the priest to address parishioners in front of the church gradually transformed into a more complex form consisting of a porch within a framed enclosure (e.g., Santo Domingo).

3.12

American Urban Baseball Parks, 1909–23. Plans.

The design of baseball parks presents the paradox of a precisely defined infield and an indeterminately shaped outfield. The type underlying the plans of all baseball parks is a symmetrical plan that requires a foul line of 330 feet, a power alley of 375 feet, and a centerfield distance of 400 feet. Taken together, the six classic major league urban baseball parks illustrated here, plus eight others, comprise a set of variations on a type. None of the fourteen ballparks built between 1909 and 1923 explicitly adhered to the type, and only one, Comiskey Park in Chicago, was symmetrical in plan. Instead, they all exhibited many idiosyncrasies depending upon their unique urban circumstances—chiefly the surrounding patterns of city blocks. Each of the early ballparks approximated the type but was replete with anomalies. As a result, each park had a unique character that required players to make subtle adjustments in play. In contrast, ballparks constructed since 1962, beyond the constraints of American downtowns, have been virtually identical multiuse stadiums, usually sitting in the center of gigantic parking lots. The unfortunate result of a conventional ballpark architecture was a standard style of play.

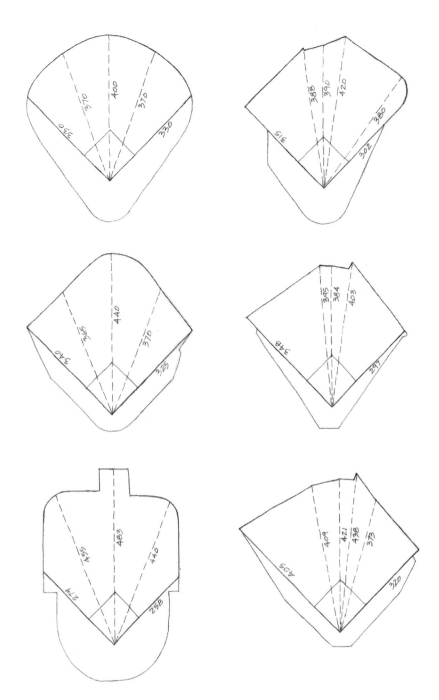

3.12

Second Floor

First Floor

Second Floor

First Floor

3.13

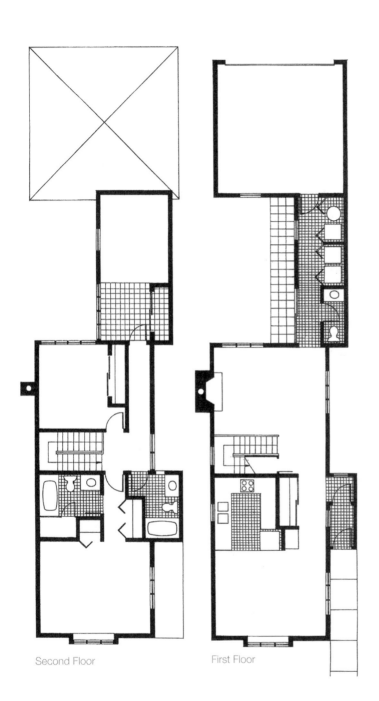

Second Floor   First Floor

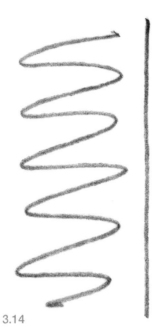

3.14

3.13
**Spinal Houses, Variants, 1998.
D. Hanlon. Plans.**

These three plans are for houses on long,
narrow lots. They are variations on a type
consisting of a spine of utilities and movement serving interior living spaces and private
exterior courts. The spine has a closed exterior wall to ensure the privacy of a neighbor's
courts.

3.14
**Spinal House Type. Schematic
diagram.**

3.15

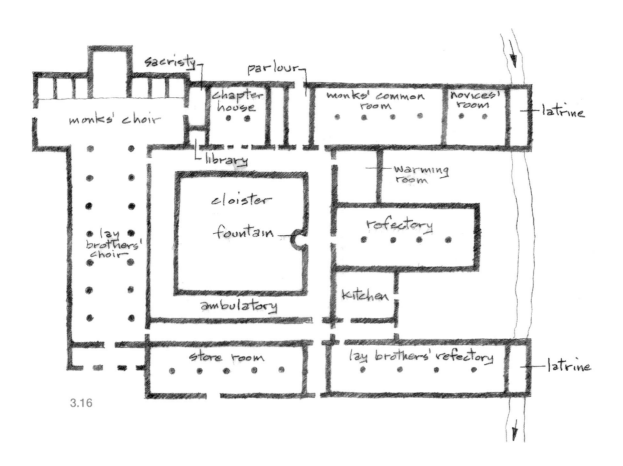

3.16

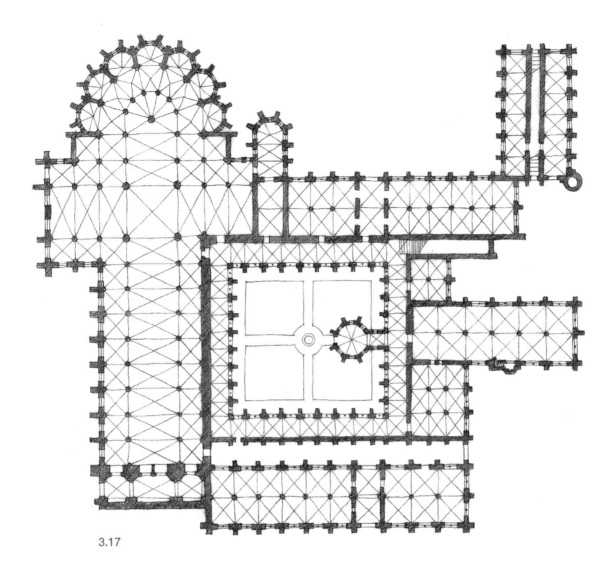

3.17

3.15
Morphology of Early Settlers' Houses in Central Texas. (After drawings by M. Imber.)

This study depicts the way Anglo settlers of the late 18th and early 19th centuries produced a variety of house forms from an iconic type—a simple rectangular volume with a gable roof—by adding porches and sheds incrementally over time. Despite considerable elaboration in form, all of the variations retain an underlying relation to the original type, indicating a deeply rooted cultural predisposition for a traditional form from another part of the country that had little to do with the realities of the climate and the landscape of central Texas.

3.16
Cistercian Monastery Type, 12th to 14th centuries. Schematic plan.

A formula dictated the design of all of the Cistercian abbeys. The principal requirement was to fit all functions rationally around a cloister and a source of water. Generally, the church was on the north side, to avoid casting a shadow into the cloister. Lower buildings ranged around the other three sides of the cloister in a standard pattern, and an orthogonal module governed the sizes and proportions of spaces. All Cistercian abbeys and monasteries were variations on this type, each deviating from it in response to the unique physical circumstances that their builders encountered.

3.17
Abbey of Royaumont, 1228–35. Plan.

At the close of the 11th century, Saint Bernard led a reformist movement of Benedictines that strove for extreme simplicity through an architecture that supported an austere monastic life. The Cistercian movement rapidly established abbeys throughout Europe, generally in wild and barren locations. Due to its ideal topography, Royaumont represents one of the purest examples of the type.

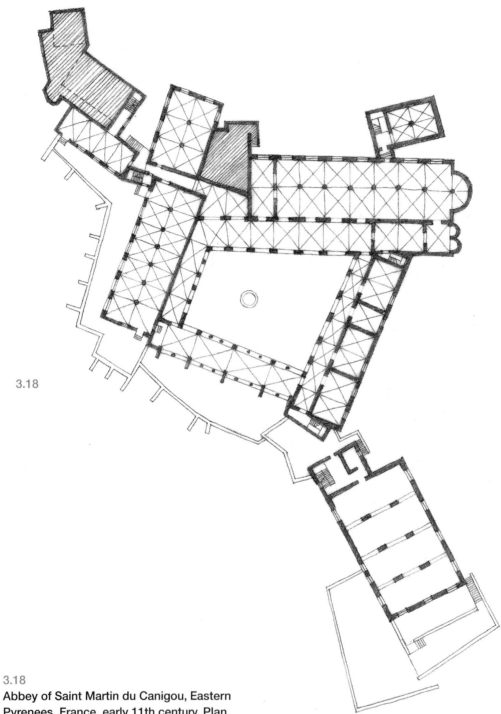

3.18

3.18
Abbey of Saint Martin du Canigou, Eastern Pyrenees, France, early 11th century. Plan.
The plan of this small abbey conformed to the type for Benedictine and Cistercian monasteries, but its designers distorted the type to fit the abbey's rugged mountaintop site. The normally serene rectangular cloister of a typical monastery, with its uniform arcaded ambulatory, became a trapezoid, each side of which is unique. Other features of the plan conformed to the underlying type but deviated from the ideal orthogonal arrangement or shifted vertically to fit the sloping site.

3.19

3.19

Abbey of Saint Martin du Canigou. View.
A view of the abbey reveals how the designer maintained
the rectangular prismatic volume of each component of the
composition by loosening the connections between them.
The interstitial spaces allowed for the distortion of the normally orthogonal plan. The result is an intriguing play between regularity and irregularity.

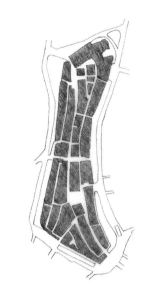

3.20

Medieval European Town. Plans.

These illustrate the three principal types
of town plan developed in medieval
Europe: the market type, the citadel type,
and the *bastide*. The market town type
emerged along trade routes and usually
developed linearly to offer the greatest
degree of exposure to the major commercial route through the town; the
market was often simply a widening of the
road. The citadel town type developed
concentrically around a defensible
position occupied by either a feudal lord's
castle or a fortified abbey. Both attracted
trade and therefore gradual commercial
and residential development on the
slopes below. While the first two types
developed gradually, the *bastide* was a
preconceived town plan, usually a grid,
designed for the efficient conveyance of
property to populate the town and its
surrounding agricultural land quickly. A
typical *bastide* had one open block near
its center as a marketplace, and though
its boundary condition was ideally regular
(a rectangle or octagon, for example), it
was more often irregular, because of
settlement patterns and topographic
features that impeded its growth. This set
of six diagrams illustrates the overall
forms of the towns and the patterns of
their streets.

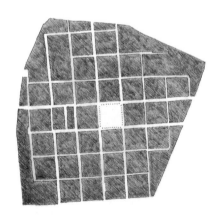

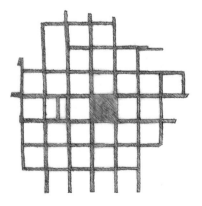

3.20

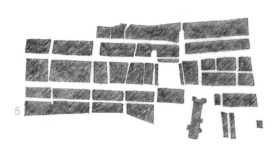

3.21

3.21

***Bastides*, France, 13th century. Plans.**

1. Villeréal, 2. Eymet, 3. Domme, 4. Lalinde,
5. Beaumont, 6. Villefranche-du-Périgord.
(After A. E. J. Morris, *History of Urban Form.*)
In southern France, *bastides* adhered to a
standard plan, or type, as a means of consolidating rural hamlets and repopulating
land decimated by war. Louis IX was respon-
sible for the construction of many *bastides* in
the Languedoc region following the Albigensian Crusade. They were predominantly
farming communities, though some had
value as market towns and military garrisons.
Despite numerous variations, the underlying
bastide type was a grid of streets within a
rectangle divided into nearly identical house
plots. Residents were required to construct
their house to cover the entire street
frontage. There was a main square at the intersection of the streets from the main gates.
A town hall adjoined the square with an arcaded ground level that provided a covered
market, and a church generally occupied an
adjacent square. Though prescriptive, the
type did not produce identical town plans. All
were variations on the type occasioned by
having to accommodate topographical and
riparian features of their specific locations. In
the seven centuries since their founding,
their individuality has increased through
gradual rebuilding, though they have maintained their original patterns and their strong
relation to the type.

3.22

Carcassonne, Languedoc, France. Plan.

Celtic people inhabited the strategic hilltop of
Carsac as early as 350 BCE, and the Romans established a garrison there in 100 BCE. Over many
centuries the town grew geomorphically around
the original citadel. By the 12th century CE Carcassonne had become one of the centers of the
Cathar heresy, a dualist system of belief similar in
some ways to Manicheanism. Since the Cathars
believed that material possessions were unholy
(including the vast possessions of the Roman
Catholic Church), Pope Innocent III declared them
heretics and initiated the Albigensian Crusade. In
1209, Carcassonne fell to Simon de Montfort, a
mercenary in the pope's employ. As with other
sieges in the Languedoc region during the crusade, this resulted in a wholesale massacre of the
town's citizens. Likewise, twenty years of war in
southern France depopulated most of the countryside. The pope confiscated the lands of the
southern feudal lords and awarded them to the
loyal Catholic northern French nobility, who then
founded new towns as a means to reestablish
agriculture and trade. Simon de Montfort located
the new town of Carcassonne, the *ville basse,* or
lower town, in the valley below the original citadel,
and, as was typical of *bastides* throughout
Languedoc, he laid it out as a simple grid and designed it to be indefensible.

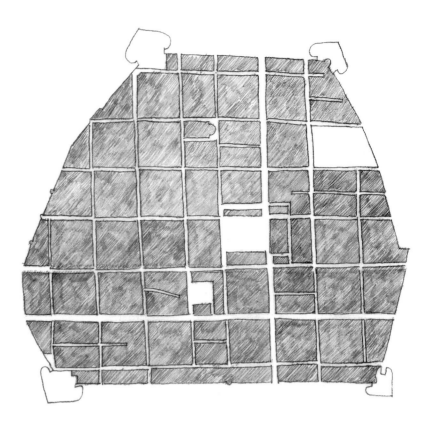

3.22

CHAPTER FOUR

THE SQUARE

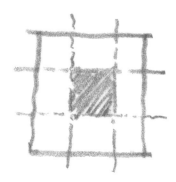

The Four-Quartered Square

Historically, the square has been the most common geometric figure used as a basis for creating building plans. Its appeal has been twofold. From a practical point of view, it offers simple numerical relationships (1:1), a clear sense of balance and orientation, and certain mathematical properties from which a designer can derive a variety of proportional relationships, such as 1:√2 and the golden section (1: 1.618...). These can then be used to subdivide the square or extrapolate it into forms of greater complexity. The square's symbolic potential has also made it popular. From the earliest forms of symbolic notation, such as cuneiform and hieroglyphics, the four-quartered square has appeared as a symbol for the perfect, primal condition of the world. This was due to the way the geometry of the square organized its interior and related it to the cardinal directions. The square was the symbol for civilization, expressing order within its boundaries—as opposed to the chaos beyond them. It was commonly represented by the intersection of two axes, originating at the midpoints of its sides and crossing at its center.

This symbol of paradise, the original uncorrupted world, persists to the present in many forms—in buildings, cities, textiles, and gardens. Architectural and urban designers have often aligned their axes with the polestar to the north and the rising sun to the east. Thus the four-quartered square indicated the role of humanity as an intermediary between the earth and the cosmos, that is, between physical and metaphysical realms.

The hostel in the Sanctuary of Asklepios at Epidaurus (4.1) appears to have been a practical application of the four-quartered square to a building plan, since it simply subdivided a large building into smaller units, first to segregate men from women and then to provide courtyards of a reasonable scale for a residential function. In contrast, the plans of the Great Stupa of Jiaohe (4.2) and the fortress palace of Datia (4.3) were architectural expressions of perfection, harmony, and comprehensive control over space and form. In the case of Jiaohe, that centralized control was religious, whereas at Datia it was secular.

A common variant of the four-quartered square particularly popular in the Greek and Roman building traditions was to distort it slightly in order to inscribe an equilateral triangle, producing a rectangle with the proportion of 2:√3 (or 1:0.866). This preserved the square's biaxial symmetry, and it could still be subdivided into four equal quadrants; however, it placed a slightly greater emphasis on one axis (usually the east-west axis) over the other. The Romans used this diagram extensively as the basis for planning provincial towns, or *castra*. Timgad, Algeria (4.4, 4.5), is one of the best preserved, but we can still find them embedded in the cores of cities throughout the Mediterranean and Europe, such as in Avanches, Switzerland, and in Florence, Italy. When the emperor Diocletian retired, he used the same model as that of the *castrum* to construct a palace at Split on the Adriatic. In the typical *castrum*, the main avenue from the west gate led to the forum; similarly, in Diocletian's palace, the west avenue led to his monumental audience chamber (4.6, 4.7).

The square continues to be popular among architects as a means for creating simple, rational plans. The combination of quartering the square and subdividing it by the golden section produces internal dimensions that are useful for a variety of spaces and functions. A comparison of two house plans—one a vernacular example from Konya in Anatolia and the other a modern house in Bergamo, Italy (4.8)—reveals precisely the same method of spatial organization. In both, an L-shaped building mass embraces a circulation zone and a square space that serves as the focus of the house. (In the vernacular house this is a courtyard, and in the Italian example it is a cubic living room.)

In the 1970s, Hiromi Fujii experimented with several variations on the internal subdivision of a four-quartered square (4.9). Of the three shown here, the first is a simple version in which each quarter has a specific function. In the second, Fujii broke down the geometry into a finer grain to create a greater variety and complexity of interpenetrating spaces based, as in the first plan, on the dimensions of the tatami mat. This plan, with its open, fluid spatial continuity, has its roots in traditional Japanese interior planning. In the third plan, Fujii explored the European approach to the use of poché, enclosed figural spaces, and an exaggerated hierarchy of served and service functions.

4.1

Hostel, Sanctuary of Asklepios, Epidaurus. Plan.

As the cult of Asklepios, the healing god, grew in Classical Greece during the 5th century BCE and became popular among Romans in the 4th century BCE, the sanctuary required new buildings to accommodate thousands of pilgrims. This hostel, one of several near the sanctuary, is a pragmatic design with individual cells surrounding four courtyards. It has two halves to segregate men from women with the only connecting passage, at its center, joining the two rooms occupied by custodians.

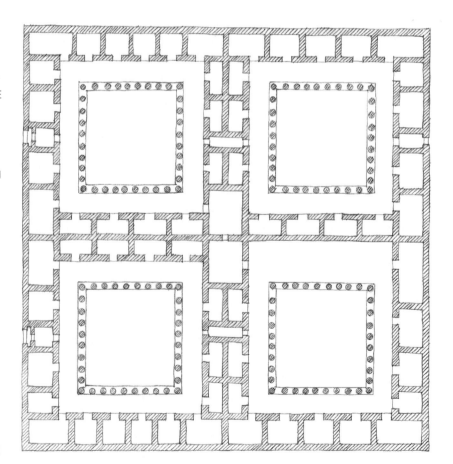

4.1

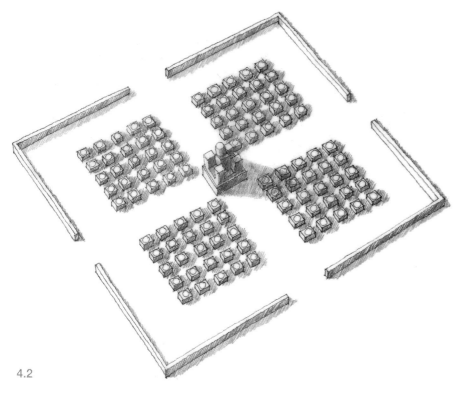

4.2

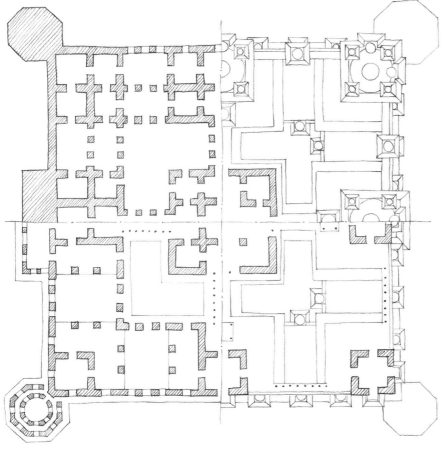

4.3

4.2

Buddhist Stupa, Jiaohe, Xinjiang, China, 1st century BCE to 14th century CE. Aerial view.

Jiaohe, sited along the Silk Road, is the largest and best preserved earthen city in the world. Due to its strategic position on a narrow 100-foot high promontory above the confluence of two rivers, it required no walls except at two gates. A wide avenue originating at the southern gate formed a spine through the center of the city leading to a temple district at the apex of the promontory. A large stupa, over 50,000 square feet in area, was at the center of the temple district oriented to the cardinal directions and consisting of four hypostyle halls (the bases of its colossal columns remain) around a central tower. All of the structures in the city, including the stupa, were of rammed earth and sun-dried mud brick. After 1,500 years of occupation, the city's occupants fled in the face of a Mongol invasion, but despite being left unprotected for 700 years since its evacuation, much of the city remains intact due to its isolation and an arid climate.

4.3

Datia Palace, Uttar Pradesh, India, 1620. Plans of four levels.

After supporting the Mughal prince Jahangir in his successful rebellion against his father Akbar, the raja Bir Singh Deo built the Datia palace/fortress to secure his homeland of Bundelkhand. The plan is a four-quartered square with corner towers and a large courtyard at its core. At the center of the courtyard is a five-story tower containing the royal apartments, with a central dome 115 feet high connected to the perimeter structure by four narrow bridges. This drawing depicts four levels of the perimeter structure (including the roof plan) at once. In the opinion of Sir Edwin Lutyens, the designer of New Delhi, the Datia palace was the most perfect in India.

4.4

Timgad, Algeria, ca. 100 CE. Plan.

Established during the reign of Trajan, Timgad was a provincial city devoted entirely to Roman citizens, particularly soldiers who had gained citizenship by fighting for Rome for twenty-five years. Derived from a military camp—a *cas-trum*—the city plan was a rectangular enclo-sure subdivided into four quadrants by two main avenues, the principal one, the *cardo,* running north-south, and the secondary one, the *decumanus,* running east-west. Consistent with its military origin, all house lots were identi-cal in size. *Cardo* means "hinge" or "pivot" in Latin, so its application to the north-south av-enue established the ritual spine of the city as the hinge of the sun in its transit from east to west. The forum occupied the center of the city with the theater behind it, while the arena for blood sports was outside the city walls, as were the suburbs for noncitizens.

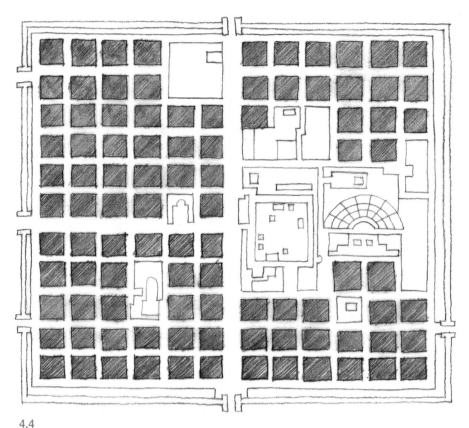

4.4

4.5

Timgad, Algeria. Composition.

The proportion of the enclosing rectangle of the city was 2:√3, that is, the rectangle inscribed an equilateral triangle. This figure was ubiqui-tous in Classical design, appearing at all scales, from small objects and architectural features to cities. Whereas the *cardo* fixed Tim-gad to a cosmological order, the *decumanus* was the principal street for daily activities—a colonnaded ceremonial avenue that originated at the western gate and led directly to the east-ern forum.

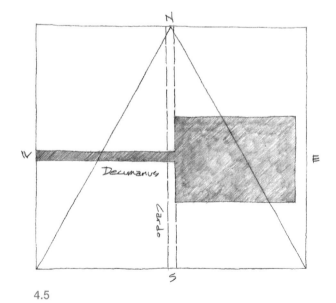

4.5

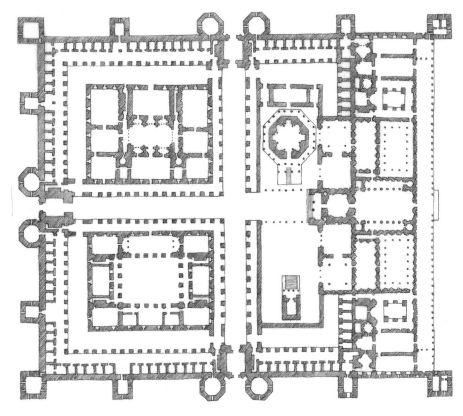

4.6

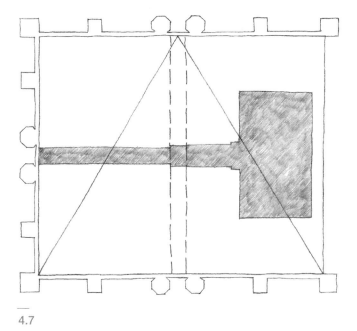

4.7

4.6

Palace of Diocletian at Split, Dalmatia, ca. 300 CE. Plan.

The plan of Diocletian's palace expressed the unified power and authority of the emperor in an era that saw a rise of absolutism in government and society. As in portraiture and sculpture of the period, architecture relied on rigid abstraction and a reduction of forms to mechanical stereotypes. Thus, the palace plan was a direct reflection of a Roman military camp, a *castrum*, in which a four-square diagram controlled all parts of the composition. A central colonnaded street led from the main gate, between the emperor's octagonal mausoleum and a temple of Jupiter, to the palace, called the *praetorium* ("headquarters"). All buildings were symmetrical, assigned a specific function, and experienced primarily as sets of formal interior spaces rather than as objects in space. This approach to planning was in stark contrast to the relaxed Hellenistic style found in Hadrian's Villa at Tivoli.

4.7

Palace of Diocletian. Proportion.

The general organization and the proportion of the palace plan were almost identical to that of the *castrum* of Timgad. The plan was a rectangle that inscribed an equilateral triangle (therefore 2:√3), and the approach from the main gate to the main palace was a colonnaded avenue corresponding to the *decumanus* of Timgad.

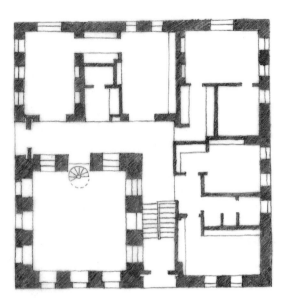

4.8

Two House Plans: Bergamo, Italy, and Konya, Turkey.

The method used to produce the plans of these two houses was identical, yet they originate in quite different design traditions. The plan at the top is for the Casa Bazzana near Bergamo, Italy, built in 1995 and designed by the high-style design firm of Citterio and Dwan. The primary living space is square in plan and separated from all other functions of the house by an L-shaped passage. The plan at the center is for a late 19th-century vernacular house in Konya, Turkey, by an anonymous architect. It, too, has the primary space of the house, the square courtyard, separated from secondary living spaces by an L-shaped passage. The diagram at the bottom shows that the two plans use an identical system of proportion. The designers subdivided a square into quarters by centerlines and then further subdivided it by the golden section. The difference between the two dimensions forms the L-shaped passage between the primary space and the secondary spaces.

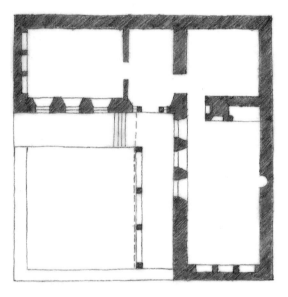

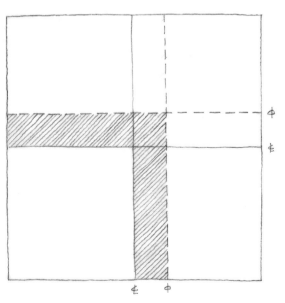

4.8

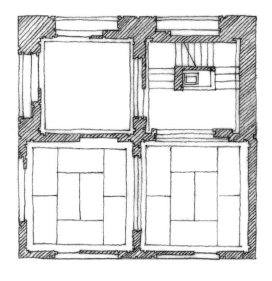

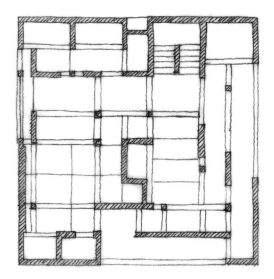

4.9

Three Variations on the Four-Square Plan, 1976. Hiromi Fujii. Plans.

These three plans demonstrate that the simplicity of the four-square diagram does not prevent a talented designer from creating complex spatial patterns. Their interest derives largely from the underlying reference to a primal diagram, a condition that produces an oscillation between stasis and dynamism in a single pattern. The top plan follows traditional Japanese interior planning precepts based on the ken, or the dimensions of a tatami mat. The center plan implies a relation to the ken as a module but deviates from its strict application for the sake of producing complex interpenetrations of spaces. The bottom example takes a more Western approach by emphasizing three figural spaces (square in plan) floating in the four-square grid, with the residual spaces as poché.

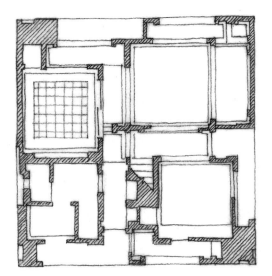

4.9

The Nine-Square Diagram

A subdivision of the square into nine squares or cells has the advantages of the four-quartered square with three additional properties. A nine-square may have a one-cell central zone with an eight-cell peripheral zone, or it can have a Greek cross with residual corner cells, or it can be a quincunx, a figure that includes the four corner cells plus the center cell (4.10).

In its simplest form, all nine cells of the diagram are identical squares of the same size. However, the nine-square diagram may appear in two other variations. The first permits changes in the proportions of the cells, allowing them to vary in size as squares and to distort into rectangles. The second either eliminates some cells or breaks the diagram and allow some cells to shift position.

In the plan of the house in Upper Kingsbury, Nova Scotia, by Brian MacKay-Lyons, the center cell—a complex solid that holds the hearth, plumbing, and stairs—contrasts with the eight peripheral cells (4.11). However, the architect does allow some distortion of the peripheral cells to differentiate living spaces. This house followed a vernacular tradition imported from Great Britain. In contrast, in a house in Edwinsford, Wales, four hearths occupy the central masonry core and all surrounding cells of the diagram are nearly equivalent. Interestingly, this plan was a late 16th-century import from Italy during the emergence of the English Renaissance under the reign of Elizabeth I. The submedieval plan of the house at Brongoronwry is the type that immediately preceded the Italian import (4.12). The Nagle House in Chicago is another example in which the cells have the same dimension but the central cell is different in quality—not a mass but instead a two-story void (4.13).

The subterranean Necromanteion at Ephyra from the 3rd century BCE (4.14) has nine identical cells, but the three central ones are joined to form a hall; note the labyrinthine entrance used to disorient pilgrims and produce the impression (enhanced by drugs and sleep deprivation) that they were entering the underworld. Henri Labrouste's design for the Bibliothèque Nationale in Paris (4.15) is a masonry shell that holds an iron cage in the form of a nine-square diagram in which all nine cells are identical volumes. Arata Isozaki implies a quincunx in the exterior form of a house in Oita, Japan, but the organization of the interior contradicts this impression (4.16). Another house of a similar size by Sverre Fehn in Sweden uses the Greek cross instead (4.17). It has a closed service core, and the arms of the cross are closed at their ends as well, but the corner cells are open to views and natural light.

A particular type of quincunx has a long tradition as the underlying diagram for monumental buildings. It is a distortion of the nine-square diagram by which the center cell is larger than the others; also, the corners diminish in size and the cells on the sides become $2:\sqrt{3}$ rectangles (4.18). To create this permutation, one superimposes four equilateral triangles on the square, their vertices at the midpoints of each side; a new grid emerges where the triangles intersect the diagonals of the square. This produces a strong hierarchy focused on the central space, a pattern that Asiatic cultures used extensively. It also appeared in Europe, particularly in Roman and Renaissance Neoclassical buildings and their derivatives. The 15th-century tomb in Agra called the Baradari of Sikander Lodi exemplifies the tradition that emerged from Central Asia and Persia (4.19). Its forest of piers creates interior avenues and pavilions surrounding the central tomb structure. In the 16th century, the same diagram produced the plan for the tomb of Humayun, a work of Mughal-Hindu hybrid architecture (4.20). It is dramatically different from the Baradari in the way in which mass and space are shaped. Piers are no longer seen as objects in space but rather as vestiges of a monumental mass that appears to have been carved away to permit passage through the building. A hundred years later, the same pattern appeared in a somewhat less complex plan for the Taj Mahal (4.21).

The plan of the Pantheon is also based on the modified quincunx; the proportions produced by the squares and equilateral triangles determine the positions and dimensions of the interior and exterior features of the great cylindrical drum (4.22, 4.23). The aedicule, a gable-roofed porch inserted into the drum, has a nine-square grid as the underlying diagram of its plan. This design became the basis for many Neoclassical projects in the Italian Renaissance, including the designs for the Basilica of Saint Peter by Donato Bramante (4.24), Antonio da Sangallo the Younger (4.25), and Michelangelo Buonarotti (4.26–4.28). The method was so successful that it persisted into the 17th and 18th centuries with the design, for example, of the Église du Dôme, part of Les Invalides in Paris (4.29).

Variants of the nine-square diagram and the quincunx were used extensively in modernist architecture as well. Louis I. Kahn used a modified quincunx in the plan of Phillips Exeter Academy Library, one similar to that of the plan of the Pantheon and Michelangelo's Basilica of Saint Peter (4.30–4.32). Kahn used the Greek cross, derived from the nine-square grid, in the Trenton Bath House (4.33), and he employed a technique of shifting cells within the nine-square grid in his proposed plan for the Adler House (4.34).

Since the nine-square diagram was ascribed cosmological significance in Asiatic cultures, many religious structures and even cities were based on its form, with each cell relating to a deity or an aspect of physical phenomena (e.g., fire, air, earth, and water). The plan of the city of Jaipur in Rajasthan is a good example: it demonstrates how the manipulation of an abstract diagram can satisfy several design requirements. Its founder, Jai Singh, was interested in investing the city with as much good fortune and power as possible, so the city plan conformed to the auspicious nine-square Prthivi Pithapada mandala. However, due to the constraints of its site, the architect adjusted the geometry, striking a balance between the tangible requirements of a physical setting and an abstract cosmological diagram (4.35).

The plan of Jaipur illustrates a key concept in design: the application of an abstract paradigm to a physical reality requires a flexible translation of a conceptual model. In the case of Jaipur, the mandala was a mental device, not a graphic one. Therefore, though the final plan deviates markedly from the nine-square mandala that served as its origin, the power of geometry persists. The city consistently aligns the pedestrian with its underlying urban idea. The architect's intention was not to represent the mandala literally as a graphic form but to create an experience of the mandala in a living urban form

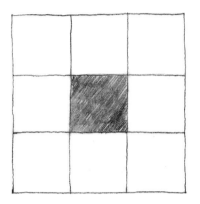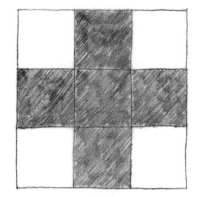

4.10

4.10

The Nine-Square Diagram.

The nine-square diagram lends itself to three interior organizations. 1. It may be seen as having two parts, a center cell and a set of eight peripheral cells. 2. Five cells related orthogonally can form a Greek cross with four residual corner cells. 3. Five cells related diagonally (the central cell and the four corner cells) can produce a quincunx.

4.11

House, Upper Kingsbury, Nova Scotia, 1986. Brian MacKay-Lyons. Plan.

Drawing on the form of a traditional salt-box common along the northeast coast of North America, the architect has designed this house as a core and shell based on a simple heavy-timber framing diagram, with the interstitial space in a nine-square. To accommodate the program, however, MacKay-Lyons has manipulated the proportions of the nine cells to produce a hierarchy of spaces. The stair, bathroom, hearth, and kitchen stove all occupy the compact central core, thus creating a stark contrast between mass and void within the house. The nine-square in this case simultaneously fixes the house within a historical context and exploits an economical method of construction.

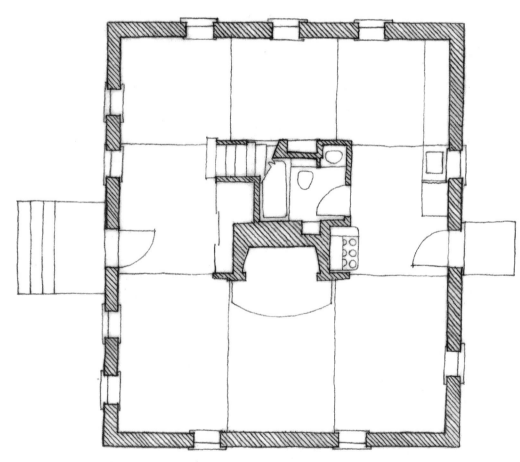

4.11

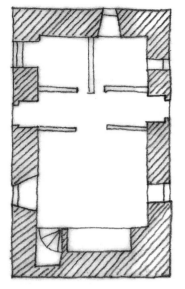
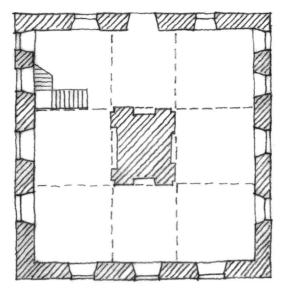

4.12

4.12

**Two Houses in Wales,
15th and 16th centuries. Plans.**

These two plans illustrate the influence of Italian Renaissance ideas on rural houses in Wales. The 15th-century house at Brongoronwry (left) has a typical submedieval plan: rectangular, with a narrow center hall, private rooms to one side, a parlor to the other, and a loft above. After the ascension of Elizabeth I to the throne, the prevailing style changed to a nine-square grid, an Italian (specifically Palladian) import. Typical of this period, the 16th-century house in Edwinsford (right) had a four-sided hearth in its center square, and aside from the orientation of the front door, there was no differentiation of interior spaces on the first floor. This dramatic interior change signaled a comparable change in the relation of the house to the landscape—it went from a building with a distinct front and back to a building to be seen as an object in the round.

4.13

**Nagle House, Chicago, 1978.
Nagle Hartray Danker Kagan.
Plan.**

The firm is noted for simple geometric Modernist designs, particularly in the many houses it has completed, and this plan reveals the flexibility of a nine-square grid as a means to organize domestic functions in a straightforward manner. Unlike the nine-square plan of a traditional house that is likely to have a heavy masonry hearth at its center, the Nagle house has a two-story void filled with natural light.

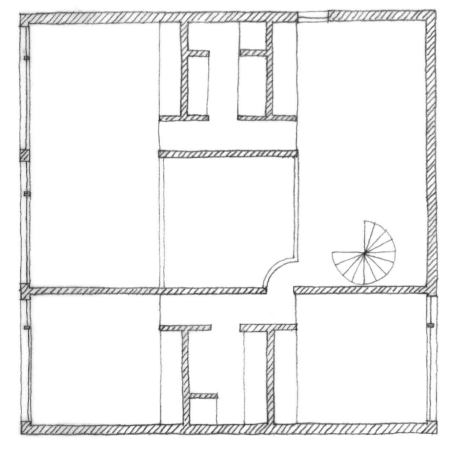

4.13

4.14

Necromanteion of Ephyra, 13th to 2nd centuries BCE. Plan.

The Necromanteion was the only oracle in Greece dedicated to consultations with the dead: residing outside of time, it could presumably foretell the future. Before the Dorian invasions, it was a Mycenaean site; it appeared in the Odyssey and was popular throughout the Classical Greek and Hellenistic periods and into early Roman times. The subterranean structure illustrated here was at the center of the sanctuary and served as the culmination of a rigorous ritual spanning several days that prepared supplicants to meet the dead. They descended a long passage to enter the underground labyrinth that led to one of the six tomblike chambers. The arrangement of the chambers and their central corridor is a nine-square in plan that, like the labyrinth, is an abstraction of the form of Hades as described in myths. After many prosperous centuries for Ephyra, the Romans exposed the oracle as a hoax and destroyed it in 167 BCE.

4.15

Bibliothèque Nationale, Reading Room, Paris, 1867. Henri Labrouste. Plan.

Though trained in the École des Beaux-Arts as a Neoclassical architect, Labrouste is best known for rationalist designs that brought industrial materials, construction methods, and aesthetics into the mainstream of cultural monuments. Labrouste was interested in the realist school of literature, led by Victor Hugo, and aspired to accomplish a similar form of expression of modern life in his architecture. He demonstrated this first in the design of the Bibliothèque Sainte-Geneviève (1845–51) that elevated industrially derived iron framing to a high art. The Reading Room of the Bibliothèque Nationale is a deceptively simple nine-square plan in which an iron frame resides within a masonry shell. Taking full advantage of cast-iron technology, the extremely slender columns rise to support nine simple pendentive-supported domes in terra-cotta that appear to be nearly weightless. In this case, Labrouste used the nine-square plan as a device for conveying a sense of serene rationalism, emblematic of the library as an institution and of the ideals of French culture as well.

4.14

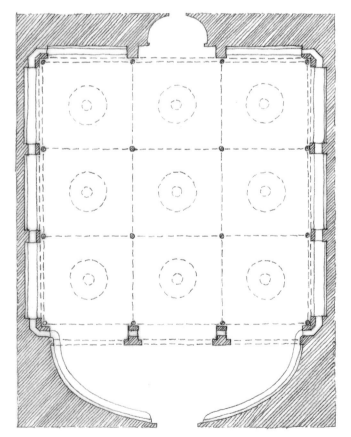

4.15

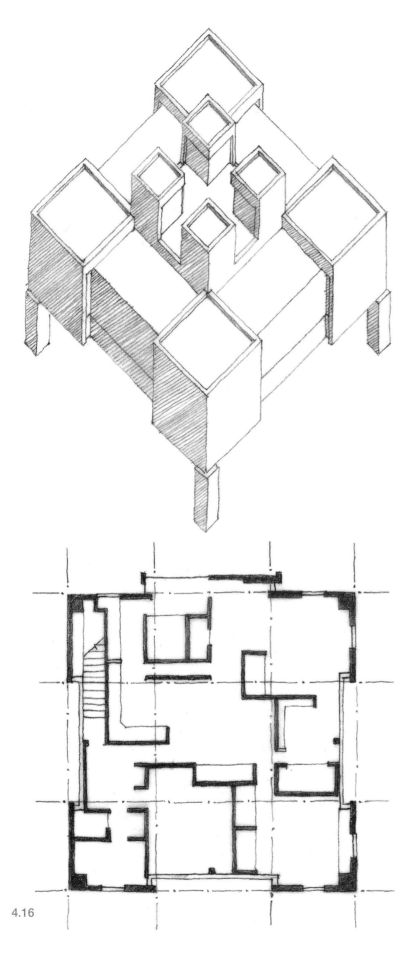

**Nakayama House, Oita, Japan, 1964.
Arata Isozaki. Axonometric and plan.**
The outer form of the house suggests a strictly
bilateral nine-square symmetry, but this turns
out to be little more than the shape of the shell.
The interior loosely obeys the nine-square diagram, corresponding to it primarily at the
perimeter but departing from it to an increasing
degree toward the center, resulting in a considerable tension between the static formal order
of the building on its exterior and the dynamic
spatial order experienced in its interior. This approach contradicts one of the tenets of Modernism—that the interior and the exterior forms
of a building should convey similar meanings.

4.16

4.17

Villa, Norrköping, Sweden, 1964. Sverre Fehn. Plan.

Though he maintained a nearly bilateral symmetry, Fehn manipulated the nine-square to produce an oscillation of space around a core, expanding and contracting, opening and closing to exterior views. He pulled the corners inward but also made them the only sources of light and views. Meanwhile, the center sections along the sides of the square are opaque but push outward to define rooms. In use, views between spaces are along diagonals surrounding the core, a system of perception in counterpoint to the orthogonal order of the plan. In this case, the architect uses the nine-square diagram to differentiate spaces without encapsulating them.

4.18

Permutation of the Nine-Square Diagram.

To increase the hierarchical structure of a nine-square diagram, Persian architects deformed the basic nine-square diagram to produce the classic design of three figures: a large central square, smaller corner squares, and intermediate rectangles in the proportion of 2:√3. The ratio of the area of the large central square to that of a corner square is thus 4:3. This proportional system was used in the Baradari of Sikander Lodi.

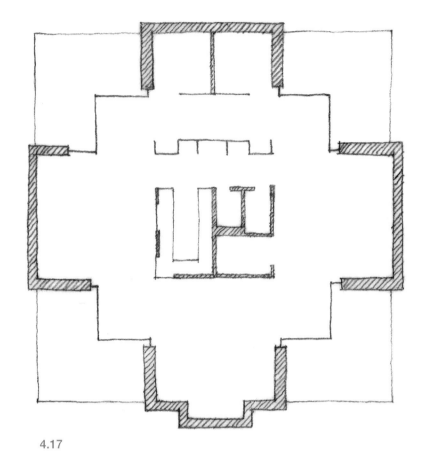

4.17

4.18

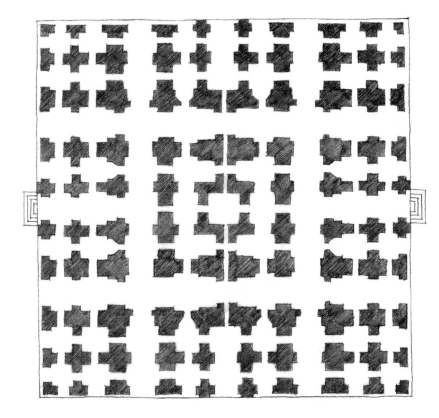

4.19

4.19

Baradari of Sikander Lodi, Uttar Pradesh, India, 1495. Plan.

Baradari translates to "twelve doorways," a term associated with pleasure pavilions in the Persian tradition. The sultan of Delhi, Sikander Lodi (1489–1517) was an Afghan Pashtun and founded the city of Agra in 1503. He built the Baradari as part of a palace complex in his capital, Sikandara, in 1495. After the Mughals defeated the Lodi dynasty in 1526, the emperor Akbar converted the Baradari to a tomb for his favorite wife, Mariam (and the mother of his successor Jahangir), whose cenotaph occupies the center chamber, surrounded by forty-two other rooms.

4.20

Tomb of Humayun, Delhi, India, 1562–72. Sayyid Muhammad and Mirak Sayyid Ghiyath. Plan.

Comissioned by Akbar, Humayun's son, the tomb was the first monumental work of architecture in India under the Mughals (whose origins were in Persia and Afghanistan). Though the architects were Persian, the building shows early signs of syncretist architecture, uniting Persian and Hindu architectural traditions. For example, though the plan of the garden is a quintessentially Persian *char-bagh* pattern (a four-square subdivided into thirty-six smaller squares), the architects surrounded the central dome of the tomb with smaller domed pavilions (*chattris*) that are Hindu in character. The plan of the tomb is a nine-square in which eight of the chambers radiate outward from a central domed chamber; they are connected to one another by orthogonal as well as diagonal passages, producing a highly complex plan. Since each of the main chambers has eight chambers radiating from it and these have subsidiary chambers as well, there are 124 vaulted chambers. Whereas the nine-square and four-square diagrams appear as pragmatic or merely convenient planning techniques in much of Western architecture, in Central Asian examples, particularly those in the Persian tradition, these diagrams are strictly symbolic, referring to the primal and perfect form of the world.

4.20

4.20

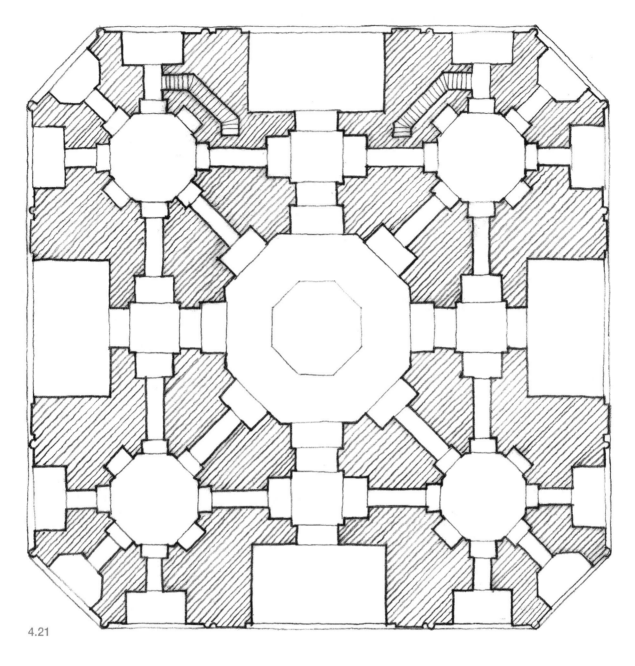

4.21

4.21
Taj Mahal, Agra, Uttar Pradesh, India, 1628–58. Plan.
The mausoleum was commissioned by the Mughal emperor Shah Jahan and contains the tombs for himself and his queen, Arjumand Bano Begum. The plan follows the Persian model established in India by Humayun's tomb, both in respect to the building, as a nine-square arrangement of vaulted and interconnected chambers, and the surrounding four-square paradise garden, a *char-bagh*. However, the plan of the Taj Mahal is simple in comparison to that of the tomb of Humayun, with a greater emphasis placed on the quality of materials and their detailing.

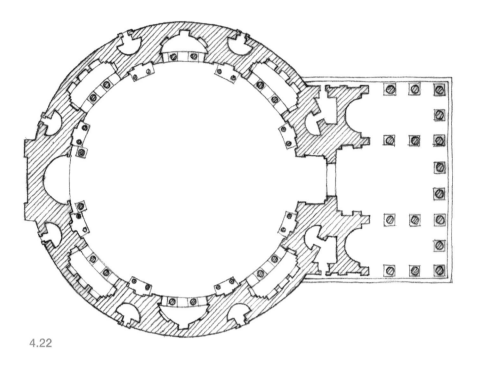

4.22

**Pantheon, Rome, ca. 125 CE.
(*possibly*) Appollodorus of Damascus.
Plan.**

The Pantheon is the best preserved building
from imperial Rome, and its dome is still the
largest ever constructed of unreinforced concrete. Its present form dates from the reign of
Hadrian, who maintained the inscription at-
tributing the original building (which burned in
80 CE) to the consul Agrippa (27 BCE). Though
stripped of all of its original facing and ornament, it survived the Christian era by being
consecrated as the church of Santa Maria dei
Martiri in 609 CE.

4.23

Pantheon. Geometry.

The unusual composition is a combination of
two entirely different building types—a single
geometric system fuses a rectangular,
columned portico and a cylindrical, domed rotunda. The portico is a simple nine-square that,
when inserted into the rotunda, corresponds
with the first row of the rotunda's distorted
nine-square. The distortion of the larger nine-
square was of an Oriental character, producing
a large center square, four smaller corner
squares, and four intermediate rectangles in
the proportion of 2:√3. The divisions of the
square that encloses the rotunda's plan determine the placement of all internal and external
niches within the thick cylindrical wall. Similarly,
the divisions of the nine-square that encloses
the portico determine the positions of all the elements (columns, niches, etc.) within it. This
geometric system served as the basis for many
later buildings in the Renaissance and the Neoclassical period, most notably Michelangelo's
plan for the Basilica of Saint Peter.

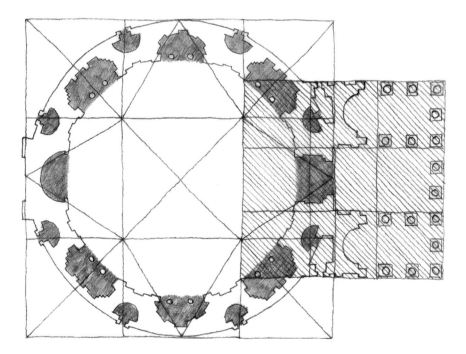

4.23

4.24

4.25

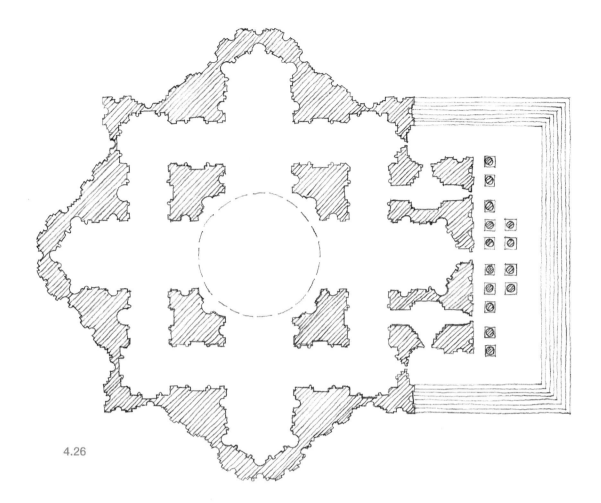

4.26

4.24
Basilica of Saint Peter, Rome, 1506. Donato Bramante. Plan.

Bramante produced a plan that was strictly centralized, with no emphasis on any one of the four cardinal directions. Having re-created the formula and the method by which the Romans had constructed the unreinforced concrete dome of the Pantheon, Bramante intended to build one much like it for the basilica, except instead of a continuous encircling wall, he planned to support the dome with four large piers. He established a strong basis for the plan, a Greek cross embedded in a nine-square grid, the corner cells of which would have supported subsidiary domes and towers. However, the corner cells were visually separated from the Greek cross, so despite a powerful central space, the spatial character of the interior would have appeared fragmented and discontinuous. This was the principal weakness that Michelangelo eventually corrected by consolidating the mass of the structure.

4.25
Basilica of Saint Peter, 1536. Antonio da Sangallo. Plan.

A succession of architects worked on the plan of the basilica after Bramante: Giuiliano da Sangallo, Fra Giocondo, Raphael, and Baldassare Peruzzi. Following them, Antonio da Sangallo's principal contribution was to strengthen the four main piers intended to support the central dome that Bramante had begun but that were too small to carry the load. Da Sangallo's plan, however, lacked the vitality of Bramante's concept and would have created an interior of vast corridors, even converting three of Bramante's elegant apses into broad semicircular ambulatories. Da Sangallo also proposed a short, wide nave and six corner towers on square bases. The four massive central piers designed by da Sangallo were in place when Michelangelo began work on the project in 1547 and were the only feature he kept from any of the plans produced by his predecessors.

4.26
Basilica of Saint Peter, 1547. Michelangelo Buonarotti. Plan.

Reluctantly, Michelangelo became the architect for the basilica at the age of seventy. His solution maintained the original Greek cross plan of his predecessors, but his plan was considerably less complex than Bramante's and da Sangallo's. Whereas earlier architects had produced elaborate plans in which the mass of the building was dispersed among many parts, such as free-standing columns, large apses, towers, and domes, Michelangelo condensed the mass into a continuous form dominated inside and out by the undulating wall surfaces.

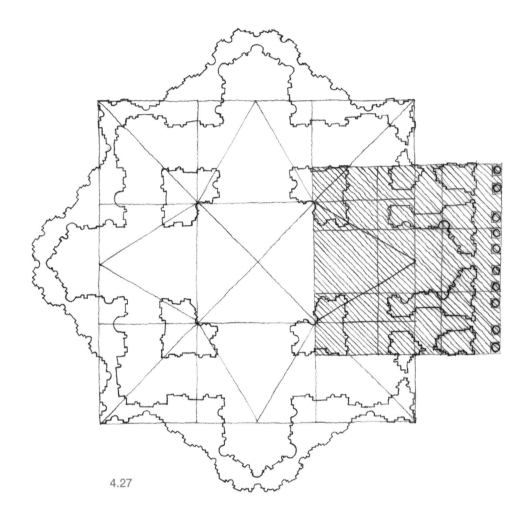

4.27

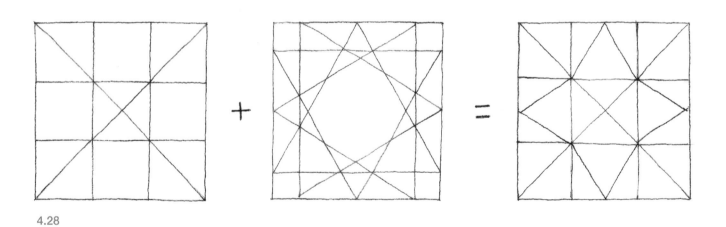

4.28

4.29

4.27
Basilica of Saint Peter. Michelangelo. Composition.

To accomplish his design objective, Michelangelo returned to the simple plan of the Pantheon as a geometric guide. In fact, the diagrams for the two buildings are identical—a fusion of a small, simple nine-square portico structure with a large, distorted nine-square in the Oriental fashion (squares and 2:√3 rectangles) for the main body. Later, Carlo Maderno's early 17th-century nave obliterated Michelangelo's portico and obscured his dome as well. Fortunately, Maderno's proposal to break into the fabric of the building and ring Michelangelo's plan with chapels was not accepted.

4.28
Basilica of Saint Peter. Michelangelo. Geometric progression.

The underlying diagram for the Pantheon and for Michelangelo's design of Saint Peter's basilica required the insertion of equilateral triangles into a square, their vertices corresponding to the centerlines of the square. The intersections of the triangles establish the corners of the large central square, which in turn create the four corner squares and the intermediate 2:√3 rectangles. This ancient planning technique was used extensively in the Middle East prior to the Hellenistic and Roman conquests and was also used from the 7th century CE onward in many Islamic buildings from India to Spain.

4.29
Église du Dôme, Saint-Louis-des-Invalides, Paris, 1708. Jules Hardouin Mansart. Plan.

Louis XIV commissioned the Église du Dôme as a royal chapel attached to the 1676 soldiers' chapel. Designed by Libéral Bruant and completed by J. H. Mansart, the plan is a derivative of the plan of the Basilica of Saint Peter by Michelangelo: a Greek cross within a nine-square grid. However, Mansart's design is quintessentially French Baroque, including a triple-shell dome in which an oculus in the innermost shell allows a view into the next shell to create an ethereal spatial illusion. Also unlike Michelangelo's continuously fluid interior, the spatial organization of Mansart's design is a formal relation of bubblelike volumes connected by orthogonal and diagonal passages. The poché that shapes these volumes appears to deform and escape from the confines of the underlying square at the front and the rear of the building to establish a longitudinal axis in an otherwise bilaterally symmetrical plan.

4.30

Phillips Exeter Academy Library, Exeter, New Hampshire, 1971. Louis I. Kahn. Plan.

Kahn was a master of complex and subtle spaces derived from simple, rigorously geometric plans. We can interpret the square plan of the library at Phillips Exeter in two ways. It is concentrically layered, but the building also has a thick shell and a spatial core, both of which contribute to the luminosity of the cubic space that appears to be suspended between them. In the abstract, Kahn's square employs several methods of subdivision: overall, it is a four-square; the core in relation to the periphery produces a nine-square; the subdivision of the space around the core produces a sixteen-square; and there is even the implication of a thirty-six-square grid. The concrete framing of the roof above the central space reiterates the nine-square motif.

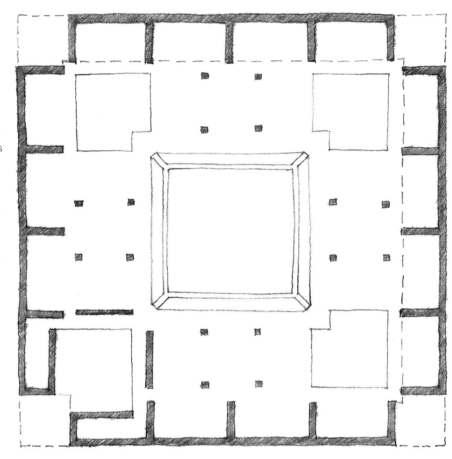

4.30

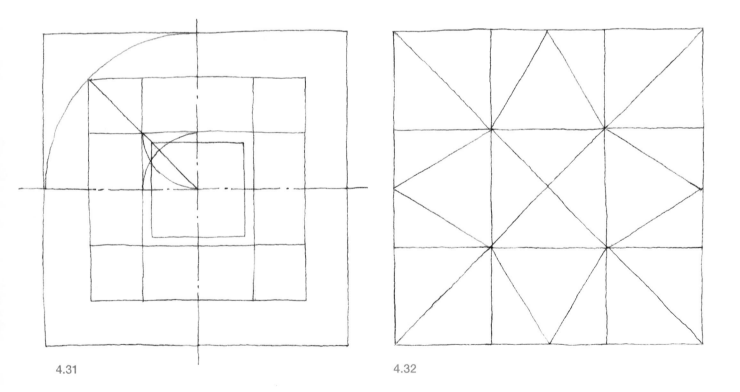

4.31

4.32

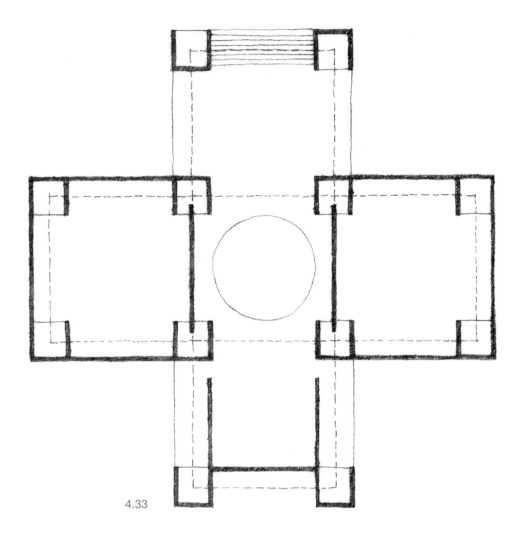

4.33

4.31
Phillips Exeter Academy Library. Geometry.

Kahn determined the dimensions of the major features of the plan geometrically rather than by the multiplication of a module. For example, the intersection of two arcs within one of the units of the central sixteen-square diagram determined the relation between the central square and its surrounding layer of stacks, and an arc from the central four-square diagram produced the dimension of the space between the zone of stacks and the perimeter wall. This method operates at numerous scales in three dimensions to create a proportional theme throughout the building of 1:√2.

4.32
Phillips Exeter Academy Library. Nine-square diagram.

Kahn used an ancient technique of subdividing the overall square plan into nine parts to produce a modified quincunx with a large square in the center, smaller squares at the corners, and intermediate rectangles in the proportion of 2:√3. In this respect, Kahn was working within the Classical tradition of architecture.

4.33
Bath House, Trenton, New Jersey, 1955. Louis I. Kahn. Plan.

Kahn used a static nine-square grid in this example, as opposed to a shifting grid (Adler House, see 4.34) or modified quincunx (Phillips Exeter Library). The plan employed the same module—a cubic pavilion with pyramidal roof—to serve several different functions. The missing corner pavilions implied the nine-square grid.

4.34

Adler House (proposal), Philadelphia, 1954. Louis I. Kahn. Plan.

Kahn experimented with several ways of using the nine-square diagram as the basis for plans. For example, the Adler House consists of five pavilions supported by boxed masonry corners. The remaining four cells of the nine-square diagram are either represented by empty square platforms, or they are implied by the shifting pavilions. Though this project remained unbuilt, he eventually used the pavilion with boxed corners motif in the Trenton Bath House.

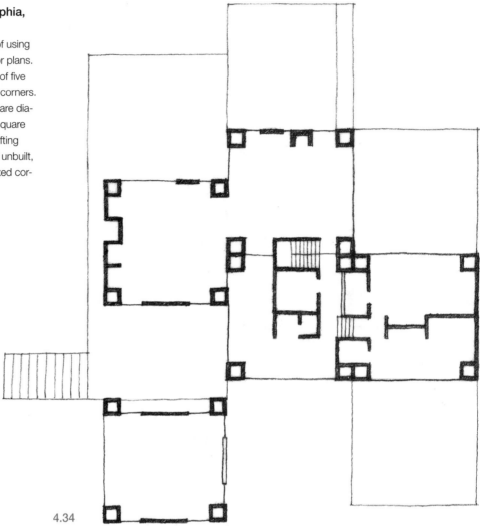

4.34

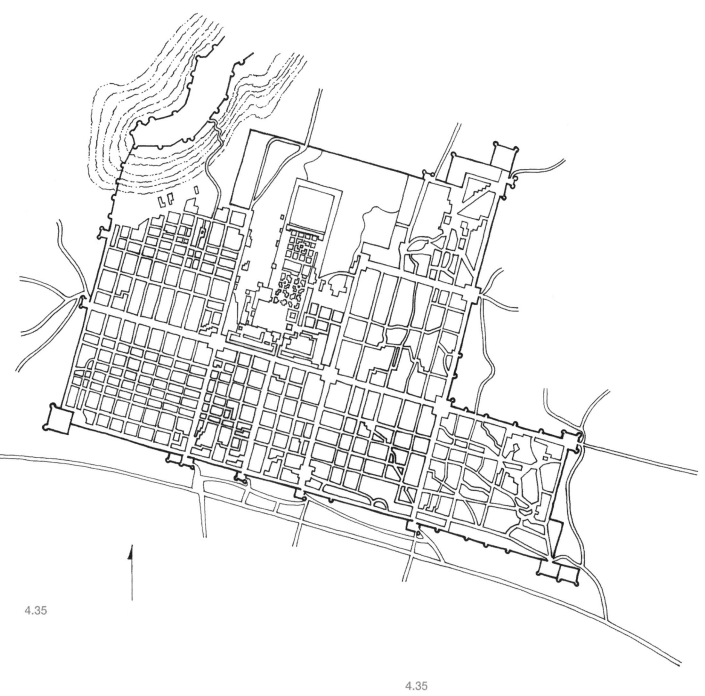

4.35

4.35
Jaipur, Rajasthan, India. 1727.
Vidyadhar. Plan.
The design strikes a balance between an abstract geometric planning diagram, a mandala, and the exigencies of a specific physical place. Since a single architect designed and constructed the city during a short period in the 18th century, we can assume that both the regular and irregular features of the plan were intentional.

4.36
Jawahar Kala Kendra, Jaipur, Rajasthan, India, 1986–92. Charles Correa.

The basis of Charles Correa's design for an arts center for Jaipur was the nine-square Navagraha mandala in which the nine squares signify the nine astrological planets. Two squares signify Ketu and Rahu, which are not physical planets but indicate the points (south and north respectively) where the paths of the moon and the sun cross. This diagram depicts the relation of exterior space (shaded) to interior space.

4.37
Vidyadhar Nagar, Jaipur, Rajasthan, India, 1984–86. Balkrishna Doshi (*sketches after Doshi*).

For his addition to the city of Jaipur, Doshi studied the combination of the four-quartered square (the traditional symbol of paradise) and the nine-square Vastu Purusha mandala.

4.38
Vidyadhar Nagar. Pattern.

A sketch of a part of the urban pattern illustrates how Doshi combined Le Corbusier's "building in the park" approach to urban design with the traditional Rajasthani form of communal courtyard housing. The former produced buildings with idiosyncratic footprints, while the latter produced regular urban blocks.

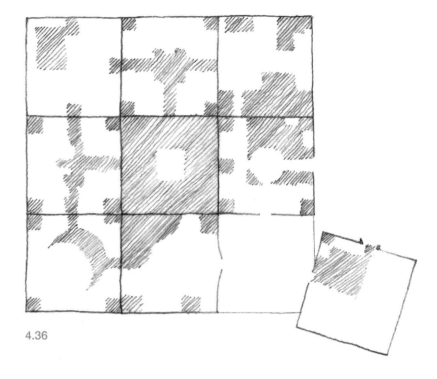

4.36

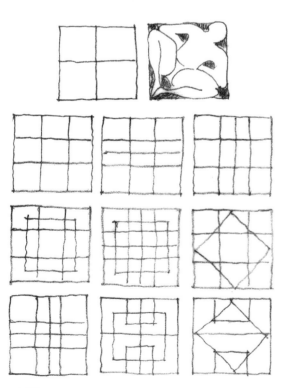

4.37

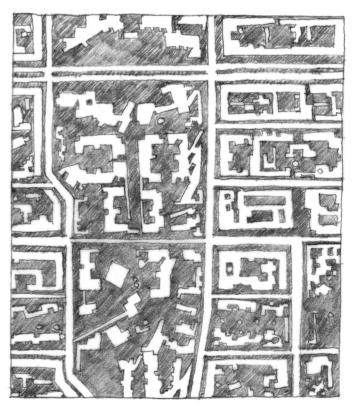

4.38

CHAPTER FIVE
LAYERING

V IRTUALLY ALL LIVING TISSUE, PLANT OR ANIMAL, IS COMPOSED OF
layers. Layering allows cells to specialize with respect to absorption, protection, sensation, growth, and other functions. As a general strategy for
order, layering is similarly useful in architecture. Layers, composed of either mass or
space, permit specialization with respect to the absorption of light, the retention of
heat, and the control of movement, as well as the segregation or integration of various functions of a building. Architects conceptualize layers in several ways. In a
plan, layering may work horizontally; in section and elevation, it may work vertically. In some buildings, layering may be concentric like the rings of a tree trunk, and
layering may be radial.

Horizontal Layering

A compelling use of layering is to control social relations. In the central Asian town
of Turpan, for example, the vernacular architecture of the Uighur people that has
developed over hundreds of years is simple in its material aspect (mud brick and timber framing) but complex in the way it orders space in a spectrum between the
entirely public realm and the entirely private realm; this is a "privacy gradient." In
the daily life of Turpan, we find seven distinct layers of space between the public life
of the street and the most intimate family spaces of a house (5.1). These layers allow
residents to control their interactions with a variety of people, depending on their
relationship to them—are they strangers, neighbors, or relatives?—and whether the
occasion is informal, formal, or ritualistic. Visitors may penetrate the layers of space
to varying degrees depending on their status in relation to the family, a custom that
all inhabitants of the town thoroughly understand.

In contrast, spatial layering may be devoted to purely aesthetic purposes, as in
Rome's Church of Santa Maria in Campitelli (5.2). Here the layers of space are
entirely for visual effect, an illusion of deep atmosphere and ambiguous scale—an
intense theatricality typical of Roman Catholic churches built during the Counter-
Reformation in Italy. Renzo Piano used horizontal layering in the Tjibaou Cultural
Center in New Caledonia as a means to differentiate between two types of spaces
(5.3). The central layer of the building is a long corridor. To one side is a set of rectangular spaces that functions as classrooms, galleries, offices, and a theater, generally
in the Western tradition of spatial organization. The spaces on the other side are

iconographic meeting rooms: tall cylindrical forms reminiscent of the traditional communal architecture of the islands. Here layering highlights the relation between two cultural forces in the contemporary society of New Caledonia. The parti of the building juxtaposes the two, integrating them to some extent but keeping them separate as well (5.4).

Two houses by the Chilean architect Cristían de Groote illustrate his interest in various methods of using layering. One plan layers spaces longitudinally, with a long corridor spine connecting a heterogeneous group of spaces in sequence (5.5). The other plan layers spaces laterally; the main living spaces are gaps between thick parallel walls that contain all services and entries (5.6). Whereas the first example establishes circulation as the primary layer, the second example dispenses with circulation altogether in favor of the rhythm of thick walls. For a small outdoor exhibition space in the Netherlands, Aldo van Eyck produced a complex set of spaces with extraordinary economy of means by layering concrete block walls that he then deformed and broke to produce a series of parallel passages (5.7). Though the walls promote a serpentine through movement, van Eyck also allows lateral movement by means of punctures and discontinuities. The extremely simple plan is a labyrinth that is nevertheless open to the surrounding landscape, so visitors experience it in two distinctly different ways.

The Australian architect Glenn Murcutt uses layered plans extensively in his work. For environmental reasons, principally the circulation of air, he prefers long, narrow houses in which every room has exposure to both of the longitudinal elevations (5.8). In his own house, he doubled this plan type by adding a second house to a preexisting house, separating the two with a narrow gap that functions as a series of thresholds, storage spaces, and ventilation volumes. The firm of Nagle Hartray used a similarly rational approach to layering in a cottage at Green Lake, Wisconsin (5.9). In this case, however, the house is built into the side of a hill to protect it from northern exposure and opens out to the south sun. The plan is a series of layers, from service spaces against the solid north wall to an open veranda on the south (5.10).

The plan of a house by the firm of Lacroze Miguens Prati in Argentina is deceivingly simple at first glance (5.11–5.14). It is a long box with a series of rooms exposed to both longitudinal elevations and to two verandas. Geometrically, it is composed of four squares. The exterior walls have complex interior surfaces that create a rhythm of correspondences across the rooms. In addition, the columns for the verandas do not correspond directly but create a secondary transverse rhythm that is seen intermittently through apertures in the thick walls. Finally, the Villa Lanza by Rudy Hunziker, with alterations by Citterio and Dwan, is a complex composition of layered spaces (5.15–5.16). Three major longitudinal layers are broken down into a finer grain of layering, and this is set in counterpoint to a rhythm of transverse layering, all of which extends beyond the boundary of the building into the landscape.

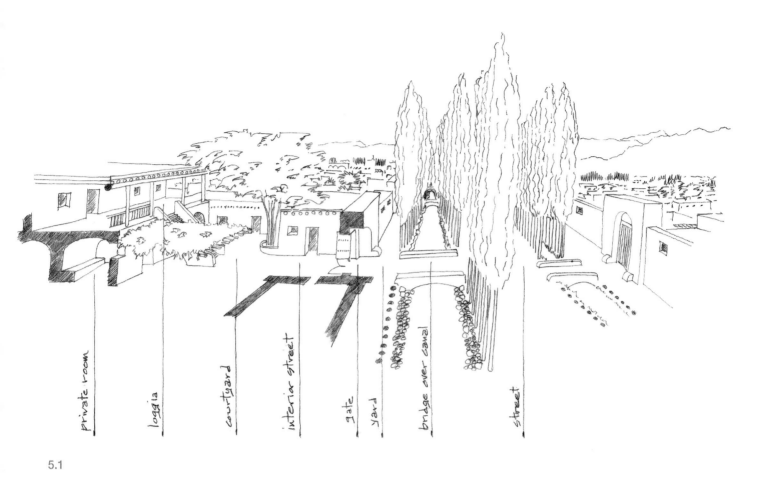

private room

loggia

courtyard

interior street

gate

yard

bridge over canal

street

5.1

5.1

Privacy Gradient, Turpan, Xinjiang, China.

The organization of this traditional Uighur town provides seven layers of space to control social relations within a spectrum from the entirely public to the entirely private, called a privacy gradient. Rows of poplars grow out of a pair of narrow canals that flank a typical street. These naturally cool the street by providing shade, shelter from wind and dust, and humidity through transpiration. Bridges across the canals, bordered by low walls, are as wide as they are long and serve as outdoor rooms; though private property, these are nevertheless directly adjacent to the public street and are thus important social spaces, in the public realm yet under private control. A narrow front yard behind the screen of trees and the canal is an informal family space within sight of the street but distinctly private in character. The monumental gate to the house compound is tall, deep, and usually in deep shadow, creating an architectural space further detached from the public realm but within sight of it. The family uses the gate as a place to lounge and to meet with guests. An interior street flanked by service buildings is a more private area controlled by the gate. This leads to the main family space, the courtyard, which also serves as a formal reception area. Typically, a stair leads from the courtyard to a second-floor loggia overlooking the courtyard; the family uses the loggia for leisure, and it leads to the most private spaces of all, the interior rooms of the house.

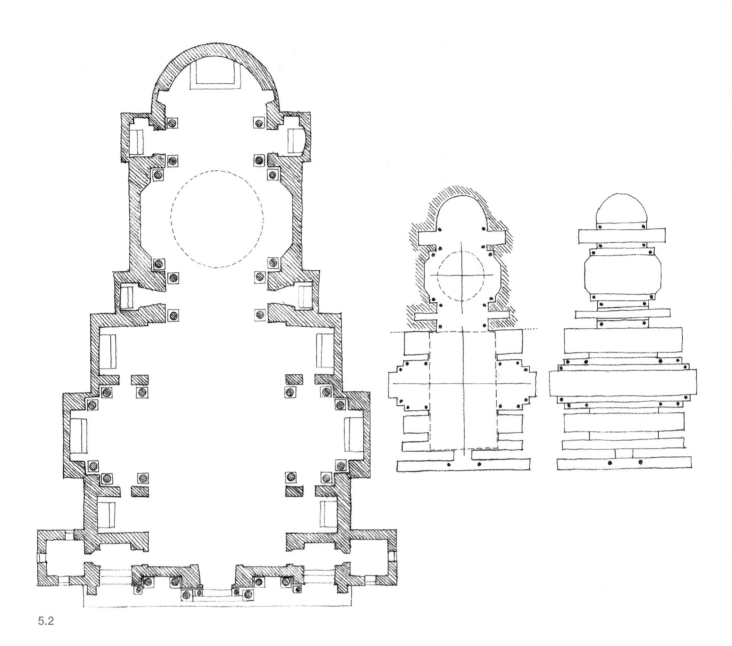

5.2

Santa Maria in Campitelli, Rome, 1662–75. Carlo Rainaldi. Plan and composition.

Rainaldi's high baroque plan has no direct predecessors in Rome, achieving an extreme degree of theatricality by means of an axial layering of space. Two methods of organization are at work in the plan: a pair of centralized spaces of differing character and a series of narrow lateral layers of space. In the first case, the plan has two centralized spatial units, the nave and the presbytery. A barrel vault flanked by six chapels forms the nave. Ten freestanding columns accentuate the middle chapels on each side, which are considerably wider and deeper than the others, thus implying a biaxial, centrally focused space approximating a Greek cross. The transition from the nave to the presbytery is a spatial constriction marked by two pairs of freestanding columns, recalling a triumphal arch. Beyond this, a dome dominates the presbytery to produce a centralized space of an entirely different character. The second method of spatial organization creates an intensely atmospheric, forced perspective by virtue of the many transverse layers of space, becoming increasingly narrow and attenuated by the freestanding columns, receding into the distance toward the altar. This effect is, in a sense, a contradiction of the first, but it unifies the otherwise distinctly separate halves of the plan.

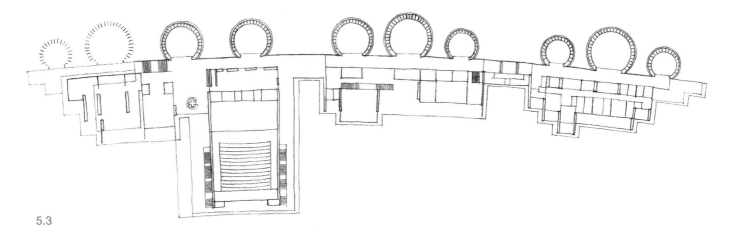

5.3

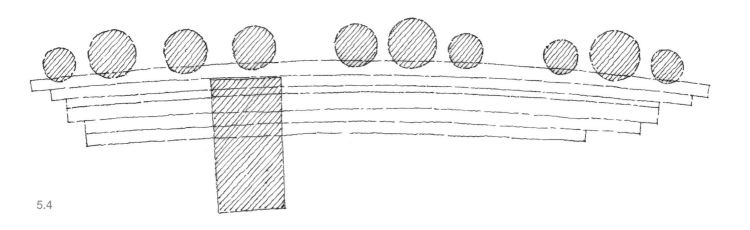

5.4

5.3

Tjibaou Cultural Center, Nouméa, New Caledonia, 1998. Renzo Piano. Plan.

Piano divided the program into two parts and assigned each a formal language and a specific position. Ritual and ceremonial spaces are cylindrical in plan and structurally reminiscent of tradition architecture in the archipelago, whereas all other spaces, such as the auditorium, classrooms, galleries, and service spaces, assume a pragmatic orthogonal geometry. These two formal types form layers on either side of a central circulation spine, its gentle curve constantly foregrounding elements of the composition as one walks down the corridor.

5.4

Tjibaou Cultural Center. Composition.

The composition of the building overall is a set of monumental objects embedded in a layered matrix. The staggered articulation of the ends exaggerates the layered form, in a manner reminiscent of Alvar Aalto's design for Baker House on the Massachusetts Institute of Technology campus.

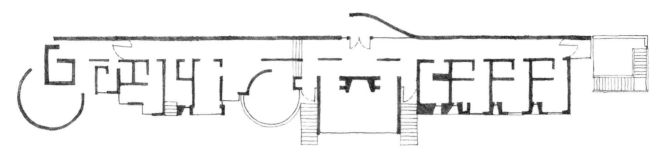

5.5

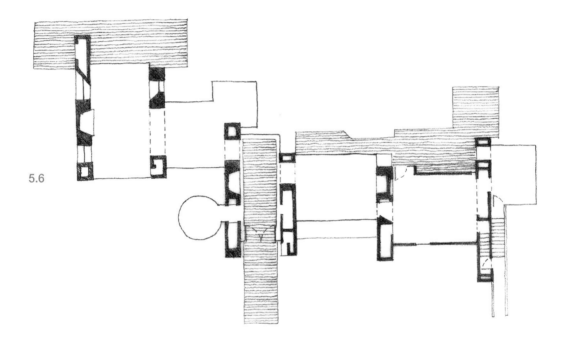

5.6

5.5

House in El Pangue, Chile, 1989. Cristían de Groote. Plan.

De Groote organized the heterogeneous collection of formal and informal spaces in the house by means of a single spinal layer of circulation. The entry wall offers little information about the private spaces it shields, peeling back to provide a sheltered entry. The entry leads to the central communal space, focused on a hearth, that divides the house into private quarters to the east and communal and service functions to the west. The circulation layer terminates at each end in two exterior features: a sheltered circular garden and a square platform.

5.6

House in Villarrica, Chile, 1993. Cristían de Groote. Plan.

An entry platform and loggia, four open living spaces, and six thick walls that contain all service functions divide this house into two halves. De Groote organized these in a series of shifting, parallel layers of alternating solids and voids.

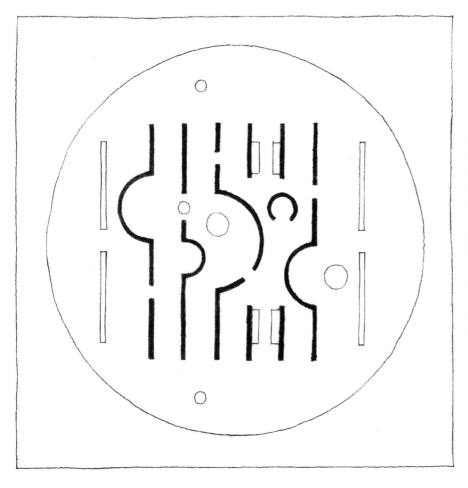

5.7

Sculpture Pavilion, Arnheim, the Netherlands, 1966. Aldo van Eyck. Plan and view.

Using a simple method of deformed parallel concrete block walls, van Eyck created a complex and varied spatial composition. One can immediately recognize the underlying organizational principle as rational, but the result is suggestive of a labyrinth. With economy of means, the architectural enclosure achieves a delicate roomlike quality, yet it is entirely open to its surroundings.

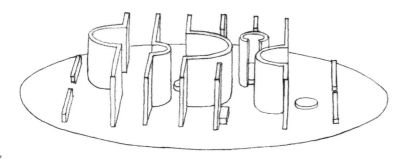

5.7

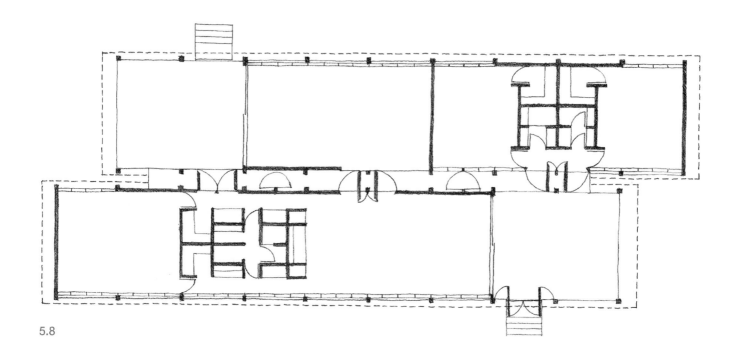

5.8

Murcutt House, Kempsey, New South Wales, Australia, 1980. Glenn Murcutt. Plan.

The architect purchased the house, originally a single bar, from a former client, and added the second bar. To ensure maximum air circulation, he repeated the technique of concentrating service functions in a compact core, permitting all other spaces to be entirely unencumbered. The narrow intermediate zone between the two buildings controls privacy and allows for ventilation of its adjacent living spaces.

5.9

Cottage at Green Lake, Wisconsin, 2003. Nagle Hartray. Plan.

The plan places service functions against a heavy north wall into a hill, with living spaces opening to the south onto a screened porch and toward the principal view.

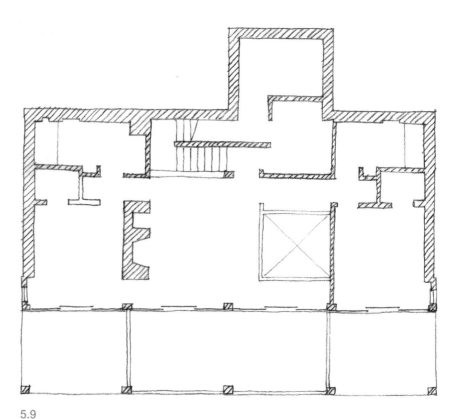

5.9

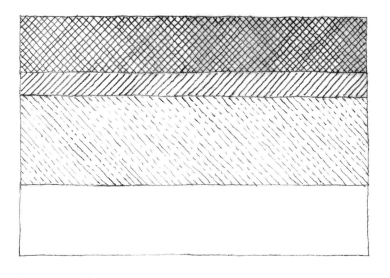

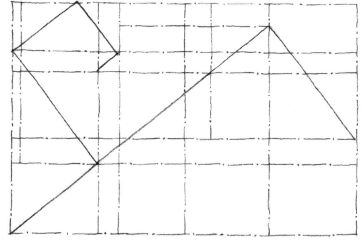

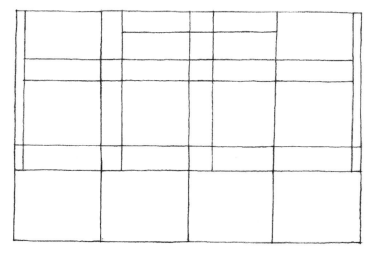

5.10

Cottage at Green Lake. Composition.
The architects organized this house in three
layers of decreasing density (i.e., with respect
to degrees of enclosure and exposure to natural light) from north to south. A tartan grid positions all features of the interior in respect to a
simple structural diagram.

5.10

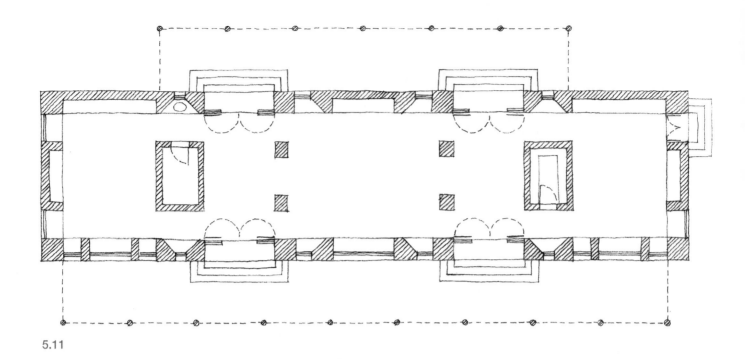

5.11

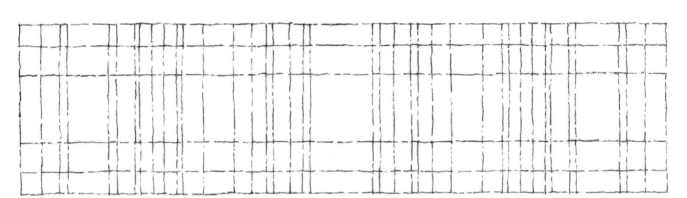

5.12

5.11
**House in El Talar, Chascomús,
Argentina, 1985. Lacroze Miguens
Prati. Ground-floor plan.**
Typical of this architectural firm, the open plan
of the house employs a rigorous geometric
pattern that organizes spaces in a simple and
direct way. The deep wall of brick has several
functions: it insulates the interior from extremes
of heat and cold, it subdues the intense sunlight, it incorporates support functions, and it
demarcates interior spaces.

5.12
House in El Talar. Tartan grid.
The two closely spaced longitudinal walls of the
building produce a tightly knit staccato rhythm
across the interior. In contrast, the transverse
correlation of the two end walls, two pairs of
columns and two enclosures, produces a simple A-B-A pattern.

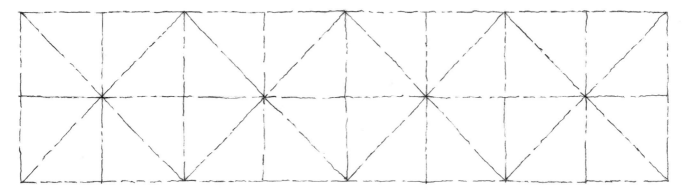

5.13

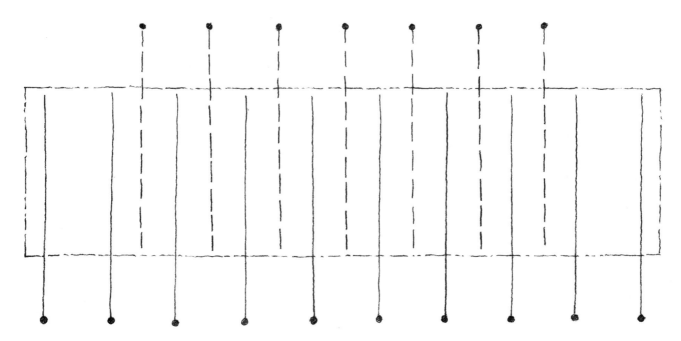

5.14

5.13

House in El Talar. Geometry.

In contrast to the complex rhythm of the interior articulation, the underlying geometry is simply a series of squares.

5.14

House in El Talar. Verandas.

The patterns of columns supporting the two verandas appear to be independent but are in fact related. Interpenetrating through the interior, each column's centerline falls midway between the centerlines of two columns on the opposite side.

5.15

Villa Lanza, Como, Italy, 1995. Rudy Hunziker with modifications by Citterio and Dwan. First-floor plan.

The plan is in the Italian Rationalist tradition, divided generally into four quarters, then subdivided further into complex registrations of spaces and formal features by means of a prominent structural system. The original owner was an art collector, so two galleries occupy half of the first floor; another quarter is given over to a formal living room, and the remaining quarter to service.

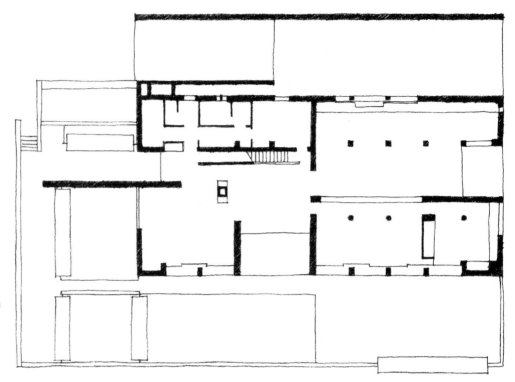

5.15

5.16

Villa Lanza. Composition.

The layering of space in the living and service quarters produces complex shifts in registrations among the compositional elements, a pattern that extends to the exterior. This pattern, however, is held within a square in which the hearth occupies the exact center. In contrast, the galleries follow a relatively simple proportional progression to form a tartan grid.

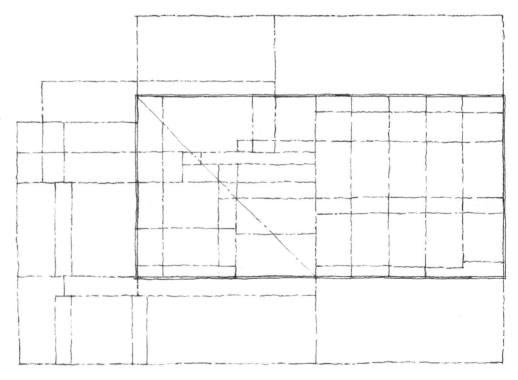

5.16

Vertical Layering

Simply placing one floor on top of another is obviously one kind of vertical layering that, as we see in many contemporary high-rise buildings, may vary from elegant (e.g., the Seagram Building) to the banal. More interesting is how vertical layering communicates an idea about the relation of a building to the ground and to the sky. This was one of the objectives of Le Corbusier's design for the Villa Savoye at Poissey, France (5.17). Following the Classical model of base-middle-top, Le Corbusier shaped each of the three layers of the house to indicate a specific function (5.18). The slender columns of the bottom layer do not merely support the building above; they appear to drive the building into the ground and force a heightened awareness of the building's relation to the terrestrial plane. The middle level is a perfect rectangular solid with sharply defined edges and a machinelike interior, serving as an icon for the ideal domestic container. Above this is a composition of forms whose shape and color form a compelling silhouette against the sky. Thus the primary living space of the house appears to hover between the earth and the sky, a metaphor perhaps for the human condition, both corporeal and spiritual. Interestingly, a Thai rice barn—a strictly utilitarian structure—has precisely the same three-part vertically layered parti (5.19): it rises from the earth on columns, contains a space ideally suited to its internal function, and has a top that not only protects it from the elements but also becomes a signature of the form against the sky. Two other vernacular structures, one a barn in Portugal (5.20) and the other a cottonseed mill in Texas (5.21) follow the same vertically layered tripartite organization. Both are rigorously utilitarian, but in their rational application of materials they are also elegant compositions of geometry, proportion, rhythm, texture, light, and shadow.

5.17

Villa Savoye, Poissy-sur-Seine, France, 1929. Le Corbusier. View.

Though Le Corbusier used the design of the Villa Savoye to demonstrate his "five points" of a new architecture and the house is a radical departure from conventional residential forms, it nevertheless has firmly Classical roots: it is divided into three horizontal layers, each of which has a specific formal character relative to its position and function. The main residential level, square in plan and crisply logical in form, may be a metaphor for the condition of the human mind, suspended between the earth and the cosmos.

5.18

Villa Savoye. Composition.

The slender, spikelike *pilotis* of the ground level not only support the building, they appear to embed it into the earth, so compositionally, this layer establishes the relation of the house to the ground. The main level is a Modernist *piano nobile* and represents an ideal life governed by reason. The structures on the roof, voluptuously curved and painted in pastels, appear in silhouette against the changing colors and cloud forms of the sky.

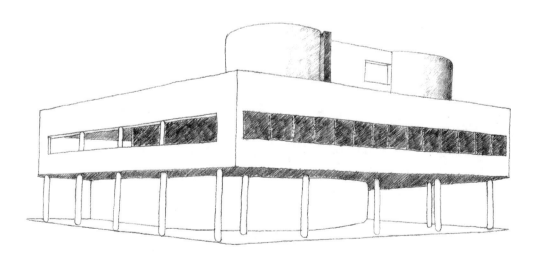

5.17

5.18

5.19

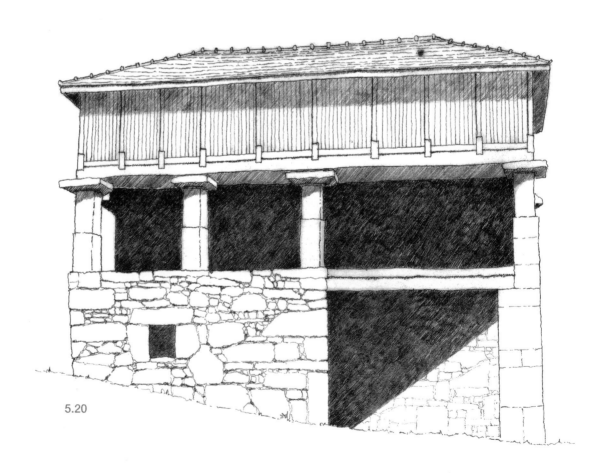

5.20

5.21

5.19

Rice Barn, Thailand, 20th century. View.

The vernacular form of the rice barn has achieved a clarity and precision of composition comparable to Le Corbusier's Villa Savoye. It, too, has three horizontal layers, each with its own distinct form relative to its position and function. The rows of columns at the lowest level simultaneously separate the body of the building from the damp ground and emphatically connect it to the earth. The main storage level is a rational, modular form—a simple box—and the roof structure, designed to shed water and provide ventilation, provides a powerful silhouette against the sky.

5.20

Granary, Portugal, 20th century. View.

This vernacular building has three horizontal functional layers. The lowest level accommodates the slope of the hillside and lifts the main body of the building off the damp ground. The second level is the threshing floor, and the uppermost level is for storage. Wide column capitals, designed to deter rats, segregate it from the lower levels, and it has a specialized enclosure system to provide ventilation.

5.21

The Daniel Gin, Lubbock, Texas, ca. 1950. View.

The three horizontal layers of this vernacular industrial building indicate three separate but related functions. The lowest level lifts the main body of the building off the ground and holds equipment. The top level is the main bin for storing cotton seed, and the intermediate level has five chutes for emptying the seed into trucks. Though the patterns of materials (corrugated steel, wood, and hardware) for each level vary according to function, the geometries, proportions, and rhythms of an underlying structure integrate them.

Concentric Layering

Concentric layering responds at the most fundamental level to a need for protection and enclosure, exemplified by the Palestinian redoubt (5.22) and the Anasazi village of Tyuonyi (5.23). In Tyuonyi, inhabitants occupied only the innermost layers of cells that surrounded the central ritual dance space. Outer cells were for food storage and defense. In buildings devoted to religious purposes, concentric layering has a different significance. A concentrically layered plan first provides a physical separation from the rest of the world by establishing an outer boundary, or several boundaries by means of multiple layers. In the case of the Nārgā Sellasē in Ethiopia (5.24, 5.25), the layers increase in density as one gets closer to the center: the outermost layer of columns is easily permeable, the next layer is less so, and the inner layer is almost closed. Orientation also changes: the outer layer has a uniform relation to the surrounding landscape (that is, no specific orientation), the second layer is oriented in four directions, and the inner layer has a single orientation. This pattern is common among sacred buildings throughout the world.

The Church of San Vitale (5.26, 5.27), the Dome of the Rock (5.28, 5.29) and the Mausoleum of Santa Costanza (5.30) have specialized structures to bring people through their outer layers into intermediate spaces, which function as ambulatories so their central spaces can be left undisturbed. The Dome of the Rock uses a progression of nested tangent circles and squares to control its proportions. The combination of the circle and square is also symbolic, the square denoting the terrestrial world and the circle denoting the cosmos above. An octagon acts as an intermediary between the circle and the square—in effect, a square becoming a circle and a circle becoming a square.

Concentric layering has an ancient tradition as a method to control privacy in houses. A Roman house at Volubilis from the 3rd century CE is a classic example of the technique (5.32). Set within a 2:√3 rectangle, the various rooms of the house form several layers of increasing regularity toward the central atrium. Though of an irregular outline, the house in al-Fustat, Cairo, from the 7th century CE achieves essentially the same effect, though its historical model is a Persian type (5.33–5.35). Main living spaces surround the central court with regular facades whereas secondary spaces occupy an irregular outer layer that fits the plan into the eccentric geometry of its site. A house in Fez, Morocco, has characteristics of both the houses of Volubilis and of al-Fustat. It follows the Roman tradition of the atrium as a perfect center but also allows the informal outer layers of spaces to conform to an irregular urban site (5.36).

Finally, Adolf Loos's design for an addition to an existing house in Switzerland is an interesting solution utilizing concentric layering (5.37). The original house was in a parklike setting, with equally pleasant views in all directions. To exploit this condition, Loos added a new layer of space on all four sides and opened the original exterior wall of the house (now an interior wall) to borrow natural light from the new outer layer of space.

5.22

Palestinian Redoubt, 20th century. Plan.

This is a small hilltop structure of dry laid fieldstone in a serpentine, concentrically layered plan, taking advantage of natural stone outcroppings to produce a defensible labyrinth. Shepherds built and sheltered in the central structure that once had a conical corbelled stone roof. To the right of it is a pen for sheep and goats.

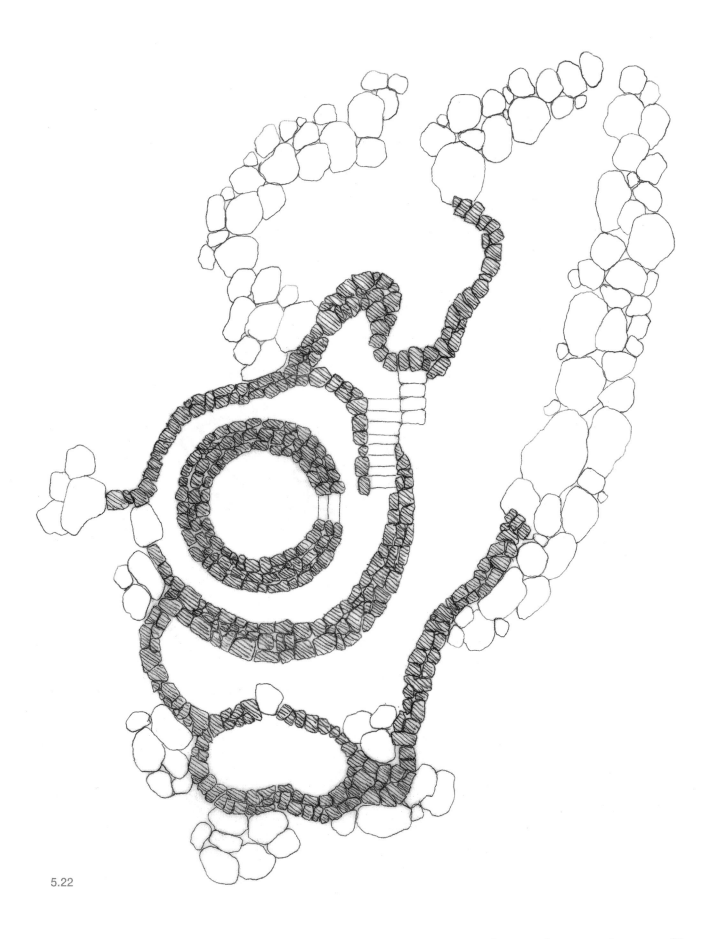

5.22

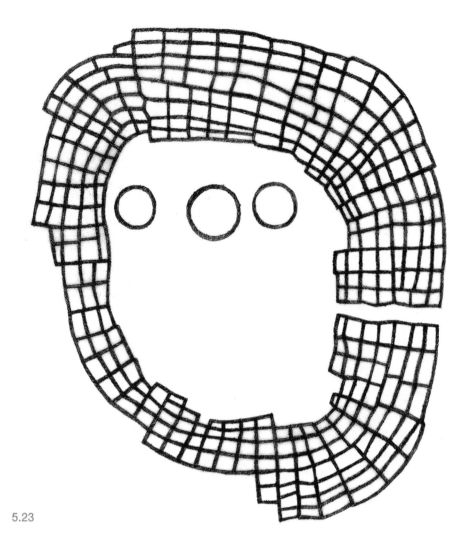

5.23

5.23
Tyuonyi, Frijoles Canyon, New Mexico, ca. 1300–1450. Plan.
The pattern of this Rio Grande Anasazi village reveals concentrically layered growth from the center outward, similar to growth rings of a tree. Its inner rings were domestic spaces, its outer were primarily for storage, and the entrance to the entire village was a narrow gap through the deepest zone of rings. Three kivas used for clan rituals occupied the center plaza. The concentric form controlled growth and established a powerful boundary between the sanctity of the community's center and the uncontrolled environment outside its walls.

5.24
Church of Nārgā Sellasē, Nārgā Island, Ethiopia, 1748. Plan.
The monastery and church of Nārgā Sellasē occupies a small island in Lake Tana at the center of the Ethiopian plateau adjacent to the imperial city of Gondar. The architecture that developed in this Christian enclave from the 4th century onward combined, by the 18th century, European, Islamic, and Indian motifs with a distinctly Ethiopian sensibility. The structure consists of three concentric rings that remain independent—their structural bays do not correspond. At the center is a square stone box, the sanctum sanctorum. Around it is a wood-framed circular prayer space sometimes closed with shutters. The outer ring is an open, colonnaded ambulatory that supports a low conical roof. All rise from a low circular stone plinth.

5.25
Church of Nārgā Sellasē. Composition.
A sense of order gets increasingly specific toward the center of the composition. The outermost ring of columns is undifferentiated. The inner circular screen wall has four segments, each of three bays oriented to the cardinal directions. Finally, the square core indicates a front, back, and two sides. The geometric relation between the square core and the circular screen wall produces four connected prayer spaces, with diagonal entries into the prayer spaces from the outer ambulatory corresponding to the corners of the core.

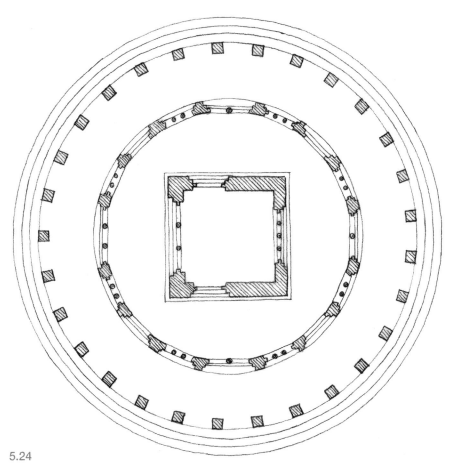

5.24

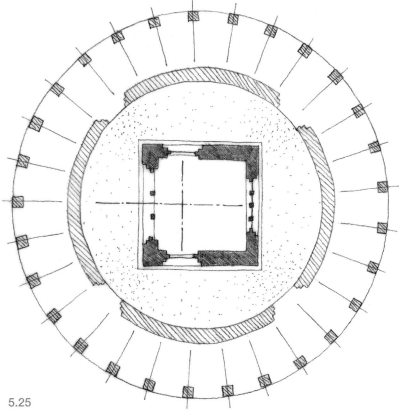

5.25

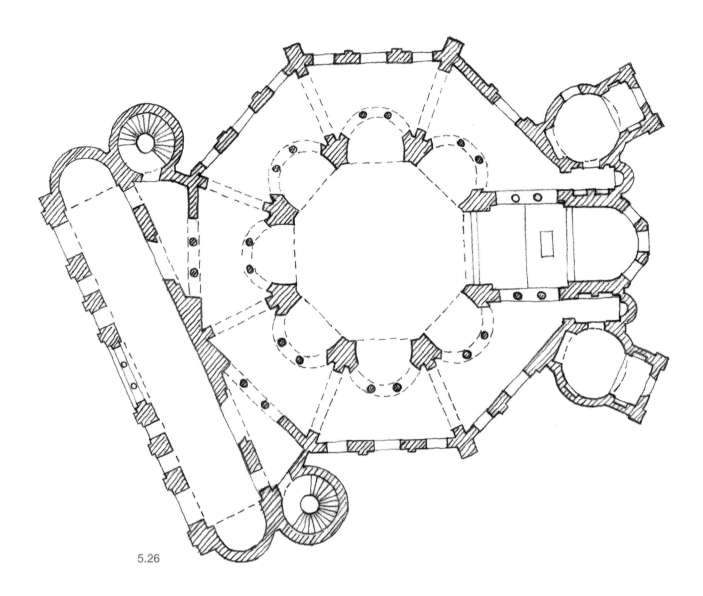

5.26

5.26
Church of San Vitale, Ravenna, Italy, 526–47 CE. Plan.

The centrally focused plan of the Church of San Vitale has two sources. As a martyrium, its traditionally concentric form marks the site of the martyrdom of San Vitale. Second, it was a refined version of the plan adopted by the Byzantine emperor Justinian, which appeared first in the Church of Saints Sergius and Bacchos in Constantinople. The centralized plan accommodated the emperor's combined roles as the central authority for the secular empire and the primary defender of religious orthodoxy. For this reason, the Byzantines abandoned the Roman basilica as the model for their churches in favor of the centralized Asiatic form. Though derived to some extent from the Church of Saints Sergius and Bacchos (completed only a few years before the construction of San Vitale began), the Church of San Vitale achieved a new dynamically fluid spatial quality. Whereas both had an octagonal core, that of San Vitale produced eight voluminous, double height, semicylindrical apses suffused with the light passing through the outer ambulatory. In the Byzantine tradition, the rough exterior shell of elemental geometric shapes enclosed an interior entirely sheathed in mosaics that reflected light from the perimeter into the center.

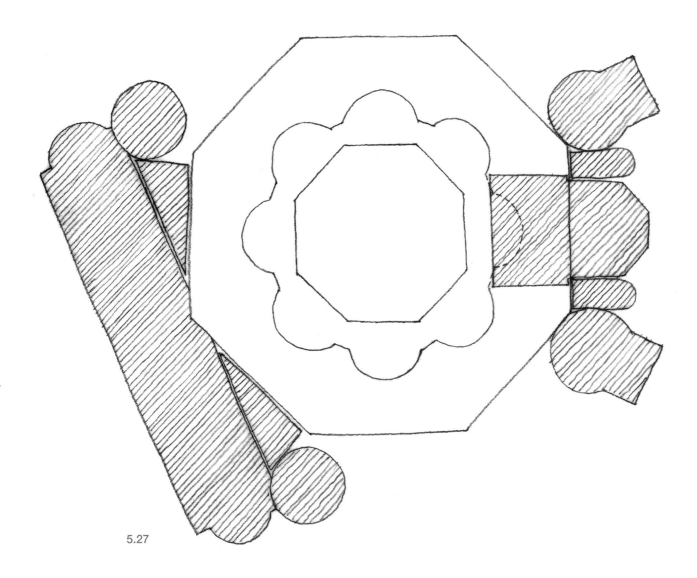

5.27

5.27

Church of San Vitale. Composition.

While the main body of the building is a concentrically layered form, the composition as a whole is a composite of several types. The narthex is a long, barrel-vaulted porch placed tangentially to one angle of the central octagon and flanked by two cylindrical towers. The triangular interstitial spaces between the narthex and the outer shell of the church are entrances. The apse that embraces the altar is a separate figure deeply embedded in the octagon, extending outward to the east and flanked by two hybrid chapels, both cylindrical and cubic. The spaces between these and the central apse become small subsidiary apses.

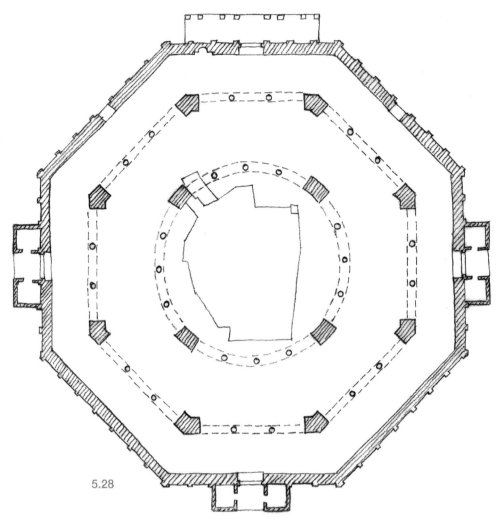

5.28

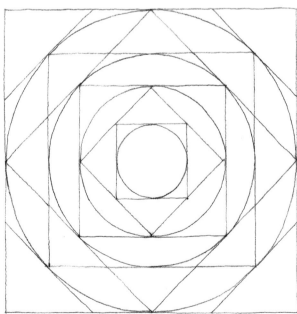

5.29

5.28
Dome of the Rock (Qubbat as-Sakhrah), Jerusalem, 688–91 CE. Plan.

The Dome of the Rock was the first monumental work of architecture in the Islamic empire. Commissioned by the Umayyad caliph Abd al-Malik and built by Byzantine artisans, it was intended to create a pilgrimage shrine for Muslims with a prestige comparable to that of the Kaaba in Mecca. However, its primary purpose was probably geopolitical and symbolic: to announce the arrival of Islam by establishing a monument of superb quality and magnificence at the center of the Judeo-Christian world. The octagonal shell is a solid wall with four entrances oriented to the cardinal directions. It encloses an octagonal arcade that in turn encloses a circular arcade surrounding the sacred rock. Together these produce three spaces. The outermost is an ambulatory, consistent with the role of the building as a pilgrimage site. The next inner space is for prayer and meditation. The central sacred space encloses the sacred rock. The dome rises directly over the rock to establish a vertical axis mundi, connecting it with the cosmos.

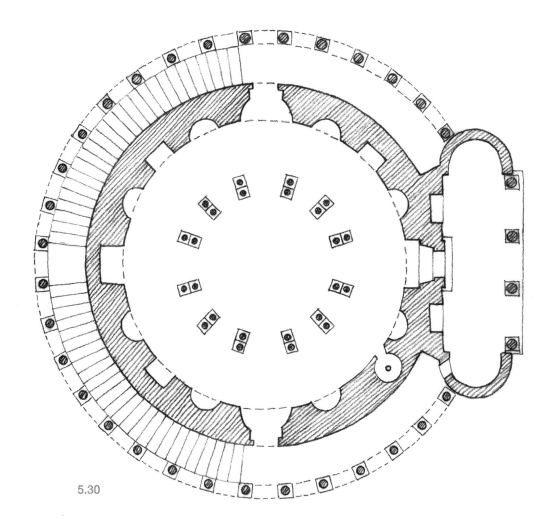

5.30

5.29

Dome of the Rock. Geometry.

A precise geometry in the design of the building was essential for conveying its meaning. All of the dimensions of the shrine are related to the sacred rock by means of a mathematical progression of nested circles and squares, a progression governed by $\sqrt{2}$. One result is that the dimension of each face of the outer octagonal shell is the same as the diameter of the circle that encloses the rock. More importantly, the system of concentric circles suggests that the power of the site emanates without limit from the center into the world and that the building is the visible manifestation of an infinite extension of spiritual power, analogous to concentric waves emanating from a pebble dropped into a still pool.

5.30

Mausoleum of Santa Costanza, Rome, 361 CE. Plan.

Originally commissioned by the emperor Constantine as the mausoleum for his daughter Constantia (d. 354), the building was completed in 361 and instead became the mausoleum for Helena, the sister of Constantine and wife of Emperor Julian. Consistent with the Roman tradition of this building type, it is circular. A porch similar to that of San Vitale in Ravenna leads into a circular barrel-vaulted ambulatory surrounding a central domed space. The variety of styles and subjects of the mosaics completely covering the interior of the barrel vault reflect the iconographic transition from pagan to Christian motifs during Constantine's reign. An arcade of twelve pairs of Corinthian columns (taken from other Roman buildings) support the central dome. Since the principal niche containing the sarcophagus of Helena is opposite the main door and two other doors create a cross-axis, the building plan is both centrally focused and axial. Pope Alessandro IV consecrated the mausoleum as a church in 1256 and relocated Helena.

5.31

Roman House, Volubilis, Morocco, mid-3rd century CE. Plan.

A 2:√3 rectangle, traditionally considered an auspicious geometry, inscribes the plan and the principal reception room. A suite of spaces centered on the atrium occupies approximately half of the plan, while beyond these are more private spaces, including the bath (lower right). The atrium is a square opening supported by a colonnade, surrounded by an ambulatory that is in turn enclosed by of the principal living spaces.

5.32

Roman House, Volubilis. Composition.

The center of the atrium is bilaterally symmetrical with four columns to each side, while the outer boundary of the ambulatory has four walls, each with its own symmetrical pattern. Though the atrium and reception room align axially, they do not correspond with the axis through the entry, vestibule, and loggia. All of the other spaces in the house comprise a heterogeneous cluster, each space adopting a shape and position according to its use. Therefore, the plan is formal where it needs to be and informal everywhere else. The four walls of the ambulatory mediate between these two orders.

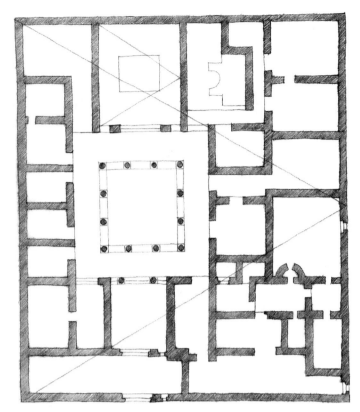

5.31

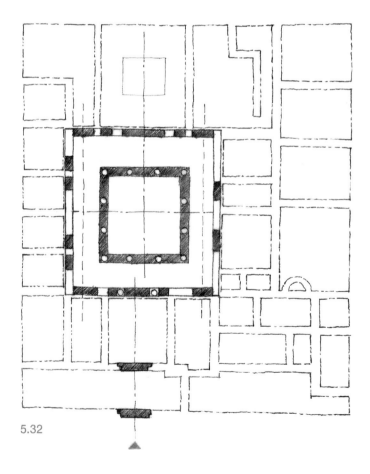

5.32

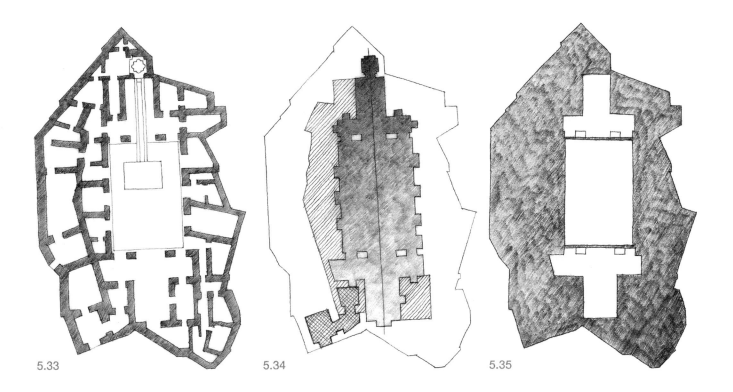

5.33

5.34

5.35

5.33
House No. VI in al-Fustat, Cairo, Egypt, 7th century. Plan

When the Arabs conquered Egypt in 639 CE, they established their headquarters in a new town called al-Fustat, now a part of present-day Cairo. The plan of this house, typical of those constructed in al-Fustat, is similar to those of ancient Mesopotamian houses, a pattern that followed several traditional design principles. In this tradition, there was no regard either for the regularity of the plan at its periphery or for its outward appearance. All interior spaces gained light and air from one or two courtyards, which were regular in plan. The main courtyard was axially symmetrical and flanked by at least two T-shaped spaces (iwans), the fronts of which each had a three-bay portico. A bent corridor led from the entrance to a corner of the main courtyard to preserve privacy. Finally, the house kept separate its use for public functions (salamlik) and for private functions of the family (haremlik). At the south end of the north-south axis there was a salsabil, a type of fountain that allowed water to tumble over a serrated stone slab into a pool, thereby cooling and humidifying the air. The water then ran down a channel from the fountain into a pool in the courtyard.

5.34
House No. VI in al-Fustat. Composition

Overall, the plan of the house provides a concentric gradation of regularity, from the strictly geometrical center through an intermediate zone of slightly irregular spaces surrounding the courtyard to entirely irregular spaces on the periphery. The entry is a suite of three small rooms with connecting thresholds that protect the privacy of the interior from the street.

5.35
House No. VI in al-Fustat. Composition.

The central courtyard has a north-south orientation and the proportion of 2:3 (32 x 48 feet). Iwans are at the north and south ends, suggesting that one was primarily for winter use and the other for the summer, as is customary among traditional houses of Arabia, Mesopotamia, and North Africa.

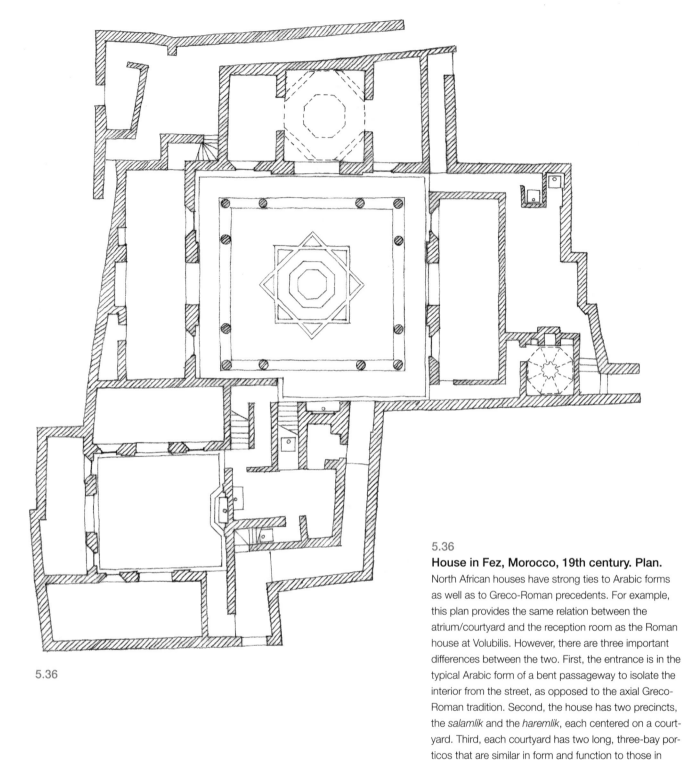

5.36

House in Fez, Morocco, 19th century. Plan.
North African houses have strong ties to Arabic forms
as well as to Greco-Roman precedents. For example,
this plan provides the same relation between the
atrium/courtyard and the reception room as the Roman
house at Volubilis. However, there are three important
differences between the two. First, the entrance is in the
typical Arabic form of a bent passageway to isolate the
interior from the street, as opposed to the axial Greco-
Roman tradition. Second, the house has two precincts,
the *salamlik* and the *haremlik*, each centered on a courtyard. Third, each courtyard has two long, three-bay por-
ticos that are similar in form and function to those in
House No. VI at al-Fustat—originally a Mesopotamian
plan type. Therefore, this plan is a fusion of several traditions in the design of houses.

5.36

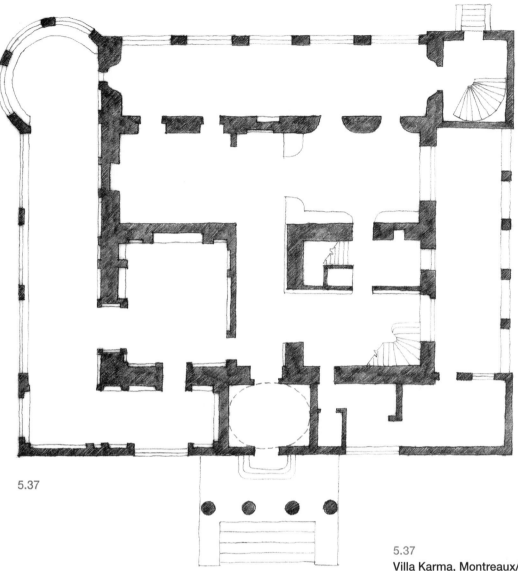

5.37

5.37

Villa Karma, Montreaux/Clarens, Switzerland, 1906. Adolf Loos. Plan.

Loos's first built commission was an addition to a house that had a roughly four-square plan with a central hall. The ground-floor plan of Loos's addition reveals a simple and clear strategy: he wrapped the existing house in a layer of spaces of nearly uniform thickness so the original core now borrows filtered natural light from the new outer layer. The closed, austere entry elevation contrasts with the other three elevations, which open expansively to the landscape, thus creating a dramatic release from darkness to light as one enters the building. Since the main axis through the relatively dark entry and central hall terminates in a niche, one is drawn laterally toward the light and views of the outermost layer of space. What initially appears to be a static, axial plan is instead experientially complex, a hint of Loos's later development of the intricate *raumplan*, a 20th-century avant-garde approach to designing interior spaces that was identical to the traditional method used in Cairene houses of the 18th century (see 3.7).

Radial Layering

Radial layering is a subset of concentric layering, the distinction being an emphasis on a radial geometry. The concentrically layered Bouleuterion of Megalopolis, for example, is a radial structure that provides everyone an unobstructed view of the speaker at the center (5.38). As a result, sitting anywhere in the building provided the experience of a double reading of spaces—both concentric and radial. The Freeman Residence by Gunnar Birkerts achieves a similar spatial ambivalence (5.39). Though the rooms of the house comprise an orthogonal plan, Birkerts superimposed a contrasting pattern that produces a second, radial reading of spaces from the center, through the orthogonal layers and into the landscape.

The medieval chapel of Santa Sophia in Benevento, Italy, has an idiosyncratic plan that is in the tradition of Classical concentric buildings such as that of Santa Costanza. However, the rotation of its columns and the modeling of its outer wall imply a radial reading of space from the center outward through the concentric layers of space (5.40). The Baensch House by Hans Scharoun offers a different interpretation of radial lay-

5.38
Thersileion Bouleuterion, Megalopolis, Arcadia, Greece, 371 BCE. Plan.

The *bouleuterion* was a Classical Greek building type used as a meeting place for the *myriad*, or all male citizens of a city-state operating under a democratic system of government. The one at Megalopolis accommodated the ten thousand voting citizens of the Arcadian confederation within a roofed enclosure 172 x 218 feet. According to Pausanias, it appeared shortly after the foundation of the city in 371 BCE and represented a major departure from the traditional design of this building type. Examples of the *bouleuterion* type in other cities, such as Athens, reveal the serious problems in planning and structure that the one at Megalopolis solved. Typically, a *bouleuterion* was a large hall in which a square grid of heavy timber columns supported the roof; since their intercolumniation was limited to a maximum of about 22 feet, the interior became a forest of columns that obstructed almost all views of a speaker who stood on the center "orchestra." The solution at Megalopolis was to arrange the columns in sets of nested U-shaped rows around the orchestra and vary intercolumniations to create a radial pattern, thus ensuring everyone an unobstructed view of the speaker. The floor was also stepped up through the U-shaped rows to improve views. Within one hundred years of its construction, democracy in Arcadia gave way to an era of tyrants. The Spartans destroyed this remarkable building in 222 BCE, leaving only its column bases.

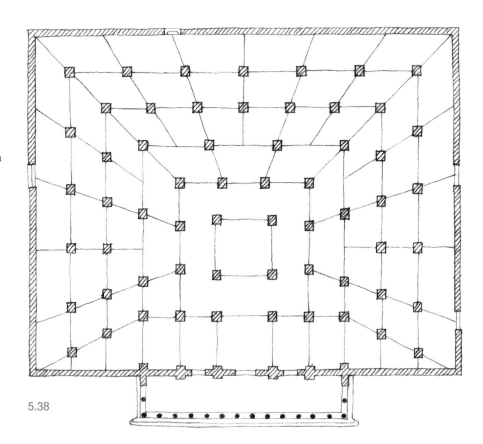

5.38

ering (5.41, 5.42). In this case, there is no implication of a center. The focus of the plan is the dining room, which opens onto a small terrace at one end of the plan. All other spaces, as well as the structure, radiate from this space like the fingers of a hand.

Layering in architectural design is appealing because it is a simple way to organize the forms and spaces of a building according to their function, and it is an easy composition for someone using the building to comprehend. It allows for an incremental transition from outside to inside, which is a satisfying experience under almost any circumstances but particularly important in religious structures. We have also seen (in the town of Turpan, for example) that a layered architecture is an effective means to control social relations. Layering tends to segregate parts of a building and to exaggerate their differences. In the case of Villa Savoye and the Thai granary, the segregation of the parts of their compositions is central to the meanings of their forms, but in other circumstances segregation may be artificial and awkward because it becomes merely a mechanical contrivance that precludes any subtlety in the relations between forms and spaces.

5.39

Freeman Residence, Grand Rapids, Michigan, 1964–66. Gunnar Birkerts. Plan.

In this plan, Birkerts explored the relation between two orientations: internal and external. Moving through the house one is always visually referencing the center of the radial plan—its centripetal force—as well as equally compelling views outward into the landscape through the orthogonal arrangement of spaces—the centrifugal force of the plan.

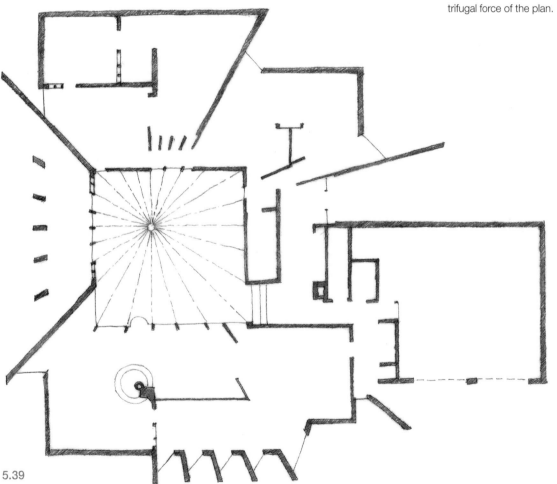

5.39

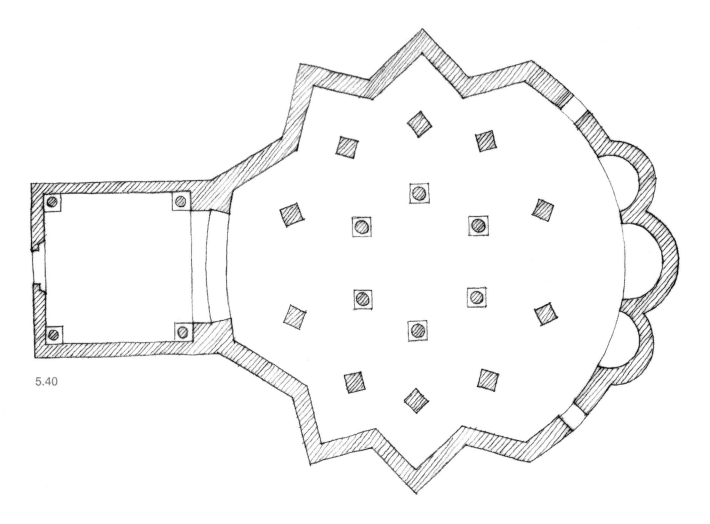

5.40

5.40

Church of Santa Sophia, Benevento, Italy, 760 CE. Plan.

The plan of this church is one of the most unusual among medieval European churches. Built by the Lombards, it is centralized in form but radial in structure and has no relation to either Roman or Byzantine precedents. The outer shell, 77 feet in diameter, is of tufa and Roman brick. It varies in form. First it is a circular plan at its entry, then a star-shaped plan at its midsection, and finally a circular plan with three shallow semicircular apses. At its center is a hexagon of antique columns, their bases placed orthogonally. This is surrounded by a decagon of piers, each of which is separately oriented in relation to the nearest wall. The three layers of vertical structure results in an equally idiosyncratic system of vaulting, first quadrangular, then rhomboid, and finally triangular.

5.41

Baensch House, Spandau, Berlin, Germany, 1936. Hans Scharoun. Plan.

Scharoun was a member of Bruno Taut's Expressionist circle and also worked within the mainstream of Modernist functionalism until he came under the influence of Hugo Häring. Häring espoused an architecture without any formal preconceptions in direct response to the place and the program that a building was intended to serve. He therefore rejected the imposition of geometry, the axial order of Beaux-Arts Neoclassicism, and the Rationalist grid, as well as Le Corbusier's belief in "pure" forms—all of which, he argued, stood in the way of the realization of a building's authentic identity. The Baensch House is one of Scharoun's early experiments with Häring's theory of design. In it we find no preconceived underlying formal order. Instead, Scharoun shaped spaces according to the movements and perceptions of their users and their relation to the exterior.

5.42

Baensch House. Composition.

Though Scharoun avoided static design devices, his method was not arbitrary. He organized spaces functionally and hierarchically, in this case fanning outward from the dining space, with service spaces against the most public perimeter wall and the major living space opening expansively to the rear private garden.

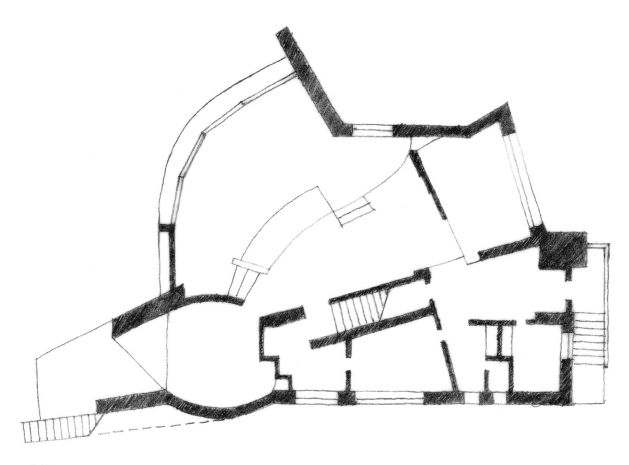

5.41

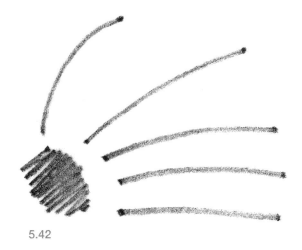

5.42

CHAPTER 6

LINEAR FORMS

Spinal

The spine of a cat is both a neural pathway and a structural armature (6.1). Similarly, architectural spines perform two functions. They are simple, easily perceived routes of movement through a complex composition and they work structurally. In both respects, a spine is an economical way to integrate a heterogeneous set of forms and functions.

Some spines are external to the architectural elements they organize. Giorgio Vasari combined various small buildings and spaces into a single form in the Uffizi in Florence with the simple and elegant device of a spinal colonnade (6.2). This also produced a unified facade to wrap around an unusually long and narrow piazza. The upper story of the colonnade was a segment of an elevated passageway that allowed the Medici to walk unmolested the entire route from their residence in the Palazzo Pitti on the opposite side of the river Arno to their midtown offices in the Palazzo Vecchio. On a smaller scale, Sigurd Lewerentz organized a set of small buildings for the Workshop Society in Göteborg, Sweden, by composing them much like a Greek agora; their principal organizing element was a spinal colonnade similar to a stoa (6.3). Carlos Raúl Villanueva followed the same principle to integrate a variety of buildings on the campus of the University of Caracas; his approach was more complex in that he adjusted the scale and rhythm of the colonnade to correspond to the various scales of the buildings attached to it (6.4). The Palace of Herod at Jericho employed a spine slightly differently. In this case, the spine ran as an exposed free-standing form (a long stair up to a temple and a bridge across a river) transversally to the compositional elements it combined, but then turned and was a fully integrated part of the palace in the form of a colonnade (6.5, 6.6).

Conversely, a spine may be an internal feature of a plan, both spatial and structural. Richard Norman Shaw's design for Greenham Lodge (6.7–6.9) and Charles Rennie Mackintosh's design for Hill House (6.10, 6.11) were similar in this respect. A central corridor controlled the relation between the formal functions and the service functions of each house. Meanwhile, one wall of the spine was the principal interior structural element that allowed free spans to the exterior walls through spaces of varying size and shape, each designed for its specific use. In the example of the Barthels Hof, an 18th-century town house in Leipzig, the courtyard was attenuated to become an interior passage extending from one street to another (6.12, 6.13). All the rooms of the house looked into this spatial spine and produced a continuous elevation, the principal one of the building.

A spine can shape a building to conform to the physical characteristics of a site, enclose exterior spaces, or frame views into or beyond the site. In the harsh climate of Saudi Arabia, the Tuwaiq Palace (which is used for recreation and meetings for the diplomatic community) wraps around an artificial oasis and encloses smaller, protected spaces for pools and terraces (6.14). Its varied program fits around a single monumental circulation spine that runs the length of the building, opening to one side or the other as needed. Similarly, in the early 1960s, the new government of Cuba commissioned the construction of several new arts schools on the grounds of a former country club near Havana. Three of the projects—the schools for music (6.15), the plastic arts (6.16), and ballet (6.17)—had serpentine plans that took advantage of their expansive sites. Among other design objectives (certainly metaphorical), the spines allowed the buildings to breathe in the hot, humid tropical climate.

At the urban scale, the spine, as a street, is ubiquitous as a means to unify a great many buildings and neighborhoods to produce a continuous spatial experience. Of course, all streets are linear, whether they are straight or curved. However, great cities as well as small towns throughout the world often use streets to achieve a higher purpose than merely permitting convenient movement. These streets become monumental by virtue of their compositional unity and simply the delight a pedestrian experiences in walking through them. For example, the Shari' al-Mu'izz li-Din Allah begins at the northern gate of the medieval quarter of Cairo and as it winds its way southward past the citadel to the Mosque of Ibn Tulun, it combines hundreds of buildings great and small in a unified but varied tour de force of an urban spine (6.18).

6.1

Cat Skeleton.

The cat has a pronounced spine terminating in the skull and to which is attached two skeletal ensembles, the thoracic cage with front legs, and the pelvis with rear legs. The spinal structure thus unifies a variety of forms and functions, establishes hierarchy, and indicates an axial relation of parts.

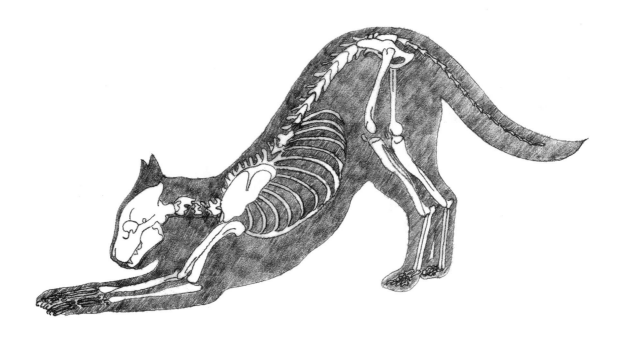

6.1

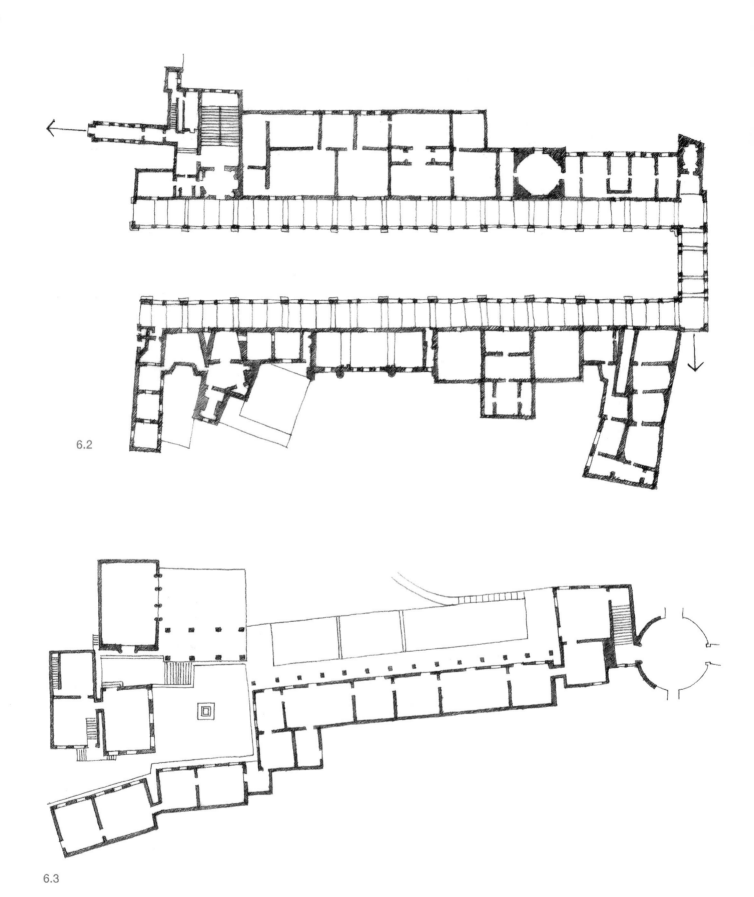

6.2

6.3

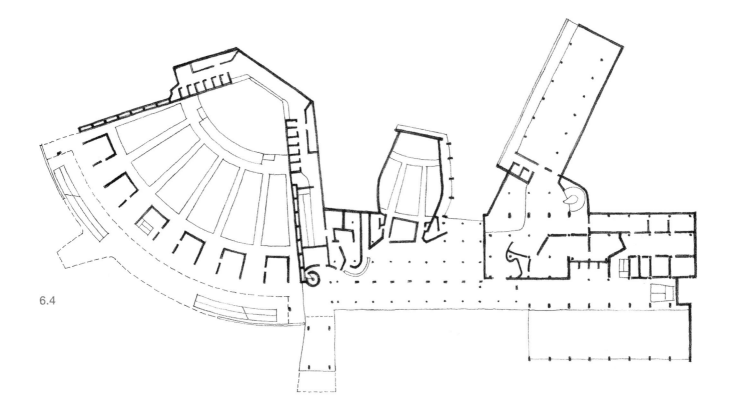

6.4

6.2
Uffizi, Florence, Italy, 1560–70. Giorgio Vasari. Second-floor plan.

Commissioned by Cosimo de' Medici and completed in the reign of his successor, Francisco, the Uffizi ("offices") served three purposes. First, it consolidated the thirteen departments of the Florentine bureaucracy into a single structure immediately adjacent to the city hall, the Palazzo Vecchio. Second, it housed the Medici's rapidly growing private collection of antiquities and art (now the sole function of the building). Third, its corridor was a segment of an elevated passageway that allowed the Medicis to walk in comfort and security above the street between their residence in the Palazzo Pitti across the river Arno to their offices in the Palazzo Vecchio (the arrows in the drawing indicate the two connections with the passage). The corridor of the Uffizi acts as a spine, wrapping around a long, narrow piazza on three sides to produce a unified facade for a highly diverse collection of rooms behind it.

6.3
Workshop Society, Göteborg Exhibition, Sweden, 1923. Sigurd Lewerentz. Plan.

In his early career, Lewerentz was a Neoclassicist who, in collaboration with Erik Gunnar Asplund, won the competition for Stockholm's Woodland Cemetery, perhaps the greatest landscape design of the 20th century. For that project, Lewerentz designed his masterpiece, the Chapel of the Resurrection (built in 1925), in a new, austerely modern but distinctly Nordic style. He had been instrumental in founding the Klara School, dedicated to an authentically indigenous method of design, and while the Chapel of the Resurrection was underway, he designed the exhibition building for the Workshop Society. Though a minor building in a large and varied oeuvre, this project is interesting because it illustrates Lewerentz's continued interest in the Classical, specifically Greek, technique of planning an architectural ensemble. The long colonnaded spine, similar to a stoa, emerges from a propylaeum-like structure, unites a series of galleries with a garden, and terminates in a court framed by gently skewed buildings, a loggia, a monumental stair, and a signature building placed on axis but slightly off center.

6.4
University of Caracas, Venezuela, 1953. Carlos Villanueva. Plan.

Villanueva's plan embeds the individual forms of a concert hall, a lecture hall, and a library into a linear spine. The spine, however, is not uniform. It varies in rhythm and proportion and incorporates a variety of secondary features that mediate between the circulation spaces and the three principal interior spaces. The result is a vibrantly layered composition that achieves unity while allowing each space to be independent according to its needs.

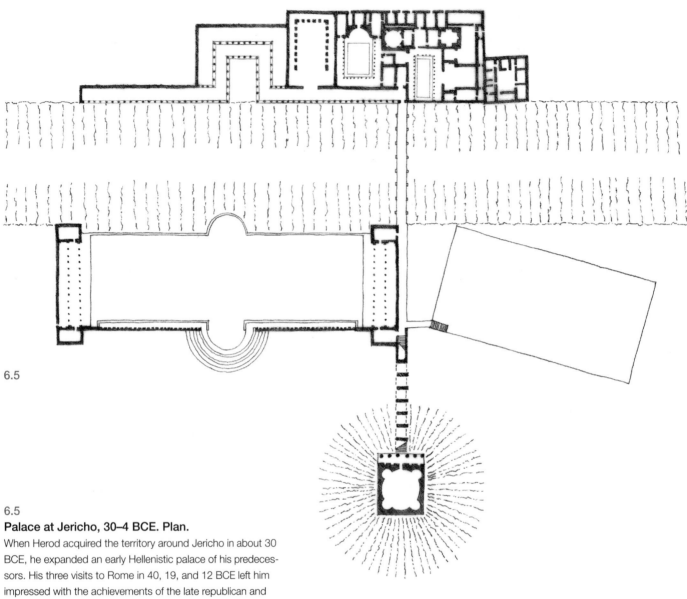

6.5

6.5
Palace at Jericho, 30–4 BCE. Plan.

When Herod acquired the territory around Jericho in about 30
BCE, he expanded an early Hellenistic palace of his predecessors. His three visits to Rome in 40, 19, and 12 BCE left him
impressed with the achievements of the late republican and
early imperial architects, and as a protégé of the Emperor Au-
gustus, he strove to transplant Roman culture to his homeland.
The palace at Jericho is one of many Herodian architectural
projects in this vein, as it exhibits characteristics of Campanian
villas and Palatine palaces. The palace at Jericho is in two parts
connected by a bridge and bracketing the Wadi Qelt, which
was reduced to a straight deep ditch. The principal palace
structures were on the north side and included several gardens,
peristyle courts, baths, and private apartments. A large garden
framed by stoas and an obliquely oriented shallow pool were to
the south of the wadi. Originating as a long colonnade within
the palace, the spine turned south to become a bridge across
the wadi, then a long staircase that climbed steeply to a temple
mounted on an artificial conical hill.

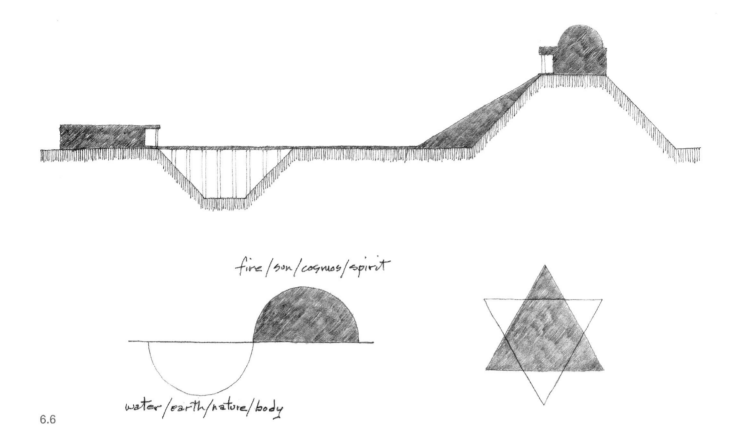

fire/sun/cosmos/spirit

water/earth/nature/body

6.6

6.6

Palace at Jericho. Section and symbolism.

To consolidate his political power, Herod needed to establish his theological credentials. The palace at Jericho played a part in this program and so invoked in its organization a key symbol of Herod's claim to legitimacy. This is found in the direct relation between the modified wadi (regularly shaped and oriented directly east-west) and the artificial hill (reminiscent of many Mesopotamian sacred mountains in the form of ziggurats). By contrasting the two and connecting them with a north-south spine, Herod was referring to an ancient Eastern mystical dichotomy: that the regenerative potential of life originated in the fusion of opposites—of fire and water—which respectively represented the sun/cosmos/spirit and the earth/nature/body. A north-south section of the palace illustrates the relation of the wadi and the hill relative to the datum of the terrestrial plane, of which the bridge and spine are an abstraction. The two principles of regeneration became a symbol consisting of two entwined equilateral triangles, which in the Hebrew tradition became the shield of David. However, the hexagram or six-pointed star appeared in Mesopotamia in the 8th century BCE, long before the rise of the Jewish state, and it persisted into medieval European culture as an alchemical symbol. The downward pointed triangle represented water, while the upward pointed one represented fire. The spine connects the similar sectional geometries of the wadi reaching toward water and the artificial hill pointing to the sun.

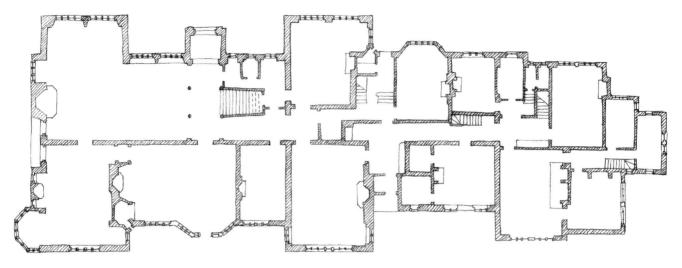

6.7

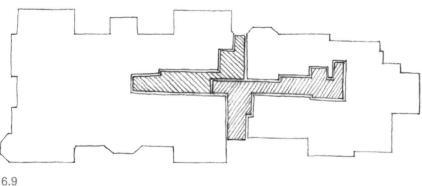

6.8

6.9

6.7

Greenham Lodge, Newbury, United Kingdom, 1881. Richard Norman Shaw. Ground-floor plan.

Shaw's clients, the Baxendale family, were members of a rapidly rising social class of businessmen in Victorian England. The Baxendales strove to express their prestige by purchasing a large country estate from the aristocracy and commissioned Shaw to design a new house appropriate to their new pretensions as landed gentry. In keeping with these ends, Shaw designed the main staircase leading down from Mrs. Baxendale's boudoir to the main salon, framed by two freestanding columns, specifically for her grand entrance at parties.

6.8

Greenham Lodge. Spine.

Since each room within the house had a specific social or utilitarian function, no two were alike. Furthermore, the traditional aesthetic of British country houses required a degree of informality despite the scale and grandeur of the building. The challenge was to strike a balance between chaos and order. Therefore, Shaw established a semblance of order by attaching the heterogeneous collection of spaces to a central structural spine and hallway.

6.9

Greenham Lodge. Served and service spaces.

Shaw divided the ground-floor plan of the house into two halves—one for formal salons, the other for service functions—each with its own circulation. These lock together at the center of the plan and break the continuity of the spine.

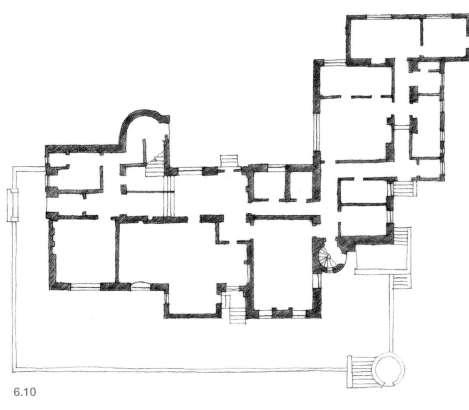

6.10

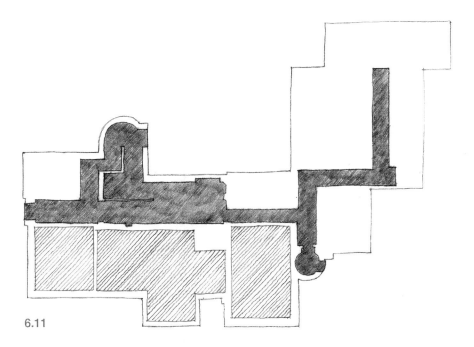

6.11

6.10

Hill House, Helensburgh, Scotland, 1903. Charles Rennie Mackintosh. First-floor plan.

By submitting his interior layout of Hill House to the client before he began the design of the exterior, Mackintosh indicated his primary interest in establishing a functional organization suitable to his client's needs. It was a practical, narrow plan that extended east to west along a bluff with all major spaces enjoying a view to the estuary of the river Clyde to the south. These were the library, dining, and sitting rooms on the first floor and the major bedrooms on the second. The nursery and children's rooms, on the other hand, were located far away in the north wing above the kitchen and service spaces.

6.11

Hill House. Composition.

Mackintosh adapted a Scottish baronial style that required an extensive center hallway to function as a spine to which he could attach a variety of individually shaped spaces. To take advantage of the site and to segregate the formal family and social spaces from children and servants, the spine needed to be quite long and complex.

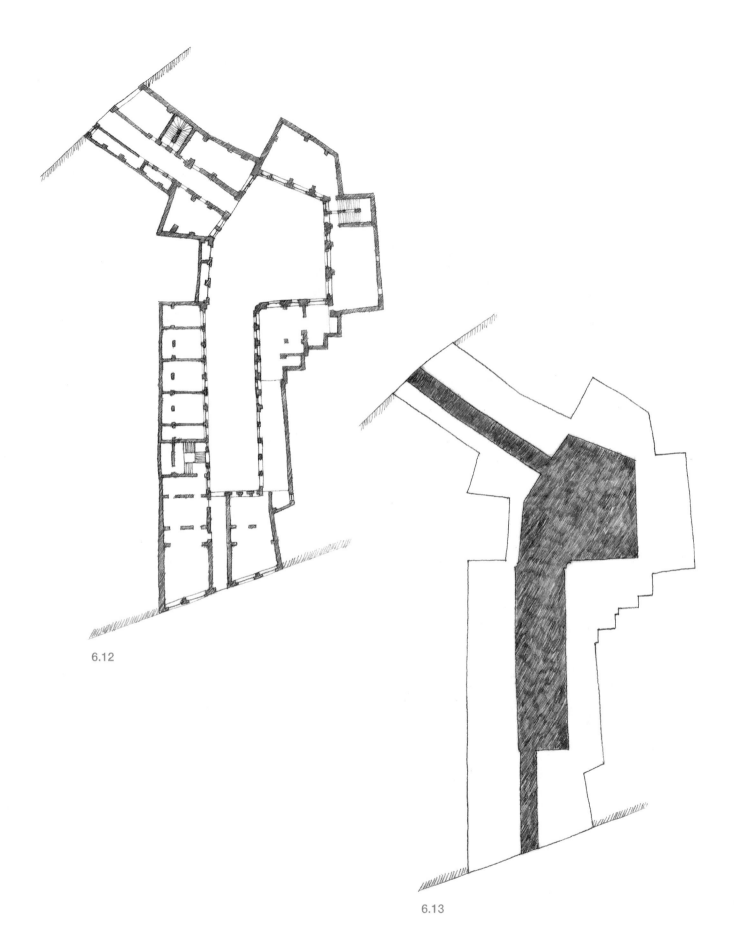

6.12

6.13

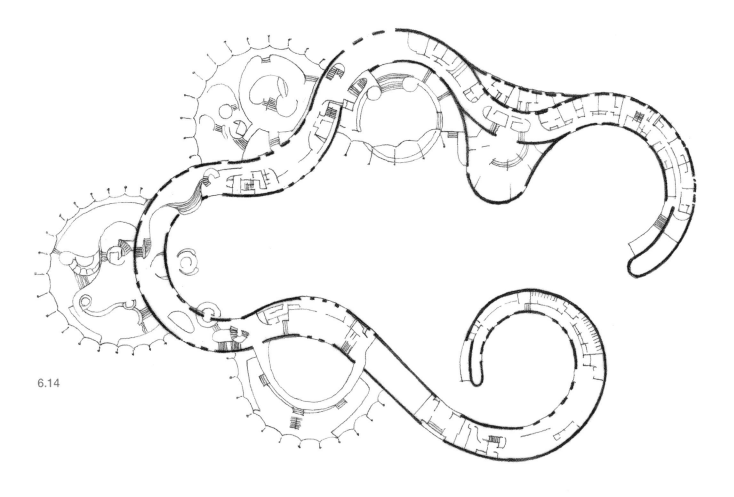

6.14

6.12

Barthels Hof, No. 8 Markt, Leipzig, Germany, 1748. Ground-floor plan.

This 18th-century house is a consolidation and adaptation of several preexisting medieval houses. Typical of merchant houses in northern Germany, the ground floor was dedicated primarily to storage and business matters. These spaces were arranged around a central courtyard that connected to two streets.

6.13

Barthels Hof. Composition.

Since the house extended entirely through a city block from one street to another, the central court became an interior street, a spatial spine in four segments on which all other work and living spaces depended for light and air.

6.14

Tuwaiq Palace, Riyadh, Saudi Arabia, 1985. Omrania and Frei Otto. Plan.

The palace is a club for the diplomatic community in Riyadh and for state receptions. To provide guest services and accommodations, its core is a limestone-clad undulating concrete wall 2,625 feet long and 39 feet high, varying in width from 23 to 43 feet. The wall partially encircles outdoor spaces for gardens and sports facilities and supports several tent structures that enclose large spaces, such as the main lounge, a reception space, a restaurant, and a multipurpose hall. The tents on the exterior of the wall are of a white Teflon-coated fabric, while blue fish-scale glass tiles sheath the inward-facing tents. The spinal form serves primarily to protect the lush central oasis from the harsh, rocky desert. It also creates a long, continuous promenade for social functions.

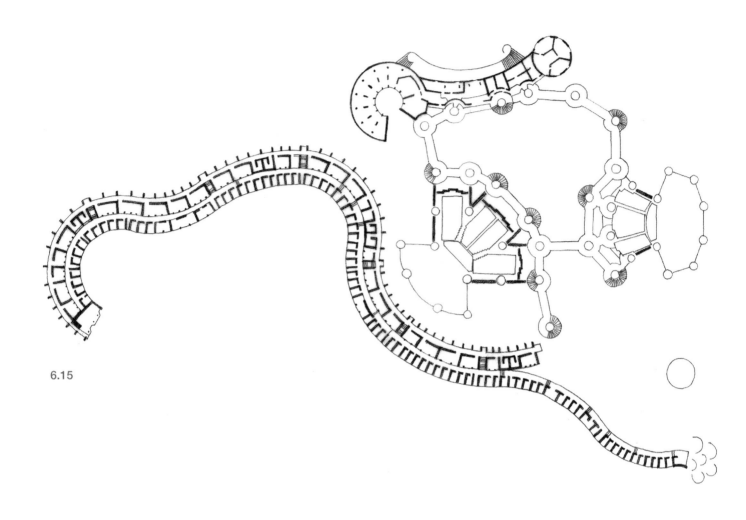

6.15

6.15
National School for Music, Havana, Cuba, 1961–63. Vittorio Garatti. Plan.
Shortly after the conclusion of the Cuban Revolution, the team of Roberto Gottardi,
Ricardo Porro and Vittorio Garatti designed five ambitious projects dedicated to the arts
on the site of a former country club near Havana. Accused of being bourgeois and individualistic, the partially constructed projects were abandoned when the Cuban leadership
aligned itself with the Soviet Union and embraced its severe collectivist architectural style.
Garatti's project proposed a formal expression of practice spaces for individuals and small
ensembles as a long cellular serpent in contrast to an archipelago of larger spaces dedicated to performances. Though the quarter-mile-long spinal form provided every practice
room with an unobstructed view into the tropical landscape and was interesting as a
metaphor of musical rhythms, it was impractical as a day-to-day means of circulation.

6.16

6.16
National School for the Plastic Arts, Havana, Cuba, 1961–63.
Ricardo Porro. Plan.
Porro designed the School for the Plastic Arts during the early romantic period of the
Cuban revolution as an expression of a new and authentic Cuban multicultural national
identity, an identity centered on a powerfully feminine and explicitly sensual African culture. He abandoned the European ideal of a mathematically constructed space in favor
of a spatial eroticism, which he believed reflected Cuba's landscape and tropical climate.
The plan suggests a tropical plant form as well as an African village—an organic composition of narrow lanes, individual buildings, and open spaces connected by sinuous,
colonnaded spines. Each of the eleven studios is an oval theater centered on the place
reserved for the live model. In contrast, the administrative spaces form a simple rectangular block that embraces a three-lobed exhibition hall. Porro used the Catalan vault extensively because it is a structural type that does not require either timber centering or
concrete, both of which were too expensive for this project.

6.17

6.17
National School of Ballet, Havana, Cuba, 1961–65. Vittorio Garatti. Plan.
The School of Ballet is one of five schools for the arts commissioned by Fidel Castro. Its plan makes explicit reference to the fluid movement of the dance by capturing nonfigural exterior spaces within its curvilinear walls in counterpoint to the figural, encapsulated interior spaces. Garatti organized the spaces along a serpentine spine shaped by alternating concave and convex surfaces. Unfortunately, the building was poorly sited in a floodplain, and the project, only partially constructed, was abandoned in 1965.

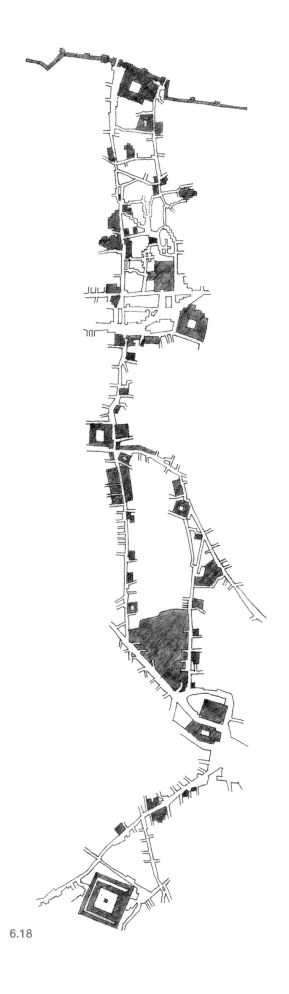

6.18

Shari' al-Mu'izz li-Din Allah, Medieval Cairo. Plan.

City streets are of course essentially linear forms, but some rise to monumental proportions to form a complete architectural ensemble. One of the great urban walks of the world is from the northern gate of the medieval quarter of Cairo (Bab al-Futuh), built by Salah ad-Din in the 12th century, south to the venerable 10th-century mosque of Ibn Tulun at the foot of the citadel. For several hundred years, this was the principal processional route for religious, military, and civic celebrations in Cairo. The plan illustrated here includes only the major architectural edifices along the urban spine, the Shari' al-Mu'izz li-Din Allah. The primary monuments were mosques, the Al-Azhar University, madrassas (schools), *wekalas* (guest houses for merchants), mausoleums, and palaces. Secondary structures were three large markets, baths (of which there were over twenty in the northern third of the route) and *sabils* (public fountains). The prestige of this great street attracted the finest architecture of several dynasties, from the Tulunids and the Ayyubids to the Mamluks.

Segmental

The principal use of a segmental composition is to organize spaces sequentially to promote movement longitudinally in a totally controlled manner. Less often, segmental buildings simply arrange identical or similar features side by side without connecting them internally. The arrangement of enclosures and tents that the Mughal emperor Akbar used while on military campaigns is typical of the sequential function of a segmental design (6.19). In addition to providing security, it conveyed authority through a hierarchy of spaces that functioned in a single way. The step well, or *baoli*, of Adalaj is a series of steps and platforms in a deep trench; its principal purpose was to create a series of subterranean spaces at various levels culminating in an octagonal pool, where people could escape the intense heat above (6.20).

The segmental form has been particularly useful for religious structures, since these often depend on rituals of a sequential nature. In the Sinai desert, Serabit el-Khadim was a set of shrines dedicated to the goddess Hathor, the protector of miners in the turquoise mines of the 14th century BCE (6.21). The complex began as a pair of shrines embedded in the side of a hill, and successive generations of miners added shrines linearly to eventually create a segmental structure aboveground. Ritually, the building required worshipers to progress from the exterior to the inner sanctum through every shrine in succession. The Temple of Horus at Edfu is also segmental but for a different reason (6.22–6.24). It was not an additive form but rather conceived as a total design. Furthermore, its sequential form was designed to function in the reverse manner of Serabit el-Khadim's: the cult figure was kept in the smallest, darkest space, accessible only to the priests, and carried out into the light through the sequence of spaces. Pharaonic tombs, such as that for Ramses VI at Luxor, were segmental primarily for security purposes (6.25). The long corridor leading to the tomb chamber was broken into segments by nine thick granite doors. Many Hindu temples of the Classic period, such as the Lingaraja Temple at Bhubaneswar, employed a standard set of structures, constructed as separate buildings, connected by specialized portals and thresholds (6.26, 6.27). These prescribed a ritualistic choreography, including offerings and performances, leading from an outdoor forecourt to the *sri mandar* that housed the cult figure of the lingam and yoni.

Segmental plans are widely used in secular buildings in the sequential type as well as the side-by-side type. A plan of Caribbean origin and a common vernacular house

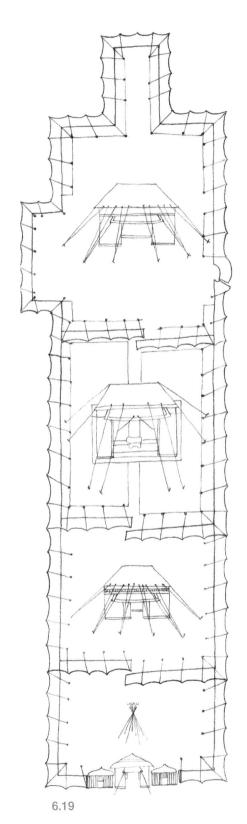

6.19

Military Campaign Tent Compound, late 16th century. Mughal Emperor Akbar. View.

This type of mobile architecture replicated the organization of a stationary palace structure with a segmental series of compounds that controlled access to the emperor based on the social standing of the petitioner. The walls of the compounds were of brightly colored fabric, and the tents were fabric replicas of palace buildings.

in the American South, the "shotgun house" is composed of a series of rooms in a row without a hallway (6.28). Similarly, two houses by Glenn Murcutt in New South Wales, Australia, use a series of interconnected rooms in a row (6.29). These houses, however, have an entrance at the center, dividing the plan into two halves, private and communal, and most of their spaces open to the side. Workers' housing in Door County, Wisconsin, uses a side-by-side plan in which access to all units is from one of the longitudinal elevations. In this case, the segmental form serves standardization (6.30). A related plan for artists' studios in Stuttgart, Germany, alternates variations of two types of units; the building as a whole imparts an impression of a segmental form without standardization (6.31).

Plans may also be segmental without the parts having a similarity to one another. The mosque, tomb, and *sabil* (public fountain) of Amir Khayrbak in Cairo unites three different building types in a sequence (6.32). The *sabil* and the mosque frame the entrance vestibule; the mosque and the tomb form a pair, though the tomb has a separate entrance as well. Nevertheless, the three form a single continuous composition with respect to their massing and their street elevation. A hospital ward in Antwerp by Frans Baekelmans also combines three separate but related elements with short corridors—in this case an effort to isolate contagious diseases (6.33). The connected basement rooms for a house in Heuport, Germany, originated in separate houses. Though not conceived as a single composition, the plan is instructive because of its cellular structure and the articulation of its five sections (6.34).

The previous examples are composed of discreet units with clear boundaries between them that rely on separate thresholds. However, this is not always the condition of segmental organizations. Some of the most sophisticated compositions allow overlapping spatial segments with only implied boundaries. For example, the Koto-in Zen Temple in Kyoto, Japan, has a series of spaces, each with a unique identity, that interpenetrate to produce a complex set of relationships, scales, and changing orientations (6.35, 6.36). Similarly, the Ninomaru *densha*, a villa within a garden attached to the Nijo Castle in Kyoto, consists of many small interior segmental spaces that blur the boundaries between six major segments of the plan. Its segmental form controls privacy and internal security and allows the serrated building form and the surrounding landscape to interpenetrate in accordance with the classical Japanese genius for integrating interior and exterior spaces (6.37–6.42).

6.20

Step Well (*Baoli*) of Adalaj, near Ahmadabad, India, 1499. Plan.

Elaborate stone step wells are unique to the architecture of the Indian subcontinent, and are especially common in the state of Gujarat. They consist of two parts: a deep vertical shaft and a staircase with platforms that lead to the shaft's bottom. In the case of the step well of Adalaj, the straight staircase descends in seven stages on a north-south axis and terminates in an octagonal space. The introduction of large platforms into the stair permitted its use as a social space and a place of refuge from the intense heat at ground level, giving the well its distinctively segmental form.

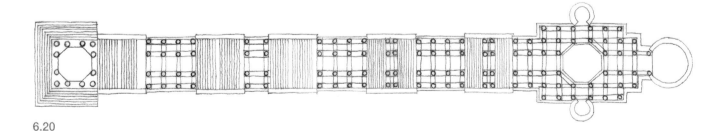

6.20

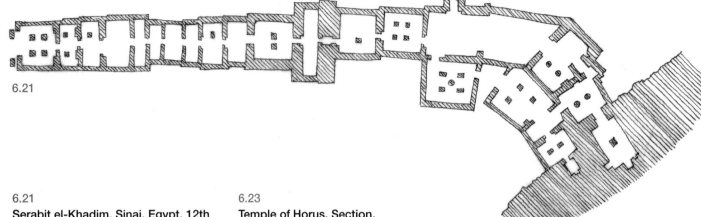

6.21

6.21

Serabit el-Khadim, Sinai, Egypt, 12th Dynasty. Plan.

This series of shrines was developed approximately from the mid-14th to the mid-13th centuries BCE in a remote area in the southwest Sinai noted for its turquoise mines. The two original sanctuaries dedicated to Hathor (the protector of turquoise and presumably of turquoise miners) occupied small caves in a red sandstone cliff, and over time, miners added twenty more small enclosures sequentially to produce a long segmental series of shrines. Unlike the great temples of the Nile Valley, Serabit el-Khadim had no initial plan but rather emerged as a segmental form through use: its plan arose from a gradual additive process. Different types of writing on the walls of the sanctuaries (including a Canaanite alphabet) indicate that various groups of miners, probably slaves, each contributed a sanctuary, adding it to those of their predecessors.

6.22

Temple of Horus, Edfu, Egypt, 257–57 BCE. Plan.

Constructed through the reigns of six Ptolemys, this is the second largest surviving temple in Egypt (after Karnak) and the best preserved. The segmental form satisfied the need for seasonal and annual rituals dedicated to the mythical life of the god Horus, his wife Hathor (including an annual symbolic conjugal visit to his temple), and the reenactment of Horus's triumph over the god Seth (which required the sacrifice of a hippopotamus). The segments of the temple followed the movement of the sun on an axis from east to west. While this temple follows a segmental plan on a longitudinal axis, we can also interpret the form as nested figures in concentric layers, or a multiple core and shell.

6.23

Temple of Horus. Section.

The section reveals a rigorously ordered sequence of spaces that diminish in scale as they approach the inner sanctum at the east end of the axis. The structural limitation of stone beams and roof slabs spanning between columns and walls produced an extremely tight rhythm of alternating masses and voids from one end of the axis to the other, a constraint that heightened the dramatic experience of movement along the axis.

6.24

Temple of Horus. Light.

The segmental form of the building not only defined the sizes and shapes of spaces, but also determined the amount and quality of light. The inner sanctum of Horus was almost entirely in the dark, surrounded by thirteen attendant chapels and storerooms. It was at the east end facing west, and as one moved out of it on axis through the chambers and hypostyle halls toward the entrance of the temple, spaces became incrementally lighter. Once each year the high priests brought the cult figure of Horus out of the darkness through the hypostyle halls and into the western court to be recharged with life by the sun.

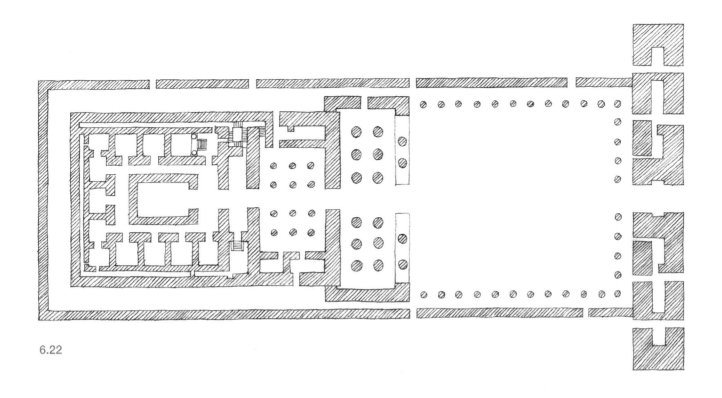

6.22

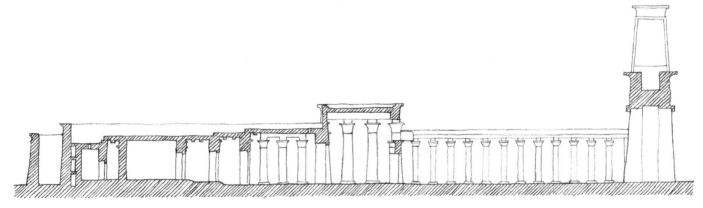

6.23

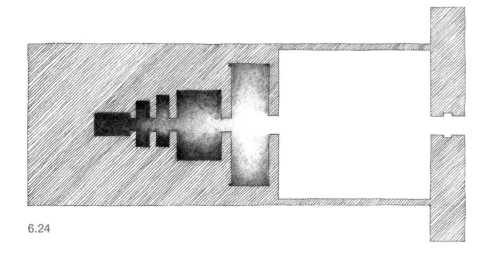

6.24

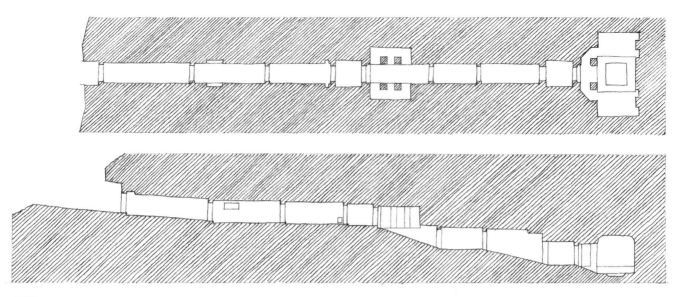

6.25

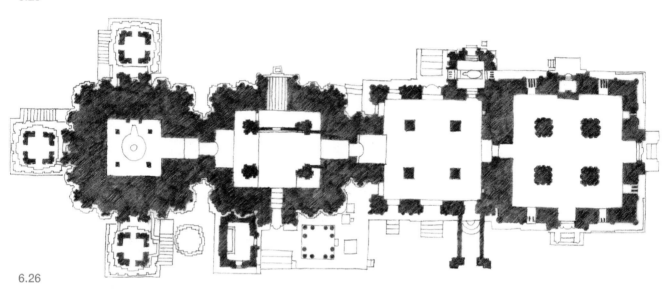

6.26

6.25

Tomb of Ramses VI, Luxor, Egypt, 20th Dynasty. Plan and section.

The tomb is from the period approximately 1186–1069 BCE. Architecturally it is no more than a passageway from the exterior to the sarcophagus chamber, its segmental form satisfying the need for security by creating nine choke points in the passageway obstructed by massive slabs of granite. The segmental form is usually used to regulate or restrict linear movement, either for ceremonial purposes or for security. This is an extreme example of the latter function.

6.26

Lingaraja Temple, Bhubaneswar, India, 11th century. Plan.

The Lingaraja Temple is the finest example of the Orissan style of Hindu architecture. Set within a walled compound among sixty-five smaller shrines, it features a 127-foot hollow tower (*shikhara*) constructed without mortar. The *shikhara* rises above the *garbha griha* (sacred chamber) which holds the cult object, a lingam that symbolizes both Shiva and Vishnu. The *garbha griha* is the oldest of four structures that comprise the segmental organization of the temple. Before it in sequence stand the *jagamohana* (assembly hall), the *natmandir* (sacred dance hall) and the *bhogmandir* (sacrificial hall). Though the ornamentation of the exterior of the temple is exuberant, its interiors are relatively plain.

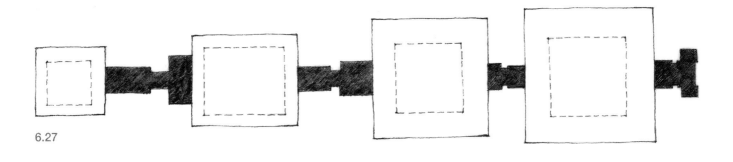

6.27

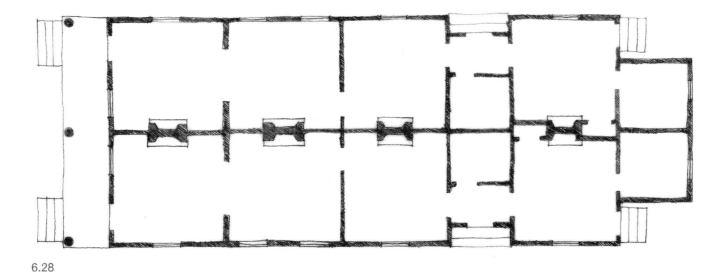

6.28

6.27

Lingaraja Temple. Schematic.

The segmental form of the Lingaraja Temple is primarily a reflection of rituals that require a sequence of increasing sacredness, from the outer sacrificial hall to the inner sacred chamber. It is also a reflection of the sequence of the temple's construction over a period of two hundred years. The gracefully tapered *shikhara* was an ancient translation in stone of a design originally in bamboo. It and the *garbha griha* were built first, after which the *jagamohana* was added. The *natmandir* and the *bhog-mandir* appeared in the 12th century. Short passageways keep the four parts separate as distinct buildings.

6.28

Double Shotgun Cottage, New Orleans, ca. 1910. Plan.

The folk term *shotgun* refers to a plan that suggests if one fired a shotgun through the front door the blast would exit the back without hitting a wall: there is no hallway, and the interior spaces are in line. It is a type of inexpensive workers' housing common in the American South from the Carolinas to Shreveport, Louisiana, with a sequence of rooms from front to back: a parlor, dining room, two bedrooms, and a kitchen (if an extra bedroom is built over the back room, the house is a "camelback"—original examples lacked indoor plumbing). The house is generally 12 to 15 feet wide, about 90 feet long and up to 14 feet high. The type appeared in New Orleans in the 1840s as an import from the Caribbean, perhaps of Haitian or even West African origin. Windows are narrow and as tall as the doors, with transoms to provide adequate ventilation in a hot, humid climate. The facade is usually elaborate, in Queen Anne, Colonial Revival or Craftsman styles.

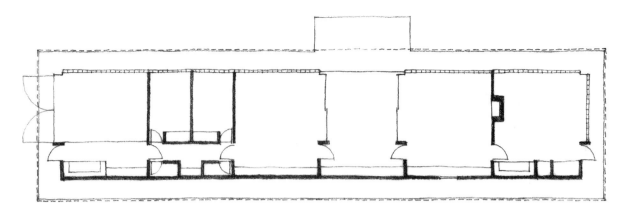

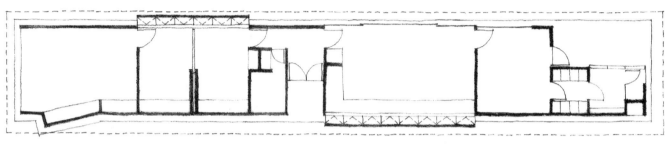

6.29

6.30

6.29

Top: Magney House, New South Wales, Australia, 1984. Glen Murcutt.
Bottom: Fletcher-Page House, New South Wales, Australia, 1998. Glenn Murcutt.
Plans.

The architect has used the segmental form extensively for houses in New South Wales, since it affords all rooms equal access to prevailing breezes, sunlight, and views. It also requires a simple, low-cost building system and minimal energy use. In these two examples, the garage is at one end and the entry and communal room are approximately in the center. Each house consists of a platform, a cellular body, and a continuous, low-pitched roof—a modernist interpretation of a time-tested vernacular design.

6.30

Workers' Housing, Door County, Wisconsin, ca. 1945. View.

In contrast to examples of segmental buildings designed for specific physical or historical conditions, this is a generic architecture that uses a segmental formal structure as a means of standardization. All segments are identical and fuse into a continuous form whose length is determined only by the number of segments needed. Within the limits of its specific function, it engages the egalitarian and utilitarian condition of its users, so despite its original purpose to house seasonal fruit pickers, it served with equal effect for German prisoners of war and is now a roadside fruit stand.

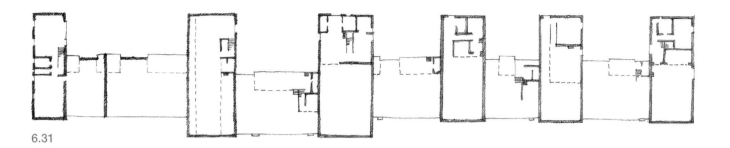

6.31

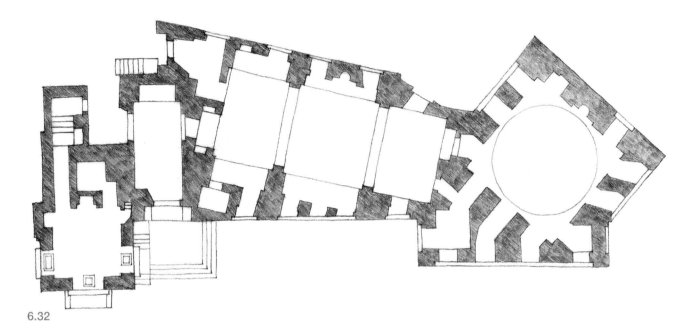

6.32

6.31
Artists' Studios, Stuttgart, Germany, 1992.
Fritz & Elizabeth Barth. Plan.

The plan implies a hierarchy of primary and secondary segments, the latter appearing to perform
a connecting function. In reality these are simply
two different types of studios. The technique results in an interesting rhythm, scale, and proportion. Note that despite their similarity, no two segments of either type are alike, producing a balance
between unity and individuality.

6.32
Amir Khayrbak Complex, Cairo, Egypt,
16th century. Plan.

The complex includes a *sabil* (public fountain), a
mosque, and the patron's mausoleum organized as
a series of spaces, each with its own orientation.
While the principal face of the mausoleum corresponds with the *sabil*, the *sabil* projects into the
street and has three faces. Its position creates the
entry and vestibule of the mosque, whose orientation is shifted toward Mecca. The plan of the mausoleum is an extraordinary example of the fusion of
two orders. The interior requires three openings on
each side of a square, while the exterior accommodates a variety of facade conditions with respect to
surrounding streets. The architect solved the problem by encasing the central space in a wall of varying thickness and then bending the apertures
through the wall so they correspond to both the interior pattern and the exterior pattern of openings.
The plan as a whole is a highly rational approach to
combining three separate structures, each with their
own identity, into a single seamless composition.

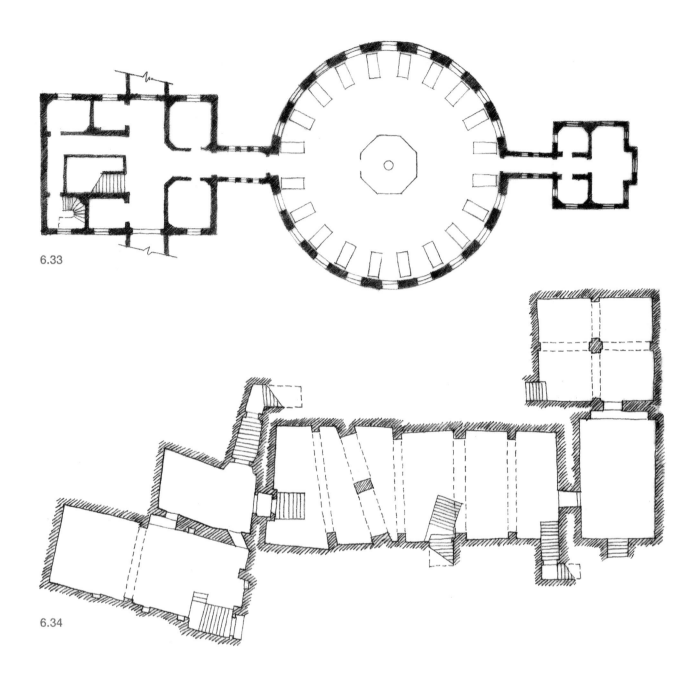

6.33

6.33

Hospital Ward, Antwerp, Belgium, 1888. Frans Baeckelmans. Plan.

This illustrates one ward in a series (note the connecting corridor) in a radial design intended to isolate patients with different diseases. In this functionalist plan, Baeckelmans segregated the ward as a whole from others and further segregated the three functions within it into three separate pavilions. The corridor that connects the various wards leads into a pavilion with two treatment rooms, stairs, a storage room, and an office. The next pavilion is the patient room in a radial panopticon design, and the third houses toilets and a bath.

6.34

House in Heuport, Germany, 19th century. Basement Plan.

This plan is doubly segmental. It has three large segments, probably derived from parts of the basements of three separate houses combined (suggested by the multiple stairs). Each segment is also itself a segmented form as a result of its structural system.

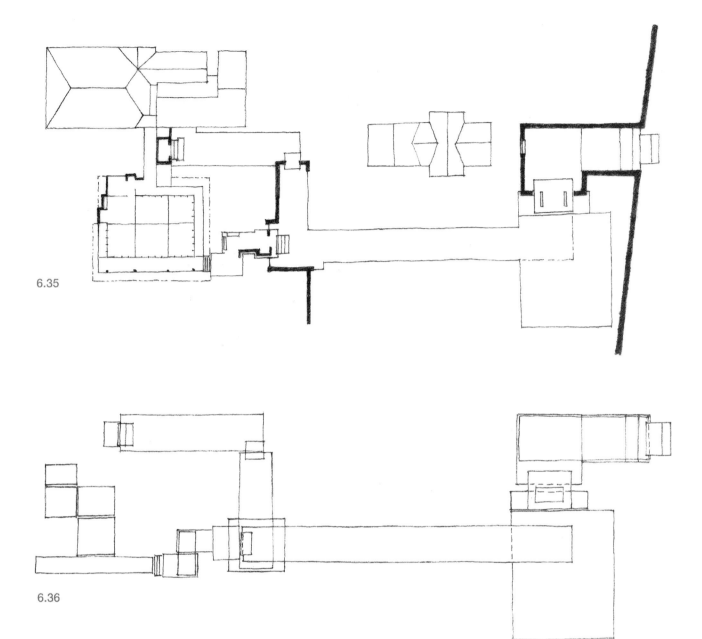

6.35

6.36

6.35

Koto-in Temple, Kyoto, Japan, 1319. Plan.

The Koto-in is one of twenty-four sub-temples in the Daitoku-ji Zen Buddhist monastic complex. The Daitoku-ji (named after a nearby mountain) is one of fourteen branches of the Rinzai school of Zen. Access to the Koto-in is from one of several avenues that run through the complex, through an enclosed gate and down an alley of maple trees. The temple is famous for its garden and the perfection of its tea ceremony.

6.36

Koto-in Temple. Processional.

The linear procession from the avenue to the temple employs a complex layering and interlocking of spaces defined by a variety of landscape and architectural features. In this regard, it is a segmental form, since each segment plays a specific role and fits with the others in a harmonious continuum. The choreography of views, spatial proportions, and shifting orientations produces the optimal relation between the pace of pedestrians and their environs.

6.37

Ninomaru Palace, Nijo Castle, Kyoto, Japan, 1602. Tokugawa Ieyasu. Plan.

Tokugawa Ieyasu constructed the Ninomaru Palace. He also founded the Tokugawa Shogunate, known as the Edo period, that lasted 250 years. Though Edo was the capital city, Kyoto was the residence of the Tokugawa shoguns and the home of the imperial court. The segmental form of the Ninomaru Palace was a direct architectural expression of a graduated system of space designed for social control. Each segment of the plan was used for the reception of visitors, who were segregated by social rank—the lowest rank in the largest, most ostentatious space and the highest in the smaller, more subtly and tastefully designed spaces. The smallest and most intimate segment (and the farthest from the main entry) housed only the shogun and the women who served him. The palace is entirely of cypress and included two security features: instead of the traditional concealment of rooms for bodyguards, they were in prominent positions, and the floors squeaked to prevent a sneak attack by assassins.

6.38

Ninomaru Palace. Building and lake.

The principal feature of the garden that surrounds the palace is an artificial lake. The composition of the palace and its landscape is principally that of the relation between the shape of the lake and the footprint of the building.

6.39

Ninomaru Palace. Interpenetration.

The segmental plan produces a complex relation between interior spaces and the landsape. Exterior space penetrates deeply into the reentrant corners of the serrated plan, while outer corners of the segments thrust equally far into the landscape. This contributes to the powerful integration of interior and exterior space and also produces the condition by which every view of the landscape from the interior also includes some part of the building in relation to it.

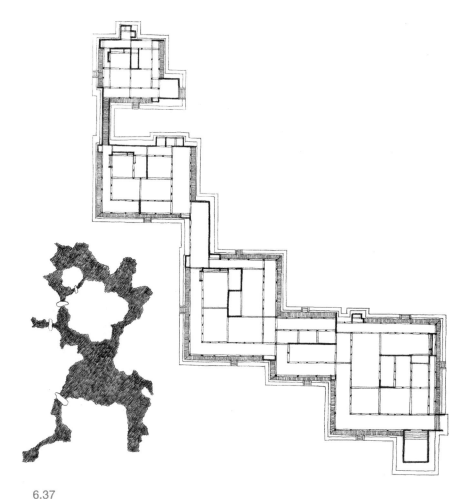

6.37

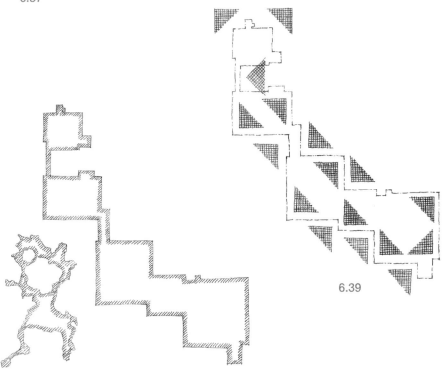

6.39

6.38

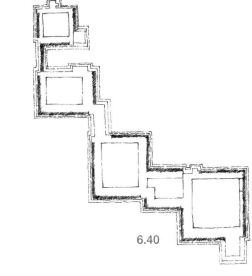

6.40

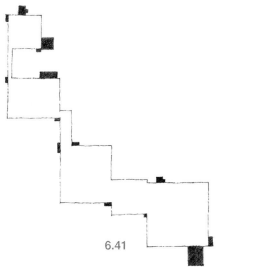

6.41

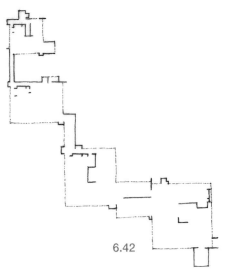

6.42

6.40
Ninomaru Palace. *Engawa.*

A basic concept in classical Japanese architecture is *en*, the "in-between." It produces a seamless gradation of space and form from inside to outside through layers, such as changing patterns of materials, modulations of natural light, and variations in degrees of enclosure. *En* is an aesthetic interpretation of a common feature of the natural landscape, the ecotone, in which flora and fauna create a gradual transition between two ecologies, the intermediate space having characteristics of both. An *engawa* is the principal means by which the concept of *en* is applied architecturally. It is the veranda on the perimeter of the building that is a feature of the building and the landscape simultaneously, that is, the in-between. It extends interior architectural space into the landscape and, as a feature of garden design, it extends the landscape into the interior. In the Ninomaru Palace, the *engawa* comprise a nearly continuous outer layer of the building, interrupted only by specialized structures on the exterior or by connections between segments designed for security. Within this outer layer is a second one devoted to service and security, and at the center of the plan are spaces for habitation, controlled by the building module, the tatami mat, of which there are approximately eight hundred.

6.41
Ninomaru Palace. Perimeter structures.

To keep interior spaces open and flexible, the architect relegated all specialized functions—such as the main entry, latrines, shrines, and guard rooms—to the perimeter, and designed them as independent structures plugged into the outer surface of the palace.

6.42
Ninomaru Palace. Stationary walls.

Movable, translucent walls, or shoji screens, modify the organization of the interior in response to changing functions. There was also a system of stationary walls, on the perimeter as well as internally, that controlled movement, security, and degrees of privacy. However, these do not enclose or even suggest rooms, but are fragmentary.

6.43

Kaedi Regional Hospital Addition, Kaedi, Mauritania, 1989. Association pour le Développement Naturel d'une Architecture et d'un Urbanisme Africains (ADAUA). Plan.

The hospital serves a large, remote sector of Mauritania near the border of Senegal. The original building is a conventional, rectangular concrete-frame structure, while the addition includes 120 beds; an operating theater; pediatric, ophthalmic, and maternity departments; as well as support and maintenance spaces within a flexible, low-cost brick structural system. Handmade brick was not within the local vernacular tradition, but its introduction in this case proved to be advantageous because it used an inexpensive, locally available material and introduced new skills to the local labor force. The structural system that emerged through experimentation employs several types of arches, vaults, and domes, erected without centering and shuttering. Gaps between bricks admit light and air. The double-shell construction cools the outer surface and reduces fluctuations of interior temperatures, and the branching form provides the necessary isolation of wards in clusters.

Branching

In nature, branching is the most efficient method of distributing and collecting energy, whether it occurs in a neural net, a tidal estuary, or the veins of a butterfly's wing. In architecture, branching plans usually produce a stronger hierarchy and centrality than can either a spinal or a segmental plan. In the five examples that follow, there is a preoccupation with surface exposure to the surrounding environment for the sake of maximizing air circulation, sunlight, or views.

The addition to the Kaedi Hospital in Mauritania is composed of double-skinned brick modules combined in clusters attached to a branching circulation system to ensure optimal air circulation and isolation for the various wards (6.43). James Stirling used a branching form for student housing at Saint Andrews University to relate all living units to communal spaces and to provide everyone with a view of the extraordinary landscape and the sea (6.44). Another housing scheme, the Anasazi village of Alkali Ridge, used a branching plan to orient individual houses to southern and eastern sunlight and to enclose three large plazas that functioned as communal spaces for daily activities, ritual dances, and clan kivas (6.45). The Smithson's proposed plan for a school connected six identical classroom units with a branching walkway surrounded by outdoor communal space; the system provided each unit its individual identity within a collective, centrally focused pattern. An interior peripheral corridor connected all of the classroom units as well (6.46). Aldo and Hannie van Eyck's addition to the Netherlands General Chamber of Audit has an internal branching circulation that terminates in spatial nodes that embrace a shared outdoor space. The new biomorphic pattern contrasts sharply with the older building's rigid geometry (6.47).

Spinal, segmental, and branching plans have an open, obvious reading of order that may be appealing in the abstract. Under certain circumstances, their forms provide advantages with respect to the organization of internal elements, whether heterogeneous or repetitive, and they may relate well to topography, views, prevailing winds, and the sun. However, linear plans tend to have extravagant circulation systems and a great degree of surface exposure to their environment.

6.43

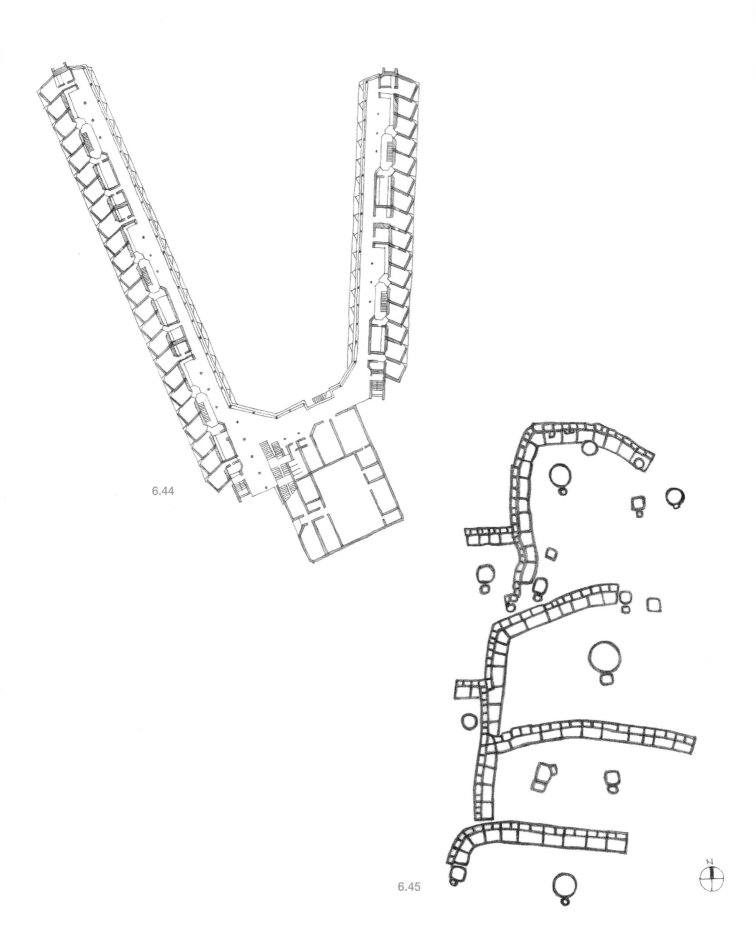

6.44

6.45

6.44

Andrew Melville Halls, Saint Andrews, Scotland, 1967. James Stirling. Plan.

Taking full advantage of views to the North Sea across the famous golf courses on its verge, two arms of dormitory rooms branch downward from a central entry and administration core at the top of a hill. Exterior panels of precast ribbed concrete set at angles create a serrated form that provides each room with a view. A glazed corridor facing into the partially enclosed space, separated from the private rooms by service and communal functions, creates a layered order for the interior of each arm.

6.45

Alkali Ridge Ruins, San Juan Valley, Utah, ca. 700–1000 CE. Plan. (After W. N. Morgan, *Ancient Architecture of the Southwest.***)**

The plans of Anasazi villages in the American Southwest exhibited a variety of responses to differences in social structures and physical contexts. The village of Alkali Ridge was a branching form divided into slender arms such that habitable spaces faced either east or south, and storage cells sheltered them on the west and north. This pattern created three plazas for the ritual spaces, the kivas.

6.46

Infants' School, Wokingham (proposal), United Kingdom, 1958. Alison and Peter Smithson. Plan.

The plan has two types of circulation. The exterior one is of an explicitly branching type from the center of the enclosure formed by the building as a whole, while the interior circulation follows the perimeter of the enclosure in a segmental pattern. The two systems intersect at six entry nodes between segments. Students would have occupied six small, identical schools, each a square in plan and facing into the central enclosure. Toilets and custodial spaces (crosshatched in this drawing) were on the outer walls of the perimeter circulation segments, adjacent to views to the outside through the ends of those segments.

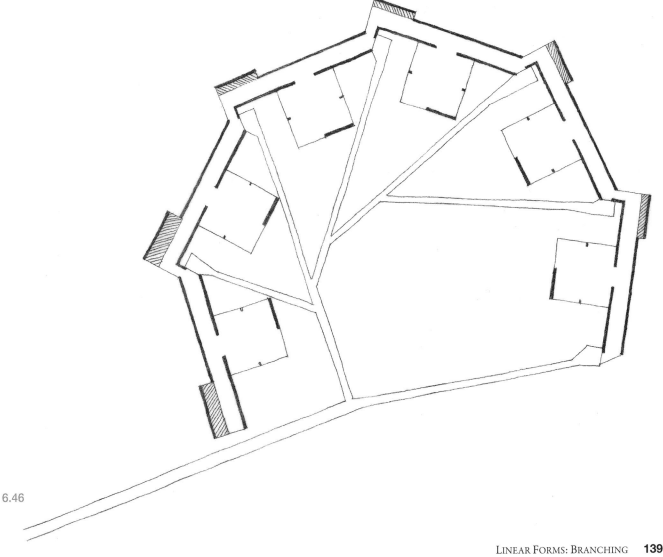

6.46

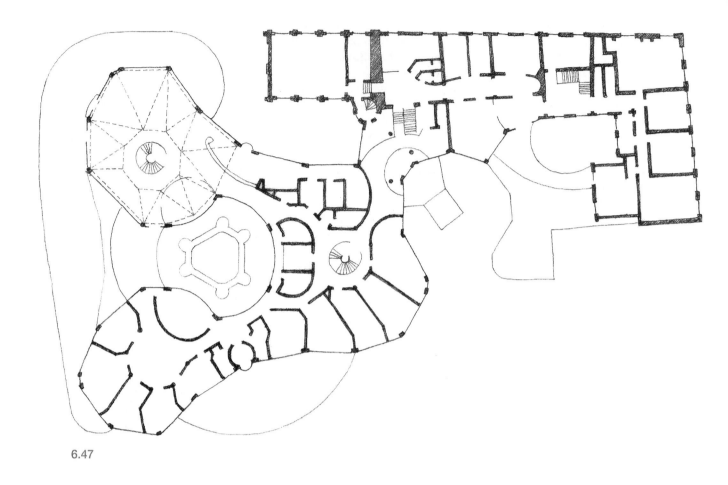

6.47

6.47
General Chamber of Audit, The Hague, Netherlands, 1997. Aldo and Hannie van Eyck. Plan.
The curvilinear plan of the new offices is an addition to the rigid L-shaped plan of an earlier building. Offices encircle a meandering circulation zone that appears to escape from the confines of the older building and split into two arms to embrace a small courtyard. One arm terminates in a vaulted library, a structural system that refers to an adjacent Gothic church.

CHAPTER SEVEN

CORE AND SHELL

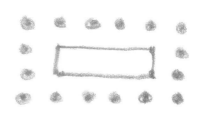

AN EGG REPRESENTS ONE OF THE MOST COMMON COMPOSITIONAL methods in architecture: the core and shell. Its shell establishes a definite boundary between the exterior and the interior, and at its center is a core imbued with special properties (7.1). Virtually all sacred sites and religious buildings follow this model, as do a great many secular buildings. Mercea Eliade, a scholar of comparative religion, identified the form as hierophany. In sacred architecture, hierophany requires two types of separation: physical and spiritual. The shell, or outer boundary, provides the physical separation that is crossed only through a dedicated portal, across a threshold, or through ritual. The core structure provides the spiritual separation and is usually associated with the vertical dimension, the axis mundi. It is remarkable that despite the extraordinary variety of religious structures in the world—whether at Angkor Wat, Beauvais Cathedral, Stonehenge, the Dome of the Rock, or an Aztec temple—the architectural formula is essentially the same.

Sacred architecture evolved from experiences people had with places in the natural world they interpreted as sacred. It is reasonable to assume that people who by necessity had an intimate knowledge of nature identified places in the landscape with unusual characteristics. These places became sacred due to a particular formal structure that reflected a fundamental principle of natural order—the primal forces of order and regeneration. People then translated these experiences into symbolic languages. Though the core and shell as a formal structure may relate metaphorically to the egg as a regenerative principle, it is certainly a practical device for separating sacred space from the ordinary world and for focusing attention on a central transformative point in space.

In addition to the egg, there are other metaphorical interpretations of the core and shell as an organizational device. Greek mythology, for example, is preoccupied on one level with the relations between mortal and divine beings, and the places where the two interacted had supernatural power. These places were usually of two types—a grotto within the earth (an aperture to the underworld) or a sacred grove of trees (trees pass through the terrestrial plane to connect the cosmos with the underworld). No doubt, these beliefs were of Indo-European origin and predated the Greeks by many thousands of years. Though a house type, the *megaron*, was the ancestor of the Classical Greek temple, there is another plausible interpretation for the temple's dual nature (a building within a building). The closed, secretive core building (the *cella*) may have been an architectural abstraction of a grotto, and the shell building, an open colonnaded peristyle suffused with light, an abstraction of the sacred grove (7.2).

The core and shell, whether used in a religious context or for secular purposes, suggests a form inhabiting another form. To emphasize this idea, some architectural traditions, such as the Byzantine, made a clear distinction between the two. In the Hagia Sophia, the building's exterior is rough and gives no indication (either in its original or present conditions) of a voluminous, curvilinear core that appears to float within and be a world apart from the rectilinear shell (7.3, 7.4).

The mosque of Ibn Tulun in Cairo from the 9th century CE uses a double wall to isolate its central space from the cacophony of the surrounding city (7.5–7.7). Within the second wall is a double colonnade facing a central kiosk. Though the kiosk functions as a fountain for ritual ablution, it is also an object of contemplation standing in a large open courtyard. It is the fusion of a cube rising from the ground and a cosmic egg descending from the sky, the two passing through one another.

Also in the Islamic tradition, the Semsi Ahmed Pasa complex by the Ottoman architect Sinan has a tomb and mosque placed on an oblique (to orient them toward Mecca) within a rectilinear enclosure of classrooms for a school (7.8). It was customary to make a distinction between two orientations, sacred and secular; the secular buildings act as a shell protecting the sacred core structure.

Thousands of Hindu, Buddhist, and Jain temples in Southeast Asia, large and small, are core and shell structures. For example, the Takeo Temple, part of the enormous complex of Angkor Wat in Cambodia, repeats the core and shell at all scales, from that of the cult object (lingam and yoni) outward to that of the temple precinct as a whole (7.9, 7.10). Each core is in effect another shell. Gateways and thresholds aligned with the cardinal directions control passages through the many shells from the periphery to the center.

The core and shell is also ubiquitous in western European sacred architecture. For example, the chapel of the Burghof, Rheda (7.11), and the crypt in the Church of Saint Germain at Auxerre (7.12) both have sacred spaces inserted into larger, protective shells with a circulation space, or ambulatory, between the two. Many of the buildings highlighted in this section follow the same principle.

The core and shell appears in secular buildings in a variety of ways. An entirely utilitarian response to organizing domestic space, typical of many vernacular traditions, is to place a heavy masonry core within a lightweight frame shell. A granary in Mali (7.13) and a *domus* in Romania (7.14) are virtually identical in this respect. Likewise, the Parson Capen House in Massachusetts (7.15) efficiently satisfies the requirements of interior space—the distribution of heat and of structure—by concentrating two hearths, the entrance, and the stair within a core in order to divide the interior space into two major spaces on the ground level, one private and the other communal. This pattern appears in a more complex way in two 20th-century examples, Le Corbusier's design for the Citrohan house type (7.16) and the design for a house in Argentina by the firm Lacroze Miguens Prati (7.17). In both, the core is a single, active, composite object that appears to inhabit the center of an otherwise open, passive, rectilinear volume.

Le Corbusier's design for the Centre Le Corbusier in Zurich (7.18), a museum originally meant to be a prototypical house, is essentially the same interpretation of a core and shell as that used for the Greek temple. Similar to the *cella* and the peristyle of the Parthenon, in the Centre Le Corbusier a lightweight steel frame building encloses interior spaces beneath and physically distinct from the roof structure. A vernacular designer in Colorado arrived at precisely the same solution to extend the useful life of his mobile home (7.19).

Two other similar projects from different origins are the 20th-century Bagsværd Community Church in Denmark by Jørn Utzon (7.20) and the 18th-century Wolpa Synagogue in Poland (7.21). They both allow a curvilinear core structure to be formally independent from its enclosing rectilinear shell structure. Utzon's purpose was metaphorical—to produce an ethereal interior atmosphere reminiscent of cloud forms. The synagogue, on the other hand, was a fusion of two architectural traditions. The exterior of the building was designed to conform to the traditional character of regional architecture, both Christian and Jewish, while the interior was derived from the spatial and decorative traditions of fabric tent structures, perhaps Ottoman or Magyar in origin.

While the core and shell may serve as a powerful metaphor, it is also a practical solution to utilitarian problems. For example, a proposal for a contemporary Arabian house had to satisfy the needs for privacy between genders and between the family and guests in a traditional society, to provide structural simplicity and economy, and to control temperatures and air circulation in a severe climate while expending a minimum of energy. The core and shell, in this case a house within a house, satisfied these requirements through a simple organizational strategy (7.22–7.24).

The formal structure of a core and shell resonates in the human psyche at a deep level because, perhaps, it replicates the primal human experience in the womb. It also satisfies a fundamental need to define an interior realm of total control distinctly separate from the uncontrollable, chaotic world. Therefore, we find it at all scales of architecture, from a simple hut focused on a hearth to great cities in which residential quarters enclose a palace/temple core.

7.1

7.1

The Egg. Section.

The egg represents the quintessential pattern of a core and shell. In addition to being emblematic of the regenerative principle, its organization is primal—the division into two functions, an outer protective boundary and an internal, hidden form. This pattern is the basis for virtually every sacred space and religious structure in human history, and it offers several utilitarian advantages for secular buildings.

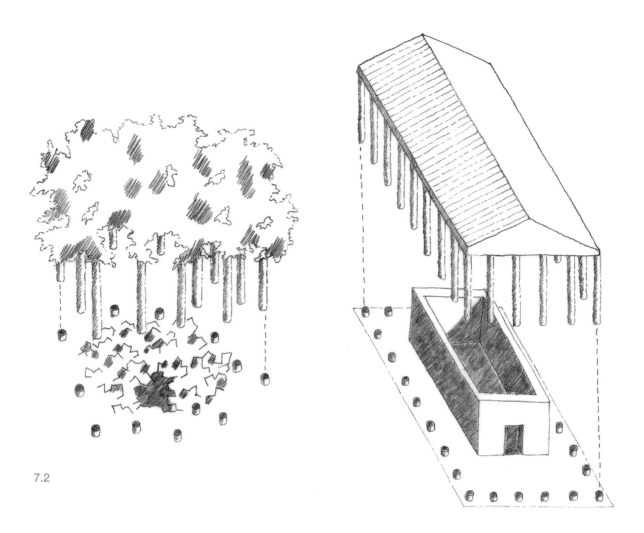

7.2

Classical Greek Temple Form, ca. 450 BCE. Schematic.

Though the form of the Classical Greek temple is likely to have evolved from the typical Dorian house, the *megaron*, a second (and not contradictory) explanation is possible. The Greeks always built temples in locations of physical and mythic power, with great attention to how they related to the landscape. For the ancients, the purpose of a temple was not merely to provide a structure in which to venerate deities. Its purpose was primarily to fix the deities to a place and thereby make allies of beings with supernatural powers. The Parthenon, for example, was not just a place for Athenians to worship Athena: it guaranteed her presence in the city. In Greek myth, gods walked the earth, and interactions between mortals and gods occurred in magical but physical places, primarily in grottoes or in groves of trees. Grottoes provided access to the Earth Mother, Gaia, as well as to the underworld. Groves of trees harbored beneficial deities by virtue of their ability to inhabit the underworld and the cosmos simultaneously. A grotto within a grove was therefore doubly powerful. The Classical temple consisted of two distinct buildings: the *cella* was a closed, boxlike form with extremely limited interior light residing within and separate from the peristyle, an arrangement of peripheral columns supporting a gable roof. As the *cella* was an abstraction of the grotto, likewise the peristyle was an abstraction of a grove of trees, their limbs combining to form a canopy overhead.

Hagia Sophia, Constantinople, 537. Anthemios of Tralles and Isidorus of Meletus. Plan.

The Byzantines abandoned the basilica as a model for Christian churches because its trabeated structure could not produce the scale and spatial unity they desired. In addition, the Byzantines blurred the boundary between the emperor's secular and religious identities to the extent that he became a semidivine intercessor, the high priest as well as secular ruler, for which the centralized church form was more appropriate. The Byzantines had access to a long Roman tradition of dome building as well as to talented Armenian and Syrian dome builders. While western Europe developed the linear basilica type that tended to emphasize structure and to organize space in modules, the Byzantines sought to subordinate structure to a single overwhelming volume. They pushed structure outside of the volume so the interior surfaces of the domes and semidomes could provide a seamless continuum of space. The sense of absolute unity the Byzantines achieved in their churches also appealed to the Ottomans as an architectural expression of Islamic ideals. So when the Ottomans finally succeeded in conquering Constantinople in 1453, their goal was to exceed the beauty and magnificence of the Hagia Sophia, a task achieved by Mimar Sinan in the Selimiye Mosque in Edirne and the Süleymaniye Mosque in Istanbul.

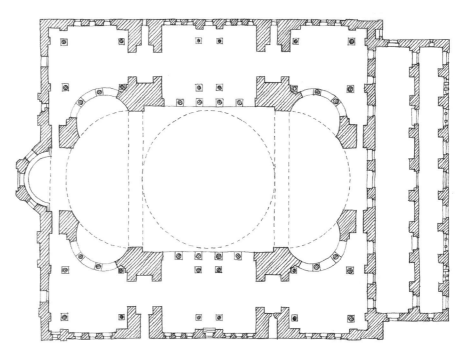

7.3

7.4

Hagia Sophia, Constantinople. Composition.

Though it burned in riots and collapsed in earthquakes over the centuries, the Hagia Sophia retained the general configuration of its architects' design objective: to invest a rigid rectangular frame with a plastic volume. The entire purpose of everything between the outer and inner forms is to accommodate the structure necessary for supporting the curvilinear surface that encloses the central volume. One consequence of this spatial concept was the need for the construction of domes and subsidiary semidomes hierarchically from the center outward. This produced an exterior form that resembled a sacred mountain—an ancient Oriental metaphor eagerly embraced by both Byzantines and Ottomans.

7.4

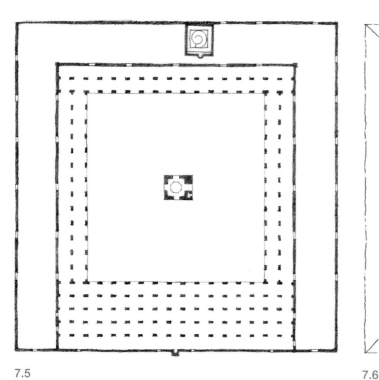

7.5

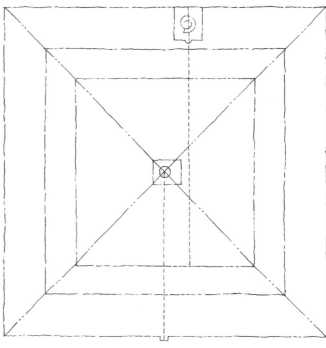

7.6

7.5
Mosque of Ibn Tulun, Cairo, 876–879. Plan.

Ibn Tulun (835–884) was a professional soldier in the service of the Abbasid caliph in Baghdad. When the caliph appointed him governor of Egypt, Ibn Tulun created a new district of Cairo (al-Qatai) and constructed a large congregational mosque there that bears his name. Though constructed by local artisans, Ibn Tulun's design has strong ties to Iraqi precedents both in planning and in ornamentation, particularly with the imperial Abbasid mosques of Samarra, where Ibn Tulun had spent his early career.

7.6
Mosque of Ibn Tulun. Geometry

The plan of the mosque is a set of three nested rectangles. The outermost is a 532-foot square that forms a high wall to isolate the mosque from the surrounding city. The mosque is a second rectangle, 381 feet wide and 460 feet long, set within the first to create an open space between them about 72 feet wide on three sides. The third rectangle is a square court 132 feet on each side. Surrounding the court is a hypostyle hall that supports a flat roof two bays deep on three sides and five bays deep on the side of the *qibla* (the wall that faces Mecca). Spatially, the hall is not cellular but rather a set of four parallel walls opened by arches. The use of a square as a planning geometry in mosques was unprecedented at the time, so despite some similarities to earlier Iraqi plans, Ibn Tulun's design was a daring experiment in purity of form within a conservative tradition. There are two monumental sculptural elements within the mosque: the kiosk in the center of the courtyard and the spiral minaret in the peripheral space. Whereas the kiosk aligns with the mihrab and reinforces the stability of the square geometry, the minaret's asymmetrical position subtly sets the space in motion.

7.7
Mosque of Ibn Tulun. Pavilion.

The pavilion in the center of the courtyard serves the practical function of a fountain for ritual ablutions, but it is also an object of contemplation. Constructed in the Mamluk period of the late 13th century, its design is indebted to that of Syrian and Anatolian styles. Surrounded on all sides by arcades, it is a symbolic form, its massive cubic base rising directly from the earth while the delicate curve of its dome, in the form of a cosmic egg and silhouetted against the brilliant sky, appears to descend from the heavens. The three tiers of structure between the base and dome imply the transformation of the two forms as if they represented the poles of the perceptible cosmos, one terrestrial and the other celestial, each becoming the other.

7.7

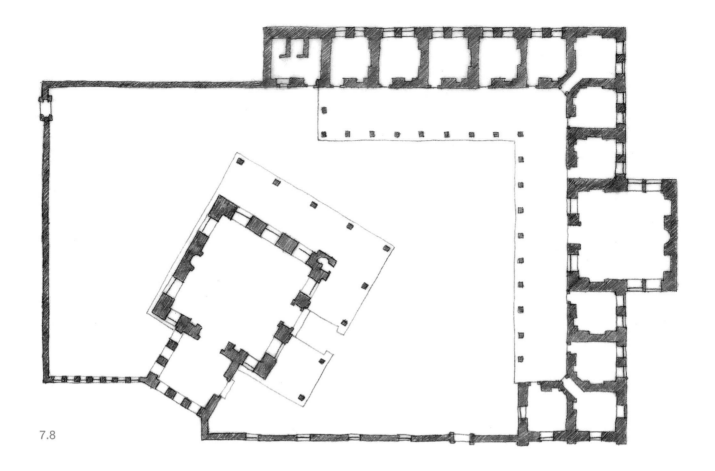

7.8

7.8

Semsi Ahmed Pasa Complex, Üsküdar, Turkey, 1580. Mimar Sinan. Plan.

This compact composition of buildings occupies a site on the eastern shore of the Bosporus opposite Istanbul. It includes a small mosque, the tomb of the benefactor, and a madrassa (a school for religious instruction), all within a walled compound. The L-shaped madrassa is part of the enclosing wall on the west and south, its twelve residential cells and a large, square classroom facing into the courtyard behind a simple shed-roofed porch. The small cubic mosque and the smaller attached tomb are oblique to the framing buildings and oriented toward Mecca. Both have entrances on their northwest sides and connect internally as well. The tomb has three windows that look directly out to the Bosporus. Sinan's design is characteristically elegant in its simplicity. The madrassa, with its wall extensions, acts as an orthogonal frame of reference for the focal elements of the composition, the mosque and tomb, which due to their obligatory orientation become figures inserted into the frame.

7.9

Takeo Temple, Angkor Wat, Cambodia, late 10th century. Plan.

This enormous group of buildings, over 328 feet on each side, rises at its center to a temple in the tradition of a five-storied mountain. It has numerous boundary layers, or shells, surrounding the central core, each pierced by monumental portals, stairs, and thresholds.

7.10

Takeo Temple. Geometry.

The plan, a cosmological diagram, is a union of nested squares and rectangles in the proportion of 2:√3, a pattern that gives preference to an approach from the east. The temple mountain occupies the center of the largest square, while the outer 2:√3 rectangle establishes the location of the eastern portal.

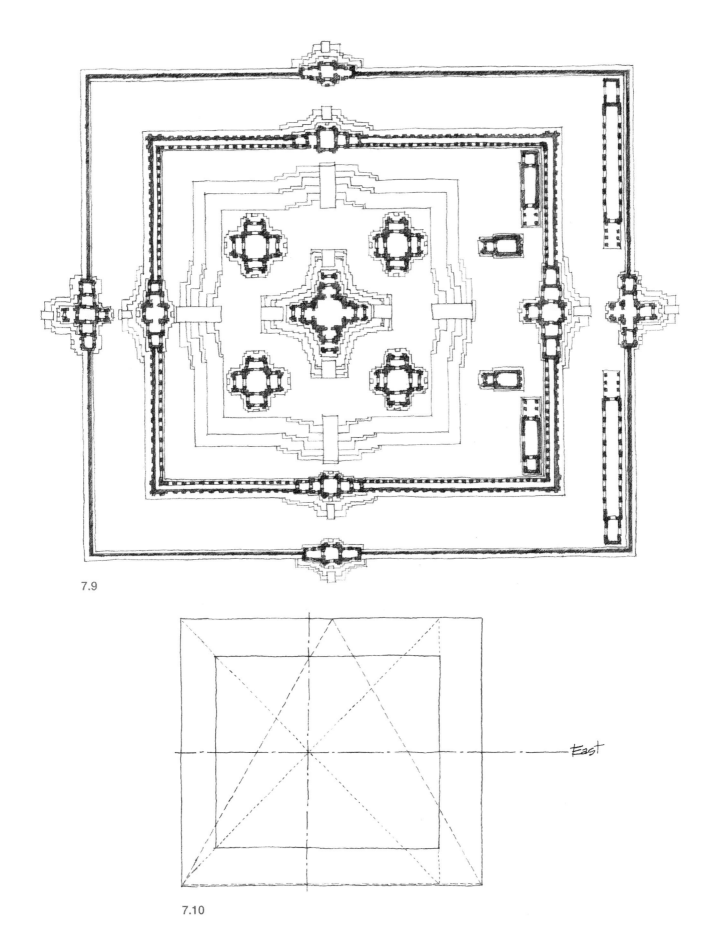

7.9

7.10

East

7.11

Chapel of the Burghof, Rheda, Westfalia, Germany, early 13th century.

The chapel within the castle occupies one entire floor of the keep, or central tower. Because the purpose of the keep was defensive, its perimeter had to be kept clear to the greatest extent possible. Therefore, the stair set into one deep wall leads directly into the chapel and from there into the perimeter corridor on the other three sides. The result is a nested structure in which the chapel stands independent of the surrounding walls of the keep.

7.12

Crypt, Abbey of Saint Germain, Auxerre, France, 9th century. Plan.

Though coordinated dimensionally with the rest of the crypt and the choir of the church above, the *confessio* of the crypt (the rectangular block) is formally a separate structure inserted into the frame of the abbey. Construction began on the crypt in the Carolingian period, and it reflects the three-aisle plan type of the period commonly found from Armenia to England.

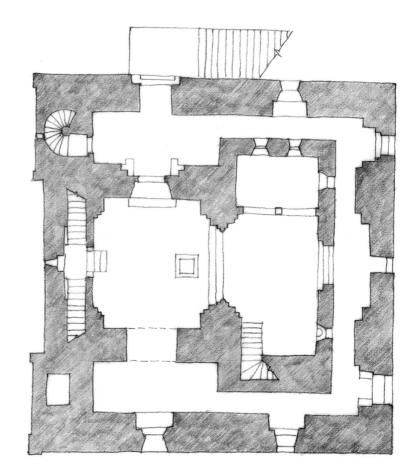

7.11

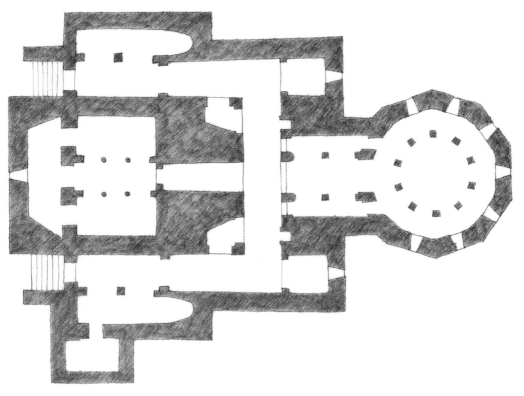

7.12

7.13

Granary of the Fali People, Northern Cameroon. Section.

The granary consists of two architectural types independent both in form and material. The central granary's flanking bins and knee-walls are biomorphic forms in clay that rise directly from the earth. In contrast, the protective canopy is an entirely separate light and airy trabeated structure in wood and thatch. Their separation controls moisture by allowing air to circulate freely around the storage units in shadow.

7.14

***Domus*, Romania, 20th century.**

The Latin term *domus* was originally associated with Roman houses but was used also to describe a house common in medieval European peasant communities from Spain to Romania. It is still in use today in some remote areas. The *domus* consisted of two separate buildings: the *foganha*, or hearth, was a masonry structure associated with the matriarchal lineage, while the *ostal* was a surrounding lightweight wood frame structure that represented the patriarchal lineage. In the Languedoc region of southern France, in the foothills of the Pyrenees, the *domus* of medieval peasants denoted not just the physical house but also the entire family, both living and dead, who resided there. In addition to simply being a practical solution to construction, the fusion of these two building types was therefore symbolic of a marriage and the very existence of the family and its historical continuity as a whole. Despite its humble form, it was of paramount importance. For example, in the inquisition following the Albigensian Crusade, some condemned heretics preferred burning at the stake to the destruction of their *domus*.

7.14

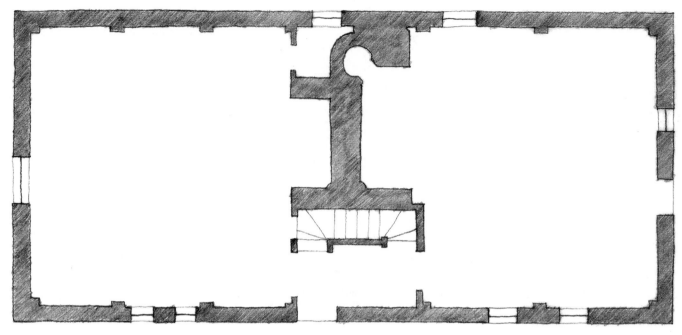

7.15

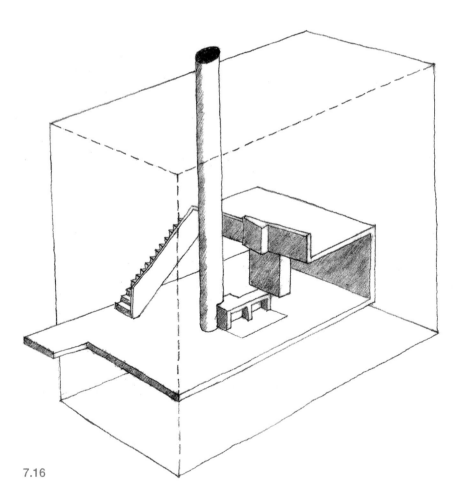

7.16

7.15
Parson Capen House, Topsfield, Massachusetts, 1683. First-floor plan.

The design of this colonial New England house is an American translation of a 17th-century English manor house, and the skill employed in its construction indicates that its artisans came from England. The frame of the house is of mortise and tenon heavy oak timbers joined with wooden nails. On the first floor, it is a parlor and hall (kitchen) plan with a monumental brick core within a wooden shell. The stair is set into the brick core and becomes an integral part of the 8-foot-wide, back-to-back fireplaces. Frank Lloyd Wright adapted this traditional idea for the core in his design of the Robie House.

7.16
Citrohan House, 1929. Le Corbusier. (After G. Baker.)

Le Corbusier consolidated several minor features of the house—stair, hearth, balcony, chimney—into a single form that occupies the center of the neutral volume of the house. He thus resolves a composition that would normally have many disparate elements into a composition that has only two: the shell of the volume and the family of forms that resides within it.

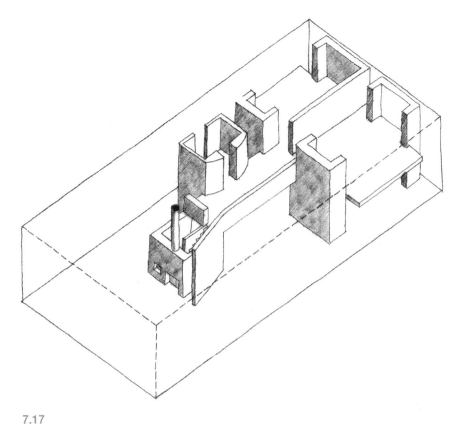

7.17

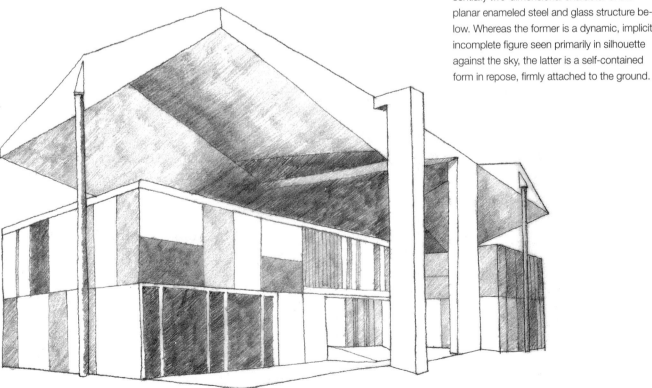

7.18

7.17

House in Gorriti Street, Buenos Aires, Argentina, 1991. Lacroze Miguens Prati.

As in the Citrohan House, all of the interior forms that explicitly and implicitly shape spaces consolidate into a single sculptural composition that resides within an architectural shell—essentially a neutral box.

7.18

Centre Le Corbusier, Zurich, Switzerland, 1965. Le Corbusier. View.

Heidi Weber, who had collaborated with Le Corbusier in the production and marketing of his lithographs, built this small museum, the last of Le Corbusier's works, shortly after he died in 1964. The basis of the design is a series of sketches Le Corbusier began in the 1950s for a house prototype. It explored several themes that recurred throughout his work, such as the prominent ramp that appears in many of his projects, including the Villa Savoye and the Villa Shodan. At a conceptual level, the building is an exposition of Le Corbusier's fascination with of the tension between three-dimensional and two-dimensional forms. In this view, we see that the composition is a pas de deux, with a vigorously three-dimensional gray steel roof form rising above and entirely detached from the essentially two-dimensional character of the planar enameled steel and glass structure below. Whereas the former is a dynamic, implicitly incomplete figure seen primarily in silhouette against the sky, the latter is a self-contained form in repose, firmly attached to the ground.

7.19

7.19

Mobile Home, Colorado, 2005. View.

Though motivated, no doubt, entirely by practicality, this American vernacular solution to extending the life of a mobile home is remarkably similar to the ancient *domus*, the Cameroonian granary, and the Centre Le Corbusier: it is a composite of two entirely different architectural forms. The idea of a building sheltering another is powerful, one that the builders of the Parthenon would have readily recognized.

7.20

Bagsværd Community Church, Bagsværd, Denmark, 1974–76. Jørn Utzon.

Utzon allowed the interior form of the Bagsværd church to be entirely independent from the exterior, in a manner similar to the Wolpa Synagogue (see 7.21). In this case, the exterior conveys a shedlike, utilitarian, and almost industrial character in precast concrete, aluminum, and glass. The stern external appearance belies the lyrical, light-suffused interior, the ceiling of which is an undulating, cast-in-place lightweight concrete shell painted white, supported by the flanking walls of the ambulatory. According to Utzon, he drew his inspiration for the ceiling from the forms and movements of clouds. The result is an extreme contrast between a hard Modernist shell of rigorous structural clarity and a soft Baroque center of indeterminate space.

7.21

Wolpa Synagogue, Poland, late 18th century. Section. (After T. Hubka.)

The Baroque period of wooden synagogues in Poland produced a type in which an elaborate, interior cupola was entirely unrelated to the rustic exterior. The synagogue at Wolpa is the greatest of these. Its curvilinear, vaulted cupola hung from the roof framing in three tiers to produce a spatial illusion of indeterminate depth, a vernacular expression in timber construction similar in spirit to what Christian architects were achieving in church architecture at the time.

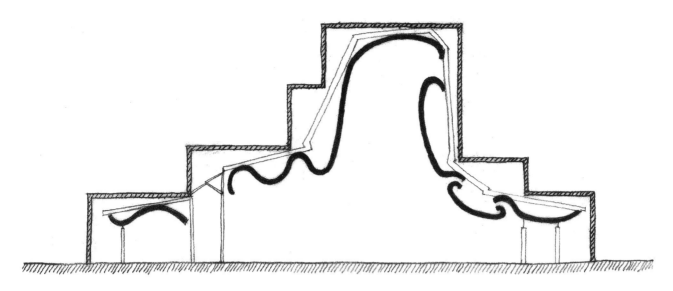

7.20

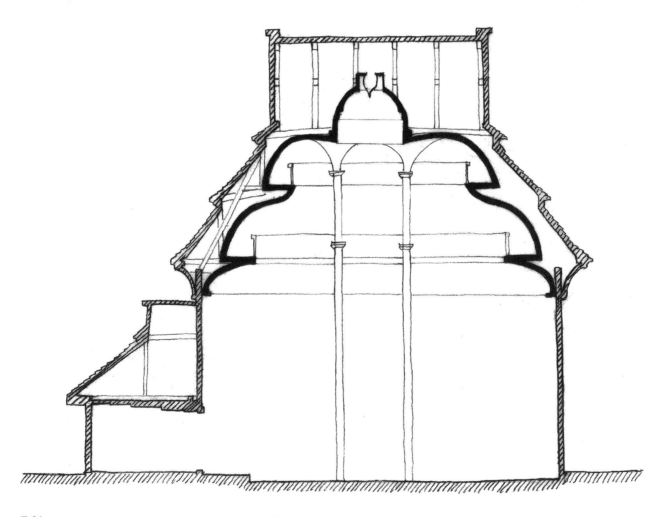

7.21

7.22

New Arabian House, Riyadh, Saudi Arabia, 2003 (competition). D. Hanlon and K. Crane. Ground-floor plan.

The challenge posed by the competition was to design a house for a middle-class family that adhered to traditional social norms but also introduced contemporary innovations with respect to organization and construction. This solution proposed a variant of the traditional courtyard house with one major difference: in response to climatic conditions, it is a core and shell interpreted as two nested boxes. The outer box is a thick static form in rammed earth, while the inner box is a relatively lightweight structure that occupies some of the space within the outer box, leaving courtyards and corridors between them partially open to the sky. These allow the interior spaces to breath without direct exposure to the sun and wind-blown dust. The plan supports Arabian social conventions, providing a reception space for male visitors at the entrance separate from a *haremlik*, or private family quarters, at the rear.

7.23

New Arabian House, Riyadh. Second-floor plan.

The most private quarters of the house are on the second floor, each room opening onto an enclosed terrace. Steel screens block the sun and airborne dust, and the traditional Arabic window type, the *mashrabiya*, transforms into a modernist idiom as a metal grilled box that protrudes through the enclosing wall. Consistent with tradition, there is a strong sense of hierarchy in the organization of the house. A back stair from the main courtyard leads to a terrace on the roof.

7.24

New Arabian House, Riyadh. Longitudinal section.

Deep walls, light shelves, and steel screens temper the climate of both interior and exterior spaces, and courtyards are rooms whose ceilings are the sky. This is a compact house whose relatively small interior spaces seem larger by virtue of their lively sectional qualities and their direct relation to adjacent outdoor rooms .

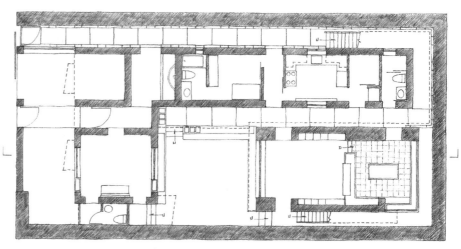

7.22

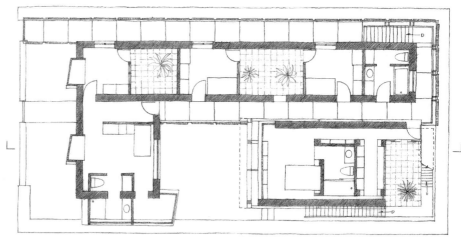

7.23

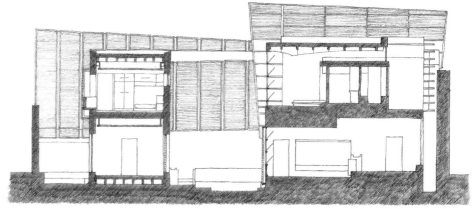

7.24

CHAPTER EIGHT

FRAME
AND OBJECT

O NE OF THE MOST COMMON COMPOSITIONAL STRATE-
gies is to combine two "families" of forms, one of them stable and the
other unstable. The stable form is an armature for the heterogeneous
collection of forms that it holds. This simple method provides both regularity and
diversity and allows change over time. In addition to its practical advantages, it is
satisfying aesthetically because, as we observe so often in nature, it combines still-
ness and movement, either actual or implied.

To perform its function, a communication tower must have a static frame to
which many types of equipment can be attached by a variety of means, in any direction, after which it must be easy to modify (8.1). In plan, the Asklepeion at
Pergamon followed the same principle (8.2–8.5). A large U-shaped colonnaded
structure on two levels enclosed the sacred space and provided the static architectural armature for an ensemble of buildings: a theater, a propylaeum, a library, a
temple (built by Hadrian as a miniature of the Pantheon), a healing center, a western stoa, and the eastern ceremonial avenue. The Sanctuary of Asklepios, with its
sacred spring, occupied the center.

Many Christian churches survived over the centuries because they adopted the
frame-and-object method. A church depended on donations from aristocratic and
wealthy families to maintain its structural fabric, but these gifts also required space
for chapels dedicated to a patron saint or for use by the families. Therefore, we find
churches with a simple core plan that allowed the attachment of a variety of smaller
buildings to their exteriors. A small parochial church in Attica, near Athens (8.6), is
almost indecipherable from the exterior due to the accretion of chapels around its
core; only upon entering the building does one see how these relate. The method is
analogous to the formal structure of a bicycle (8.7). A bicycle has two families of
forms. One is the rigid frame that is seldom if ever modified and, short of a major
accident, does not wear out. The other family is a set of accessories (seat, wheels,
gears, etc.) that vary as the bicycle ages.

Another church that used a similar method was the 11th-century Église Notre-
Dame-la-Grande at Poitiers, France (8.8). In addition to the outer layer of variable
chapels, this church has an inner layer of groin vaults that form an ambulatory. As a

result, the church is composed of four formal layers that increase in irregularity from the center outward: the central nave, the ambulatory, the enclosing wall, and the chapels (8.9, 8.10).

Another interpretation of the frame-and-object composition is to differentiate between two forms: one that is stable and establishes the frame of the plan and another that either occupies or penetrates the first as an alien form. The great Italian Renaissance painter Andrea Mantegna designed his house in Mantua predicated on an opposition between the rectangular frame of a cubic brick block and the pure cylinder that inhabits its center (8.11, 8.12). Similarly, in an early design for the Governor's Residence in Chandigarh, Le Corbusier appears to have set several playfully biomorphic objects loose in a square cage (8.13). They seem to have been caught, like fish, in the tight column grid. A set of four plans—three theaters and a church—illustrate four ways of thinking about the relation of the interior object to its enclosing frame (8.14). The Ziegfeld Theater had a symmetrical, biomorphic shape at its center, and everything between it and the outer shell of the building was poché (8.15). The concert hall of Göteborg, Sweden, by Nils Eriksson also has a symmetrical object at its center; however, for acoustical reasons the object has its own shell, and the space between it and the outer shell of the building is open to allow the inner shell to vibrate (8.16). In the Salzburg Convention Center Theater by Juan Navarro Baldeweg, the interior object seems to be breaking free of its frame, the stress of the action appearing to distort them both (8.17). Finally, the plan of Our Lady of the Angels Cathedral by Raphael Moneo has allowed the central figure to disintegrate its frame, which is now fragmentary and almost residual (8.18). In a more reserved fashion, the 21st-century house by Johnsen Schmaling has an efficient and economical plan for a small budget (8.19). It also has something to say about formal logic; as with all of their work, the architects suggest the genesis of the final form in the relations of its parts. In this case, a cubic form presses into a receptive bar. The zone of their union is the zone of most movement in the house (8.20).

A third interpretation of the frame-and-object method is the "bowl of fruit" parti (8.21, 8.22). The stable form is a container that only partially controls a heterogeneous group of objects—just as a collection of fruit can change, but the bowl itself cannot. The Monastery of Saint Catherine in the Sinai is an example in which the encircling wall permitted the interior buildings to be shaped and oriented in any way that was convenient (8.23, 8.24). A similar approach appears in a competition entry for the reconstruction of the souks in Beirut (8.25, 8.26). An arcaded building wraps around three-quarters of the site. Restored buildings as well as new ones jostle in the center, producing a variety of urban spaces similar to the district's historical character.

Contrast between frame and object is also a common compositional device in art, represented here by two works: the pool in the Barcelona Pavilion (the building by Mies van der Rohe and the sculpture by Georg Kolbe) and a print by Suzuki Harunobu (8.27, 8.28). In both, a fluid form, implying movement, is in the foreground of a stationary orthogonal architectural frame. In the plan of the Dominican Convent, Louis I. Kahn interpreted this compositional device as a U-shaped, cellular container in which several objects have apparently accidental (but actually carefully contrived) intersections (8.29). Fifteen years later, James Stirling repeated the theme in his proposal for the Berlin Science Center (8.30). It, too, has a cellular container (in this case, an obvious reference to a stoa) and a heterogeneous set of other buildings rendered in plan almost as typological cartoons. Similarly, the plan for a woodcarving museum in Inami, Japan, by Peter Salter contrasts the inanimate frame of the traditional Japanese plan with the apparently startled herd of small buildings escaping from it (8.31).

The frame-and-object parti is one of the most useful compositional techniques because it allows a designer to organize a variety of elements informally without imposing an artificial geometry on them. While the frame provides some degree of regularity in the plan, the objects that it contains are free to create varied connections and spaces between them. The composition as a whole can achieve a balance between stability and instability, either allowing for change over time or implying it.

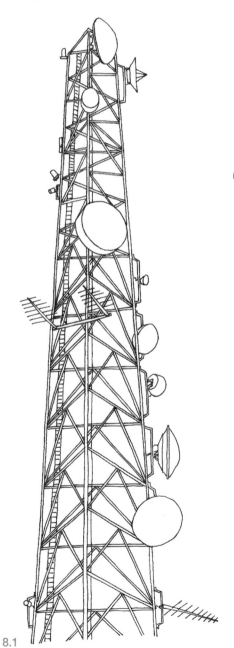

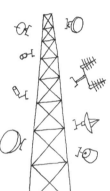

8.1

Communication Tower. View.
The design has two parts: a static frame and a family of interchangeable components, allowing it to transform over time. This produces a dual form, one that is simultaneously stable and dynamic.

8.1

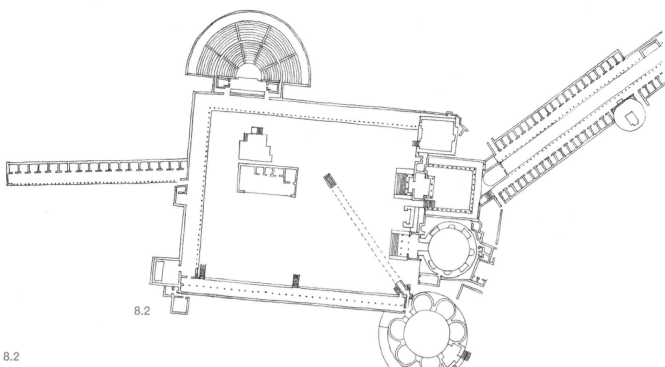

8.2

The Asklepeion, Pergamon
(Bergamo, Turkey), ca. 128 CE. Plan.

The ancient sanctuary of the god of healing, Asklepios, was a center of culture for people of wealth and leisure, and a meeting place for philosophers, politicians, writers, and rhetoricians from throughout the Hellenistic world. The Roman emperor Hadrian conducted an extensive remodeling of the sanctuary in the 2nd century and built several important structures. His direct involvement in the project is evident in the design of the Temple of Zeus-Asklepios, a copy of the Pantheon on a reduced scale. It was one of several buildings he added to the eastern precinct of the sanctuary, including a library, a treatment center in the form of a rotunda, and the propylaeum. The Temple of Asklepios, with its sacred spring, is at the center of the enclosure. A vast colonnaded enclosure (with a gallery below it on the south side) was equipped with continuous stone benches for the conduct of the principal therapeutic regime of the spa, the interpretation of dreams.

8.3

The Asklepeion. Schematic plan.

A continuous colonnade on three sides of a large court acts as an armature that holds a set of object buildings. Four are embedded in the open side of the compound, while three (the theater, stoa, and a ritual chamber of undetermined function) are attached to the exterior.

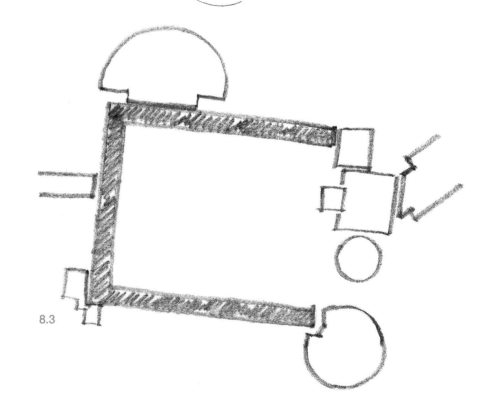

8.3

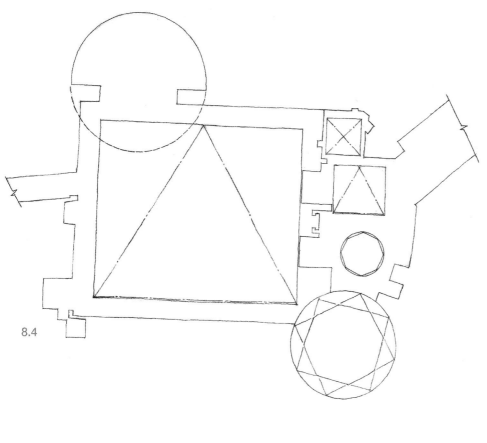

8.4

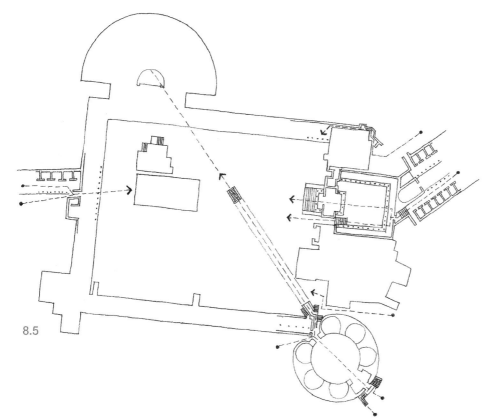

8.5

8.4

The Asklepeion. Geometry and proportion.

A geometric figure governs each of the principal elements of the composition. The central court inscribes an equilateral triangle, as does the propylaeum; the library is square in plan, the cylindrical Temple of Zeus-Asklepios and the lobed rotunda are organized internally by octagons, and the theater is a hemicycle.

8.5

The Asklepeion. Circulation.

The processional way led to the inner court of the propylaeum, which served as the main entry to the sacred precinct. The lobed rotunda provided six alcoves for healing but also led to a subterranean passage on axis with the theater that delivered patients to the center of the courtyard adjacent to the sacred spring of Asklepios. Subsidiary entries brought people from the western stoa through a gap between the rotunda and the Temple of Zeus-Asklepios and into the framing colonnade around the library.

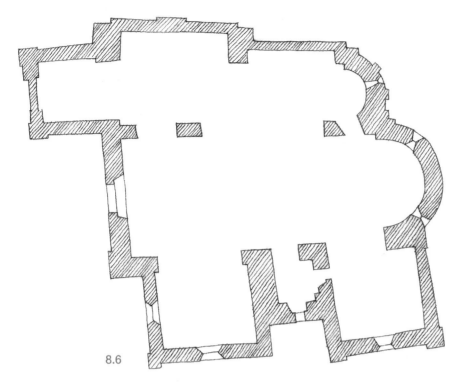

8.6

8.6
Parochial Church, Attica, Greece, ca. 18th century. Plan.

This is one of many small stone Greek Orthodox churches in the countryside near Athens. The plan drawing emerged from direct observation, not from documentation. As the plan suggests, it is difficult to discern what the organization of the building might be from the outside, as it appears to be an undulating wall without repetition or order. Even what turns out to be the principal apse appears on the exterior as just another projection of the enclosing wall. However, upon entering, the order becomes clearer. At the center of the composition is a simple barrel-vaulted nave terminating in an apse, its longitudinal walls opening to six flanking chapels. The chapels are large in relation to the nave and crowd around it, obscuring its form.

8.7
Parochial Church, Attica, Greece. Composition.

To understand the eccentric composition of the church, the construction of an analogy is useful. The plan is analogous to a bicycle. Despite differences in their appearance, the church and a bicycle share a formal structure, or underlying compositional strategy. Both rely on two types of forms, one static and the other dynamic. Similar to a bicycle's frame, the church relies on a standard formal type (as do virtually all other small churches in the region) that comprises the static element of the composition: a simple nave and apse. In contrast, there is a dynamic family of chapels, analogous to the accessories of the bicycle, which may be added or subtracted as needed. Historically, this is how the church survived. It depended on the construction of the chapels by benefactors over time as a means to preserve its core structure. The partial foundations of prior chapels on the exterior indicate that, as with bicycle accessories, older chapels were replaced with new ones.

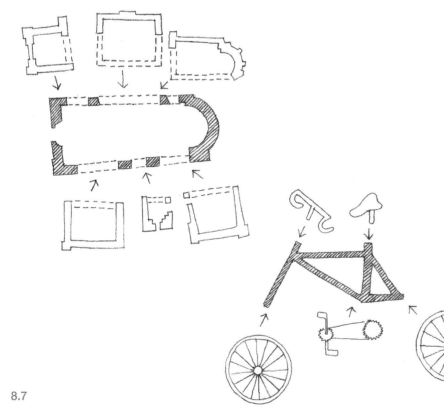

8.7

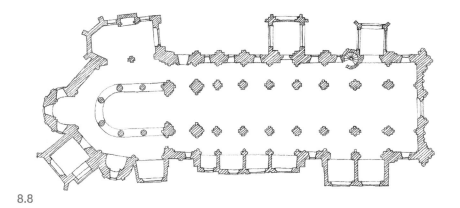

8.8

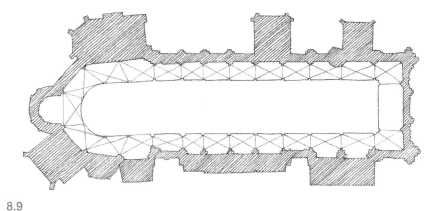

8.9

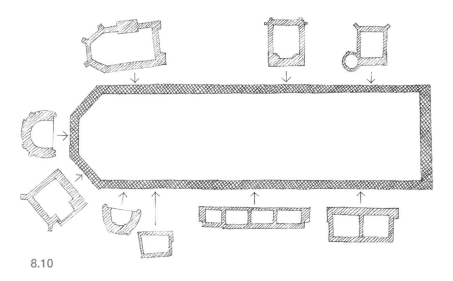

8.10

8.8
Église Notre-Dame-la-Grande, Poitiers, France, 1090. Plan.

Since it lacks a crossing and transepts, the plan of this Romanesque church allows the narthex, nave, choir, and sanctuary to be a continuous space. Four large compound piers indicate the narthex and two pairs of even larger piers suggest the choir. The plan emerged in the 11th century with three aisles seven bays long. A barrel vault covers the central aisle, with groin vaults over the side aisles and a dome rising over the last bay to support a bell tower. The nave ends in a sanctuary surrounded by an ambulatory with three semicircular chapels. In the 12th century the church extended westward to produce a narthex with the addition of two new bays of greater dimensions than the originals, and the facade appeared at this time as well. In the 15th century, and continuing through the 16th century, patrons began to build the peripheral chapels around the sanctuary and along both sides of the nave.

8.9
Église Notre-Dame-la-Grande. Layers.

The plan has four layers of different characters. While the innermost layer of space is a relatively uniform figure defined by a barrel vault over pairs of piers, the next layer, an ambulatory, employs groin vaults to produce a modular space. The third layer is the enclosing screen wall of stone and glass, interrupted at intervals by the fourth layer of chapels.

8.10
Église Notre Dame-la-Grande. Composition.

The primary composition of the church is a static frame to which is attached a heterogeneous family of forms, in this case a variety of chapels that were contributed by wealthy donors. The original frame of the building could not accommodate these, so the chapels are outside the church and punch through its screen wall to the interior. The secondary compositional characteristics are a layered order and a core and shell.

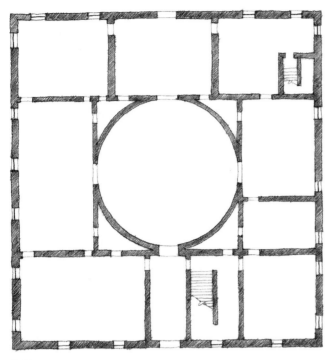

8.11

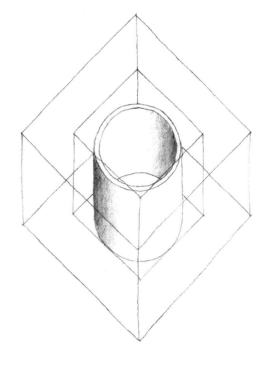

8.12

8.11
House of Mantegna, Mantua, Italy, 1476. Andrea Mantegna. Plan and schematic axonometric.

One of the most individualistic and influential painters of the Italian Renaissance, Andrea Mantegna served for nearly fifty years as the court painter for the Gonzaga family of Mantua. His design for the house he built for himself in 1476 reflects the precision, rigidity, and austerity of form for which his paintings were famous. Its composition is extreme in its simplicity: a brick cylinder pressed tightly into a cubic void at the center of a rectangular brick block. Leon Battista Alberti, a close associate of Mantegna, may have influenced the design of the house. Alberti, like Mantegna, was an admirer of Roman architecture, and both were avid collectors of Roman sculpture. When Mantegna built his house, Alberti was working in Mantua, since Duke Ludovico II of Gonzaga had commissioned him to design the Basilica di Sant'Andrea (begun in 1472). The forms of Sant'Andrea, with its triumphal arch facade and barrel-vaulted nave, as well as Mantegna's house, with its bold geometry in brick, make explicit references to Roman precedents such as the markets of Trajan and the Basilica of Maxentius.

8.12
House of Mantegna. Courtyard view.

Mantegna organized the cubic and cylindrical volumes of the house with extreme simplicity and abstraction.

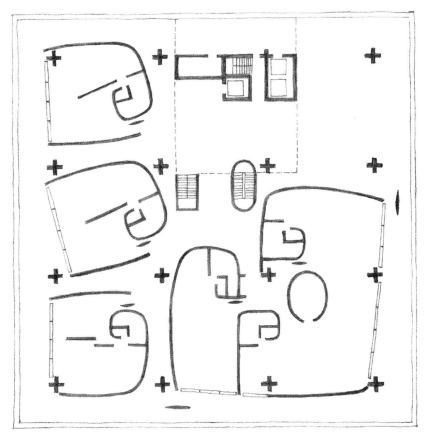

8.13

8.13
Governor's Residence, Chandigarh, India, 1952. Le Corbusier.

In this early design for the residence, Le Corbusier used a compositional technique that he applied to many projects. He created a Cartesian space defined by a simple boundary and a grid of columns (accentuated by their cruciform section) and then inserted freestanding objects. The result was a play between two types of spaces: the whole spaces that were within the objects and the fragmentary spaces that were residual, or between the objects (see 9.44 and 9.45).

8.14
Four Plan Types for Theaters.

These diagrams summarize the plan strategies exemplified by the Ziegfeld, Göteborg, Salzburg, and Los Angeles building plans that follow. The Ziegfeld is an egg-shaped bubble of space that occupies the center of an otherwise solid box, packed with service functions. The Göteborg example segregates the theater and service functions into two zones such that the theater stands as an independent object within an interior space. The Salzburg example places the two functions side by side so the theater, though rooted to its service functions, becomes an object on the exterior. Finally, the Los Angeles example fragments service functions such that the main space is only partially figural. These four plans represent their designers' clear strategic decisions with respect to how people perceive the principal space.

8.14

8.15

Ziegfeld Theater, New York City, 1927–1966. Joseph Urban and Thomas White Lamb. Plan.

Designed as a legitimate Broadway theater, the Ziegfeld was later used as a movie theater and a television studio. Its audience hall is a symmetrical ovoid bubble of space shaped by the poché of surrounding walls and service functions. The deep proscenium stage appears as another symmetrical ovoid figure superimposed upon the first.

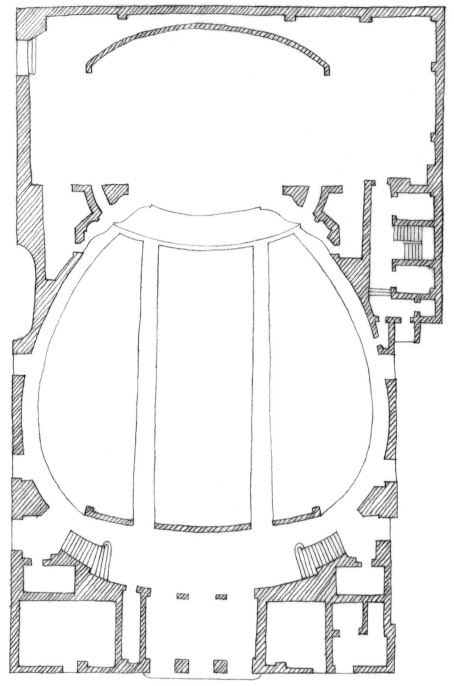

8.15

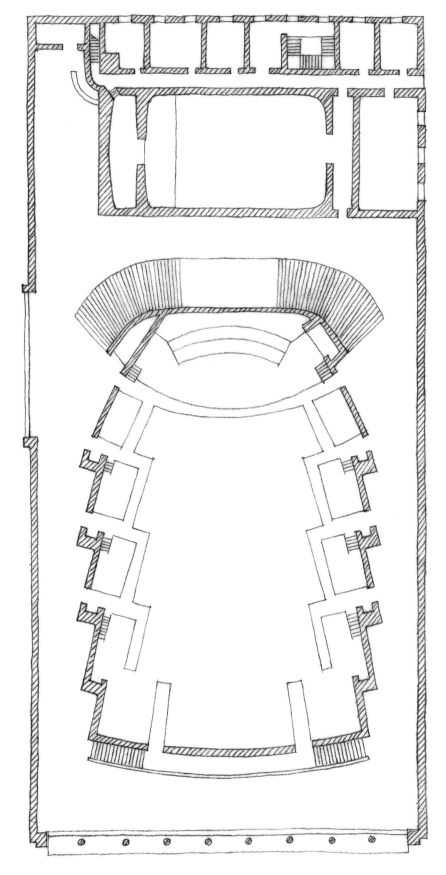

**Concert Hall, Göteborg, Sweden, 1935.
Nils Einar Eriksson. Plan.**

The concert hall shares the cultural center of Göteborg with three other monumental buildings: the art museum, the municipal theater, and the municipal library. Eriksson restrained his modern functionalist approach to design on the exterior to be compatible with the Neoclassical style of the three older buildings nearby. However, the interior is strictly functionalist. Eriksson conceived the concert hall as a musical instrument—literally, not metaphorically. All service functions are at the rear of the building, entirely apart from the performance space sheathed in Canadian maple panels as if it were a violin. The formal result is a highly sculptural object suspended in a void. He separated the performance space from the rectangular box of the building to completely control its acoustics, considered by musicians to be among the best in the world (so good that it is often used for high-quality recordings).

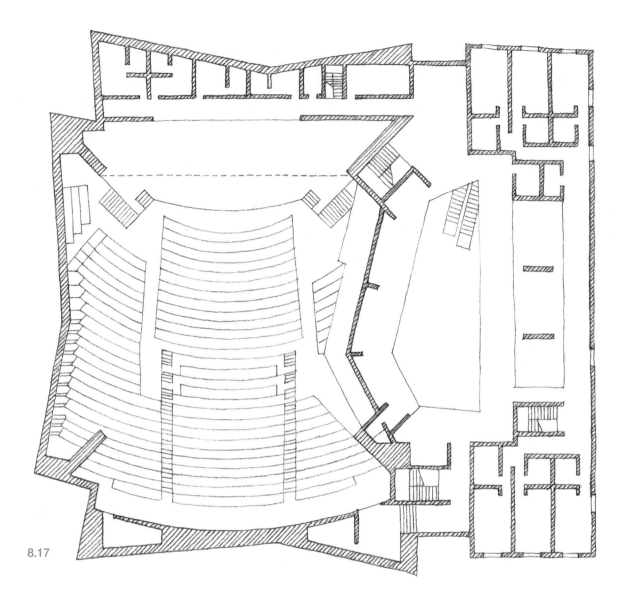

8.17

8.17
Convention Center, Salzburg, Germany, 1992. Juan Navarro Baldeweg. Plan.
The architect set the angular forms of the main hall in high contrast to the sedate rectangular enclosure of the service functions. The angular forms indicate the importance of the theater space on the exterior of the building as well as in the main double-height lobby. The result is as if two buildings are side by side with a shared circulation zone between them.

8.18
Our Lady of the Angels Cathedral, Los Angeles, California, 1997–2000. Raphael Moneo. Plan.
Because the plan seeks to strike a balance between several objectives, it assumes a hybrid form. Consistent with the traditional iconography of Roman Catholicism, this church maintains the cruciform plan. However, to promote the active participation of the parishioners in the liturgy, it is also a centralized plan. Likewise, it maintains a traditional axial orientation, relating the baptistery to the altar, yet it conveys a modernist sensibility toward flux and change by avoiding static symmetry. Peripheral chapels and the ambulatory that serves them turn from the inside outward to preserve the simplicity of the main space. The result is a highly dynamic plan in which primary and secondary features interlock in unexpected ways.

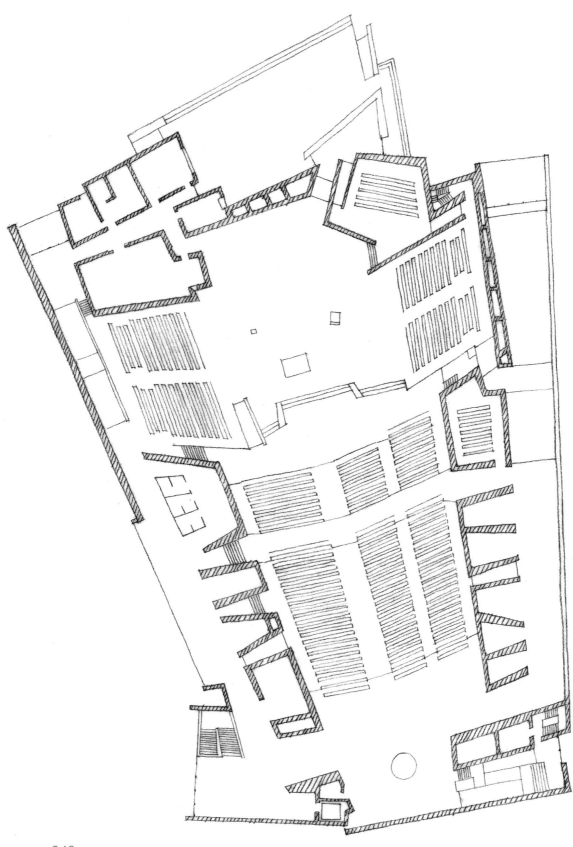

8.18

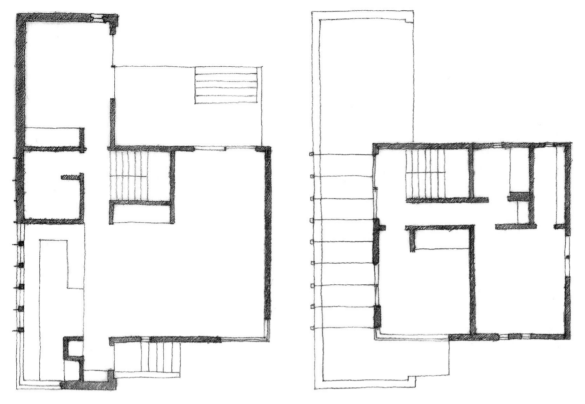

8.19

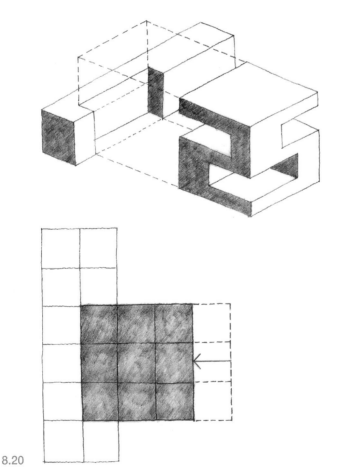

8.20

8.19
Urban Infill House 02, Milwaukee, Wisconsin, 2004. Johnsen Schmaling Architects. First- and second-floor plans.

This small, inexpensive house is sophisticated in its form and in the detailing of simple materials. Its compact plan relies on a 48-inch construction module that maximizes the use of standard manufactured construction products. Unrepentantly Modernist, the house nevertheless fits well into the scale and character of a typical working-class neighborhood. The interior spaces seem larger than their actual dimensions because the architects opened the corners of rooms to fenestration, recognizing that the largest perceived dimension of a rectangular space is its diagonal.

8.20
Urban Infill House 02. Composition.

The design concept is a two-story sculpted wood and glass cube inserted into a one-story bar of concrete block and glass, a relation controlled by an underlying modular grid. Though the two parts integrate internally, one's perception of the house externally is of the cube as a figural object in contrast to the neutral bar. Designed as a prototype, these two parts, as well as the construction details, may rotate and flip to produce variations depending on the circumstances.

8.21

8.21
Bowl of Fruit. View.
(*After E. Ash.*)

The compositional strategy shared by many
buildings and groups of buildings is analogous
to the relationship between a bowl and the fruit
it contains. The bowl is a static, invariable form,
whereas the fruit is a dynamic set of variable
forms. The bowl establishes the place of the
composition by defining a boundary and relatively simple formal conditions. In contrast, the
fruit produces complex and unstable formal
and spatial relationships.

8.22
Bowl of Fruit.
Schematic section.

The spaces between forms of the fruit are ten-
uous, implying that the composition is subject
to change over time. The bowl, on the other
hand, imparts stasis and permanence.

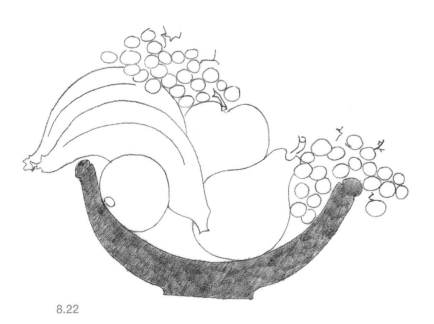

8.22

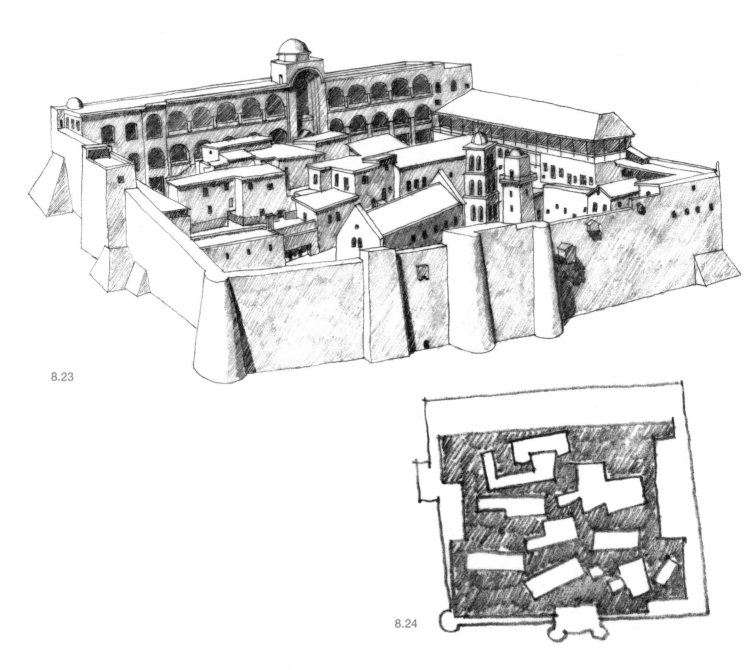

8.23

8.24

8.25

8.23

Monastery of Saint Catherine in the Sinai. View.

The monastery is at the foot of Jebel Musa, otherwise known as Mount Sinai. Established in the mid-6th century by the Byzantine emperor Justinian, it is a fortified compound devoted to maintaining shrines and relics associated with Mount Sinai and Saint Catherine of Egypt. Though Christian, it came under the protection of Muhammad when the Arabs conquered the Sinai and was later under the protection of the Ottoman sultans. Within its enclosure, there is a small Fatimid mosque.

8.24

Monastery of Saint Catherine. Composition.

As a fortified monastery, it has a rigid, roughly rectangular boundary wall. The loose collection of buildings of its interior, an accumulation over many centuries, does not conform to a preconceived plan. Compare this plan to the proposal for Beirut and the projects by Louis I. Kahn (Dominican Convent, 8.29) and James Stirling (Berlin Science Center, 8.30), all of which utilize the "bowl of fruit" parti.

8.25

Reconstruction of the Souks of Beirut, 1994. D. Hanlon and T. Proebstle. View.

A competition entry for the reconstruction of the historical center of Beirut included a heterogeneous collection of buildings from a variety of historical periods that survived the civil war in Lebanon. There was no attempt to rationalize or regularize the composition of buildings in its center; the "bowl of fruit" parti established order instead. The bowl became a continuous arcaded building that absorbed several peripheral structures, established a boundary to the city quarter, and allowed a diversity of architectural forms and spaces to persist within its enclosure.

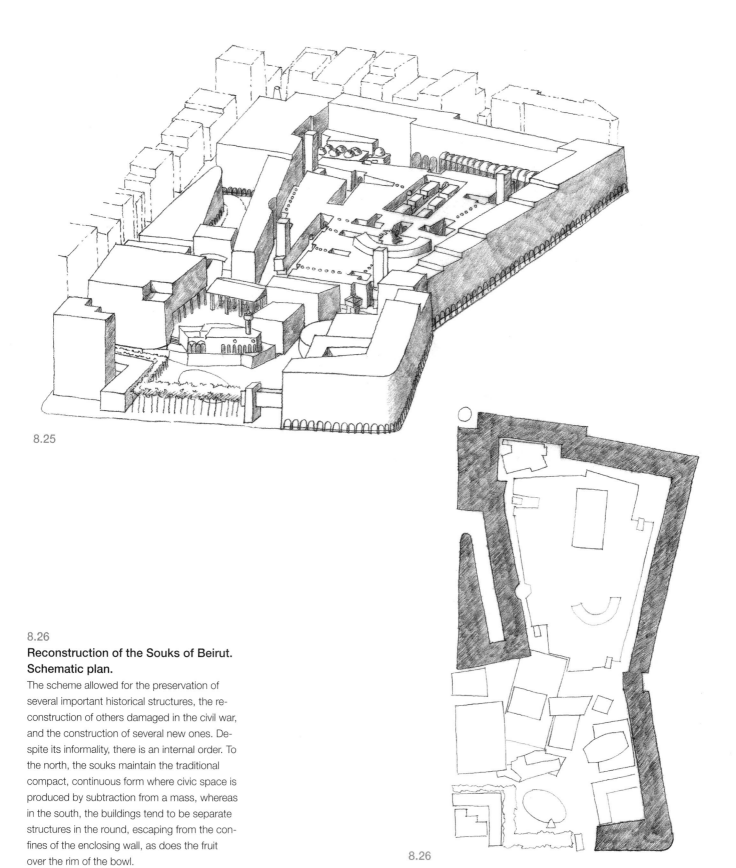

8.25

8.26

Reconstruction of the Souks of Beirut. Schematic plan.

The scheme allowed for the preservation of several important historical structures, the reconstruction of others damaged in the civil war, and the construction of several new ones. Despite its informality, there is an internal order. To the north, the souks maintain the traditional compact, continuous form where civic space is produced by subtraction from a mass, whereas in the south, the buildings tend to be separate structures in the round, escaping from the confines of the enclosing wall, as does the fruit over the rim of the bowl.

8.26

8.27

8.28

8.27

Alba (Dawn), 1925, by Georg Kolbe.

Mies van der Rohe placed this bronze sculpture at one end of a shallow reflecting pool in
the Barcelona Pavilion. He, like many European
artists and architects of the early 20th century,
found Japanese art compelling. Like Suzuki
Harunobu's *Lady on the Veranda*, the fluid form
of the sculpture casts its shadow against the
rear wall and its reflection on the water. The
contrast of a curvilinear form against a rectilinear frame is one of the most common compositional techniques in art and architecture. Mies
used it in a more abstract way in his design for
a brick courtyard house in which the building is
the sensual object against the backdrop of a
square-grid courtyard (see 1.24).

8.28

Lady on the Veranda after a Bath,
Edo Period, Japan. (After Suzuki
Harunobu.)

The compositional technique of contrasting a
curvilinear object against a rigid spatial frame appears in much of classical Japanese art. In this
piece, the rotated woman's body in flowing fabric
produces a whirlwind of space around her that
pushes against the precise, minimalist orthogonal architectural frame in which she stands.

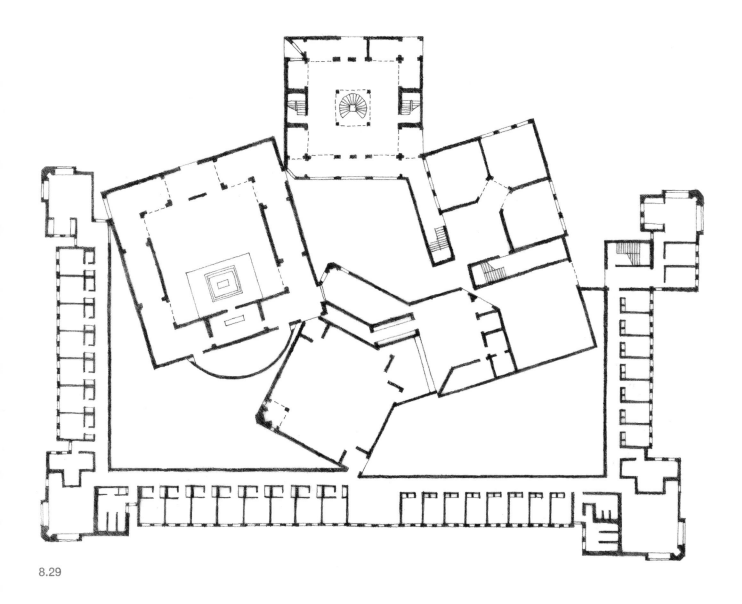

8.29

8.29
**Dominican Convent, Media, Pennsylvania, 1965–68 (unbuilt).
Louis I. Kahn. Plan.**

Vincent Scully and Kenneth Frampton have both cited Kahn's interest in the plan of the
Campo Marzio in Rome as depicted by Giovanni Battista Piranesi. Piranesi's plan depicts a
Roman preoccupation with individual building typologies at the expense of any unifying organizational principle. It was the precise connections between otherwise autonomous
building forms and how, perhaps, this compositional technique could express the fragmentary and anecdotal experience of modern life that interested Kahn. Kahn divided the program for the Dominican Convent into two parts, one static and the other dynamic. Individual cells and their service spaces comprise a static U-shaped shell. This shell of monastic
cells constitutes the essential structure of the community. It barely contains and controls
five idiosyncratic buildings that jostle in the embrace of the cells. Connections at the corners of the large buildings imply interpenetrations and overlapping relationships as in a still
life composition, a technique that creates tension between the formal internal symmetries of
the individual buildings and the implied informality of their connections. The buildings
(chapel, refectory, library, and meeting rooms) do not relate otherwise in plan or form; each
is a distinct architectural type, and the spaces between them are unambiguously residual.

**Science Center, Berlin, 1981. James
Stirling and Michael Wilford. Plan.**

This competition entry is remarkably similar to
Louis I. Kahn's plan for the Dominican Convent
created fifteen years earlier. The strategy is the
same: to divide the composition into two formal groups and to set off five large figural buildings joined at their corners against a datum of
small cellular units. In this case, each of the figural buildings represents a historical type, and
one is an existing symmetrical Neoclassical
building. Unlike in Kahn's plan, where the building types are abstract and esoteric, in the Stir-
ling/Wilford design the types are virtually cartoons of a castle keep plan, a semicircular
Odeon plan, a cruciform church plan, a hexagonal tower plan, and a Greek stoa plan.

8.30

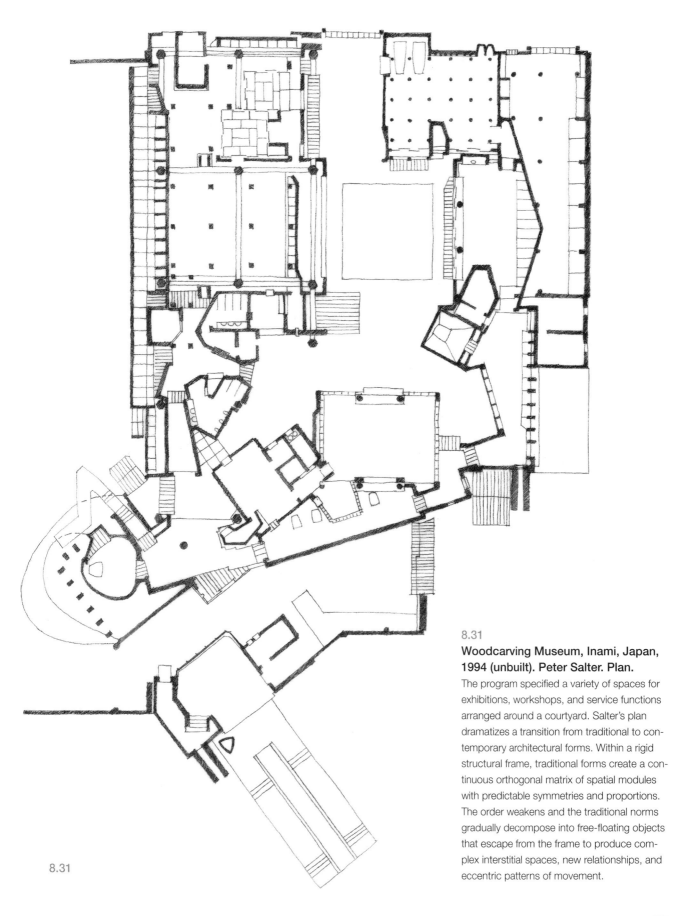

8.31

Woodcarving Museum, Inami, Japan, 1994 (unbuilt). Peter Salter. Plan.

The program specified a variety of spaces for exhibitions, workshops, and service functions arranged around a courtyard. Salter's plan dramatizes a transition from traditional to contemporary architectural forms. Within a rigid structural frame, traditional forms create a continuous orthogonal matrix of spatial modules with predictable symmetries and proportions. The order weakens and the traditional norms gradually decompose into free-floating objects that escape from the frame to produce complex interstitial spaces, new relationships, and eccentric patterns of movement.

8.31

CHAPTER NINE

CLUSTERS

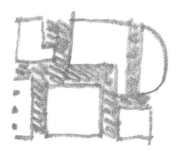

O NLY RARELY IS AN ARCHITECTURAL DESIGN COMPOSED of a single figure. It is generally a combination of either similar or dissimilar figures arranged in either regular or irregular groupings. Though there is considerable latitude for interpretation, for the sake of understanding the choices available examples have been organized in four groups:

- Similar figures in a regular grouping
- Similar figures in an irregular grouping
- Dissimilar figures in a regular grouping
- Dissimilar figures in an irregular grouping

Despite their differences, one or more of five conditions govern these compositions:

1. Radial focus on a central point

2. A shared axis as a centerline

3. Perpendicular relations of their sides or axes of symmetry

4. Parallel relations of their sides or axes of symmetry

5. Tangential relations of their sides or axes of symmetry

9.1

Types of Clusters.

The four basic compositions of clusters are, from left to right similar figures in a regular grouping, similar figures in an irregular grouping, dissimilar figures in a regular grouping, and dissimilar figures in an irregular grouping.

Despite their differences, one or more of five conditions govern these compositions:

1. Radial focus on a central point
2. A shared axis as a centerline
3. Perpendicular relations of their sides or axes of symmetry
4. Parallel relations of their sides or axes of symmetry
5. Tangential relations of their sides or axes of symmetry

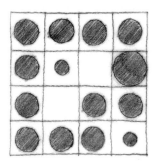

9.1

178

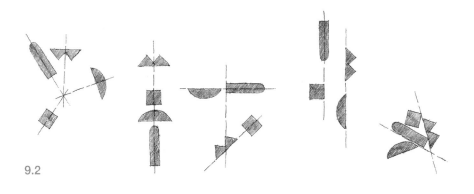

9.2
Five Compositional Conditions.
Radial, Axial, Perpendicular,
Parallel, and Tangential. (After
Borie, et al.)

Similar Figures in a Regular Grouping

Similar figures may be identical, but they may also be variations of a figure related by geometry, proportion, hierarchy, and orientation. Though much of the discussion of similar figures in a regular grouping will concentrate on plans, we can find the pattern in the three-dimensional volumes of buildings as well. A corner bar in a small Iowa town is a row of buildings built successively, all of the same geometry and proportion but differing in size (9.3). The Monastery Church of Gračanica in Kosovo is a single, compact form comprised of the same structural motif at various scales, culminating in a central cupola (9.4). And the Raja Birbal Pavilion at Fatehpur Sikri, India, is a composition of cubes; the repetition of a single figure is so powerful in its simplicity that the missing cubes are as evident and important as those we can see (9.5–9.7).

In plan, the 14th-century Jami Masjid in Gulbarga, India, relies entirely on a square grid (9.8). Cubic volumes with hemispherical domes comprise the central zone. An outer zone two cells deep produces an ambulatory, and the main dome rests on a cube of nine cells. A section of the 16th-century Der alte Bau in Geislingen, Germany, reveals a similar modular approach in the design of this utilitarian building, a warehouse (9.9). The precut heavy timbers for its frame were, in effect, a kit of parts. The construction of buildings such as these depended on notes and dimensions of freehand drawings rather than detailed measured drawings. Therefore, consistent dimensions were of great advantage in the fabrication of the parts and the framing of the structure.

By not applying a module uniformly, a designer can produce larger spaces that contribute as much to the formal structure of a plan as the modules themselves. For example, the Souk el-Oued in Algeria is entirely composed of a single cubic module based on the optimum size of a hemispherical dome made of sun-dried mud brick (9.10, 9.11). Just as the dimensions of the cubic module determined the design of all interior spaces of every house, so too did they determine the shapes of the courtyards. This is true of the orphanage in Amsterdam by Aldo van Eyck as well, and not by coincidence, since van Eyck based his theory of social space on a study of the urban morphology of towns in North Africa (9.12). In these he found a system that balances a sense of unity with variety. Candilis-Josic-Woods shared van Eyk's experience and his views, and experimented with this casbah theme in the design of the Free University of Berlin, a continuous matrix of structure that alternates open and enclosed spaces in a more complex pattern (9.13). In a similar vein, the museum dedicated to Mahatma Gandhi, designed by Charles Correa, has a square structural grid of columns that allows for a free flow of space through interior and exterior volumes (9.14, 9.15). In his designs for houses, Ulrich Franzen also used the method of situating interior volumes within an underlying grid, allowing voids between these volumes to accentuate the form of the house as a whole; the Dana House (9.16) and the Bernstein House (9.17) demonstrate how this apparently simple system can produce subtle spatial relations within a rationalist plan. Louis I. Kahn probably never saw the plan of the Anasazi village of Ramah, but his plan for the Yale Center for British Art (9.18) bears an uncanny resemblance to that of Ramah (9.19). Both employ interconnected square cells within a continuous rectangular outer boundary and an irregular interior boundary that produces a courtyard focused on a cylindrical object (a monumental stair in the museum and a kiva at Ramah).

In the previous examples the grid that controls the figures in the composition is obvious, but this is not always the case. The figures in the plan of the Henny House by H. P. Berlage are individual rooms, each shaped according to its specific needs (9.20). However, they are all subject to a 160-centimeter (5-foot 3-inch) square grid. In a somewhat looser manner, the American Academy of Arts and Sciences by Kallman, McKinnell & Wood organizes similar spaces in a variety of sizes and proportions within a nearly uniform column grid. The varying pattern of columns and poché defines the hierarchy of the composition (9.21–9.23).

One of the challenges that sometimes arises in the design of a building is to create a set of regular figures from a program in which a variety of spaces have quite different spatial requirements and then to organize those figures in a regular grouping to produce a compact plan. Usually, this is in response to the shape of the site or the need for a complex but efficient internal circulation. The plan for the 17th-century São Bento Monastery in Rio de Janeiro combines many different types of spaces by forcing them to conform to an orthogonal pattern and then packing them together tightly (9.24, 9.25). Deep walls accommodate variations in structure, for example, the one that mediates the church and the cloister. Raphael Moneo used a similar technique to organize the heterogeneous galleries, circulation, and support spaces in the Beck Addition to the Museum of Fine Arts in Houston (9.26, 9.27). Persian architects also

9.3

Small Town Tavern, Iowa. View.
This small vernacular building illustrates the essence of the compositional theme of similar figures in a regular grouping. It consists of three buildings constructed sequentially as additional space was needed (note the slight change in the wood siding from one part to another). The vernacular designer adhered to a simple gable-roofed motif to produce a unified composition that nevertheless varies in scale and detail, decreasing from front to back to create a restrained but playful grouping of related forms.

9.3

employed the technique extensively in the design of houses. The architect of the Rasoulian House used the continuous elevation of the central courtyard to regularize all of the adjacent spaces by projecting the structural pattern of the courtyard elevations into the body of the house (9.28, 9.29). The Razvian House plan went further, submitting all spaces, despite their varying functions and forms, to the rule of an underlying module (9.30–9.37). Though considered a mosque, the building constructed by Amin Hodja in Turpan, China, has been a school and a hostel for travelers as well (9.38–9.41). To allow functional flexibility, interior spaces are generic cells on three sides around a covered court; the fourth side contains the monumental structures of a minaret/tomb tower, two tombs, the entrance, and a courtyard.

Similar figures in a regular grouping do not need to conform to an orthogonal grid; they may be curvilinear. The oldest known form of architecture is that of Malta. In the Hajar Qin Temple of the late 4th millennium BCE, biomorphic capsules of space fit together in a roughly radial pattern around a central gallery facing outward to a peripheral wall (9.42). In a typical Tayaba house of northern Benin, nearly identical cylindrical structures connect to form a ring around a central granary, the space between them roofed to create a tightly secured compound (9.43).

9.4

Monastery Church of Gračanica, Kosovo, ca. 1320. View.

The plan of this Serbian Byzantine church is a rectangle resolving into a quincunx above—a central brick tower/dome embraced by four smaller corner tower/domes. However, the clear hierarchy and harmonious proportions of the exterior do not reflect the organization of the interior, which is not centralized and symmetrical. The architect was primarily concerned with the sculptural qualities of form rather than any correspondence between the spatial logic of the interior and the massing of the exterior. The repetitive forms of the exterior building up toward the center convey the metaphor of the Cosmic Mountain. Materials are sandstone and limestone of different colors, with courses of Roman brick.

9.4

9.5

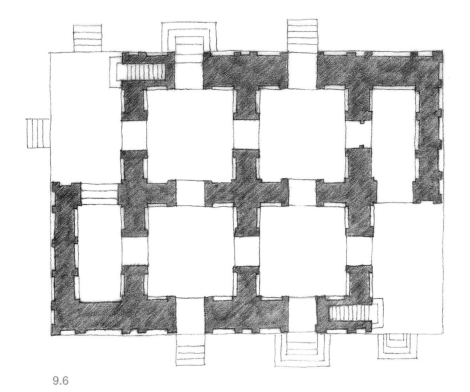

9.6

9.7

9.5

Raja Birbal Pavilion, Fatehpur Sikri, Uttar Pradesh, India, 1571. View.

The Mughal emperor Akbar ordered the construction of the city of Fatehpur Sikri in 1571 and abandoned it fourteen years later. The reason most often cited is a lack of water, but it could have been a shift in the geopolitical landscape of his empire. Nevertheless, the city is a magnificent achievement in urban design and unlike any other. Laid out on a gigantic square modular grid, it employed many subtle and elegant design features with respect to scale, proportion, hierarchy, and shifting orientations. The relations of the various buildings to the open spaces that surround them are superbly conceived and executed. The Raja Birbal Pavilion is one of these buildings. Constructed for one of Akbar's most trusted advisors, the Hindu Brahmin Birbal, the pavilion is one of the smaller structures in the entire urban composition, but it controls a critical juncture in the axial alignments of open spaces and larger structures.

9.6

Raja Birbal Pavilion. Ground level plan.

The ground level plan reveals the pavilion's adherance to the modular grid of the city. It is composed of four cubes and two half-cubes, all on a plinth.

9.7

Raja Birbal Pavilion. Volumetric analysis.

Since the pavilion is a three-dimensional extension of the two-dimensional grid of the city, its cubic form appears to rise from the grid. One way to understand it is as one large cube containing eight smaller cubes, two of which are missing. The two half-cubes of the ground plan and the plinth are an addition to this figure.

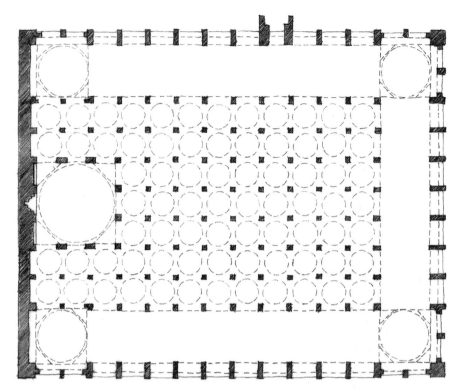

9.8

Jami Masjid, Gulbarga, India, 1367. Plan.

In the Deccan, Mughal architecture ignored local Hindu traditions and employed features drawn directly from Iranian precedents. The plan of this congregational mosque, for example, is rigorously cellular throughout and lacks the customary courtyard. Even the outer barrel-vaulted ambulatory conforms to the module of the inner hypostyle hall. Light and air enter through the periphery and through a clerestory surrounding a dome rising above the *qibla* (the wall that indicates the direction of Mecca).

9.8

9.9

Der alte Bau, Geislingen, Germany, late 16th century. Transverse section.

In this case, the similar figures of the composition are the spatial modules revealed in section. The utilitarian medieval warehouse, typical of market towns across northern Europe, consists of precut timbers to fit a modular spatial design. The timber framing—a kit of parts—consists of an orthogonal system of columns, beams, purlins, and rafters, plus a secondary order of diagonal bracing. On each floor, the pieces of structure are standardized. Note that the center bay has no bracing in order to maintain a clear passage for goods down the length of the building.

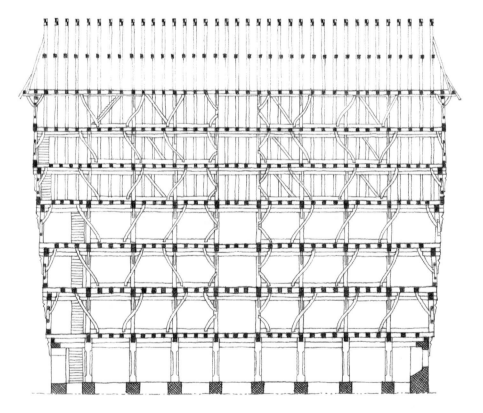

9.9

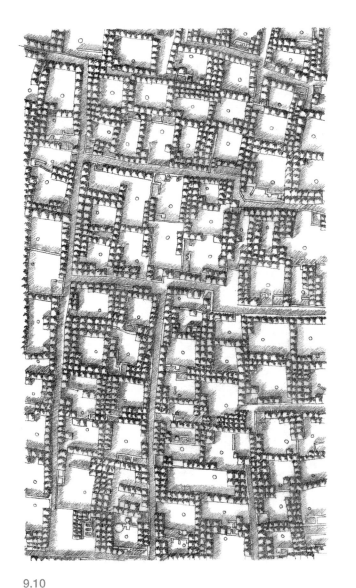

9.10

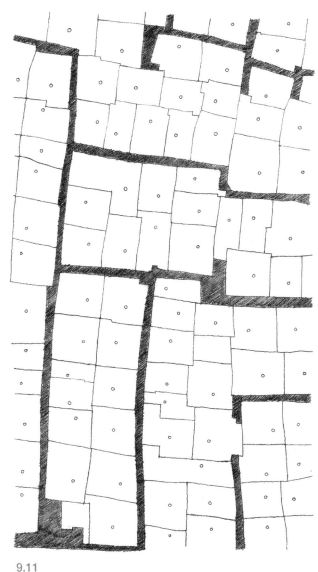

9.11

9.10
Souk el-Oued, Algeria. Aerial view.

A structural/spatial module, a cubic volume surmounted by a hemispherical dome, is the basis for the form of this town. The structural limitations of sun-dried mud-brick construction determined the dimensions of the module. The module extends to all open spaces as well, since its replication defines the boundaries of those spaces. The result is a roughly orthogonal plan for the town oriented to the cardinal directions; the streets, lanes, and cul-de-sacs are residual spaces in the urban pattern. Note that each house has its own well.

9.11
Souk el-Oued. Property plan.

Despite the uniformity imposed by the structural/spatial module, no two house compounds are the same. The module does not impose conformity, but instead provides a unifying theme with which individuals may construct innumerable variations. In a hot, dry climate replete with blinding sandstorms, it is important to create an urban form that is compact. Therefore, like communities across North Africa and the Middle East, Souk el-Oued is a settlement composed entirely of courtyard houses that directly abut one another and thereby individually and collectively take advantage of specific exposures to sun and wind.

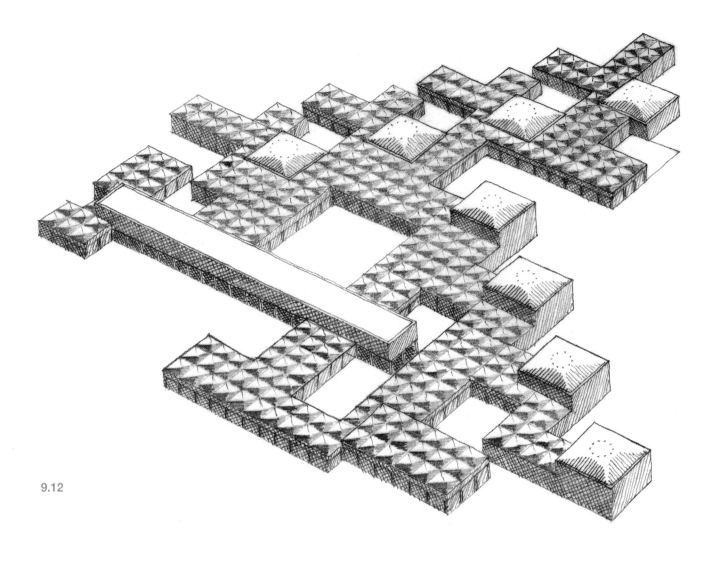

9.12

9.12

Orphanage, Amstelveenseweg, Amsterdam, 1955–60. Aldo van Eyck. View.

Van Eyck's orphanage exemplifies the architectural interpretation of mid-20th-century structuralist theories of linguistics and anthropology. Reacting against the mechanistic manifestations of post–World War II functionalism, van Eyck joined like-minded theorists such as Jaap Bakema, Georges Candilis, Giancarlo De Carlo, Alison and Peter Smithson, and Shadrach Woods to form Team Ten. These architects espoused a return to humanism through architectural interpretations of patterns of language and of primal structures of communities such as those they had studied in North African cultures. Team Ten's structuralist approach drew upon the theory of language as an open, limitless system of compositional opportunities based upon a limited vocabulary and grammar. This was combined with anthropological observations of traditional settlements such as the casbah that produced complex, labyrinthine patterns composed of variations upon simple formal themes. Likewise, the strictly modular pattern of van Eyck's design for an orphanage belies an extensive internal variety, with great emphasis placed on the grammar and syntax of the architecture, that is, the threshholds and intermediate spaces that produce multiple interpretations of the form.

9.13

Free University, Berlin, Germany, 1974. Candilis-Josic-Woods (with M. Shiedhelm). Partial roof plan.

George Candilis, Alexis Josic, and Shadrach Woods, who worked together from 1955 to 1968, were influential members of Team Ten and the younger generation of the International Congress of Modern Architecture (more commonly known by its French acronym CIAM (Congrès International d'Architecture Moderne). Candilis and Woods worked on housing projects in the French colonies of North Africa after World War II, where they studied the urban and housing forms of indigenous Islamic communities. They met Josic while working in the office of Le Corbusier on the design of the Unité d'Habitation. Whereas the CIAM approach to urbanism separated the functions of the city mechanistically, Candilis, Josic, and Woods espoused a more organic web of functions based on the ordinary living habits of residents. The Free University was their major experiment in the creation of an urban structure that permitted variation within a unifying grid of circulation. Compare this plan to the plan of Souk el-Oued (9.10).

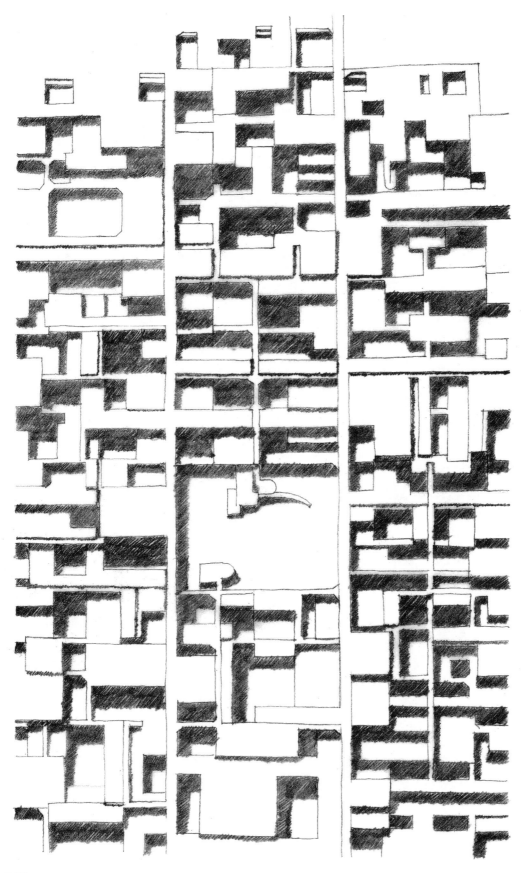

9.13

9.14

Gandhi Smarak Sangrahalaya, Ahmadabad, India, 1958–63. Charles Correa. Plan.

This museum occupies part of the Sabarmati Ashram that Gandhi founded in 1915 (after his release from prison) and in which he lived until 1933. It is now devoted to the preservation and exhibition of documents related to Gandhi's life and work. Correa created a matrix of interior and exterior spaces bound by a square grid to suggest Gandhi's ideal of the self-sufficient village. Also consistent with Gandhian precepts, the cellular form achieves unity in variety—from the four-square central courtyard to the open, irregular perimeter that engages the surrounding landscape.

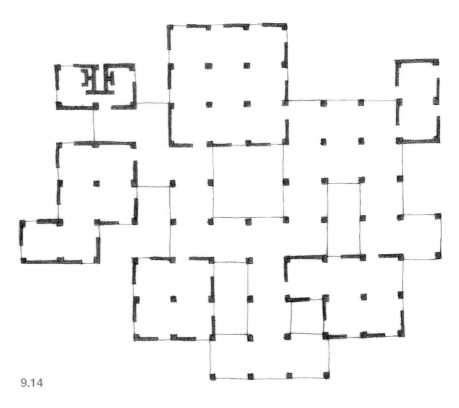

9.14

9.15

Gandhi Smarak Sangrahalaya. Composition.

Six aggregated pavilions define interior spaces, each composed of from two to nine cubic units. Correa used the same structural system, but without enclosing walls, to create the covered open spaces that weave between the enclosures. At the heart of the composition is the four-square courtyard open to the sky, reminiscent of the village center.

9.15

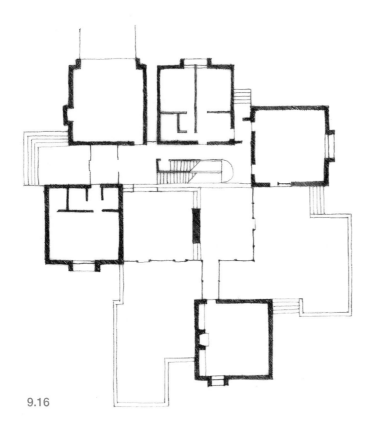

9.16

9.16
Dana House, New Canaan, Connecticut, 1963. Ulrich Franzen. Plan.
Franzen composed the house of five brick boxes embedded in a glass core. Four are living spaces, and the fifth is a garage. The geometry of the core suggests that the four living spaces originated within it and migrated outward, leaving a void behind in which the stair is a sculptural object. Apertures in the boxes and through the spaces between them control views into the surrounding landscape.

9.17
Bernstein House, Great Neck, New York, 1963. Ulrich Franzen. Plan.
Franzen used a repetitive geometric module to establish a brick bearing-wall structural system. However, he designed and combined the modules to satisfy the program and to provide spatial variety. For example, he subdivided one module for service functions, used a second as a frame for a sculptural stair, and combined three others to produce a monumental living space. Finally, one module remains open to provide a sheltered outdoor space.

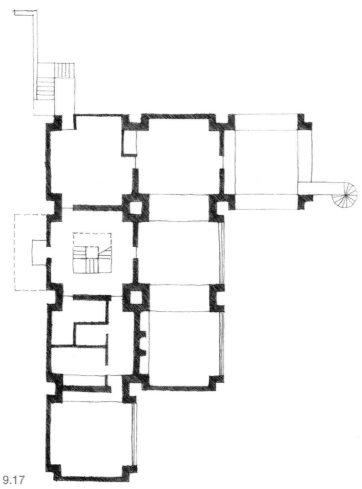

9.17

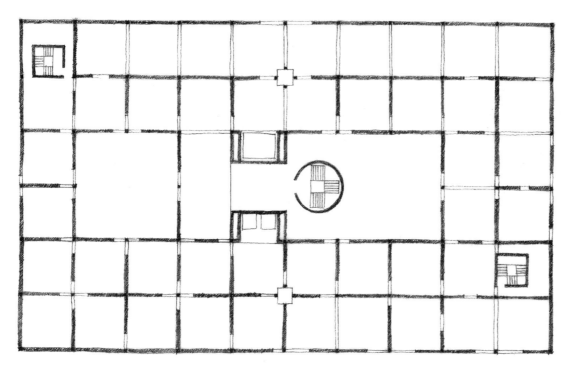

9.18

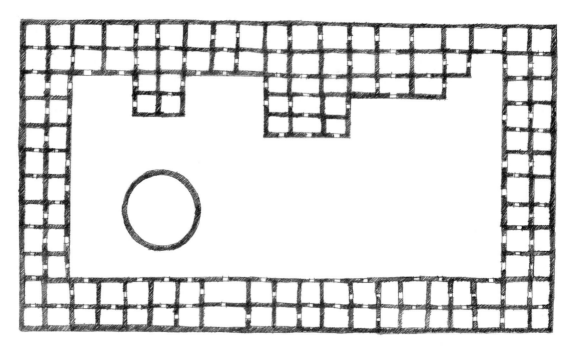

9.19

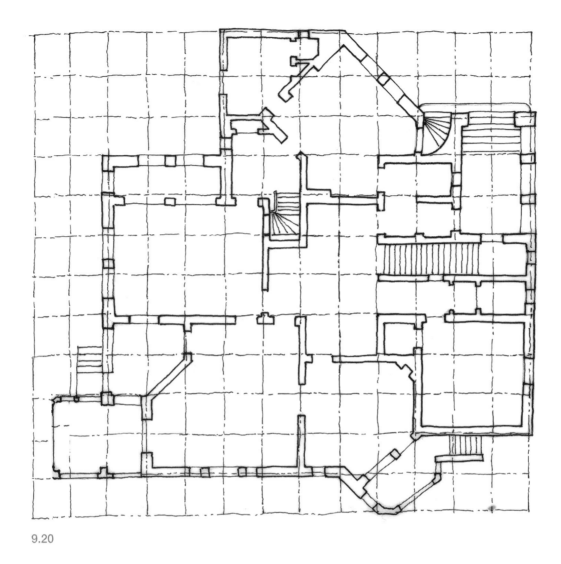

9.20

9.18

Yale Center for British Art, New Haven Connecticut, 1964–1975. Louis I. Kahn. Plan.

Located across the street from Kahn's first major commission, the Yale University Art Gallery, the Center represents Kahn's mastery of the use of natural light and his restraint in spatial organization and the use of materials. The cellular plan focuses on two courtyards, its simple geometry belying the complexity of natural light that saturates the various galleries, filtering through rooftop skylights and concrete coffers and apertures between the galleries. Finely detailed concrete framing with infill panels of white oak, stainless steel, and glass reinforce one's perception of the structural grid and the spatial module.

9.19

Village of Ramah, Ramah Valley, New Mexico, 1275–1325. Plan. (After W. Morgan, *Ancient Architecture of the Southwest.*)

Ruins of Anasazi settlements in the American Southwest exhibit varied responses to the landscape, climate, and social structures. This Zuni example is unusual due to its complete enclosure (probably in response to the need for defense) laid out orthogonally with great precision. However, it is similar to all others of the period by virtue of having only two types of building form: spaces for habitation or storage are rectangular cells, whereas ritual spaces are cylindrical kivas. The arrangement of domestic spaces, all facing into the common court, their backs to the outside world and focused on the single kiva, produces a powerful statement of communality.

9.20

Villa Henny, The Hague, Netherlands, 1898. H. P. Berlage. Plan.

This project was contemporary with Berlage's signature building, the Amsterdam Stock Exchange. His design of the house was controversial due to the raw quality of the brick, used in the interior in the same manner as it was on the exterior. Berlage organized the complex plan on a 160-centimeter module but did not allow the grid to dictate the placement of every feature. For example, the 45-degree rotation of the front reception room creates a flow of spaces around the two-story central hall. Thus, the grid is not evident as one explores the spaces of the house, but rather acts as an invisible ordering principle for Berlage's design process.

9.21

**American Academy of Arts
and Sciences, Cambridge,
Massachussetts, 1981.
Kallman, McKinnel & Wood. Plan.**

The plan is a set of rectilinear spaces and
groups of spaces superimposed upon an
orthogonal grid of square piers and columns.
Inconsistencies in the grid produce hierarchy
and a complex shifting of symmetries that in
turn create a layering and interpenetration of
interior spaces. The manner in which the
architects combined disparate spaces without attempting to standardize them, and the
way the deep poché of walls becomes highly
sculptural by fusing a variety of minor functions, recalls the design method of some
19th-century British architects, notably that
of Norman Shaw and Edwin Lutyens.

9.22

**American Academy of Arts
and Sciences. Spatial matrix.**

Despite its orthogonal order, the plan does
not attempt to impose a regular grid or to
force the disparate elements of the program
into a repetitive dimensional system. Instead,
the pattern allows the grid to shift and deform in support of objectives of hierarchy
and orientation and allows each programmatic element to float on this idiosyncratic
grid. Even the dominant set of interior piers
is incomplete, serving not to define the
center but to indicate gateways and
directions of movement.

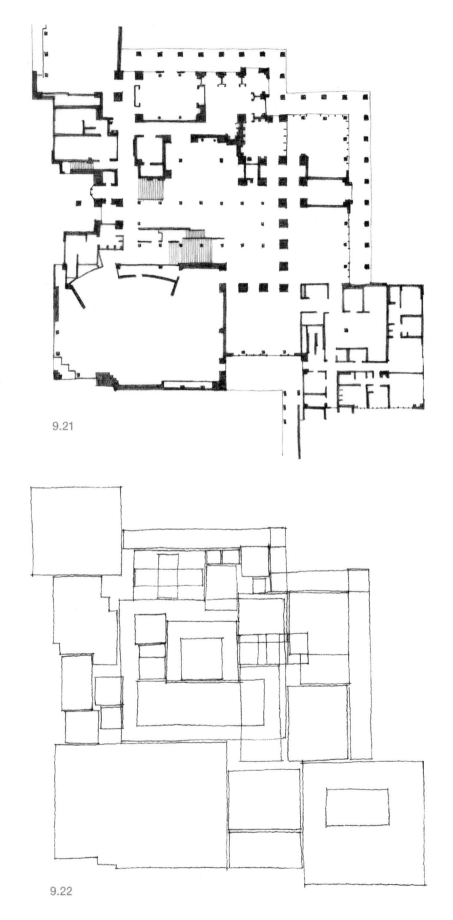

9.21

9.22

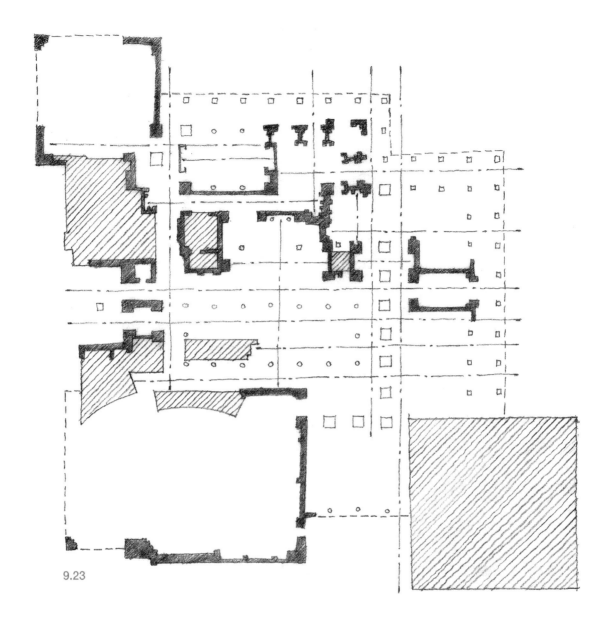

9.23

9.23

American Academy of Arts and Sciences. Walls, service spaces, and axes.

The plan exhibits a family of complex walls in poché that combine small but important elements, including structure, which are critical to the system of shifting orientations, symmetries, and readings of transparency. Service functions (shown here crosshatched) are grouped not just for efficiency but also to contribute to the shaping of major spaces. Finally, some axial views pass through the building while others terminate within it in order to organize the diverse spaces from the point of view of a moving pedestrian.

9.24

São Bento Monastery, Rio de Janeiro, Brazil, 1617–41. Francisco Frias. Plan.

Frias was a military architect employed, in this case, to design a Benedictine monastery. The eight side chapels were not original but appeared in the late 17th century. Otherwise, the existing plan is faithful to Frias's rationalist approach to design, an approach consistent with the austere rule of Saint Benedict. Frias was not inventive in his design, but followed a standard approach to Benedictine planning—a compact, economical and pragmatic arrangement of functions within an orthogonal frame. Ornament (added later) was another matter. The interior of the church, in particular, is extravagantly Rococo in style.

9.25

São Bento Monastery. Composition.

The composition has two zones and is strictly hierarchical. The church, surrounded by its attendant spaces, such as the sacristy, dominates one zone. The other zone is residential, with monks' cells, chapter house, refectory, and kitchen clustered around the cloister.

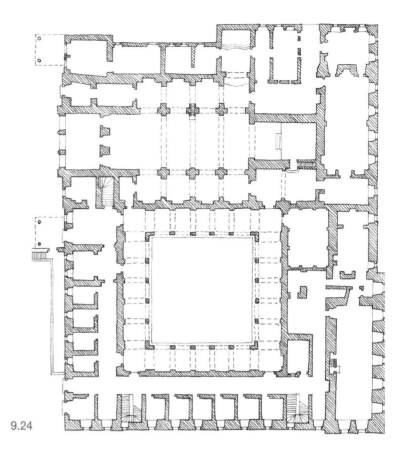

9.24

9.25

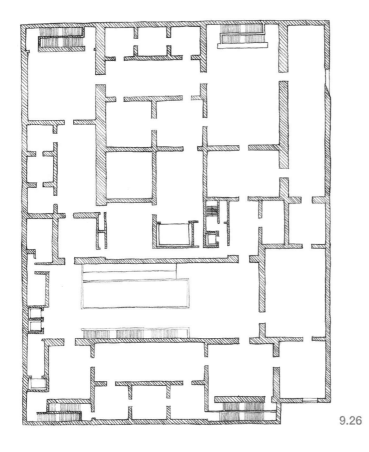

9.26

9.27

9.26
Beck Addition, Museum of Fine Arts, Houston, 2000. Raphael Moneo. Second-floor plan.

The museum addition completely fills a city block and pulls away from one corner only for the entrance. Its plan provides a variety of gallery spaces within a simple rectangular frame, with a central monumental circulation space and four peripheral stairs. Natural light enters primarily through large rooftop structures.

9.27
Beck Addition. Composition.

Moneo suppressed the appearance of structure to emphasize the purity of individual gallery spaces. These comprise a heterogeneous set of rectangular rooms, most of which have a plan proportion between 1:1 and 1:2. Though the plan appears labyrinthine, circulation is simple: a peripheral route connects the major galleries, from which secondary routes connect smaller galleries.

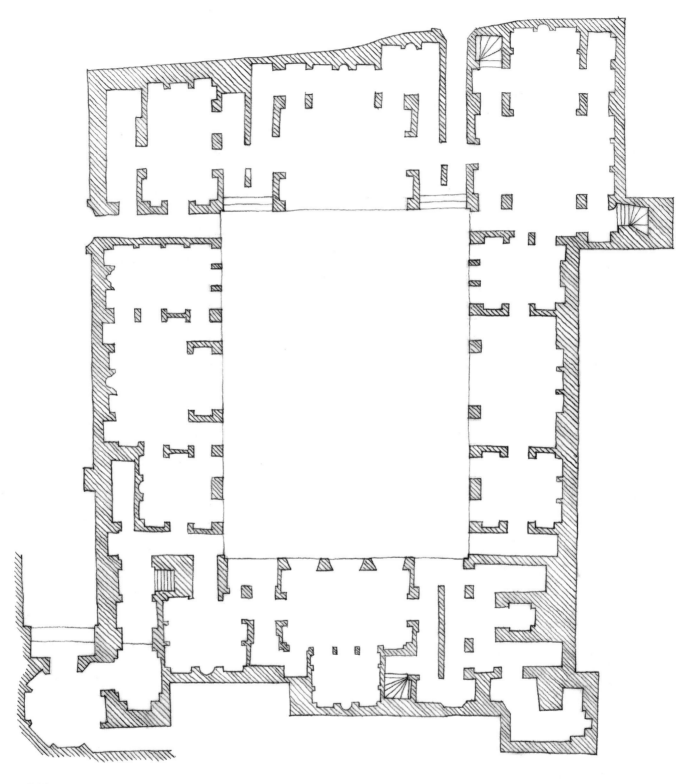

9.28

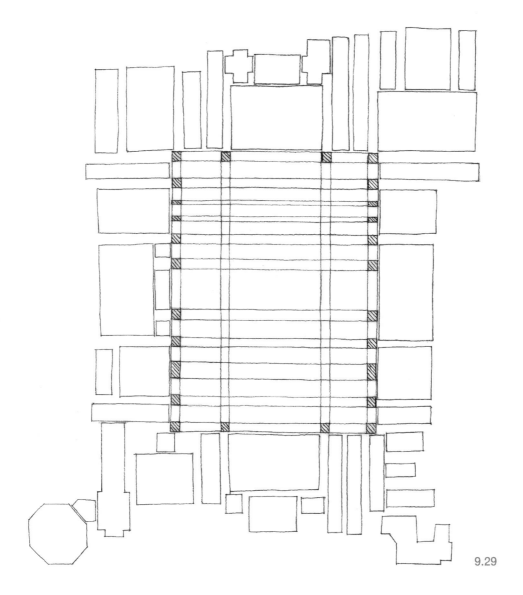

9.29

9.28
Rasoulian House, Isfahan, Iran, 19th century. Plan.

The house is a traditional Persian four-iwan courtyard plan, in which the iwans are spaces enclosed
on three sides, open to the courtyard and aligned
axially to the cardinal directions. These are living
spaces used in relation to the season and the time
of day to take full advantage of sunlight or shade.
The entry at the southeast corner unites approaches from a street and an alley, first into an octagonal room, then a crooked passage, then a rectangular room, and finally through an L-shaped
passage into a corner of the courtyard. From this
entry point one views the largest dimension of the
courtyard, its diagonal, and the elevation of the
principal iwan at the opposite end of the space.

9.29
Rasoulian House. Composition.

Two pairs of elevations enclose the courtyard. The
north and south elevations are simple three-bay
designs, whereas the east and west elevations are
more rhythmically complex. Therefore, the courtyard, as the principal room of the house, is regular
and formal in its configuration. In contrast to the
perfection and abstraction of the courtyard and its
attendant reception spaces, the subsidiary rooms
comprise an irregular, informal, and heterogeneous
grouping, each space designed according to its
specific function

9.30
Razvian House, Isfahan, Iran, 19th century. Plan.

This large house is unusual due to its perfectly orthogonal plan composed of rectangular rooms that all open to some degree to courtyards, which are the main rooms of the house. A lattice of passageways controls privacy and allows for the circulation of air around living spaces.

9.31
Razvian House. Courtyards.

There are five courtyards, three associated with the private family quarters (the *haremlik*), and two for the public precinct (the *salamlik*).

9.32
Razvian House. Passages.

The lattice of passageways allows for the movement of people through the house without passing through the center of the courtyards, a pattern that provides for discreet service to the formal spaces surrounding the courtyards and for the circulation of air between courtyards. The public entrance is at the southwest corner of the plan.

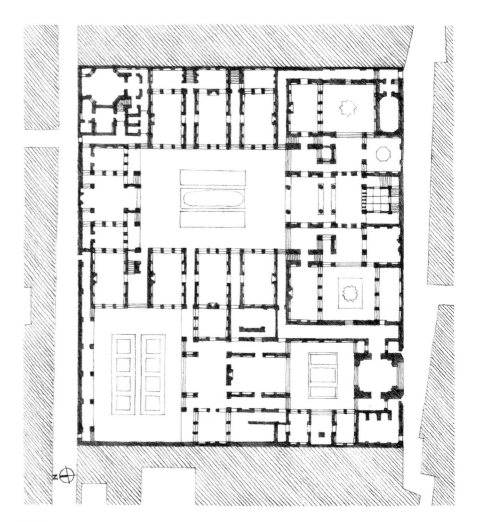

9.30

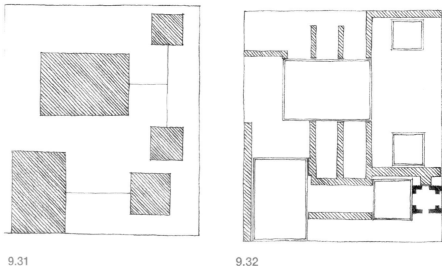

9.31   9.32

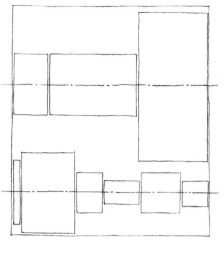

9.33

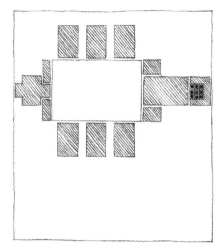

9.34

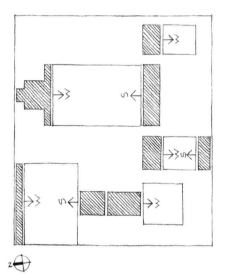

9.35

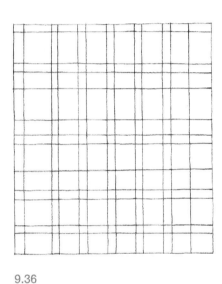

9.36

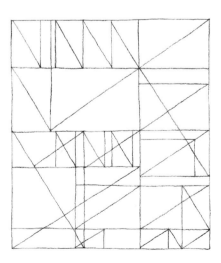

9.37

9.33
Razvian House. Dual axes.

The two sections of the house, *salamlik* and *haremlik*, each have an axis of symmetry that links their respective spaces sequentially. The *salamlik* is for the reception of male guests, and its sequence of interior spaces and courtyards controls the degree to which a guest is permitted within the house, on the basis of his relation to the family. The separate composition of family spaces has its own formal order.

9.34
Razvian House. *Haremlik.*

The private quarters center on the main courtyard of the house. At the south end of the axis is a wind tower that, in conjunction with the courtyard, ensures the constant movement of air through interior spaces. Rooms surrounding the courtyard allow the family to situate itself comfortably according to the season (north or south) or the time of day (east or west).

9.35
Razvian House. Seasonal spaces.

The principal seasonal spaces are on the north and south sides of the courtyards. Winter rooms have their backs to the north and face the sun. Summer rooms have their backs to the sun and face the shaded courtyard.

9.36
Razvian House. Tartan grid.

Though the house has a great variety of spaces, large and small, they are all controlled by an underlying grid that emerges from a rational and pragmatic approach to structure.

9.37
Razvian House. Proportion.

A proportional system ensures an organic unity of the many spaces within the house. The ratio of 1:1.5 governs the shape of each of the many rectangles that comprise the pattern of organization in the plan.

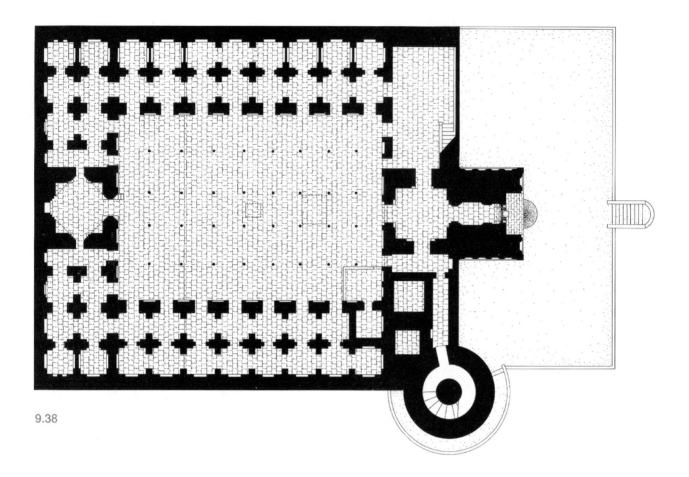

9.38

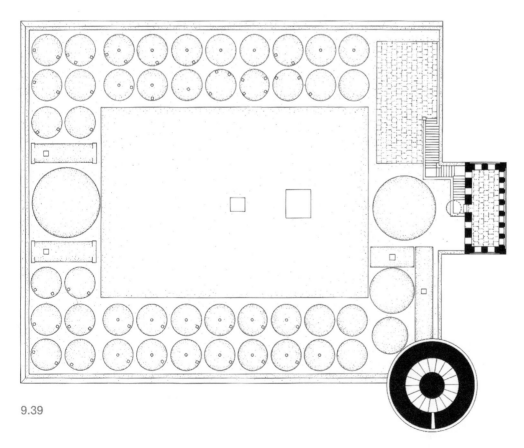

9.39

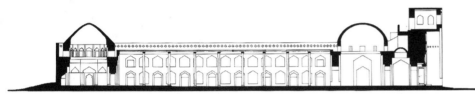

9.40

9.41

9.38

Amin Hodja Mosque, Turpan, Xinjiang, China, 1776. Plan.

Turpan is one of a string of oasis towns that was once a segment of the Silk Road across the northern edge of the Taklimakan Desert in Central Asia. The plan of the Amin Hodja Mosque conforms to the Central Asian type in which a double layer of domed brick cells surrounds a central courtyard. In this case, the courtyard has a flat roof supported by slender timber columns. Functionally, the building served several purposes. In addition to being a mosque, it was a madrassa, or school, and served as a caravanserai, or hostel for traveling merchants. Across Central Asia, these three building types shared virtually the same plan, consisting of a standardized spatial module. The main axis runs from the entrance on the east facade to the mihrab at the west end, approximating the direction of Mecca.

9.39

Amin Hodja Mosque. Roof plan.

The minaret/tomb tower rises at the southeast corner, and a roofed terrace over the entry is accessible from a small courtyard beside the entrance. The small cubic modules that surround the central space have hemispherical domes pierced by small apertures oriented to celestial events such as the position of the moon or planets on specific dates. These were an integral part of the program of teaching that took place in the spaces below. In a sense, the building is an astronomical observatory as well.

9.40

Amin Hodja Mosque. Elevation and section.

The minaret consists of a central brick column surrounded by a thick brick shell, the stair between the two winding up to a small room at the apex. Ornament on the exterior of the minaret is entirely brick patterning. The minaret also served as a marker for the two tombs at its base, similar to tomb towers in Persia and Turkistan, and may have functioned as a lighthouse, since even a small lantern at its top could have been seen by caravans miles away across the desert.

9.41

Amin Hodja Mosque. Axonometric.

This "worm's-eye" axonometric of the *qibla* (the wall that faces Mecca) and its adjacent cells reveals the powerful modular character of the interior, that is, of similar figures in a regular grouping.

9.42

Hajar Qin Temple, Malta, late 4th millennium BCE. Plan.

The twenty-three temples on Malta are the oldest standing form of architecture on Earth. Cult figures found within them suggest the worship of female fertility deities. Their creators constructed the temples of limestone megaliths weighing up to twenty tons. The typical temple plan includes several hemispheric chambers, or apses, that branch off from a narrow central corridor. Timber framing and hides probably covered the incomplete corbelled domes above the major spaces. As in other prehistoric cultures, the design of these sacred buildings may have originated in ordinary dwellings or underground burial chambers. However, Hajar Qin is unusual among Maltese temples because it has a central corridor that passes entirely through the structure. The composition is of similar, roughly elliptical volumes arranged in a regular branching pattern.

9.43

Tayaba Compound, Northern Benin. Plan and section.

This West African house is virtually a diagram of the family. It is also an efficient response to a hot, dry, dusty climate and is easily defensible. There are five cylindrical units for family members, four smaller ones for supplies and agricultural implements, and a central granary. The circular compound composed of nearly identical units is common in much of Africa, but this one employs a roof spanning from the peripheral structures to the central pillar.

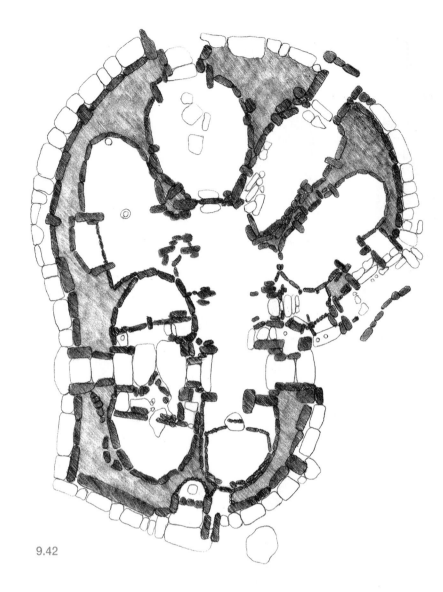

9.42

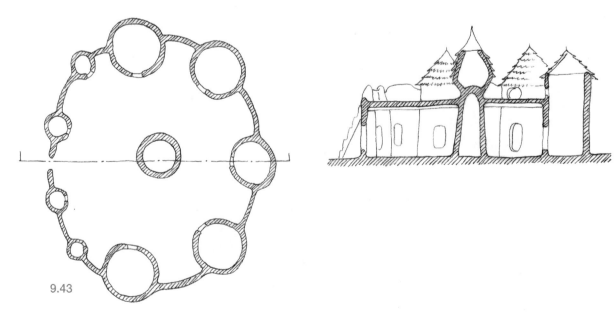

9.43

Similar Figures in an Irregular Grouping

In the following examples we can see that an irregular grouping is not arbitrary or capricious; it can be as rational as a design based on an orthogonal grid (and in most cases more so). An irregular grouping can respond directly to the constraints of a site without attempting to impose an artificial order on the given condition. It can also respond well to complex social conditions that require variable relations between private and public space. Often, a regular grouping of figures is not suited to these circumstances.

A house in northern Cameroon (9.44, 9.45) and a part of the town of Labbezanga, Mali, (9.46, 9.47) demonstrate the use of similar figures in an irregular grouping to produce complex social spaces. The Cameroonian house employs cylindrical structures to enclose interior spaces. However, the principal living area is the interstitial outdoor space between these buildings, and its complexity controls the relations among the various members of the extended family within the compound. The town in Mali has three types of buildings: two sizes of cylindrical structures and a rectangular one combined with low walls to create family compounds that interlock and overlap to produce larger clan compounds. The curvilinear plan is a traditional way of providing protection as well as a strong central focus for each building group. Though also composed of circular units in plan, the Husain-Doshi Gufa in Ahmadabad, by Balkrishna Doshi, is a semi-subterranean structure devoted to the sculptural possibilities of curvilinear space (9.48). The different sizes of the more or less hemispherical modules of space provide variety, but their similarity provides a sense of fluid spatial unity.

In contrast, a farmhouse in Apulia, Italy, is a compact composition of similar rectangular spaces in which there appears to have been no need to submit individual elements in the composition to a unifying spatial concept (9.49). Each space satisfies only its individual requirements, resulting in a form that is an amalgamation of eight autonomous but similar figures. Pueblo Bonito in Chaco Canyon, New Mexico, was a combination of two figures—a rectangular cell and a cylindrical cell (9.50, 9.51). They made a clear distinction between secular and religious functions and consequently appeared in the plan in different configurations. The rectangular cells were for domestic use, either as living spaces or for storage, and formed a matrix surrounding the two main plazas. In contrast, the cylindrical kivas were for ritualistic purposes and occupied a variety of positions in the composition: some were within the matrix of rectangular cells, some were on the margins of the matrix, and some were freestanding.

Two examples show how architects made the most of highly irregular sites by allowing the grouping of similar compositional elements to form irregular connections and interstitial spaces. A house in Cairo from the 18th century fits between a main street and a back alley (9.52, 9.53). Created from the acquisition of several smaller houses within a densely developed urban neighborhood, the architect's solution was to arrange the traditionally rectangular rooms around an irregularly shaped central courtyard, all of them facing inward except for the main reception rooms (*salamlik*), which face outward to the street. The Baqeri House in Gorgân, Iran, sits on a large, irregular urban site (9.54–9.59). It, too, has access to two streets, one for the formal entry and two others for secondary or service entries. All living spaces conform to a standard format, with minor variations for different functions. Their disposition within the irregular frame of the site is particularly interesting. What appears at first to be arbitrary is actually a carefully contrived series of courts and thresholds, as well as frontal and oblique relations among buildings. These control social relations among members of the family, their servants, and visitors, and they optimize the perceptible space by accentuating diagonal views through the courts.

Two projects demonstrate how an irregular grouping of similar figures can create a dynamic relation between the internal organization of a composition and its context. An apartment house by Hans Scharoun in Berlin at first glance appears to have two halves that are mirror images of one another (9.60). Closer inspection, however, reveals that despite a strong similarity there is no direct one-to-one

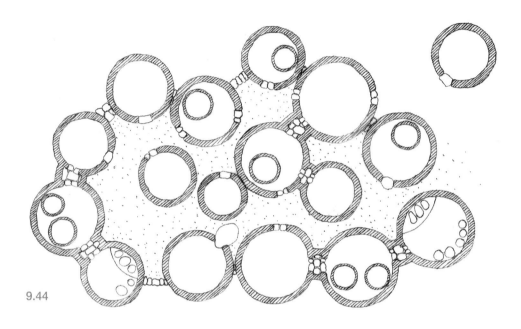

9.44

9.44

House Compound, Northern Cameroon, 20th century. Plan.

The standard construction technology—a sun-dried mud cylinder with a conical grass roof—serves both residential and storage functions in this compound. These relate to one another informally but connect to produce a single entry into the central courtyard.

9.45

House Compound, Northern Cameroon. Courtyard schematic.

The principal living space of the house is the least figural. It is a meandering interstitial space that weaves between the cylindrical components. This is the opposite of the effect found in the courtyard houses of many other cultures that rely on a rigidly geometric figural space to control the composition of irregular spaces that surround it.

9.45

correspondence between the two halves; each unit on a typical floor is unique, and even service spaces, such as lobbies and stairs, differ. The irregular contour of the elevation provides a variety of views to the surrounding city. Roberto Menghi's Franchetti House in Sardinia is a composition of similar rectangular blocks in clusters around a shared courtyard. Designed for a large Italian family, branches of which can occupy individual clusters, it resembles a Sardinian village surrounding a piazza (9.61–9.66). The single anomaly is the kitchen, a cylindrical object that thrusts out into the courtyard to signal its dominant role in the daily life of the family. Menghi thus achieved a delicate balance between the need for semi-independence among the branches of the family and the need for a strong sense of community

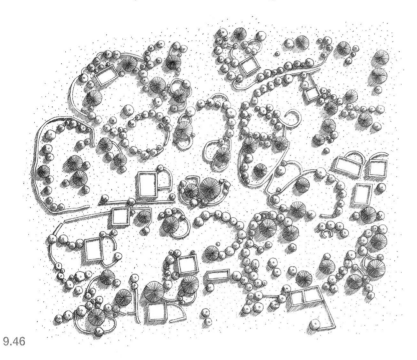

9.46

9.46

Labbezanga, Mali, 20th century. Aerial view.

In an aerial view of a portion of the town, we can see a mixture of two house forms, the traditional cylindrical structures and the rectangular form influenced by Western methods of construction. Weaving between them is a pattern of low serpentine walls that serve as property boundaries and livestock pens. The three forms together create a network of family compounds in a formal language that employs similar figures in irregular groupings.

9.47

Labbezanga, Mali. Schematic of compounds.

A mapping of compounds reveals a complex overlapping of boundaries to denote familial and clan affiliations. These produce a hierarchy of clusters with an interstitial space for efficient movement between them.

9.47

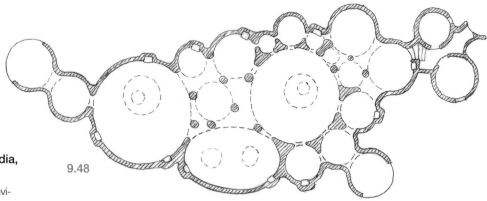

9.48

9.48

9.48
Husain-Doshi Gufa, Ahmadabad, India, 1992–95. Balkrishna Doshi. Plan.

Located on the campus of the Centre for Environmental Planning & Technology in Ahmadabad, the Gufa (cave) is an underground art gallery dedicated to the work of the painter and sculptor M. F. Husain. The building is a lightweight concrete shell enclosing biomorphic spaces lit from above through conical roof structures. In plan the composition of similar cellular spaces is in essence linear, leading the visitor through the gallery from one end to the other.

9.49
Farmhouse, Selva di Fasano, Alberobello, Italy, 18th century. Plan. (*After E. Allen.*)

The *trulli* of Apulia, in the Salentine Peninsula of southern Italy, are of dry-stone construction; the inner and outer surfaces of walls and domes are of dressed limestone with a rubble fill. The local dry-stone technique originated in the early 17th century as a means for the local baron to avoid taxes he owed his king. The baron prohibited the use of mortar so that his subjects could quickly dismantle the roofs of houses (the basis of the tax) upon the approach of the tax collector. By the 18th century, the tradition of *trulli* construction had reached a high degree of craft. This is an area of marginal farmland, with little wood, thin soil, and a lot of limestone, found loose in the fields or in solid slabs just below the surface. The thick walls and domes of the *trulli* used as much of the loose stone as possible to produce cubic spaces with conical roofs, a structural technique that worked for a variety of functions, such as housing, storage, winemaking, olive oil production, and sheltering animals. Planning the structures simply required the accumulation of any number and size of cubic cells necessary—no underlying modular or proportional system was needed. This resulted in a cluster of similar objects in a generally orthogonal but irregular grouping.

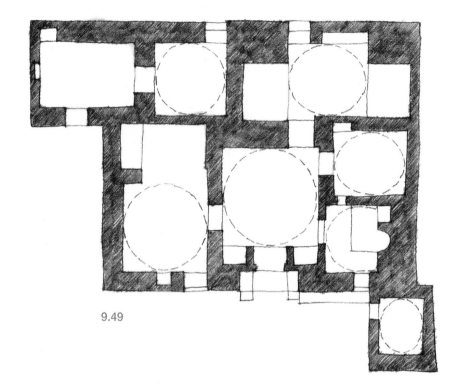

9.49

9.50
Pueblo Bonito, Chaco Canyon, New Mexico, 935–1075. Anasazi. Plan.

The largest of the ceremonial centers in Chaco, the D-shaped plan of Pueblo Bonito overlooked the wide canyon, with its long, straight wall oriented toward the south and a curved back sheltered from the north against a cliff face. Cellular domestic spaces comprised most of the architectural massing of the town, while the cylindrical kivas served the ritual activities of various clans. Inhabitants used the two large plazas for daily activities and, more importantly, for ceremonial dances.

9.51
Pueblo Bonito. Composition.

Pueblo Bonito had three types of space: roughly orthogonal cells for domestic use, ritual space (kivas), and open plazas. Most of the kivas were in the matrix of domestic spaces; a few were partially in the matrix; and some were floating free within the plazas, independent of the housing.

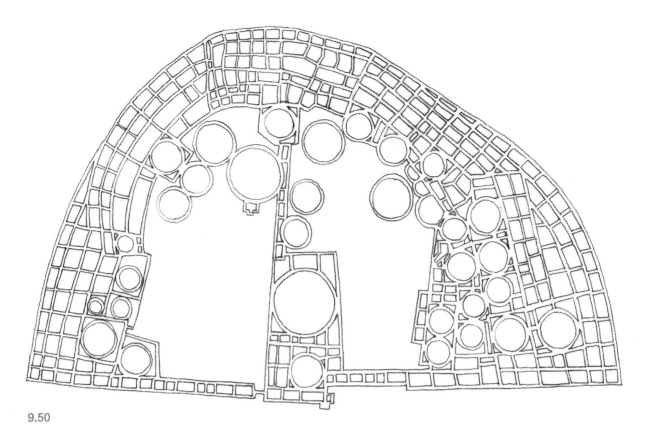

9.50

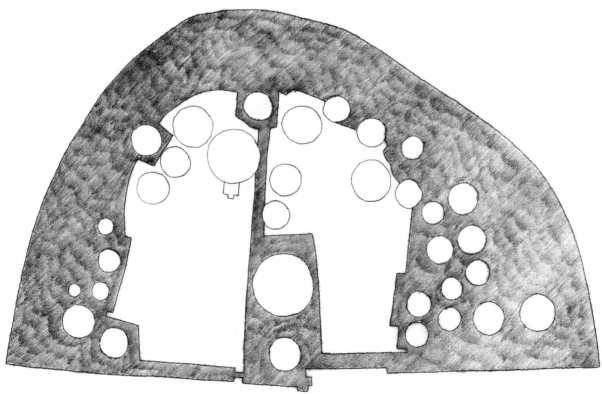

9.51

9.52

**Al-Razzāz House, Cairo, Egypt, 18th
century. Second-floor plan.**

This Mamluk house is a composite of several
small preexisting houses and additions—a typical way in which houses for growing, prosperous families could organize domestic space in
a densely built urban settlement. The result is,
in effect, several semi-independent houses
joined to enclose a shared courtyard. The
method suited the structure of the family by
providing for its two principal needs: social co-
hesion and physical security.

9.52

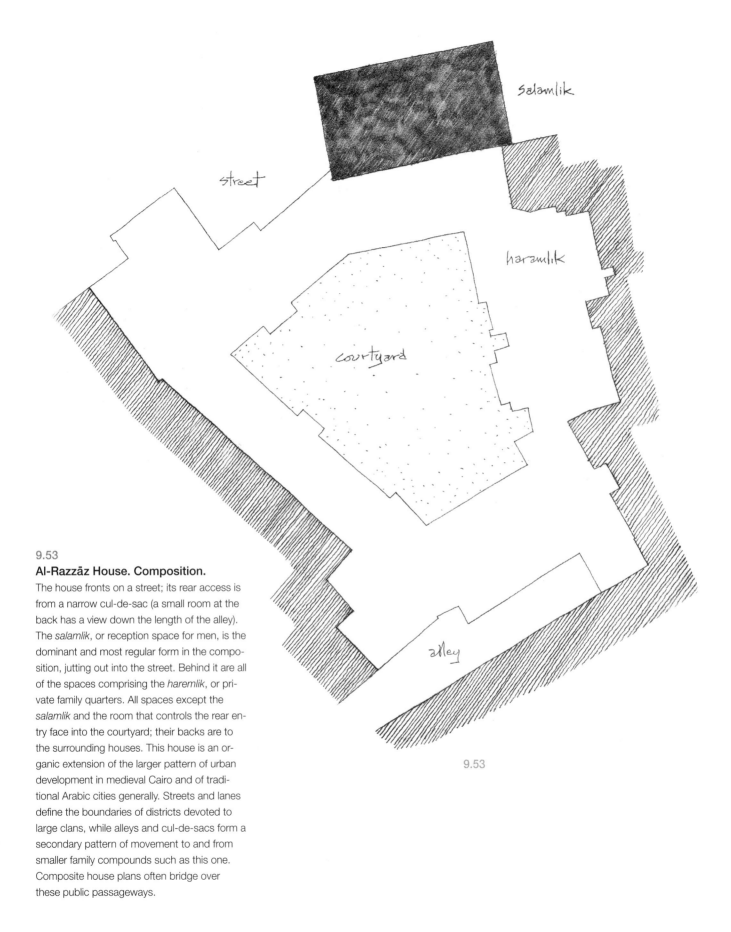

salamlik

street

haramlik

courtyard

alley

9.53

Al-Razzāz House. Composition.

The house fronts on a street; its rear access is from a narrow cul-de-sac (a small room at the back has a view down the length of the alley). The *salamlik*, or reception space for men, is the dominant and most regular form in the composition, jutting out into the street. Behind it are all of the spaces comprising the *haremlik*, or private family quarters. All spaces except the *salamlik* and the room that controls the rear entry face into the courtyard; their backs are to the surrounding houses. This house is an organic extension of the larger pattern of urban development in medieval Cairo and of traditional Arabic cities generally. Streets and lanes define the boundaries of districts devoted to large clans, while alleys and cul-de-sacs form a secondary pattern of movement to and from smaller family compounds such as this one. Composite house plans often bridge over these public passageways.

9.53

9.54
Baqeri House, Gorgân, Iran, 19th century. First-floor plan.

This house has an extensive courtyard system that organizes public, communal, and private functions of the household, provides a controlled sequence of movement or an architectural promenade, and controls light and air in a hot, dry climate. All interior spaces are open to at least one courtyard. The house is a two-story, thick bearing-wall structure in brick with three entrances: one on the main street through a gateway, past a porter's lodge, and into a reception court; a second midway through the house primarily serving members of the family; and a third at the rear for service.

9.55
Baqeri House. Building blocks I.

The house takes full advantage of an irregular site by breaking up the program into separate blocks of rooms (crosshatched) that sit on raised platforms (shaded). Together they shape the residual space into the five courtyards. All living spaces on the first floor are about 3 feet above the courtyards.

9.56
Baqeri House. Building blocks II.

The building blocks are in two groups. Four blocks joined by screen walls define the periphery, creating one large courtyard in the center. Then a pair of building blocks produces a figure that subdivides the central courtyard into five smaller courtyards.

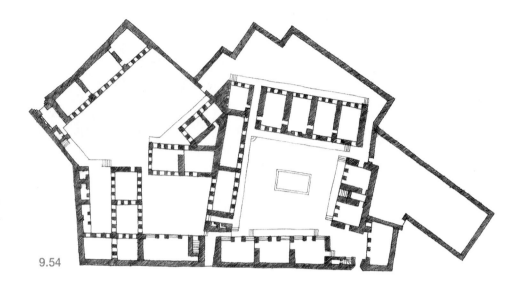

9.54

9.55

9.56

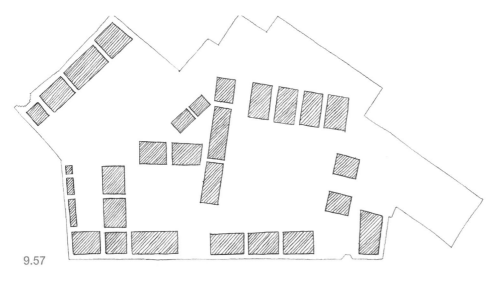

9.57

9.58

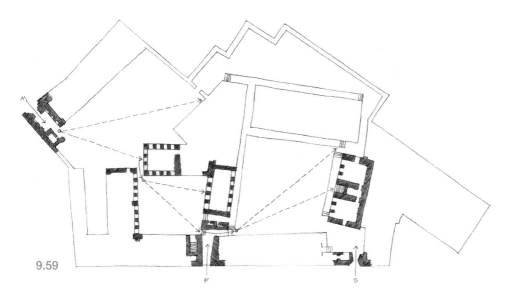

9.59

9.57

Baqeri House. Room proportions.

All rooms adhere to a set of proportions in plan: 1:1, 1:1.5, 1:2, and 1:3.

9.58

Baqeri House. Connections.

Exterior spaces (courtyards and surrounding streets) connect by gateways at courtyard corners, creating thresholds that complete their geometries.

9.59

Baqeri House. Architectural promenade.

A carefully designed sequence of spaces controls movement from the main entrance through a succession of three principal courtyards. Each courtyard is entered in succession at a corner, from which two views present themselves. The first is a view diagonally across the space to reveal its largest dimension, and the second is toward the building that dominates the courtyard. These experiences connect by narrow, deep spaces, each of which places the viewer in the optimal position to appreciate the next pair of views.

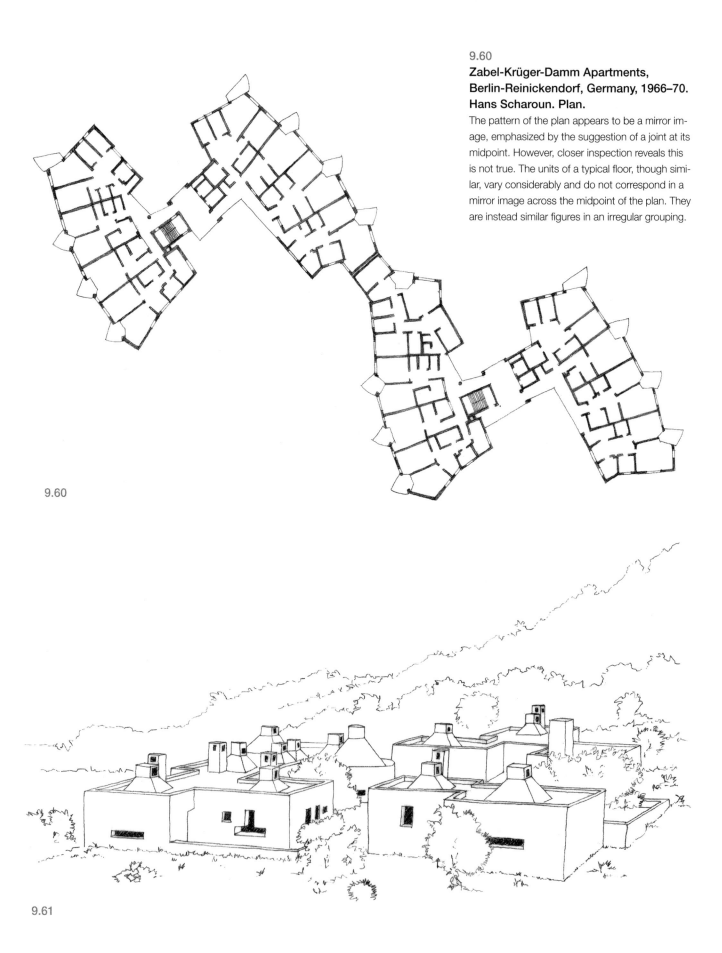

**Zabel-Krüger-Damm Apartments,
Berlin-Reinickendorf, Germany, 1966–70.
Hans Scharoun. Plan.**

The pattern of the plan appears to be a mirror image, emphasized by the suggestion of a joint at its midpoint. However, closer inspection reveals this is not true. The units of a typical floor, though similar, vary considerably and do not correspond in a mirror image across the midpoint of the plan. They are instead similar figures in an irregular grouping.

9.60

9.61

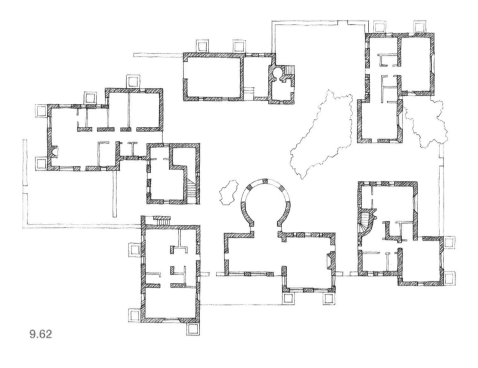

9.62

9.63

9.61

Franchetti House, Sardinia, 1970.
Roberto Menghi. View.

The house is in a rugged, rocky landscape, its mass broken into six separate buildings that loosely enclose a courtyard. Though organized orthogonally, the similar forms are in an irregular grouping to relate to both the immediate and the distant landscapes. This composition achieves several objectives. The group of buildings simulates the appearance of a vernacular Sardinian village. Separate houses accommodate the various branches of the extended family, allowing them to occupy the house separately and periodically. In a hot, dry climate, breaking the mass of the house into smaller parts enhances the circulation of air around and through the interior spaces. Finally, separating the parts of the house creates a set of entry courts between them, much like open-air vestibules for the central courtyard that frame views inward as well as outward into the surrounding landscape.

9.62

Franchetti House. Plan.

The plan achieves a delicate balance between the formality implied by the orthogonal arrangement of precisely shaped stone volumes and the informality of their open relation to the surrounding landscape. The single geometrical anomaly in the composition is the cylindrical kitchen with a conical roof, which juts into the central courtyard to signal its unifying function in relation to the extended family. Across the courtyard from the kitchen is a bath. The buildings are of thick stone bearing walls with deep-set windows to control sunlight and have rooftop ventilators to draw warm air out of the interior spaces without the use of mechanical equipment.

9.63

Franchetti House. Composition.

The relation of massing and exterior spaces forms a composition of interlocking volumes. The irregularities in the massing produce varied spaces around the courtyard that have definite shapes despite being open to the landscape.

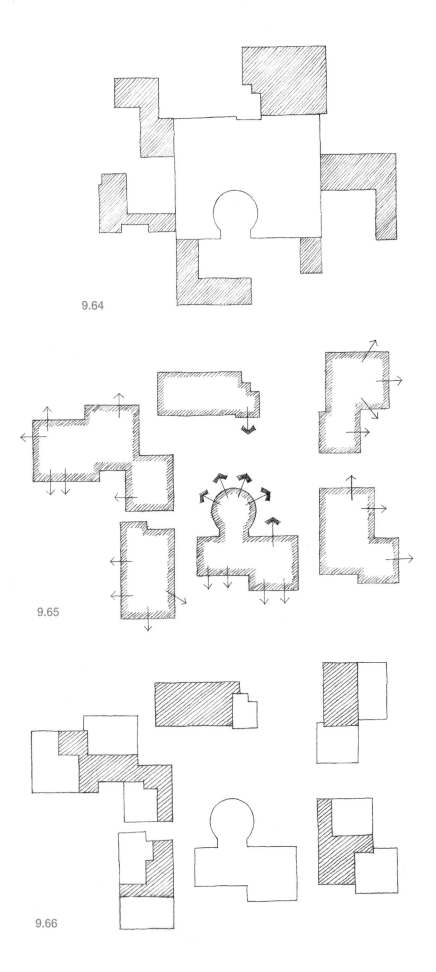

9.64

Franchetti House. Entry spaces.
One can approach and enter the house via the courtyard from any direction. The six vestibule spaces between the building masses produce a variety of entry conditions for the courtyard, and while it is usually in brilliant sunlight, the smaller vestibules provide intimate exterior spaces in cool shadow.

9.65

Franchetti House. Views.
Most of the views from the living spaces are toward distant views, not the courtyard. Only the kitchen, the communal living room, and the bath look into the central courtyard.

9.66

Franchetti House. Service spaces.
Menghi subdivided the building volumes into service (crosshatched) and served spaces, organizing them compactly and in continuous groupings. Service spaces provide additional privacy for individual rooms within the separate houses that comprise the cluster of buildings.

9.64

9.65

9.66

Dissimilar Figures in a Regular Grouping

Some compositions consist of a group of figures in which no two are alike or even similar. To unite them, designers generally resort to one of two techniques. One figure may be assigned a dominant role and all others either physically attached to it or related to it in a subordinate condition with respect to size, shape, or position. Or the figures may all relate to an exogenous ordering principle, like a datum or a grid. The first two examples in this section illustrate these techniques. The group of architectural features in a courtyard in Turpan (a stair, a small doorway to a subterranean room, a bench, and a passageway to an adjacent courtyard) comprise a pleasing composition because all are subordinate to a large triangular form. They are not appendages of the triangular form but rather modifications of it, despite the fact that they retain their individual identities (9.67). On the other hand, the shed, bin, and barn in Iowa are not related to one another in size or shape, but they form a comprehensible composition by virtue of their shared relation to a datum, an imaginary line in the foreground (9.68).

The 15th-century house of Andrea Mantegna (9.69) and the 18th-century Abbey Church of Saint Gall (9.70) each place a circular figure within a rectangular frame. Though the two figures are not geometrically related, this compositional technique is successful in both buildings by virtue of the dominant position of the circular figure and the way it forces the subordinate rectangular figure to accommodate it. The more complex plans for *hôtels particuliares* of the 17th and 18th centuries—the Hôtel d'Amelot (9.71), Hôtel de Beauvais (9.72–9.74), and the abbot's residence in Villers-Cotterêts (9.75, 9.76)—are successful because in each case an axis unites a sequence of central ritual spaces to create a composite form that serves as an armature for the surrounding secondary spaces. The axis is broken in the early 20th-century Länderbank in Vienna, but a strong hierarchy controls diverse components centered on a central rotunda (9.77, 9.78). A similar effect may emerge through an accretion of forms, as in the Monastery of Hakhpat in Armenia (9.79, 9.80). Its original 10th-century church is a symmetrical, centrally domed structure with two flanking half-domes that create a longitudinal axis. The axis was extended with the addition of a *gavit*, or assembly room; the other three additions to the rear of the church then became clearly subordinate to the axial armature of the church and *gavit*.

One method of composing dissimilar figures in a regular grouping is bricolage. Borrowed from the French, *bricolage* is a term originally used to describe surprising, unplanned events, such as the unintended action of a billiard ball or the unanticipated behavior of a quarry in hunting. More generally, it came to mean a creative use of whatever is at hand. The Russian Constructivists, such as Vladimir Tatlin and Alexander Rodchenko, preferred bricolage as a method of producing art because it was consistent with the revolutionary, antiacademic spirit of the early 20th-century avant-garde in Russia. They used the detritus of ordinary life to compose sculpture that had no recognizable formal pedigree and no material quality based on class. The form emerged spontaneously by experiment rather than from a preconception. Design by bricolage usually produces compositions of dissimilar objects in a regular grouping.

In the latter half of the 20th century, artists and architects adopted bricolage to describe a certain kind of additive compositional technique. Whereas collage adds

9.67

Courtyard, Turpan, Xinjiang, China, 1987. View.

The composition of this vernacular design elegantly unites several architectural elements—a stair, a bench (on the stair landing), an opening to a subterranean space, and a passage through the stair to a second courtyard—into a composition of dissimilar figures in a regular grouping. As is typical of vernacular architecture, the designer has drawn on a deep background in construction and everyday use to produce a single sculptural ensemble from dissimilar forms and functions. Each part of the composition is an individual form yet related to the others by means of an underlying similarity of geometry and proportion. Though each element appears to be a direct, minimalist solution to a problem, the composition as a whole transcends mere pragmatism to achieve an organic unity.

9.68

Shed, Bin, and Barn, Iowa, 2000. View.

There was clearly a decision to arrange these three dissimilar buildings close together and in a regular grouping. Aside from possible practical considerations, the compactness and regularity of the composition heightens the visual impact of the varying scales, geometries, and proportions of unadorned solid forms in the flat landscape.

one form to another, partially obscuring what is already there, bricolage is a method of organizing parts of a composition so that each remains entirely visible and whole, and the articulations among the parts are clearly visible as well. This, then, was an aesthetic goal distinct from a composition in which all parts were subsumed within a single image. Bricolage achieves a compositional unity, but one in which all parts of the composition retain their individual identities. Aesthetically, the result was much like early forms of machinery in which there was no attempt to mask or enclose the mechanism, so all of the parts and their relations were plainly visible. For example, note the difference between the early 20th-century Grinnell GEM washing machine (9.81) and the late 20th-century Sears Series 70 washing machine, in which the parts are enclosed in a form of packaging (9.82).

Some of the architectural motifs in James Stirling's buildings make strong references to Russian Constructivist art and architecture, principally the work of Konstantin Melnikov. For example, the Leicester University Engineering School of 1959 is composed as a bricolage (9.83, 9.84). Stirling appears to have designed a separate form for each part of the building program and then combined the forms so each retains its individuality. The building is a mechanical composite, each part of which is presumably designed optimally for its function alone. As with the Grinnell GEM washing machine, a sense of compositional unity emerges from the hierarchy of forms, their contrasting shapes and patterns, and the ways in which they are joined.

Russian and German architects, refugees of World War I, had brought similar ideas with them to England in the 1920s and 1930s. Likewise, William Edmond Lescaze had introduced Russian modernism (as a style, stripped of its political ideology) to the United States in 1932 in his tour de force design for the PSFS Building in Philadelphia. So Stirling's use of bricolage was not new in 1959; it just seemed new when placed in opposition to the prevailing glass-box aesthetic of the late 1950s.

The second technique of composing dissimilar figures in a regular grouping is to relate them all to a datum. A small section of the bazaar in Kashan, Iran, reveals a consistent pattern by which a variety of buildings, large and small, are attached to the central spine, a continuous interior street (9.85). The means of attachment is in all cases another shorter street or corridor that is symmetrical to the building to which it leads. All of these buildings are packed together with small shops filling the spaces between them and fronting on the passageways (9.86). A second example is perhaps the greatest of the medieval Armenian monasteries, Sanahin (9.87–9.91). Though constructed over a period of three hundred years and comprising nine buildings of various sizes and different functions, the composition achieved a remarkable coherence. This is due to a rule created at the outset and followed scrupulously throughout its long history. The entire plan is based on a nine-square diagram; as each building was added, it fit incrementally into the diagram. The sophistication of the system derived from the flexibilty by which each building could relate to the diagram and to its predecessors, an approach handed down through many generations of architects. Collectively, these architects produced a great work of art.

9.67

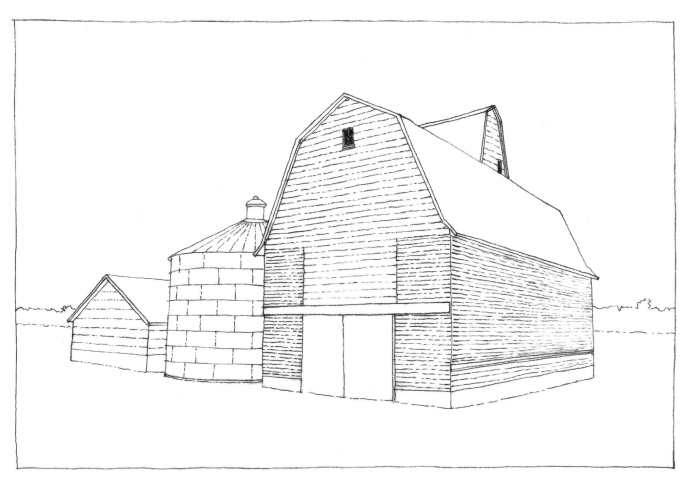

9.68

House for Andrea Mantegna, Mantua, 1476. First-floor plan.

Mantegna was the designer of his own house, but his friend, Leon Battista Alberti, may have influenced the design. Compositionally, Mantegna's design is a curious achievement. It imparts the impression of rigorous regularity despite the fact that no two spaces are alike, not even the small interstitial spaces between the central cylindrical court and its cubic frame.

9.70

Cathedral of Saint Gall, Saint Gallen, Switzerland, 1755. Peter Thumb. Plan.

The Baroque cathedral of Saint Gall appeared in the 18th century as an adjunct to one of the greatest Benedictine Carolingian abbeys of Europe, founded in the 7th century. In contrast to the Gothic and Renaissance approaches that organized space in modules, Thumb sought to achieve a new fluidity of space. He conceived the form of the church as a robust structural frame set within a fragile screen wall. Allowing light to enter through the outer screen and between the deep piers of the frame into the central space, Thumb produced a theatrical effect of layers of mysteriously luminous space receding into the distance. He reinforced the illusion by inserting a cylindrical volume at the center in lieu of transepts, a figure in its own right but also a deformation of the rectangular frame. With a typically Baroque delight in contradiction, Thumb designed the cathedral to appear simultaneously linear and centralized.

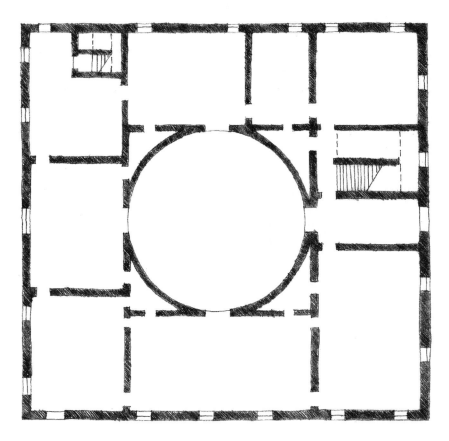

9.69

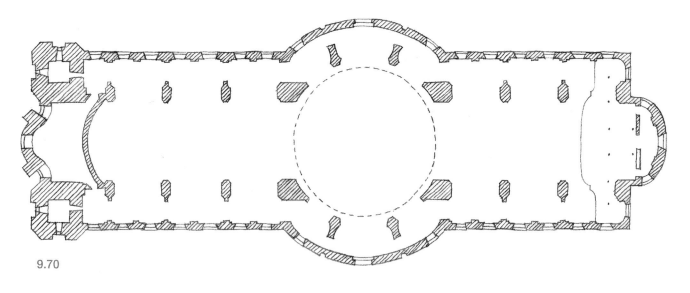

9.70

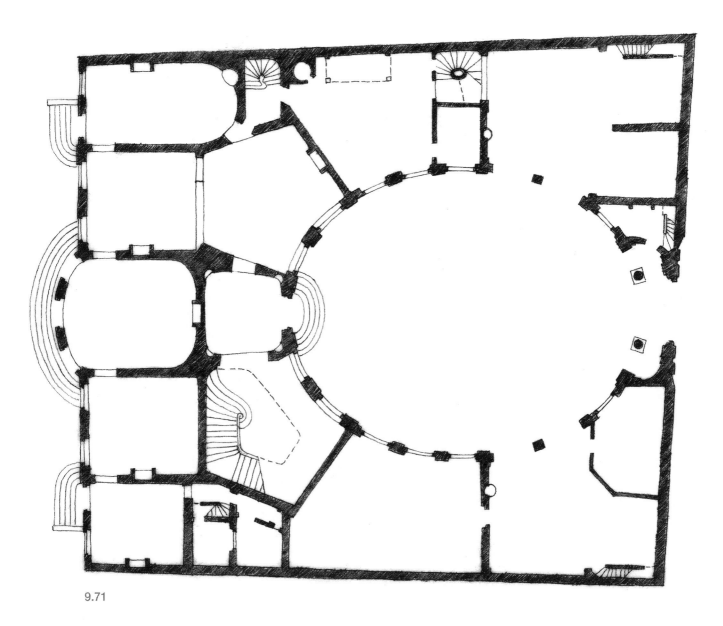

9.71

9.71
Hôtel d'Amelot, Paris, 1712. Germain Boffrand. Plan.
In 18th-century France, the method of planning a *hôtel particulaire*, or an urban house for the upper class, was typically to make a distinction between spaces dedicated to formal or ceremonial functions and those that accommodated domestic and service functions. The former were figural and arranged axially, whereas the latter became an inhabitable poché. The obsessive application of this general idea was the architectural reflection of an intensely hierarchical social structure, one that not only segregated social classes, but for the upper class alone also alienated the rigid choreography of public manners from a hidden, messy domestic life. In this case, the large elliptical entry courtyard leads through a foyer and a series of salons to a rear garden. All service functions are subordinate to this formal core.

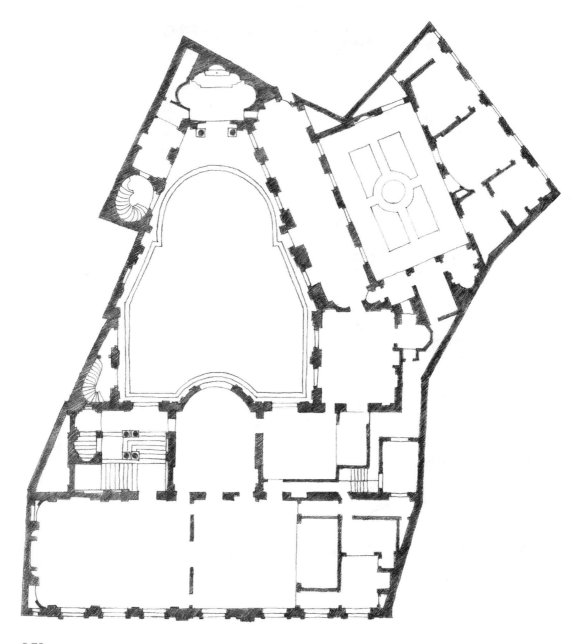

9.72

9.72
Hôtel de Beauvais, Paris, 1655. Antoine Le Pautre. Plan.

The plan is a distortion of a conventional 17th-century organization for large urban houses requiring an axial arrangement of formal salons, courtyards, and extensive service spaces. The distortion was a creative response to an irregular building lot unsuited to the building type.

9.73
Hôtel de Beauvais. Composition.

The composition embeds a set of figural spaces in a matrix of small subsidiary spaces and poché. The challenge for the architect was to align the individual axes of symmetry with one another. Le Pautre turned a severe limitation to his advantage by creating the distinctive shape of the principal courtyard. Though it is in response to the constraints of the site, its shape creates a forced perspective that makes it appear considerably larger than its actual dimensions.

9.74
Hôtel de Beauvais. Site.

The property consisted of fragments of a medieval urban pattern, and it faced on two streets. Le Pautre exploited this condition to provide a formal entry facade on the primary street and service access on the secondary street.

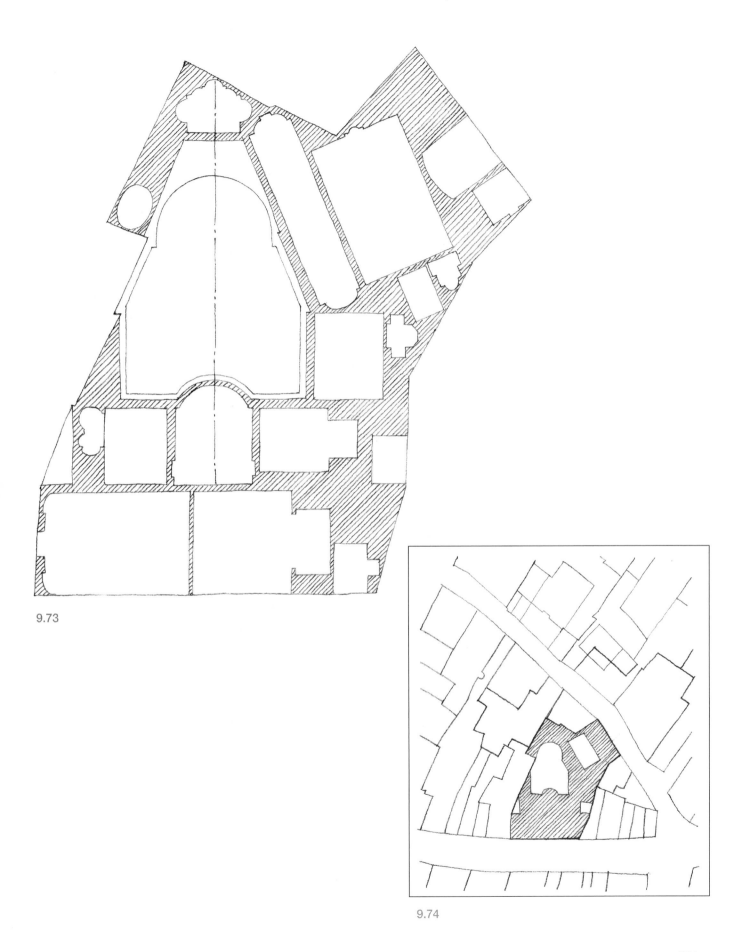

9.73

9.74

9.75

Abbot's Residence, Villiers-Cotterêts, France, 1765. François Franque. Plan.

An example of an 18th century urban *hôtel particulaire*, the abbot's residence requires the composition of a great variety of spaces within an irregular boundary. Aside from the entry processional, these spaces need not relate to one another in a consistent fashion. Poché operates at two scales: secondary and tertiary spaces produce an inhabitable poché between the primary spaces and the outer boundary of the plan. At a smaller scale, walls of varying thickness produce the second type of poché that shapes the figural spaces.

9.76

Abbot's Residence, Villiers-Cotterêts. Composition.

The composition makes a distinction between public and private functions of the house. Highly stylized and ritualistic public functions of the abbot's residence are in a regular grouping—an axial and symmetrical promenade from the forecourt, through the *cour d'honneur* and the vestibule to the stair. In contrast, private spaces comprise an irregular grouping around this spine, performing together as an interstitial poché, with each space maintaining its unique geometry and orientation.

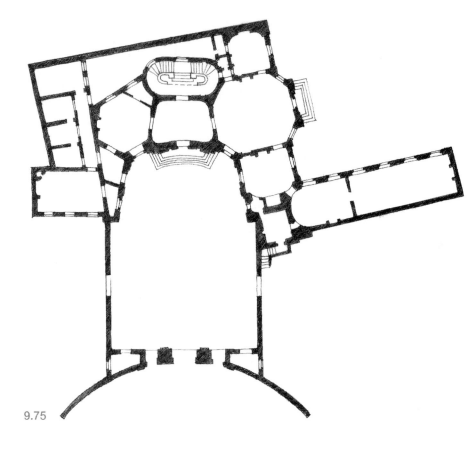

9.75

9.76

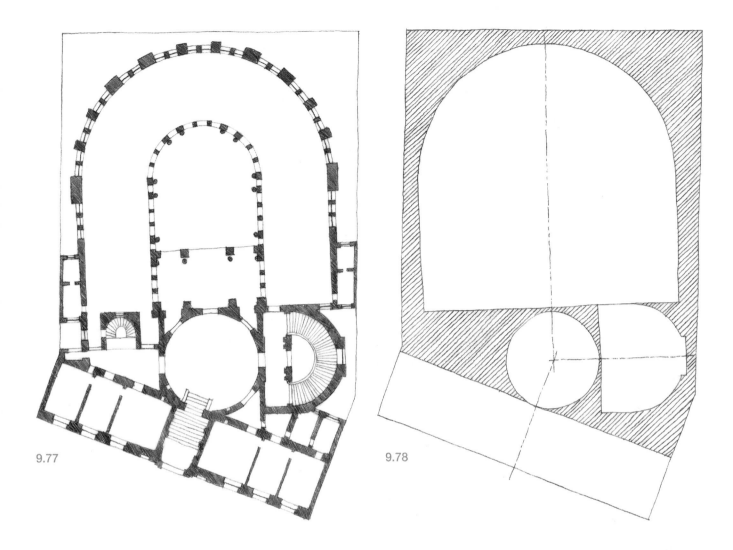

9.77
Länderbank, Vienna, 1884. Otto Wagner. Plan.
Wagner's early career was as a classical revivalist, but in 1895 he published a book, *Modern Architecture*, in which he espoused a functionalist architecture based on the organization of plans according to programmatic needs and the use of new materials and methods of construction, rather than preconceived notions of order. Architects in the United States, such as Louis Sullivan, William LeBaron Jenny, and others had pioneered these ideas, but they were radical in Europe. Wagner was also an influential teacher and one of the founders of the Secessionist movement, along with artists and designers such as Gustav Klimt, Josef Maria Olbrich, and Josef Hoffmann. The plan of the Länderbank illustrates Wagner's functionalist approach to organizing a program, in which he devoted a single form to each function of the program and then connected them mechanistically. For example, the office building facing the street has a form suited to it alone, distinct from the forms assigned to the central rotunda, the stair, and the banking hall.

9.78
Länderbank, Vienna. Composition.
Wagner's technique of breaking the program into pieces, designing a form for each piece, and then assembling the result predated similar experiments among the Russian Constructivists and those of other western European architects such as James Stirling (his design for the Leicester University Engineering School, for example). Unlike these architects, however, Wagner relied on a Classicist technique to organize the disparate parts of the composition by pinning them together with axes of symmetry.

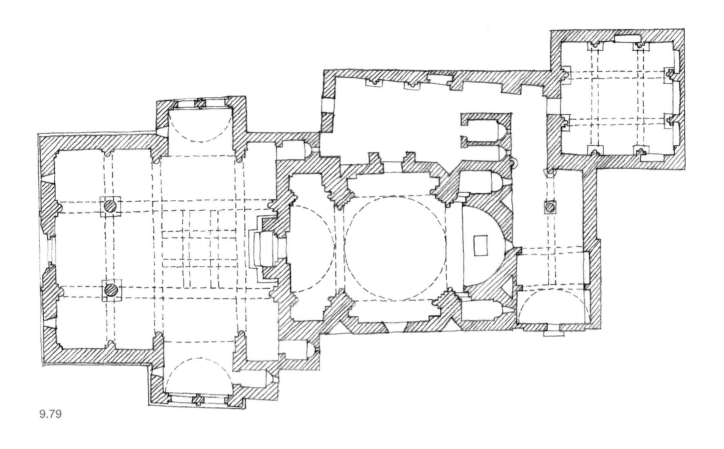

9.79

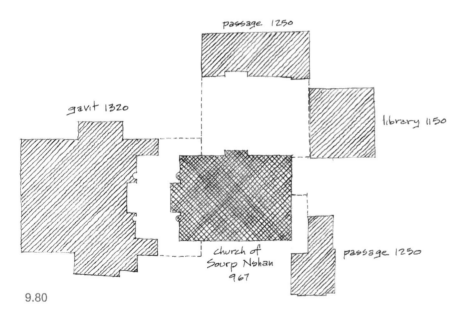

passage 1250

gavit 1320

library 1150

Church of
Sourp Nshan
967

passage 1250

9.80

9.79

**Monastery of Hakhpat, Lori, Armenia,
10th to 14th centuries. Trdat. Plan.**

Hakhpat was a major center of philosophy, theology, literature, arts, and sciences in medieval Armenia. The Sourp Nshan (Holy Cross) Church was the first structure to be built (967) in this complex. Trdat, the architect of Hakhpat, was also the architect for the reconstruction of the dome of the Hagia Sophia in Constantinople after the earthquake of 986. Armenian architects were at the forefront of structural and spatial innovations in the Middle East during the early medieval period and worked for the Arabs in Syria and Iraq at this time as well. Four intersecting arches framed into three walls and two large columns support the roof of the main space to produce a roughly nine-square plan. The pattern repeats at a smaller scale within the central square to support a lantern at the apex of the dome. The floor of the *gavit*, or assembly space, is entirely paved with the gravestones of the monastery's sponsors, the royal Ghiurichian family.

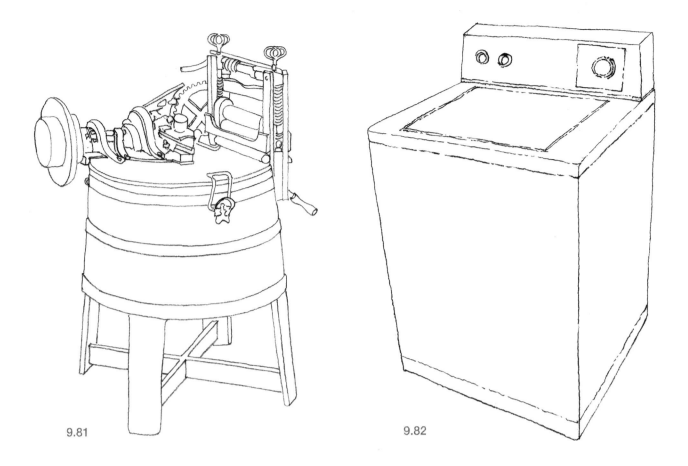

9.81

9.82

9.80
Monastery of Hakhpat. Composition.

The church is a compact, centrally planned structure with a large dome supported by four piers with engaged columns. A library in a nine-square plan appeared adjacent to the church in 1150; a hundred years later, the monastery added two passages to combine the church and the library into a single structure. Finally, in 1320, the *gavit* rose in the front of the church.

9.81
Grinnell GEM Washing Machine, 1918.

When large appliances began to enter the American home, there was no attempt to disguise their purely mechanical function. Machines were modern, and the more mechanistic they appeared, the better. Concurrently, this attitude was reflected in the artistic avant-garde's interest in bricolage as a design method, by which every part of a composition and its relation to every other part was evident. The architectural pioneers of bricolage were the Russian Constructivists, who translated the bold experiments of sculptors into buildings by designing specific forms for each part of the architectural program and then assembling the parts so each retained its individual identity.

9.82
Sears Series 70 Washing Machine, 1990.

As packaging of mass-market consumer products assumed greater importance in the second half of the 20th century, attitudes toward the appearance of machines changed correspondingly. The mechanism disappeared into opaque, hard shells that displayed only the controls and the company logo. Having a visual sense of how the machine worked was no longer desirable. This spartan aesthetic was reflected in a changing taste in architecture that projected values of simplicity, cleanliness, safety, and efficiency. As with the evolution of washing machines, the new architectural aesthetic of mute boxes drastically reduced the amount and quality of visual information that buildings conveyed.

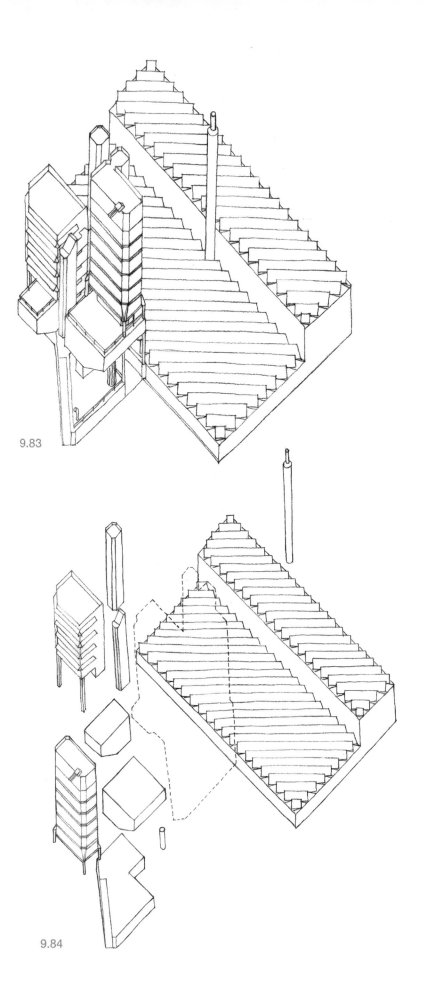

9.83
**Leicester University Engineering
School, Leicester, UK, 1959. James
Stirling. Axonometric.**

Stirling's project derived from some of the
Russian Constructivists' work in the early 20th
century, and he used bricolage as a compositional technique. In addition, Stirling made specific references to formal motifs of the Rus-
sians, such as the shapes and positions of the
fully exposed lecture theaters that originally appeared in Konstantin Melnikov's design for the
Rusakov Workers' Club of 1928.

9.84
**Leicester University Engineering
School. Exploded axonometric.**

Each part of the composition maintains its distinct identity within the overall composition. They
are both formally and physically separate forms
implying an almost nostalgic image of mechanism in the context of the minimalist mainstream
of post–World War II modernist architecture. The
building's popularity, and the aesthetic in general, increased in the 1960s as people became
accustomed to images of lunar landing modules
and similar machines that appeared to be intricate composites of exposed components.

9.83

9.84

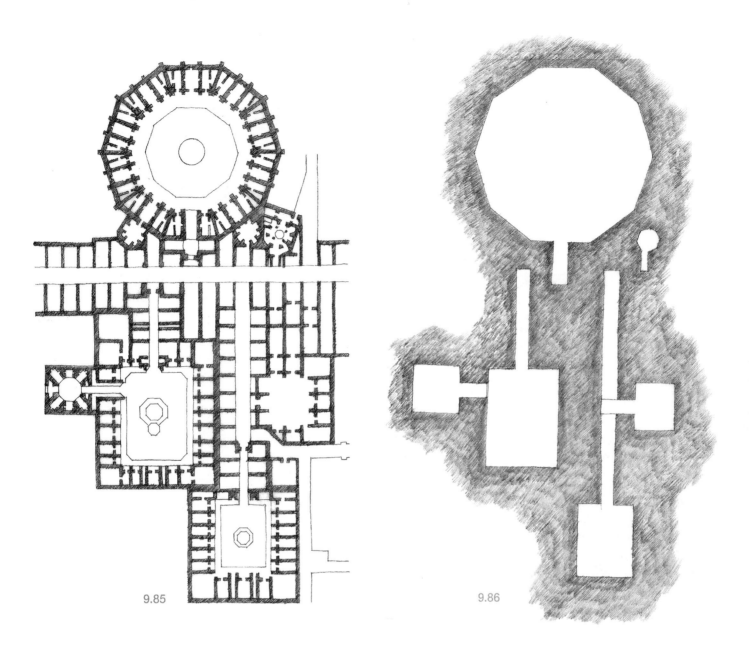

9.85

Bazaar, Kashan, Iran, 18th to 20th centuries. Plan.

The bazaar is a linear, segmental form consisting primarily of small shops to which are also attached many large specialized structures, including mosques for the merchants, baths, hotels (caravanserais), and schools (madrassas). The shops comprise the principal spine of the bazaar but also occupy every interstitial space between the larger structures. All open space is internal to these structures, so no buildings are freestanding.

9.86

Bazaar, Kashan. Composition.

The *waqf* is an organization common to bazaars throughout the Islamic world. An endowment of properties such as the ones in this plan, the rents from it support the neighboring religious and social institutions, such as mosques and schools. In this case, all of the major specialized structures attach to the spine by means of alleys, never directly, in order to give small shops greater exposure to pedestrian traffic, primarily on the spine, and secondarily along the alleys.

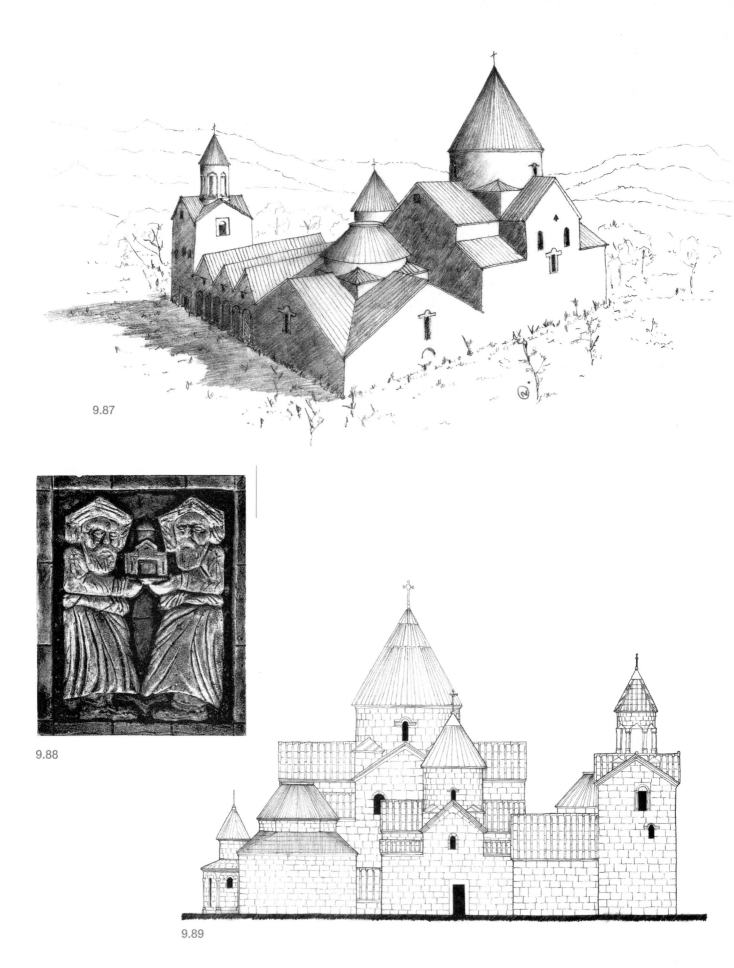

9.87

9.88

9.89

9.87

Sanahin Monastery, Alaverdi, Armenia, 932–1235. View.

The monastery of Sanahin is a masterpiece of medieval Armenian architecture and was for several centuries a major center for medieval scholarship in the arts and sciences. Despite being composed of nine buildings constructed over three hundred years, it achieved a remarkable unity of design. It is entirely of stone, including the roofs, in a compact composition that fuses several distinct building types into a single continuous form.

9.88

Sanahin Monastery. Dedication.

A stone plaque set into the west elevation illustrates the 10th-century architect of Sanahin offering his client and founder of the monastery, a Kyurikid prince, a model of the project. This is one of the earliest known depictions of a scale model of an architectural project.

9.89

Sanahin Monastery. North elevation.

The heterogeneous grouping of buildings at Sanahin appears unified for four reasons. First, the architects restricted the massing of the various buildings to simple three-dimensional geometric figures such as cubes, cylinders, and cones. Second, all of the buildings obeyed a traditional system of proportion. We can see this in its elevations, such as the one shown here, where each part of the composition relates to all others with respect to similar dimensional ratios. The third factor was hierarchy. The composition is an elegant assemblage of forms varying in scale and ascending to a crescendo in the center. The fourth technique used to achieve unity is evident in plan, a process of design explained in succeeding illustrations of the morphology.

9.90

Sanahin Monastery. Plan.

The monastery is a composite of separate buildings in a compact pattern oriented to the cardinal directions in which connections between the buildings are direct, varied, and logical. The architects worked with several traditional building types. The two churches, oriented west to east, employ a central dome with four vaulted flanking spaces, of which the eastern one is a deep apse. As is typical of Armenian churches, these buildings employed a subtractive method to create interior space (see 10.2). A *gavit* is a space used as a meeting hall, its form derived from that of a traditional Armenian wooden house composed of four or six columns supporting a conical or pyramidal roof. The *gavits* at Sanahin are also cemeteries for the remains of monks, so their floors are entirely paved with gravestones. The library is the purest and simplest building geometrically, a cubic structure with a conical roof. The transition from its square base to the conical roof is an octagonal structure, its form derived from that of a tent. The academy is an open passage from the *gavit* of Saint Asdvadzadzin to the rear courtyard; students once sat on stone benches along its two sides. The Chapel of Saint Gregory is a cylindrical structure with four small apses, and the bell tower is a three-story stone block with a small open cupola.

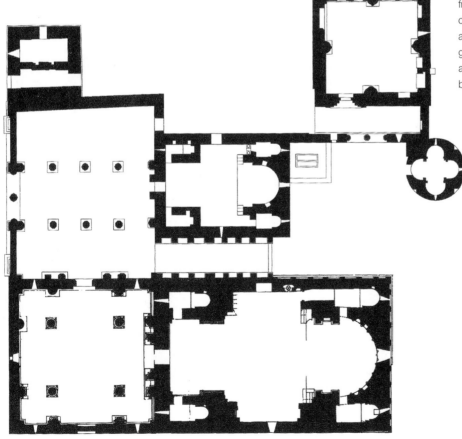

9.90

9.91

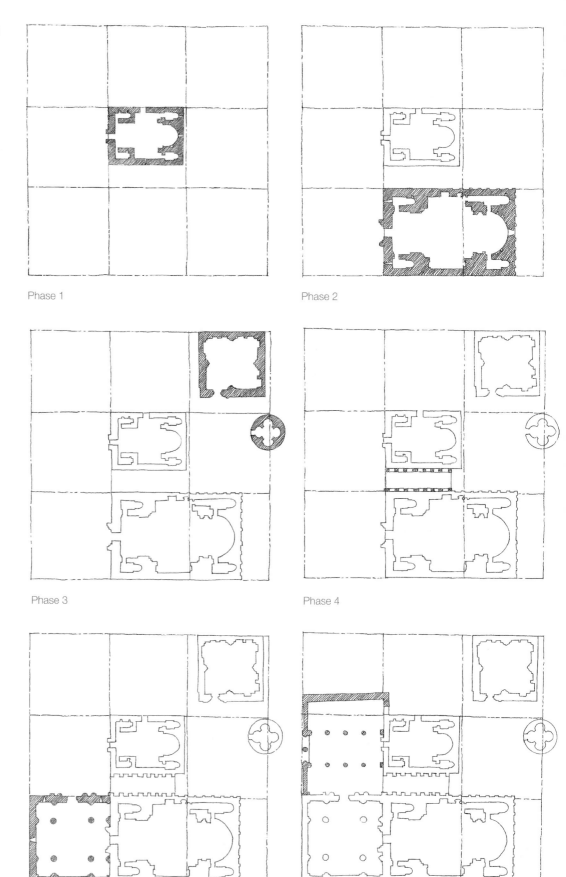

Phase 1

Phase 2

Phase 3

Phase 4

Phase 5

Phase 6

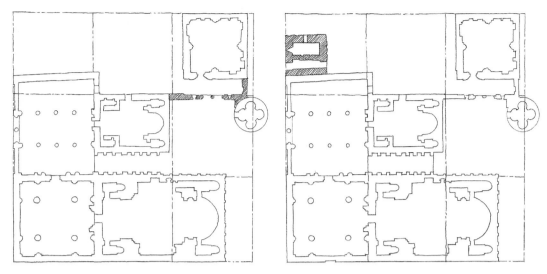

Phase 7   Phase 8

9.91

Sanahin Monastery. Morphology: The nine-square diagram.

The fourth method by which the architects of Sanahin were able to maintain its compositional integrity over three hundred years and eight separate building campaigns was to subject the entire plan to an underlying nine-square diagram. Though the separate buildings each had unique requirements as to size and form, they all fit within the diagram. The *gavit* of Saint Amenaprkitch in the southeast corner of the plan represents the norm, since it perfectly fits a single square. Other buildings either occupy parts of their assigned squares or push into adjacent squares. The single anomaly is the Chapel of Saint Gregory, which appears to have pivoted out of its cell and attached itself to the library portico. Morphologically, the strategy the architects used at Sanahin is interesting because though all parts of the composition are subject to the rigorous, abstract order of a nine-square diagram, the development of the plan allowed for considerable flexibility and variation depending on the requirements of each building.

Phase 1: 934, Church of Saint Asdvadzadzin

Phase 2: 962, Church of Amenaprkitch

Phase 3: 1063, Library and Chapel of Saint Gregory

Phase 4: 1090, The Academy

Phase 5: 1181, *Gavit* of Amenaprkitch

Phase 6: 1211, *Gavit* of Astvadzadzin

Phase 7: 1220, Library Portico

Phase 8: 1235, Bell Tower

Dissimilar Figures in an Irregular Grouping

Some compositions do not rely on a geometric armature or a datum to relate either similar or dissimilar figures; neither do they rely on a single figure that is hierarchically dominant as a means to control all others. Instead, as in the example of a still life by Jean-Siméon Chardin, *Jar with Apricots*, the integrity of the composition emerges entirely from relations of shape, size, contour, orientation, color, and texture among various forms, and in particular from the figural character of the spaces between them (9.92).

A house compound of the Gurunsi people in Burkina Faso (9.93) and the Winton Guest House by Frank Gehry (9.94) share a compositional strategy much like that of Chardin's still life. Differences in the forms and the uncomfortable relations between them are paradoxically what produce a coherent composition. Hugo Häring avoided any underlying geometrical relation among the elements of his designs, arguing they were an artificial and arbitrary contrivance. Instead, his compositional method allowed each figure to achieve its own character, to some degree in competition with the others. A 1948 proposed plan for a house illustrates how his technique results in a great degree of formal and spatial ambiguity; the various relations seem to compete for dominance, but none succeed (9.95, 9.96). Reima and Railli Pietilä worked in a similar vein but on a larger scale in their design for Mäntyniemi, a residence for the president of Finland near Helsinki (9.97). Service spaces tend to be in small, more or less orthogonal clusters, forming figures that bracket a main serpentine route through the building from end to end. In contrast, the boundaries and geometries of major spaces are less distinct.

The plan of the 15th-century Palace of Albrechtsburg, Germany, deforms the largest, presumably most important spaces to accommodate a few minor, geometrically precise spaces, thus undermining one's presumption about its compositional hierarchy (9.98). The minor spaces are the most figural and embed themselves in the less clearly defined major spaces. For his design of the Art Tower in Mito, Japan, Arata Isozaki also used the motif of embedding a figure in a host. In this case the host is not a figure, however, but a matrix of galleries, service spaces, and circulation (9.99, 9.100).

Topographic conditions sometimes prevent the use of a geometric armature for placing a variety of structures. Two structures that are part of a complex called the Great Zimbabwe incorporate massive stones in situ but then proceed to create complex spaces with massive stone walls often with indeterminate boundaries (9.101, 9.102). The "hill structure" or acropolis of the Great Zimbabwe is similar in this respect to the acropolis of Pergamon (9.103, 9.104). In both examples, the importance of the interstitial spaces—those between the major spaces and monuments—goes beyond merely allowing for movement. They comprise a countervailing force to the major figures in the plan, a continuous spatial system that expands and narrows in accordance with approaches to and thresholds into the major spaces, thus altering one's perception of the scale of the surrounding buildings.

The Sanctuary of the Oracle of Delphi is substantially different (9.105–9.108). It has an open space for a processional from the main entrance at the bottom to the amphitheater at the top that traverses the mountainside, winding between freestanding figures: treasuries, temples, and sacrificial altars. Each of these is independently sited on one of a series of terraces to relate to the processional (generally on an oblique to one's approach), but also to the topography and to views of the landscape beyond. Though the Temple of Apollo is a dominant figure, smaller figures in this composition are independent.

Though the four types of clusters are ostensibly about the organization of forms, either similar or dissimilar and in either regular or irregular groupings, the underlying purpose of cluster organizations is to rationalize their relations, that is, the spaces between them. In some cases, these spaces are figural and direct extensions of the forms themselves (e.g., Souk el-Oued), producing a continuous, unambiguous pattern of masses and voids. In others, the spaces are nonfigural and residual (e.g., Pergamon), creating a relationship between masses and voids that is ambivalent and unpredictable. These are contested spaces subject to the varied internal orders and orientations of the forms that surround them.

9.92

9.92

***Jar of Apricots*, Jean-Siméon Chardin, 18th century. (After Chardin.)**
This pencil sketch emphasizes composition at the expense of the luminous and playful color of Chardin's exquisite still life. His skill of composing varied forms in a disarmingly informal style is without equal.

One needs to savor his *Jar of Apricots* . . . before discovering its resonances, which are not only visual but tactile: how the tambour lid of the round box accords with the oval shape of the canvas itself and is echoed by the drumlike tightness of the paper tied over the apricot jar; how the horizontal axis of the table is played upon by the stuttering line of red wineglass, fruit, painted fruit on the coffee cups; how the slab of bread repeats the rectangular form of the packet on the right, with its cunningly placed strings; and how all these rhymes of shape and format are reinforced by the subtle interchange of color and reflection among the objects, the warm paste of Chardin's paint holding an infinite series of correspondences.

—Robert Hughes,
Nothing If Not Critical

9.93
House Compound, Gurunsi People, Burkina Faso, 20th century. View.

The composition of this compound has a striking similarity to the technique that Frank Gehry used in the Winton Guest House (9.94). Instead of imposing a unified form on the house, its designers have allowed each function to determine an appropriate form and then allowed the house to assume an order based on change over time. Whereas Gehry only implies this in his design, in the case of the Gurunsi it is explicit and pragmatic. The house is a direct reflection of the family structure, each member or branch identified by an individual structure focused inward toward a shared space. The tree serves a symbolic function similar to the central hearth form in Gehry's house, so despite the heterogeneous character of the family—its functions expressed by an open, discontinuous presentation to its surroundings—it relates to its site through a single central, unifying feature.

9.94
Winton Guest House, Wayzata, Minnesota, 1986. Frank Gehry. View.

Gehry separated the programmatic elements, designed them individually, and recombined them into a cluster. The result is an architectural still life in which the character of each form depends upon its relations to all others. The small building periodically accommodates visiting members of a family. The clustering of a heterogeneous set of forms around the central hearth is perhaps a metaphor for the family as a cluster of individuals who constantly negotiate their individual identities and relationships.

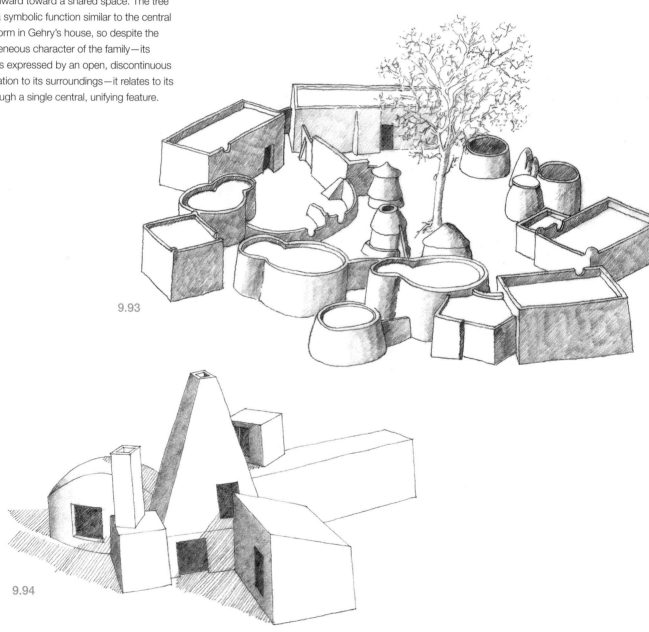

9.93

9.94

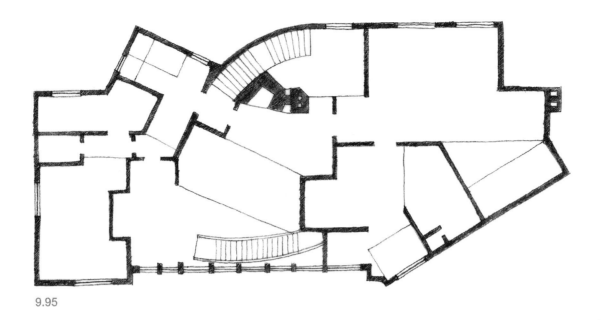

9.95

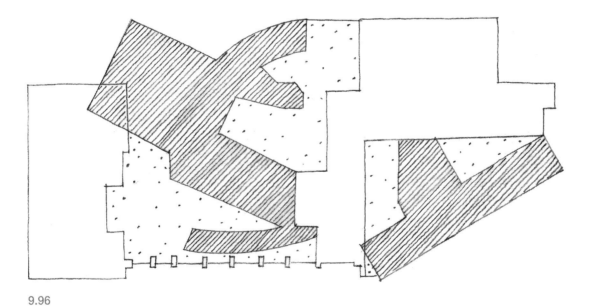

9.96

9.95

**Unbuilt House, ca. 1948. Hugo Häring.
Plan.**

Häring's theory of architecture as a "habitable
body" led to the use of what might appear at
first to be disjunctive geometries and orientations. Since the order of Häring's architectural
space is always local, never universal, one is
constantly engaged in relating one's own body
to that of the building.

9.96

Unbuilt House, Häring. Composition.

On closer analysis, one can see that Häring
composed the plan of this house as two sets
of figures: one a pair of regular orthogonal
forms, the other a pair of irregular oblique
forms, both set against a background of interstitial spaces.

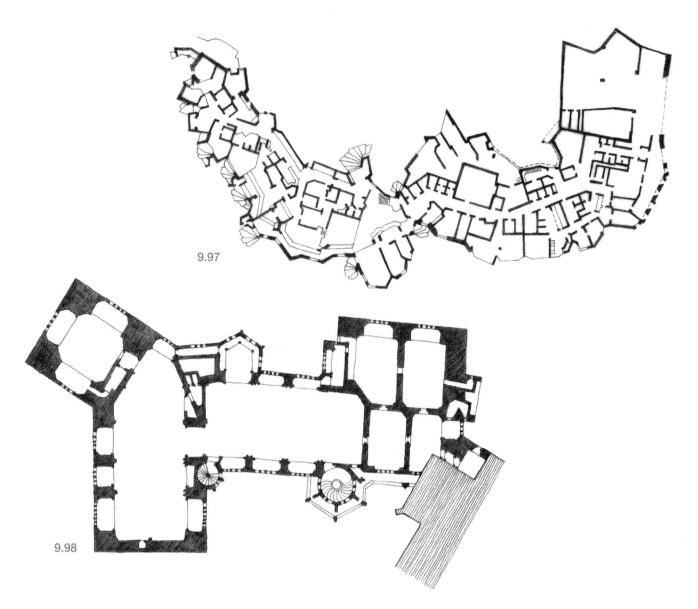

9.97

9.98

9.97

Mäntyniemi: Residence for the President of Finland, Helsinki, 1993. Reima and Railli Pietilä. Plan.

In contrast to mainstream functionalist Modernism, the work of the Pietiläs reflected their interest in phenomenology and the specific characteristics of the culture and landscape in Finland. Their designs tended to avoid orthogonal geometry and did not merely conform to the landscape but rather related to it expressionistically. The materials of this 22,000-square-foot house are primarily stone, birch, and concrete. The serpentine plan, with its highly irregular geometry, not only allows many different views of the rugged landscape but also creates views back to the house in relation to the landscape, similar to the technique used in some of the great Japanese imperial villas, such as Katsura and Ninomaru densha.

9.98

Palace of Albrechtsburg, Germany, 1471–85. Plan.

The composition does not subordinate its parts to an overall organizational structure but instead allows each part to maintain its unique character. This does not result is a lack of order, however. There is a clear sense of hierarchy among its elegantly modeled primary, secondary, and tertiary forms, resulting in a bricolage. This is also a good example of an articulated skin, since the deep wall varies considerably in thickness, transparency, and detail as it encloses the entire composition and absorbs several objects, such as stairs, bay windows, and service spaces.

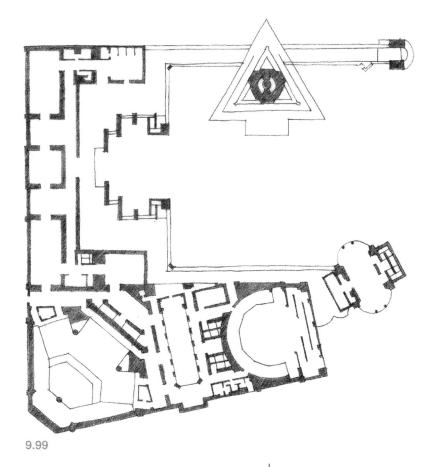

9.99

9.99
Art Tower, Mito, Japan, 1990. Arata Isozaki. Plan.

The art museum illustrated here is part of a large cultural complex that includes a tower that dominates the center of the small resort city of Mito. It was constructed to mark the city's one hundredth anniversary, and the city dedicates 1 percent of its annual budget to exhibitions and events held there. The architect's stated goal was to create an art gallery that could accommodate a wide variety of exhibitions simultaneously. Gallery interiors are extremely simple with respect to materials and lighting, their character determined primarily by their diverse sizes and proportions. Isozaki believed that that gallery interiors should be neutral backdrops for art, and the architecture reflects this concept: the architectural matrix of rectangular galleries and support spaces serves as an orthogonal poché for a few pieces of the program (such as the theater and the concert hall, designed as idiosyncratic architectural objects).

9.100
Art Tower. Composition.

Isozaki's composition indicates his desire to combine a heterogeneous collection of functions within a single building envelope and exaggerate their individual forms. The result is a play between positive and negative objects. Positive objects are detached, such that their form is evident externally; we see three of them surrounding the courtyard. Negative objects embed in the building and are discernable primarily from within; we see three of them in the thick wing of the building at the bottom of the plan. The six objects are dissimilar and arranged in an irregular grouping, since the identity of each one depends on its unique form and the orientation of its internal axis of symmetry. Overall, the building form does not provide a dominant unifying order, since it is simply a neutral matrix for the objects.

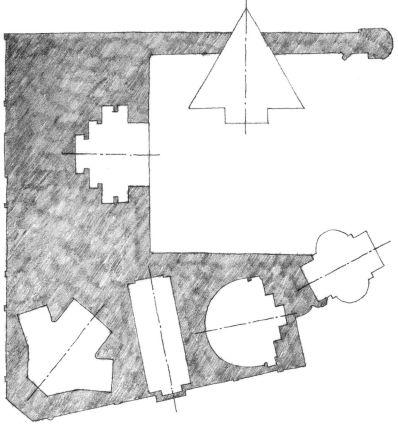

9.100

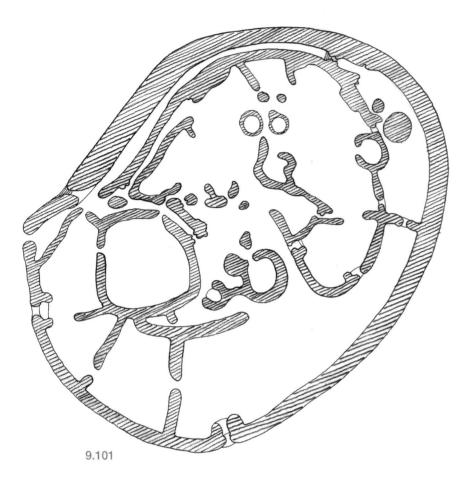

9.101

9.101
Great Zimbabwe, Zimbabwe, 13th to 15th centuries. Plan of the Great Enclosure.

The ruins of this complex of massive stone walls undulate across almost 1,800 acres of present-day southeastern Zimbabwe. The extensive ruins of Great Zimbabwe were probably the work of a Shona culture, a Bantu speaking ethnic group uninfluenced by non-African cultures. It is the largest prehistoric structure south of the Sahara. Among hundreds of curvilinear stone structures, the Great Enclosure was most likely the residence of an elite class of ruler/priests. The granite block walls, laid as dry stone, taper to 36 feet in height and display a high degree of sophistication in their design and craft.

9.102
Great Zimbabwe. Plan of the Hill Complex.

Unlike the Great Enclosure, the Hill Complex incorporates many colossal granite boulders in its design. The amount of skilled labor required to construct the walls of both buildings was considerable; their complex curvilinear design was a sophisticated architecture. It must have resulted from a profound cultural predisposition toward a particular way of shaping and perceiving form and space in relation to the landscape and the climate. Unfortunately, acting on racism and greed, early European explorers looted or destroyed virtually all of the archaeological evidence that could have identified the builders of the Great Zimbabwe.

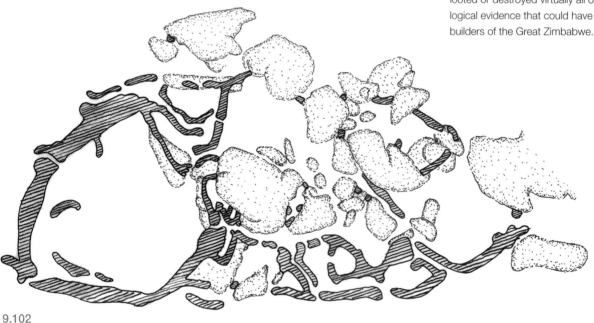

9.102

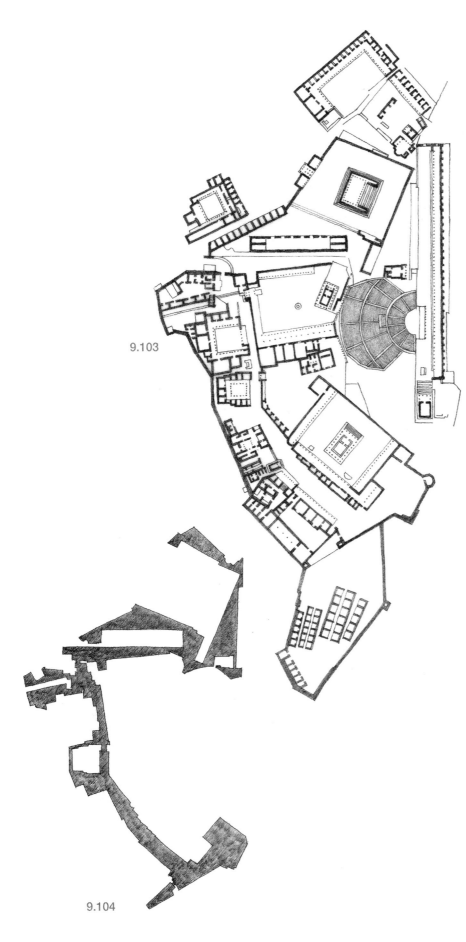

9.103

9.104

**Acropolis of Pergamon,
3rd century BCE. Plan.**

Under the rule of the Attalid dynasty (283–129
BCE), Pergamon ruled a vast area of Asia Minor and became one of the most influential
centers of Hellenistic culture. The Attalids allied
themselves with Rome and Thrace against the
Macedonians, and the city was eventually in-
corporated directly into the Roman Empire
upon the death of the last Attalid ruler. The
Acropolis of Pergamon was a composition of
standard Hellenistic building types, including
several temple precincts, a library, five palaces,
an arsenal, an agora, a theater, and a stoa. All
parts of the composition were designed to fit
into the irregular topography of a rocky ridge
overlooking the Caicus River Valley, but each
part was designed as an independent entity
with its own internal organization and orientation. As a result of the varying orientations and
geometries of the autonomous precincts, the
spaces between them became a complex set
of passages and civic spaces that wove
through the acropolis and led downhill to the
city below. Therefore, unlike Miletus, the designers of Pergamon made no attempt to subordinate its parts to a preconceived geometric
matrix, but rather allowed the city to develop
geomorphically, taking advantage of varying
views of the landscape, changing topography,
and differing qualities of light, and thus producing a complex composition of dissimilar objects
in an irregular grouping.

9.104

**Acropolis of Pergamon.
Circulation spaces.**

A figure/ground of the circulation spaces
shows that though it serves all of the major figural spaces and monuments of the acropolis, it
is a continuous figure in its own right. Its varying shape provides approaches and thresholds
that modify the perceived scale of buildings
with oblique views and forced perspectives.

9.105

Sanctuary of Delphi, Greece. Plan.

Delphi is a sacred site of great antiquity. In the Minoan culture, it was a place where mortals could communicate with the Mother Goddess. The conquering Dorians transformed it into the principal site of the Apollonian cult and secondarily into that of Dionysus. The precinct rests on a steep, south-facing slope enclosed by a wall that explicitly separates it from the outer, profane world. Among the contentious Greek city-states, Delphi was one of the few places of neutrality and refuge because it was the site of the most important oracle in the ancient Mediterranean world. At first glance, the plan appears chaotic, but its organization conforms to its ceremonial functions and the topography.

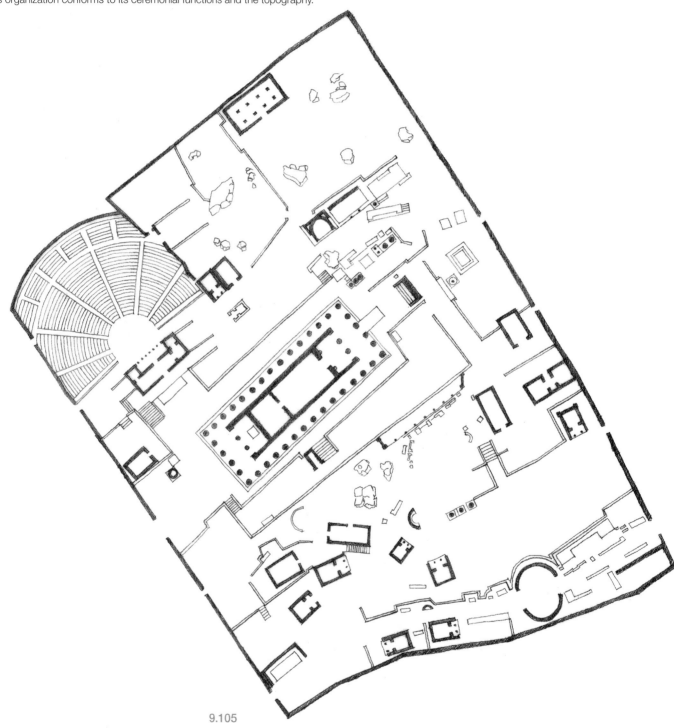

9.105

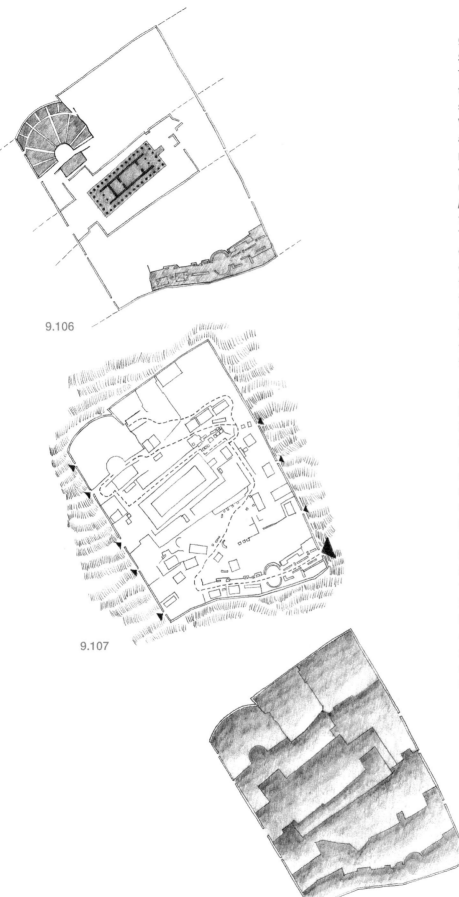

9.106

9.107

9.108

9.106
Sanctuary of Delphi. Precincts.
The sanctuary had three precincts. Lowest on the hillside was the main entry leading to a street flanked by sacrificial altars. This Sacred Way linked Delphi to the Sanctuary of Demeter at Eleusis. Halfway up the slope was the Temple of Apollo within an enclosure of retaining walls. The *cella* of the temple had four segments, the easternmost of which was the *pronaos*, in which supplicants would make offerings and present questions to the oracle. The next space was the *naos*, occupied by the officiating priests of the cult. The sibyl, the vehicle of the oracle, occupied the third space. The fourth space faced west and served as a place for rituals devoted to Dionysus for three months of the year. At the top of the slope was the third precinct within the sanctuary, with the theater embedded in the hillside overlooking the Temple of Apollo and the valley beyond.

9.107
Sanctuary of Delphi. Path.
In addition to the main entry at the southeast corner of the sanctuary, eight others pierce the encircling wall. These are minor, however, because the series of altars, treasuries, shrines, and temples that culminate in the theater originates at the principal gate where the internal path connects to the Sacred Way.

9.108
Sanctuary of Delphi. Terraces.
The rugged terrain of the mountainside coalesces within the walled precinct into interlocking terraces defined by retaining walls, staircases, and ramps to create a series of outdoor rooms or stages designed for specific rituals and ceremonies associated with the buildings along the uphill serpentine route.

CHAPTER TEN

SUBTRACTIVE SPACES AND THE DEEP WALL

THE CONVENTIONAL APPROACH TO DESIGNING AN ensemble of spaces is to consider the mass of a building as a thin shell enclosing volumes added one to another. However, the opposite approach is possible as well: space can appear by subtraction rather than addition. The Monastery of Geghard in Armenia illustrates the literal and figurative interpretations of this concept (10.1). Three of the chapels are subtractive spaces, excavated from a cliff face. There are no actual walls and no building exterior for these, only volumes that appear by the extraction of mass. In contrast, the main church stands in the open air, and its assembly space, the *gavit*, was partially excavated and partially in the open air. However, the plans of those structures in the open suggest that their interior volumes resulted from subtracting mass from an imagined solid block of stone similar to those in solid rock. This was the traditional Armenian method of shaping interior space, as shown in the five typical church plans presented here (10.2). The conceptual basis is a solid block of masonry from which the architect has subtracted mass to produce interior space. A plan of a royal bath in the city of Fatehpur Sikri in India (10.3) reveals a similar approach, as does the plan of the 18th-century Williams-Wynn House in London by Robert Adam (10.4), where the volumes of all of the formal reception rooms appear to have been sculpted out of a solid, leaving behind a complex poché.

We may also imagine the 12th-century keep of Dover Castle to be a solid masonry cube, 95 feet on each side, its interior space resulting from subtraction (10.5–10.8). The pattern changes for each of the four main levels, but the principal living spaces are consistently in the center, with ancillary spaces on the periphery. Similarly, the plan for a group of madrassas and mausoleums built in Cairo by the Mamluks in the 13th and 14th centuries suggests that the main spaces appeared by the subtraction of mass from a solid block, leaving behind a poché that incorporates all of the secondary functions (10.9, 10.10). This approach was common in Arab

Islamic architecture, because in that tradition there was no need for any correspondence between the forms of a building's interior and those of its exterior. For example, from the exterior of the Sultan Hassan Mosque in Cairo, one has no idea of the form of the volume at its center; likewise, when in that space one is entirely alienated from the surrounding poché as well as from the exterior form of the building (10.11, 10.12).

A more figurative interpretation of subtractive space is the use of a "deep wall." The plan of a house in Kandahar, Afghanistan, reveals the deep wall to be a traditional device in some cultures (10.13, 10.14). The house as a whole is a deep wall surrounding the courtyard, while interior living spaces are the result of carving out the deep walls, an idea repeated in the configuration of each room: every room is composed of a deep wall surrounding a central open space, and niches carved out of the wall hold all of the family's possessions. The Afghan house is thus an example of a self-similar object in which the same idea manifests itself at different scales. Louis I. Kahn used the deep wall extensively in his work for two reasons: it provides a clear hierarchy between the primary space at the center and subsidiary spaces on the periphery, and it creates opportunities to manipulate natural light through its thickness. Two among many of his projects serve to illustrate the strategy. The First Unitarian Church and School in Rochester, New York, embeds the school spaces within a deep wall to protect the sacred space in the center (10.15). Kahn used the same idea for his proposal for the Hurva Synagogue in Jerusalem, in which the deep wall is composed of chapels (10.16). In both cases, the principal source of light for the central space is from the roof; the deep wall provides a secondary source of light.

The deep wall is useful for modern residential projects also. Luigi Snozzi created a deep wall around the living spaces of an apartment building in Lugano, Switzerland, by locating all of the service functions—kitchens and bathrooms—on the periphery (10.17, 10.18). Natural light enters the central spaces through gaps that serve as private terraces between these solid forms. A freestanding house in Argentina by Lacroze Miguens Prati uses a series of deep walls both longitudinally and laterally to organize structure, to control natural light, and to incorporate all of the subsidiary and service functions of the house (10.19–10.22). The result is a powerfully layered spatial form.

In pre-modern examples, design by subtraction relied on massive forms and the extensive use of poché to create figural interior spaces. We experience these spaces as cavities in the body of the building. This indicates a fundamentally different attitude toward architectural space than what we find in much of conventional modern practice. Conceptually carving out space from a form suggests a preference for a particular sculptural quality of space that the additive approach (which is generally devoted to maximizing the quantity of space) cannot provide. Though contemporary architects have largely abandoned the extensive use of poché, the deep wall provides some of the benefits of subtractive space, such as embedding secondary functions in a mass that can then be used sculpturally either as an object in its own right or as a means to shape spaces.

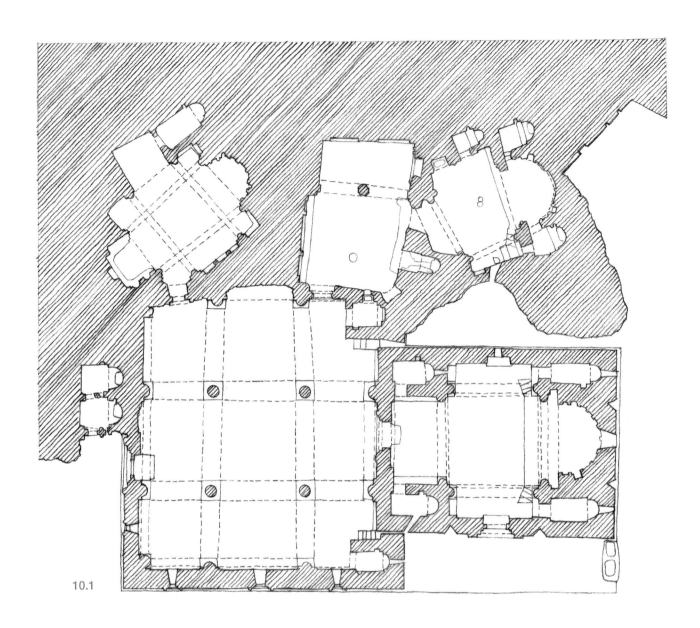

10.1

Monastery of Geghard, Kotayk', Armenia, 12th to 13th centuries. Plan.

The construction of buildings as volumes in solid rock occurred in many locations around the eastern Mediterranean and the South Asian subcontinent: Abu Simbel on the Nile; the burial chambers of Naqsh-e-Rustam in Persia; various sites in Phrygia, Lycia, and Pamphilia in Asia Minor; Buddhist shrines in India; Petra; and sites in Greece and Palestine. Though they have a precise architectural interior comparable to a building in the open, they have no exterior other than a facade and are negative forms, as distinct from the positive forms of buildings in the round. Geghard is a particularly interesting example, since it unites positive and negative forms. One component of the architectural ensemble, the square-planned *gavit* that serves as a meeting hall and the entrance to the church, is partially negative and partially positive. Furthermore, this structure leads directly to the entirely positive form of the church as well as to the entirely negative forms of the smaller chapels cut out of the rock. In the open air, we can perceive a building's orientation simply because we see it in relation to the landscape and light. However, the negative forms dispense with orientation since they are not forms in space and because their illumination comes from apertures directly above. The church and the *gavit* also have a direct connection with one another, as if the church inserted itself into the *gavit*. In contrast, the chapels connect to the *gavit* by means of specialized articulating spaces, as if they plugged into it.

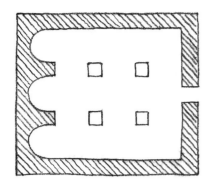

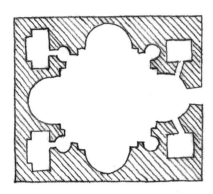

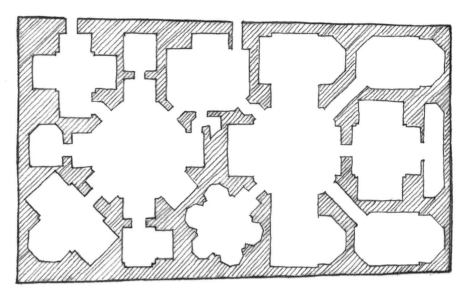

10.3

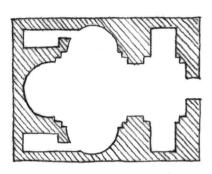

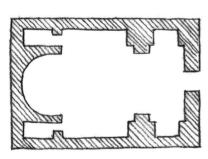

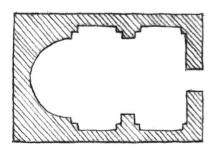

10.2

10.2

Medieval Armenian Church Plan Types. Schematic plans.

Though varied in detail, the plans of medieval Armenian churches reveal a consistent attitude toward architectural space. Conceptually, Armenian architects produced space by subtracting mass from a solid, even if the building was an object in the open air. This was in direct contradiction to the development of medieval architecture in western Europe, where space became increasingly modular and extended. Cathedrals of the High Gothic eventually became translucent skeletal frames. In contrast, these examples illustrate a predilection for a massive form in the round that encloses a compact figural space.

10.3

Baths at Fatehpur Sikri, Uttar Pradesh, India, 1570. Plan.

The spatial conception of the baths at Fatehpur Sikri is in direct opposition to that of the palaces they serve and to the organization of the city as a whole (see the Raja Birbal Pavilion, 9.5). The entire ensemble of palaces, pavilions, kiosks, gardens, and pools is an extrapolation of a two-dimensional square grid. The city's trabeated structure is an additive, modular approach to design in which we perceive architecture as a positive figure in space. The baths of Fatehpur Sikri are the only exception to this rule. Conceptually, they are solid blocks of masonry from which space emerges by subtraction, and the unique shapes of their interior spaces are not perceptible on their exterior. These are two entirely different ways of creating and perceiving architectural form and space.

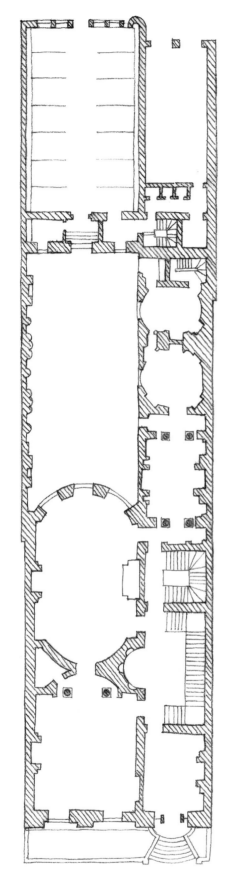

10.4

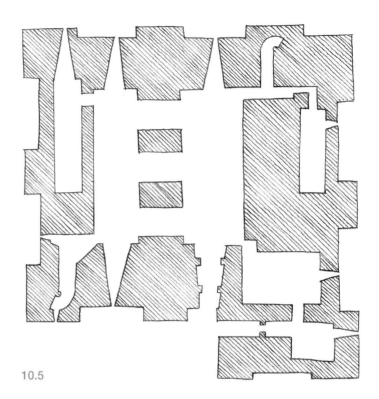

10.5

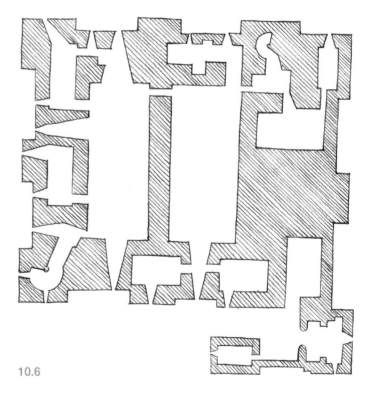

10.6

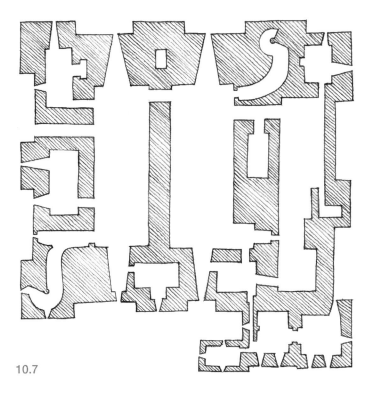

10.7

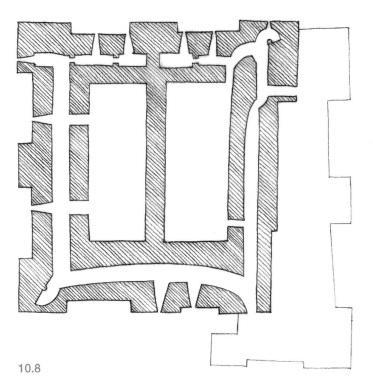

10.8

10.4
Williams-Wynn House, Saint James Square, London, 1775. Robert Adam. Plan.
The intention of the plan was to create a hierarchical sequence of spaces, each with a unique character, to support a formal social choreography. Within two parallel longitudinal bays, the spaces vary with respect to axes of symmetry, proportions, and orientations. The plan suggests that interior volumes result from the subtraction of mass from the whole, leaving figural spaces and residual poché.

10.5
Dover Castle Keep, Kent, United Kingdom, 1180–90. First-level plan.
There is evidence of an Iron Age earthworks and an Anglo-Saxon fort on the site of the castle. William the Conqueror made some additions, but it was Henry II who built the castle keep in the 12th century as a 95-foot cube. Conceptually, interior spaces appear to be the result of carving out a massive block of stone. The royal apartments were on the second level, consisting primarily of two great halls surrounded by ancillary spaces. Two winding stairs at diagonal corners served all four levels. Louis I. Kahn expressed an admiration for the luminous quality of castle interiors, produced by sunlight penetrating an extremely deep poché, an effect he strove to re-create in many of his projects.

10.6
Dover Castle Keep, Second-level plan.

10.7
Dover Castle Keep, Third-level plan.

10.8
Dover Castle Keep, Fourth-level plan.

10.9

Madrassa and Mausoleum Group, Cairo, 13th and 14th centuries. Plan.

From left to right: Madrassa of Sultan Qala'un, 1285
Mausoleum of Sultan Qala'un, 1285
Madrassa of al-Nasr Muhammad, 1304
Mausoleum of al-Nasr Muhammad, 1304
Madrassa of Sultan Barquq, 1386
Madrassa and Mausoleum of al-Kamil, 1225

Mamluk sultans constructed these connected buildings, which occupied the western half of the wide north-south avenue at the center of the 10th-century city of al-Qahira, the medieval core of Cairo. The orientation of the principal interior spaces toward Mecca does not correspond with the alignment of the secular street. Likewise, the facades of the buildings have little to do with the organization of their interiors. All entrances are via corridors that penetrate deeply into the building mass and require at least one turn before entering the main spaces, a technique that emphatically separates the sacred spaces from the secular city.

10.9

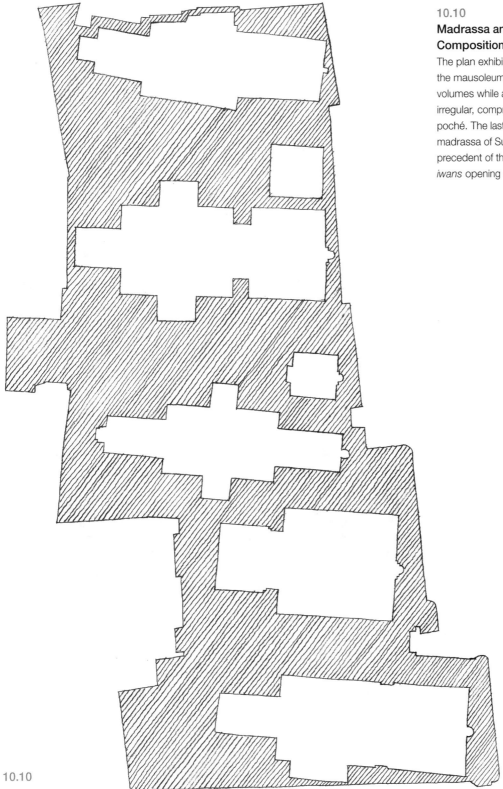

10.10

Madrassa and Mausoleum Group, Cairo. Composition.

The plan exhibits a strong hierarchy of spaces: the mausoleums and madrassas are large figural volumes while all subsidiary spaces are small and irregular, comprising a continuous enveloping poché. The last mosque built in the series, the madrassa of Sultan Barquqs, follows the precedent of the Mosque of Hassan, with four *iwans* opening onto a central paradise garden.

10.11
Sultan Hassan Mosque-Madrassa, 1359. Plan.

The Sultan Hassan complex is the apotheosis of Cairene Mamluk architecture. Paired with the al-Rifā'i Mosque, it marks the southern terminus of a long spine of secular and religious structures that runs through the medieval core of Cairo (see 6.18). The two buildings share a *maidan*, or large open market space, and form a gateway to the citadel. The Sultan Hassan Mosque is a four-*iwan* type, that is, a huge cruciform plan. The *iwans* housed teachers of the four schools of theological law, and according to an ancient custom, the central space represented paradise. The deepest *iwan* faces Mecca, and beyond it is the mausoleum. Surrounding these is a labyrinth of rooms, courts, and corridors that forms the madrassa, a theological school.

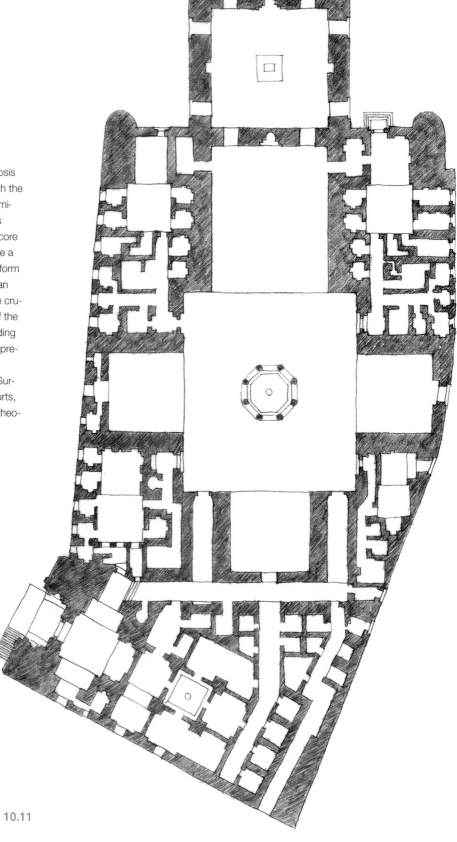

10.11

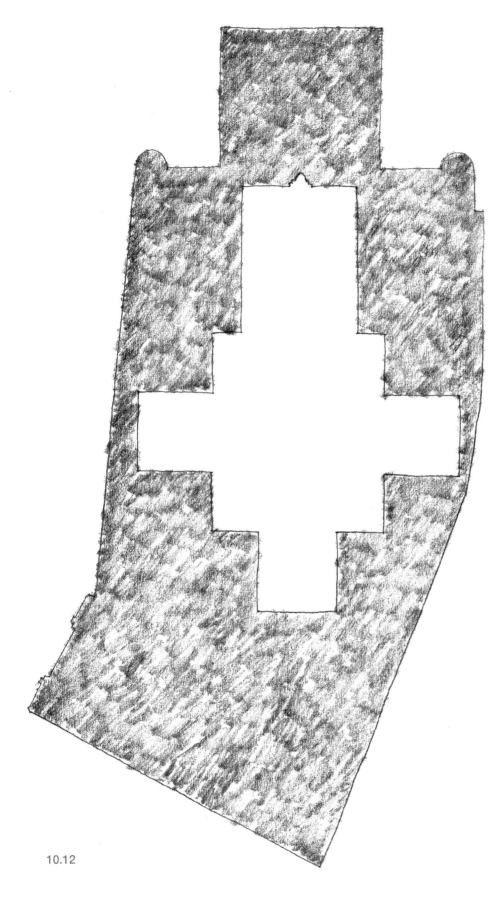

10.12

Sultan Hassan Mosque-Madrasa. Composition.

Typically, Islamic architecture emphasizes the perfection of an interior space with little or no regard for its correspondence with the exterior or the site. The Hassan complex is one of the best examples of this custom, since in addition to the imposition of the immense central space unrelated to the world outside, the maze of spaces that surrounds it comprises a thick inhabited poché with no formal relation to either the center or the periphery. It could be argued that the site was entirely unsuited for this architectural program. The solution was to force a preconceived form into it and to allow all of the variable elements of the program to inhabit the residual space.

10.12

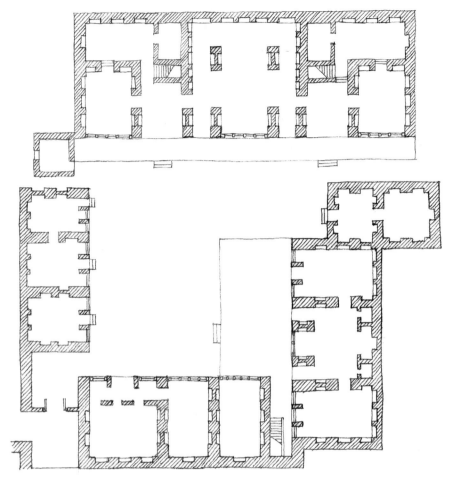

10.13

10.13
Compound House, Kandahar, Afghanistan, 20th Century. Plan. (After Hallet & Samizay.)

This urban house is an arrangement of rooms all facing into a central courtyard, separated from it by movable wooden shutters. The main entry is at the lower left into a small vestibule court that leads to a diagonal view of the main courtyard. Private family rooms are on the opposite side of the courtyard, raised on platforms. Its mud brick walls are thick for climatic purposes, and people sit on cushions and carpets on the floor rather than on furniture. Most of the rooms do not have specific functions; the family uses them for leisure, eating, or sleeping in response to diurnal and seasonal cycles.

10.14
Compound House, Kandahar. Composition.

The urban Afghan house is an example of a self-similar object; it uses the same pattern of organization at two scales. The house, taken as a whole, is a deep wall enclosing the principal room, the courtyard. Individual rooms are, in effect, large niches in the deep wall that permit a variety of household functions. Similarly, each room within the house is a deep wall surrounding an open central space, its carved niches providing storage for all domestic accoutrements used in that room.

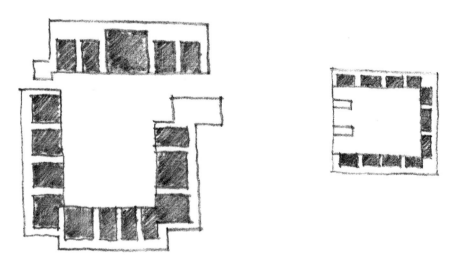

10.14

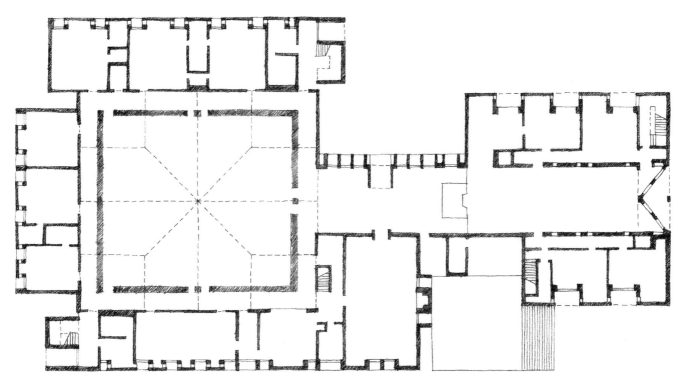

10.15

10.15
First Unitarian Church and School, Rochester,
New York, 1959–69. Louis I. Kahn. Plan.

Kahn's parti is similar to that of the Unity Temple in Oak Park, Illinois, that Frank Lloyd Wright built in 1905. Both architects used a bipartite organization by which a central entrance loggia separates the formal ceremonial space from support functions. The forms of both buildings are austere, elaborated cubic compositions—Wright's in concrete, and Kahn's in brick. However, Kahn's program was more complex, with the inclusion of a school. His insight was to avoid the obvious approach. Instead of juxtaposing the congregational space and the school as separate institutions, he wrapped the school around the congregational space, separating the two functions with an ambulatory that shares the light entering from above through four corner towers. This was consistent with one of his favorite motifs, the thick protective wall surrounding a sacred, top-lit center. While the rooms of the school serve as a thick wall, Kahn repeated the motif at a smaller scale in the outer wall of the school by shaping it as a series of deep niches holding recessed windows. In short, the building is a self-similar object, using the deep wall at two scales. Together with the skylights, the technique guarantees that all natural light entering the building, either laterally or vertically, reflects off several interior surfaces before illuminating the interior.

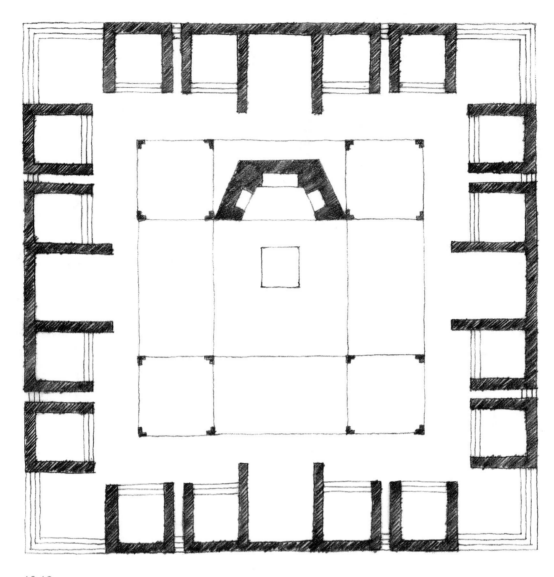

10.16

10.16
**Hurva ("the ruins") Synagogue, Jerusalem, Israel (first proposal), 1968.
Louis I. Kahn. Proposed plan.**

The original synagogue on this site, in a 19th-century Ottoman style, was blown up
during the Arab-Israeli War of 1948. Between 1968 and 1973, Kahn produced three
plans for its reconstruction, each of which would have left the ruins of the old synagogue in place as a memorial garden and located the new structure on an adjacent
site. He once again utilized the motif of a deep outer wall protecting a sacred center
illuminated from above, this time through four inverted pyramids at the corners of the
space. The outer wall would have appeared to be 40-foot-high stone piers on the exterior; on the interior they were to serve as alcoves for meditation or individual prayer.
An ambulatory, which could have also been used as additional prayer space for the
Sabbath and festivals, mediated between the outer wall and the central space.
Kahn's design seemed too forceful for the context, as it would have stood in high
contrast to the historical core of the Old City of Jerusalem and would have competed
in importance with the nearby Western Wall. Eventually, the synagogue was recon-
structed as a copy of the original.

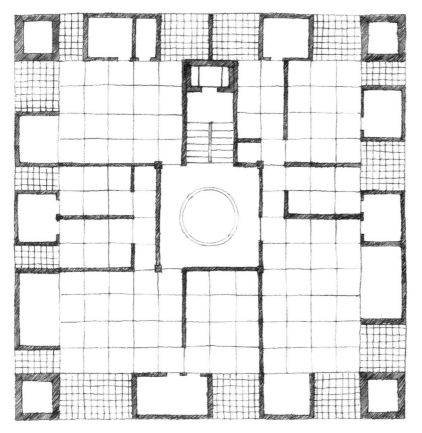

10.17

10.17

Apartment House "Martinelli," Lugano, Switzerland, 1971. Luigi Snozzi. Plan.

Four hollow corner piers, with all of the baths, kitchens, and terraces between them, create a deep wall on the exterior of this project. The interior residential units vary in size and configuration within the limitations of a square module, and at the core is a skylit atrium. As a result, every interior room has at least one terrace that acts as an exterior room wedged between bath and kitchen units. These units, which form the deep wall, also modify the sunlight and increase privacy.

10.18

Apartment House "Martinelli." Composition.

The strategy of placing all baths and kitchens on the exterior of the building in a deep wall creates an opportunity for varying the pattern of the building's elevations depending on the planning of individual apartment units. As long as plumbing chases are placed vertically, the locations of baths and kitchens may slide laterally through the deep wall.

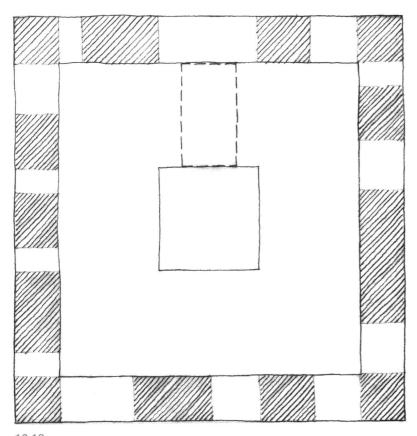

10.18

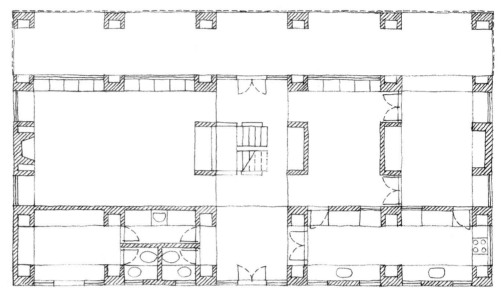

10.19

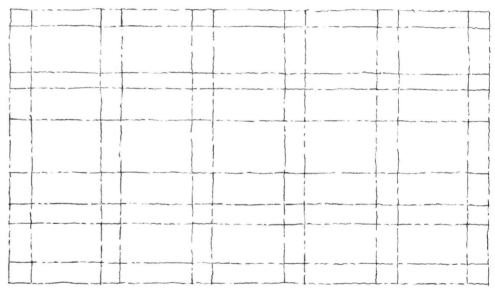

10.20

10.19
House in San Isidro, Buenos Aires, Argentina, 1981. Lacroze Miguens Prati. Ground-floor plan.
A grid consisting of twelve pairs of load-bearing brick piers resolves the demands of the program and the context. On the north side, the piers form a veranda that buffers the interior from the summer sun and serves to expand interior living spaces. In contrast, on the south side the piers fuse with infill brick walls to form a dense bar of service spaces. Between these two zones a series of screen walls containing fireplaces and closets demarcate the principal ground-floor living spaces.

10.20
House in San Isidro. Tartan grid.
The grid produces three zones from south to north and five zones east to west, a system that provides for a variety of spaces without losing a sense of wholeness and continuity.

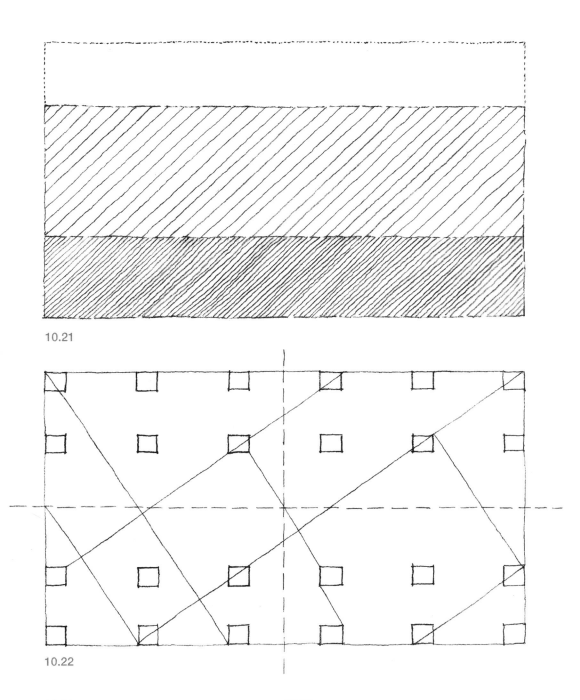

10.21

10.22

10.21

House in San Isidro. Spatial Layering.

Layering of space from south to north (that is, from back to front) is the principal organizational concept of the house. The degree of mass in the house diminishes from south to north, and consequently, the degree of light and openness increases in that direction as well.

10.22

House in San Isidro. Proportion.

Regulating lines reveal that one encounters the same proportion at all scales of the grid of piers— from the space between a pair of piers to large ensembles. This proportion operates in section and elevation as well.

CHAPTER ELEVEN
ARTICULATED SKIN

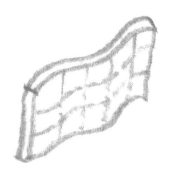

CONSIDER THE ARCHITECTURE OF OUR OWN BODIES. We require an entirely predictable arrangement of internal organs, bones, and muscles: any deviation from the norm is an anomaly, and often fatal. Our skin is a different matter. From person to person, there are great differences in texture and color. There is also considerable variation in the skin of a single individual; in addition to variations in texture and color, there are variations in sensitivity, elasticity, and porosity. A person's skin varies in contour to produce eyelids, nose, lips, and ears, and it has many other features embedded in it, such as hairs, pores, glands, and nails. Even eyes evolved from photosensitive skin, eventually becoming specialized structures. The muscles of our face allow us to communicate by distorting our flexible skin. So we find that while internally human bodies are highly standardized, the architecture of our skin is articulated to make each person a unique individual. Our skin is the physical boundary between the world and ourselves; it provides protection and regulates our temperature and water content, it allows us to sense the environment, and it is a highly malleable substance for expression. Not content with what nature provides, many of us add colors, designs, and even hardware to our skin to achieve even greater personalization.

We may consider buildings analogously when their design is heavily invested in the unique properties of the boundary between internal spaces and the surrounding environment—in other words, the architectural skin. In some cases, such as Herod's fortress of Masada, the building is almost entirely composed of the boundary condition, in this case a wall that varies in thickness and function (11.1). The Masada wall had many specialized structures embedded in it, and even the large palace structures were internal extensions of it. Not far from Masada is the fortress of Krak des Chevaliers, a 12th-century crusader castle (11.2, 11.3). It, too, had an articulated skin, a wall that varied considerably in character depending on its orientation, and also a variety of specialized structures—such as towers, ramparts, and various buildings—embedded in it. Unlike Masada, the skin of Krak des Chavaliers folded back upon itself to create the principal entrance. A leper colony in Chopta Taluka, India, has almost all of its functions embedded in a peripheral structure that acts as a deep wall protecting a courtyard from the harsh environment (11.4). The wall acts much like a thick skin that varies in porosity to protect the courtyard. The al-Hakim Mosque is in a dense neighborhood of Isfahan, Iran (11.5–11.9). In addition to providing interior spaces suitably oriented for prayer, the building needs to segregate its central courtyard from its noisy and dirty surroundings. The design solution was to construct two circuit walls, one within the other. The outer wall accommodates the intricacies of the neighborhood and is therefore highly irregular in shape. The inner wall, however, is composed of a bilaterally symmetrical set of piers and columns forming a rectangle in the proportion of 2:√3; the four sides of the courtyard comprise the principal elevation of the mosque. A variety of prayer spaces are set between these two walls, and the entire ensemble of these forms a thick skin, ensuring the requisite purity and tranquility of the courtyard.

Many buildings are suited to a standard plan of their type, while their exteriors often offer the greatest latitude for design. The principal opportunity to shape the architectural character of such a building is in its articulated skin, most often its facade. The Palazzo Rucellai in Florence by Alberti and Rosselino is a case in point (11.10). Its interior, a composite of several medieval houses, follows a plan conventional for its type. The identity of the building resides entirely in its facade, which is an essay in stone on the most advanced theories of proportion and form of the time. The pattern of apertures and pilasters on the facade has nothing at all to do with the actual structure of the building or the organization of interior spaces. In this respect, it is a scenographic diagram, a stage set for the small piazza in front of it. Similarly, the facade of the Ca d'Oro was applied to a basic box that contained a standard Venetian palace plan (11.11, 11.12). In this case, the division into two parts corresponds to a division of the interior, but the architect exaggerated the differences between parts on the exterior for pictorial purposes. Despite its apparent simplicity, the facade of the Ca d'Oro employs a complex visual device—a set of multiple centerlines that animates the elevation, never allowing one's eye to come to rest as it surveys the many relations among the parts.

John Nash used an articulated skin for a different purpose in his design for a curved row of upper-class houses called Crescent Park in London (11.13). Similar to the Rucellai, it had a facade that created a theatrical backdrop for the space before it, but the house interiors it screened from view were not necessarily standardized. In fact, Nash had little concern for how individual clients designed their houses. For him, the architecture of the Crescent was entirely that of the facade. Another articulated skin that, in its uniformity, masks a variety of spaces behind it, is that of the Reliance Building, designed by Charles B. Atwood (11.14). Though built in 1895, it is still one of the most elegant tall buildings in Chicago by virtue of its delicate, undulating skin. Otherwise, it has a standard arrangement of rooms surrounding a central core.

Another way in which the skin of a building can come to dominate its identity is by projecting the interior organization onto the exterior. In the most interesting cases, this is not a matter of fact but rather a technique of clever compositional exaggeration. One elevation of a courtyard for the 19th-century Sabsiri House in Cairo is a playful composition of a variety of apertures obviously designed for a pictorial effect by which elements seem to advance or recede depending on their scale and complexity (11.15). Edward Godwin had a similar interest in his composition of the facade of the "White House" in Chelsea, London, for James McNeill Whistler (11.16, 11.18, 11.19). He exaggerated apertures in size, both large and small, as well as in complexity, and set them off against a datum string course to suggest a foreground and a background on a perfectly flat surface. This was a painterly device entirely consistent with the work of Godwin's client. Whistler often inserted an artificially high horizon line behind his monumental portrait figures, such as that of Mrs. Frederick R. Leyland, to create an uncomfortable spatial illusion, as if the floor were tilted forward and the space surrounding the figure were flattened as a consequence (11.17). Another example is the Seigneurale of Segovia, the mayor's residence in that city, built in the 16th century (11.20–11.24). It retains strong Moorish influences in its completely tiled facade punctured by windows of various shapes. As in Godwin's design, the position of some windows in relation to a horizon line breaks the uniformly flat surface in two, the upper surface appearing to be slightly behind the other. Apertures correspond to spaces of the interior behind them, but they are proportioned and detailed to reinforce a pictorial impression on the facade. The effect is similar to a Cubist landscape in which the ground plane tilts downward from a horizon with the sky rising above, both compressed into a shallow space.

An articulated skin can be a forceful expression of movement as well. Basic to understanding the form of the chapel of Notre Dame du Haut at Ronchamp by Le Corbusier is to recognize it as a pilgrimage church with an ambulatory on the exterior (11.25). Its orientation in respect to one's initial approach and the undulation of its skin, alternating between concave and convex surfaces, induce a clockwise circumambulation. A variety of patterns and forms eventually lead to a seating area in front of the outdoor altar, rewarding the pilgrim for following the building's implicit rotation. The late 20th-century Sainsbury Wing of the National Gallery of Art in London, by Venturi, Rauch, Scott Brown & Associates, uses an articulated skin to draw pedestrians along Pall Mall toward the original 19th-century building that faces Trafalgar Square (11.26). The skin of the new addition is articulated with Neoclassical pilasters similar to those of the older building, but these compress as they approach the older building as if the skin were crumpled, thus expressing, in a touch of Postmodernist irony, its role as a historicist veneer on a modern structure.

One of the tenets of Modernism in the early 20th century was that the skin of a building should be essentially passive, that it should be simply a factual projection of the interior organization of the building onto the exterior. It should not be expressive in its own right or have an identity independent of the rational arrangement of spaces behind it. This attitude derived from admiration for the machine as an "honest" form that conveys is true character without the application of arbitrary stylization or personal taste. In addition, particularly among European theorists, it reflected an egalitarian and socialist political ideology. A purely factual public image of a building absolved it of any suggestions of social class, history, or dated cultural conventions. Since the skins of buildings determine the character of streets and other public spaces, the character of the public realm suffered. Not all architects subscribed to the "hair shirt" theory of design espoused by hardcore Modernists, and in the late 20th century the inevitable overreaction resulted in a variety of efforts to revitalize the character of architectural skins. Unfortunately, many Postmodern projects lacked the intellectual and aesthetic rigor of their predecessors and now appear flippant and shallow.

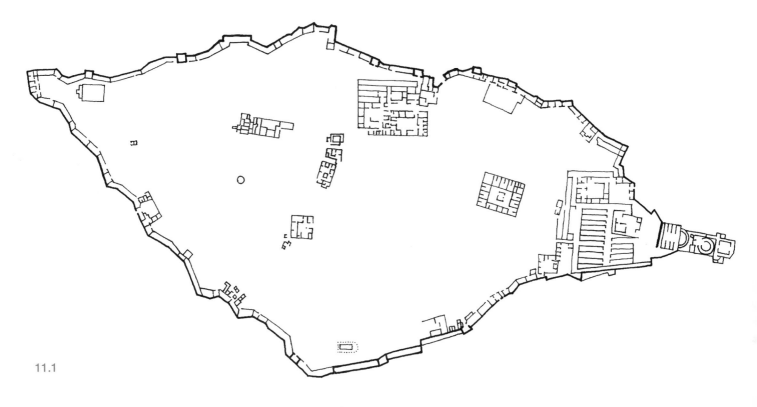

11.1

11.1

Masada, 1st century BCE. Plan.

Masada ("fortress" in Hebrew) occupies a high, isolated plateau in the Judean Desert overlooking the Dead Sea. A rhomboid in shape, the fortress is approximately 1,968 feet long and 984 feet wide. Most of the architecture on the plateau consists of a casement wall along the edge 4,593 feet long and 20 feet wide that contains many storerooms, barracks, bastions, and towers. Herod seized the site around 42 BCE and used it initially to secure his family and administration when he traveled to Rome in 40 BCE. He built two palaces within the fortress, one of which consists of three terraces with pleasure pavilions on the northern promontory overlooking the valley below. The western palace beside the main gate was for administrative and ceremonial functions. There were also extensive storehouses and cisterns capable of sustaining thousands of people for long periods. Because of its large size and complexity, Masada is a good example of an architecture that is in essence an articulated skin; all of the principal architectural features of the site fit into the encircling wall—the skin—or are extensions of it.

11.2

Krak des Chevaliers, Syria, 1170–1250. Plan.

Built on the foundations of an earlier Kurdish castle, the Krak des Chevaliers dominated a strategic pass between the Mediterranean and the inland cities of Homs and Hama on the Orontes River. A castle that the Kurds erected fell to the Count of Toulouse in 1099, and then the crusaders, led by Tancred of Antioch, began a process of strengthening and enlarging the castle until it could house a garrison of 2,000. The Krak passed into the hands of the Count of Tripoli, who handed it on in 1142 to the military-monastic Order of Hospitallers. They held it for 130 years until they surrendered it to the Mamluk sultan Baybars on April 8, 1271. The castle stands on a massive outcrop of the Gebel Alawi overlooking the river valley, with two concentric walls enclosing a moat. The inner wall is considerably higher than the outer one, so the defenders could always dominate their besiegers. Folding back upon itself to create a long, serpentine entry passage, the outer wall has a variety of structures built into it to produce an articulated skin.

11.3

Krak des Chevaliers. Schematic plan.

The articulated skin folds to create the entrance. Though connected and to some degree continuous with the skin, the central buildings are a separate composition of rectangular structures.

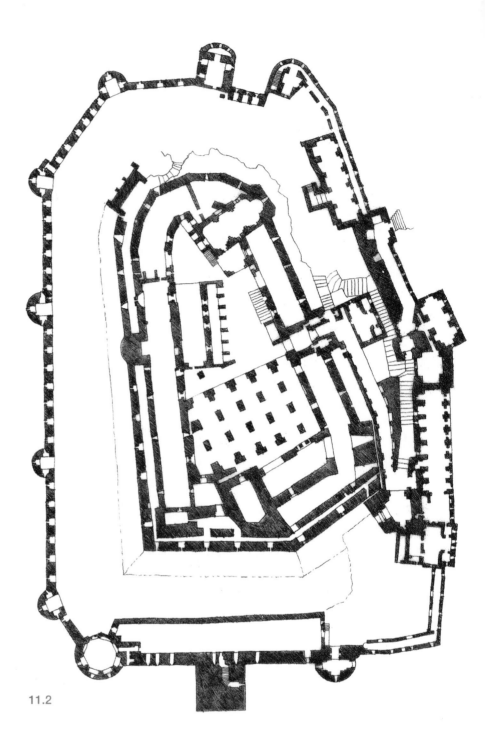

11.2

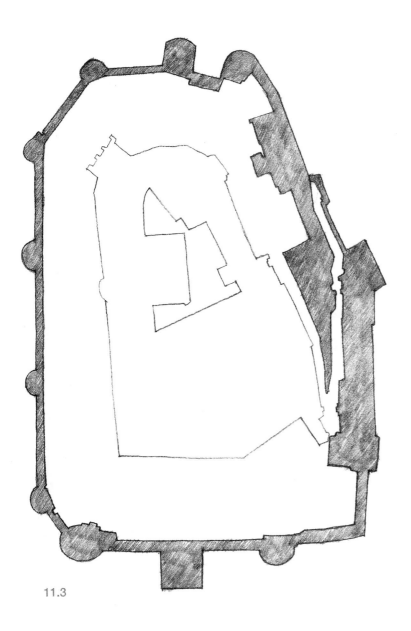

11.3

11.4

Leper Colony, Chopta Taluka, India, 1985. Per Christian Brynildsen and Jan Olav Jensen. Plan.

The plan consists of two sets of forms. One set comprises a thick wall that protects a courtyard from the harsh environment. The other is a collection of sculptural forms within the courtyard, each with a specialized function. Though the wall is in effect a skin of uniform thickness (constrained by the simple masonry construction), it nevertheless allows for a variety of spaces, including residences for patients and staff, offices, and treatment rooms. The skin is semipermeable, open or closed to the exterior or to the interior depending on the requirements of specific functions. This accomplishes two objectives: it establishes a powerful sense of place by defining a boundary around a communal space, and it provides diversity and individuality. Within the courtyard, even the most prosaic activity—sitting or bathing—uses an abstract form that imparts a sense of ritualistic importance.

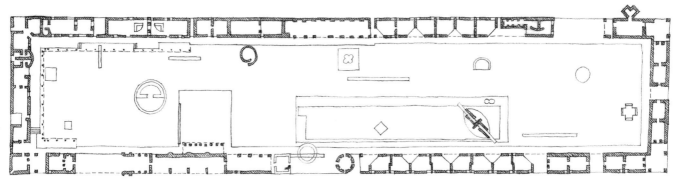

11.4

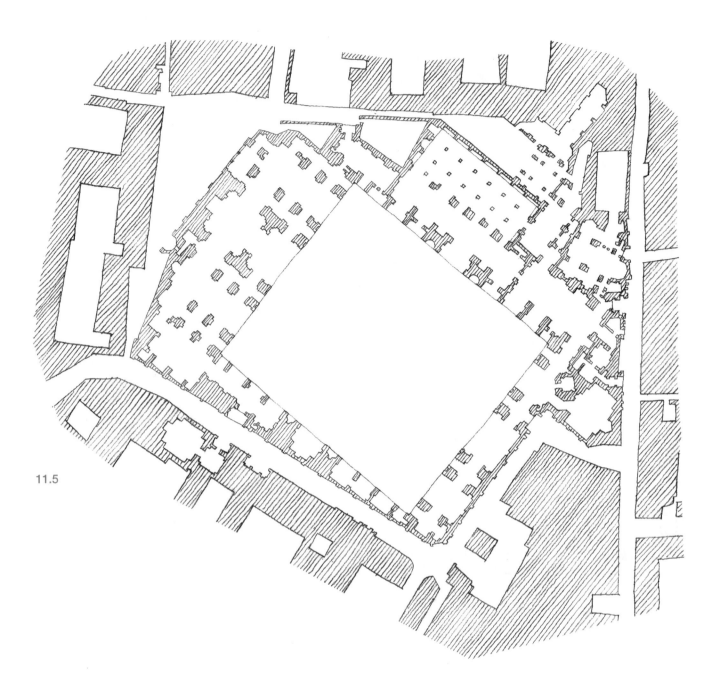

11.5

11.5

Al-Hakim Mosque, Isfahan, Iran. Plan.

The problem posed in the design of the al-Hakim Mosque involved inserting a regular figure into an irregular space. Its plan reflects its context: a tight-knit neighborhood of residential and commercial buildings. There is no *maidan*, or open space associated with a principal facade; in fact, there is no formal facade on the exterior of the building. Its form mediates between the need to accommodate the highly irregular character of its boundary condition relative to the city and the need for a sense of purity and perfection conducive to prayer at its core. The result is a gradation of form from a conditional boundary to an unconditional center.

11.6

Al-Hakim Mosque. Two walls.

The building solves the problem of its context by means of
two walls. An outer wall encloses the mosque and fits into all
of the irregularities of the context. It sits directly at the edges of
surrounding streets and is thus a continuous elevation seen
close up and in scale with the elevations of buildings directly
opposite it across the narrow streets. It deforms to fit the void
provided for it and deforms further to provide numerous small
entrances. The inner wall has an entirely different character. It
is of a monumental scale and encloses a regular geometric
figure, a rectangle subdivided into four quadrants according to
the Persian model of paradise. Whereas the outer wall has
small apertures in scale with the narrow streets they face, the
organization of the inner monumental wall depends on four
monumental *iwans*, or ceremonial gateways.

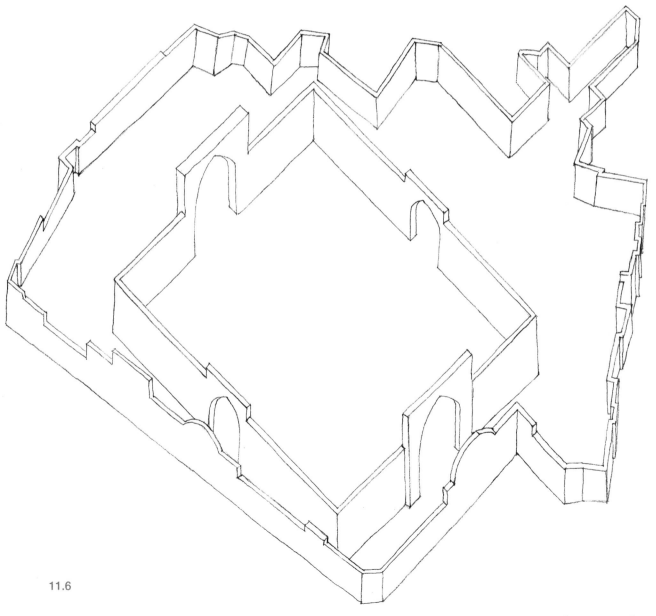

11.6

11.7

Al-Hakim Mosque. Entrances.

The space between the outer and inner walls
contains prayer halls and passages that connect the center to the periphery. Eight entrances serve people who approach the
mosque from the surrounding streets. These
entrances lead to passages that often turn several times before finally penetrating the inner
wall. As a result, someone entering the
mosque is absorbed into a series of close,
slightly disorienting and relatively dark, winding
spaces and then released into the expansive,
brightly lit *sahn*, or inner courtyard.

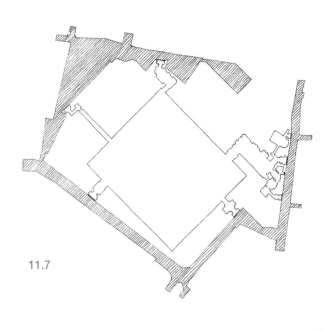

11.7

11.8

Al-Hakim Mosque. *Sahn*.

The *sahn* is a rectangle in the proportion of
2:√3. This proportion is true of the courtyard as
a whole, but also of each quadrant formed by
the central axes of the four *iwans*, the longitudinal axis establishing the mosque's orientation
toward Mecca. The wall that encloses the *sahn*
is the true monumental facade of the mosque,
a facade that is in the interior of the building
rather than on its exterior. Though the prayer
halls surrounding the *sahn* vary in form and
structure, they all resolve into two pairs of elevations for the *sahn*, a pair for the short sides
and another for the long sides. Together they
form the continuous facade of the inner wall.

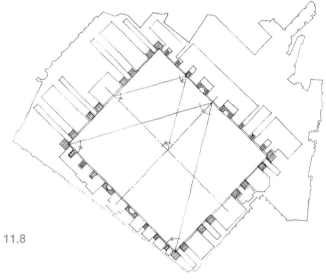

11.8

11.9

Al-Hakim Mosque. Ordering systems.

Two formal systems provide order for the
mosque: the structural grid of the *sahn* and the
qibla, or wall that indicates the direction of
Mecca. The two are directly related. When one
stands in the *sahn*, the correspondences of
structure across the space between the pairs
of enclosing elevations create a powerful organizing force—a tartan grid. This grid relates
directly through its principal centerline, through
the main prayer hall to the primary prayer
niche, the mihrab, in the *qibla* wall. Subsidiary
mihrabs in the continuous *qibla* serve to orient
worshipers in other prayer halls.

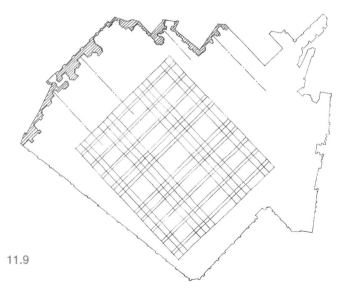

11.9

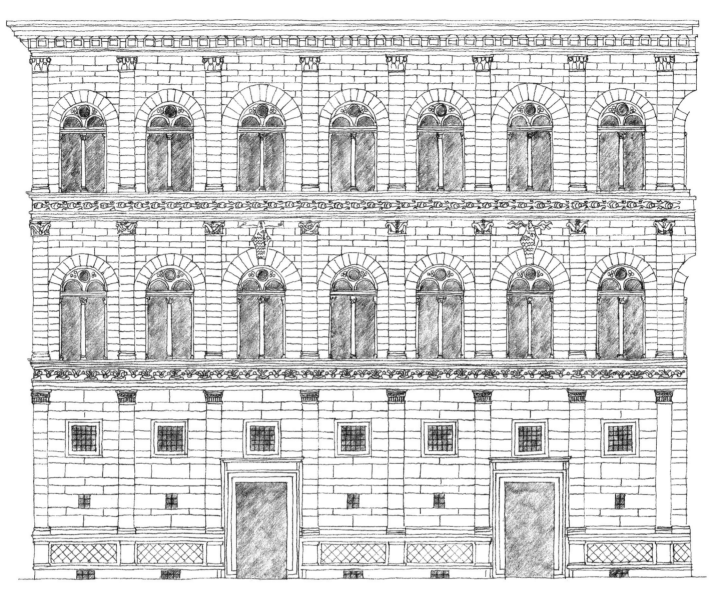

11.10

Palazzo Rucellai, Florence, 1446–51. Leon Battista Alberti and Bernardo Rossellino. Elevation.

The design by Alberti, executed by Rossellino, is only the thickness of the facade, the building's skin. Since the plan of the palazzo is a conglomerate of five preexisting medieval houses (three on the Via della Vigna Nuova and two behind them), there is no correlation between the internal organization of the building and its Renaissance skin. The facade is therefore a scenographic device intended to accomplish two objectives: to demonstrate a rationalist approach to design based upon Alberti's interpretation of Classical compositional principles, and to form one wall of an urban room, the Piazza Rucellai, in concert with the Loggia Rucellai, a companion piece designed by Alberti. The building skin is of *pietra forte*, a fine-grained sandstone. The detailing of the pilasters, rustication, ornament, and openings is nearly flat, thus creating architecture that is, in effect, a two-dimensional diagram of Alberti's theory of proportions.

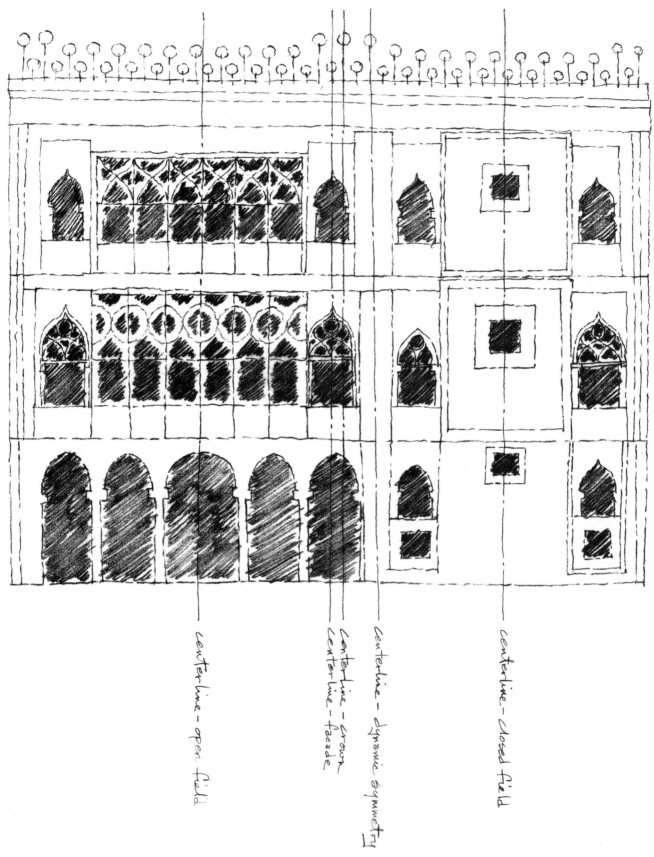

centerline - open field

centerline - crown
centerline - facade

centerline - dynamic symmetry

centerline - closed field

11.11

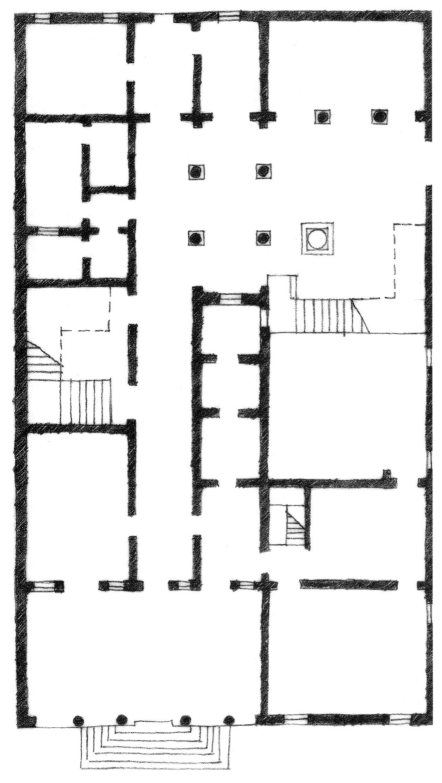

11.11
Ca d'Oro (Palazzo Contarini), Venice, 1430. Giovanni and Bartolomeo Bon. Elevation.

The composition of the principal elevation of the palazzo is an exercise in multiple centerlines, the purpose of which is to produce a pattern that visually oscillates. The first centerline establishes the dynamic symmetry of the facade by dividing the left, open portion from the right, closed portion. Though of unequal dimensions (the open portion comprises about 60 percent of the facade width) the two are comparable in visual weight because the simplicity and density of the closed portion balances the complexity of the open portion. A centerline for each of the two portions balances them individually. The pattern of merlons at the crown of the building creates a fourth centerline by virtue of the three taller merlons approximately at the center. This is not, however, the centerline of the facade. That fifth centerline passes through the fifth bay from the left. The result is a visual oscillation: though the composition as a whole is stable, our perception can never entirely come to rest because we subconsciously strive to identify the true centerline of the facade. Two notes of interest: the end bays on the *piano nobile*, or second level, are identical, which stabilizes the entire composition within the visual equivalent of parentheses. And the merlons were symbols of an ermine, the large white weasel emblematic of authority, dignity, purity, and honor, and thus associated with Venetian nobility and the owner's social status.

11.12
Ca d'Oro. Plan.

The plan reveals that the interior of the palazzo was entirely conventional for its time. Thus, the facade was clearly a compositional exercise in its own right, a work of art comprised of an articulated skin applied to a box.

11.13

11.13

Crescent Park, London, 1821. John Nash. View.

In addition to being an accomplished architect, Nash was a successful real estate developer. In this project, as with several others (e.g., Carlton House Terrace, Cumberland Terrace, Regent's Street and Park), Nash created an architecture that was little more than skin deep. By this means, he emphasized the theatrical character of urban spaces to serve the aspirations of his upper-class clientele. The uniform wall of Crescent Park masks a great variety of interior spaces behind it. The strictly conformist modularity of the wall allowed those who invested in the project to purchase any number of bays behind which they could construct their own houses in any way they wanted. The curve serves two purposes: it allows a viewer at any point to see the entire repetitive pattern of the design, and it gracefully embraces a park in which the principal social functions of the neighborhood occurred.

11.14

Reliance Building, Chicago, 1895. Charles B. Atwood (D. H. Burnham & Co.). View.

The Reliance Building is the most compelling example of the emergence of a new type of construction in Chicago in the late 19th century, a lightweight skin hung from a steel frame. Atwood's elegant composition took full advantage of a new technology by which the exterior skin did not have to support the building nor relate to the frame. The skin is glass and terra-cotta panels, its slender verticals and the narrow spandrels and mullions accentuating its transparency and lightness. Furthermore, the skin is nearly flat, with minimal projections and indentations, and therefore casts minimal shadows. The result is a highly rhythmic surface that folds around the frame like a piece of intricately lined paper. Atwood exaggerated this effect by stretching the windows (i.e., widening them) as they project outward in bays and contracting them between bays and at the corner. (Over fifty years later, Alvar Aalto used windows graphically in a similar way to accentuate the curvature of the Baker House at the Massachusetts Institute of Technology—see 13.21.) Atwood was not immune to the historical eclecticism of his time. Note that he emphasized the corner as a cluster of extremely slender columns rather than one large one, recalling a similar Gothic device.

11.14

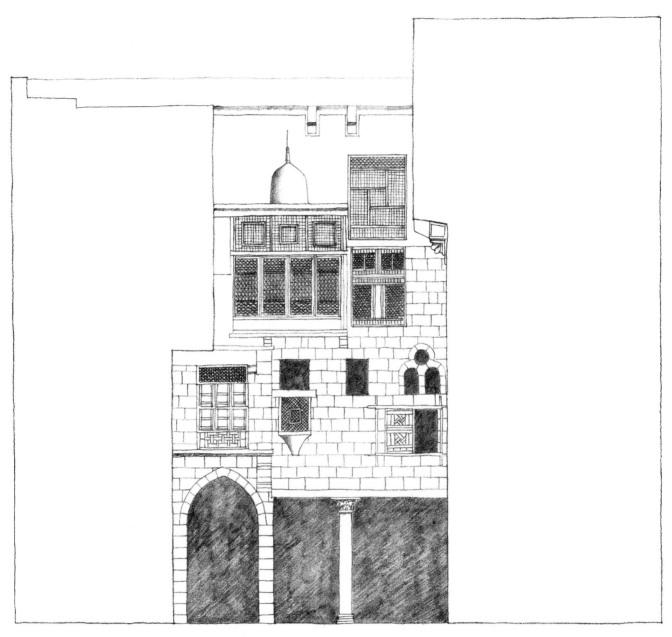

11.15

11.15

Sabsiri House, Cairo, Egypt, 19th century. East courtyard elevation.

This exuberant composition allows each element to be an entirely self-referential anecdote. However, it is not sufficient to say that the various openings and details merely correspond to the exigencies of interior organization. There is no attempt to enforce a unifying order, as each form and even each void is an object against the dressed stone background. Their varying scales and complexities imply a depth of field, some advancing and some receding in relation to the neutral wall surface. One's eyes never come to rest on a single element — a painterly approach to design by which a two-dimensional surface is treated as a sensual object in its totality rather than in its parts.

11.16

11.16

"White House," Chelsea, London, 1878. Edward Godwin. Elevation.
Godwin was an active member of the circle of avant-garde artists in Chelsea who
shared Whistler's radical ideas about art. It is not surprising, therefore, that his design
for Whistler's house bears a striking resemblance to the compositional ideas that
Whistler used in his paintings. Godwin approached the design of the facade in a
painterly fashion, arranging windows, doors, and ornament as if they were figures on
a canvas and playing the figures off against one another and against an artificial datum, or horizon line.

11.17

Portrait of Mrs. Frederick R. Leyland, 1873. James McNeill Whistler.

Whistler was a leader of a group of artists who believed art had its own rules of form and meaning beyond conventions of representation. Japanese and Chinese prints became fashionable in England and Europe in this period. Whistler enthusiastically adopted the pictorial technique common in these prints, flattening space by tilting down the horizontal plane of the floor so it became continuous with the background and emphasizing the foreground figure as a silhouette. In his portrait of Mrs. Leyland, for example, the floor and rear wall became a single plane. Their intersection is merely a horizontal band, a datum that establishes a relative scale in two dimensions. The figure appears to float in space before it, its scale determined by its relationship to the dark band.

11.17

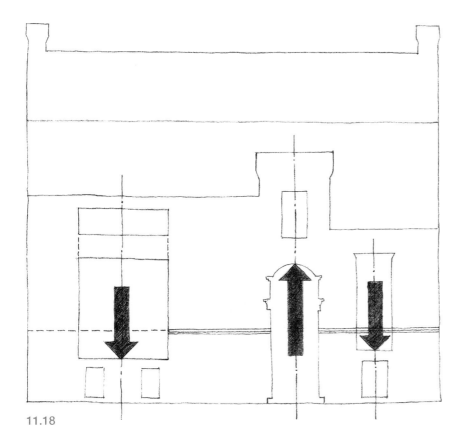

11.18

11.18

"White House," London. Vertical forces.

The three major figures in the composition alternate in their apparent forces: downward, upward, and then downward through the datum. Subsidiary figures on vertical axes reinforce each one: two small windows on the left, one window in the center above the main door, and a single window on the right.

11.19

"White House," London. Figures and datum.

Similar to Whistler's portrait of Mrs. Leyland, Godwin's facade allowed figures (in this case, windows and doors) to float in front of or behind a horizontal datum, rest on it, or break it. Note that by exaggerating the size of windows and doors--making them both larger and smaller—he creates an impression of deep space on a perfectly flat plane.

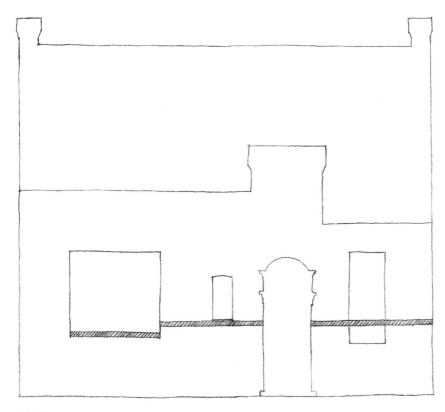

11.19

11.20

11.20
**Seigneurale, Segovia, Spain,
16th century. Elevation.**
The facade of this house for the mayor of
Segovia was entirely clad in tiles of subtly shifting patterns, a technique derived from Moorish
precedents. Its composition is highly complex.
Because interior spaces focused almost entirely
on a *cortile*, or courtyard, the disposition of exterior windows on the facade did not have to
correspond to interior functions. Therefore, the
architect could arrange them for an aesthetic
objective, which was to produce a dynamic visual balance within a heterogeneous grouping
of objects on a two-dimensional plane, as in an
early 20th-century nonobjectivist painting by
Piet Mondrian or Kasimir Malevich.

11.21
Seigneurale, Segovia. Vertical sections.
The architect divided the facade into three vertical sections by the dimension of the tower
and the centerline of the principal window. The
center section is wider than the two equal
flanking sections, thus producing an A-B-A
rhythm and a centerline for the entire composition. Diagonals of these sections (at 30-degree
angles) pass through all of the apertures on the
facade except the tower window.

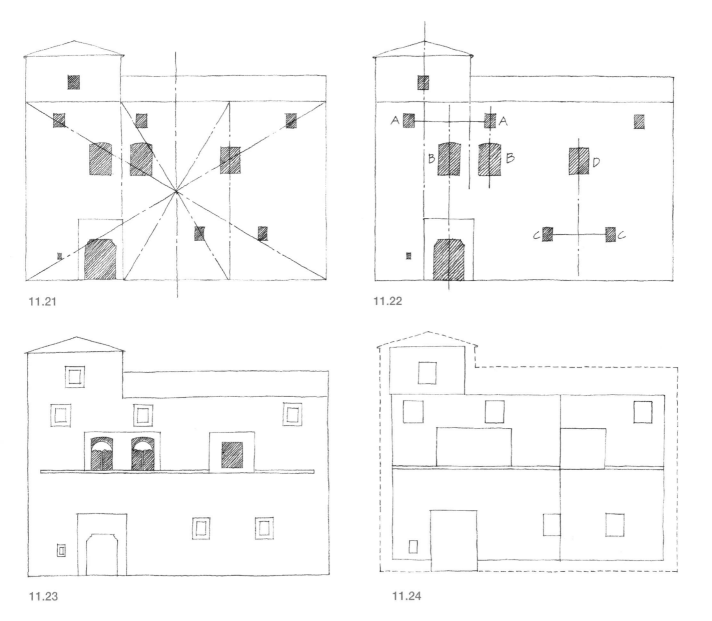

11.21

11.22

11.23

11.24

11.22
Seigneurale, Segovia. Window centerlines.

The architect grouped windows in pairs and connected them via centerlines with other features. The two windows A-A are symmetrical about the left window of pair B-B, which is in turn on axis with the entry. Pair B-B is symmetrical about the right edge of the tower. The tower window aligns with the left edge of the entry, and the two windows C-C are symmetrical about the centerline of window D.

11.23
Seigneurale, Segovia. Horizon line.

Apertures are arranged hierarchically, with the three most prominent windows on the string course and the secondary windows floating around them. The pair with the palm tree motif appears to have no sill and so implies that it slides behind the "horizon" of the string course. The largest window that appears to be in front of the string course therefore contradicts the position of the upper portion of the facade plane established by the palm tree pair. This device, in conjunction with subtle alterations in the patterns of tile fields, produces a sense of spatial depth on a smooth, two-dimensional surface—a purely pictorial invention.

11.24
Seigneurale, Segovia. Repetition, extension, and similarity.

The architect composed the entire field of the building facade of rectangles in a highly abstract pattern, allowing for repetition (the secondary windows), extension (the sliding of the primary windows along the string course), and similarity (changes in scale but not proportion between the entry and the secondary windows). The principal window divides the field as a whole into four quadrants, no two of which appear to be on the same plane.

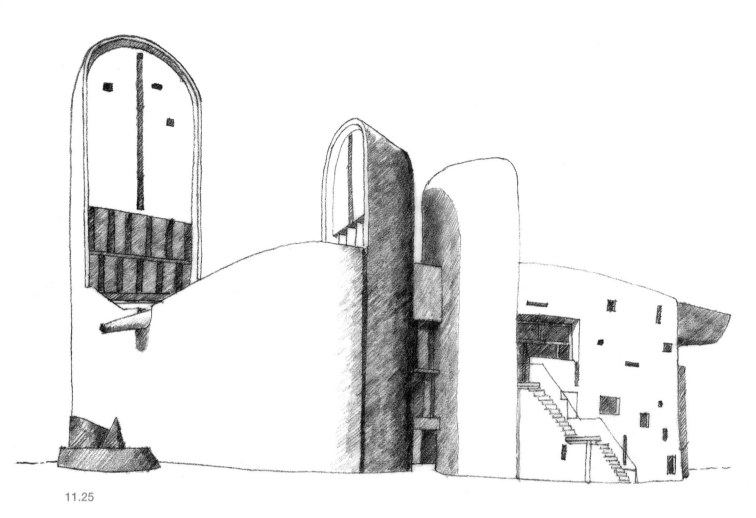

11.25

11.25

Notre Dame du Haut, Ronchamp, France, 1955. Le Corbusier. View.

Built on a hilltop previously occupied by a 19th-century chapel, Notre Dame du Haut was a complex solution to the problem of integrating a program and its site. Because it is a pilgrimage chapel, not a congregational church, Le Corbusier's design emphasized its outer surface—an articulated skin—above all other qualities. In his travel journal, Le Corbusier described his impression of the approach to the Parthenon from a distance atop the Athenian acropolis. He wrote that it disappeared from view as he ascended the acropolis, but upon reaching the summit, it appeared suddenly up close as a monumental object. Furthermore, it was on the oblique in relation to the entrance to the acropolis (the propylaem), so it presented itself as a three-dimensional object in space. Le Corbusier used the same method at Notre Dame du Haut. One first sees it from afar as a white object against the landscape. It then disappears from view as one ascends the hill, hidden behind trees and a low convent building, then finally reappears at a monumental scale close up. Likewise, the sharp prow of the form turns slightly to the right of the approach to induce a clockwise circumambulation of the building, culminating in the outdoor liturgical space. To emphasize the implied rotation of the building, the articulated skin is a composition of alternating concave and convex surfaces.

11.26

11.26

Sainsbury Wing of the National Gallery of Art, London, 1991.
Venturi, Rauch, Scott Brown. View.

The late 20th-century museum addition is a deformed mimicry (this is not meant pejoratively—
just factually) of the original early 19th-century Neoclassical building by William Wilkins. Typical
of Postmodernist mannerism, the new building reveals itself as an ornamental skin stretched
over a rather ordinary box—in Robert Venturi's parlance, a "decorated shed." In this sketch, the
dual character of the Sainsbury Wing is in juxtaposition with the original building. The skinlike
exterior appears to have stretched around the corner, then compressed and crumpled as it
neared the older building, the pilasters eventually piling up on one another.

CHAPTER TWELVE
METAMORPHOSIS

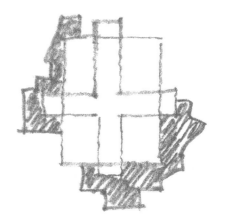

NORMALLY, WE ASSUME BUILDINGS RESULT FROM A single program of design and construction, and that their forms are durable enough to withstand fluctuating circumstances over time. Exceptions to this rule are instructive, however, because they suggest a design method that embraces change, rather than resisting or defying it. Though many buildings incur minor adaptations to new technologies or social conventions, some buildings experience radical change. This goes well beyond adaptive reuse to challenge the core identity of the building and to suggest an evolving cultural phenomenon within a dynamic historical context, rather than a static idea fixed in time. Such buildings are particularly valuable because they provide a historical narrative in their forms—a story—not just a snapshot of a historical moment.

The plan of the Great Mosque of Isfahan in Iran contains a record of the evolution of the mosque as an architectural type in that part of the world (12.1). The model for the earliest Arabic mosques was Muhammad's house—a simple walled enclosure containing a courtyard and a hypostyle hall—and the first version of the Great Mosque, constructed in the 8th century, followed this Arabic pattern (12.2). When the Abbasids overthrew the Umayyad caliphate, Persian ideas came to dominate all of the arts and sciences of the Islamic Empire, including architecture. The plan of the Great Mosque changed accordingly to a four-iwan type that emphasized two axes through the central courtyard; each of the four iwans housed one of the four traditional schools of Islamic law (12.3). Beginning in the 12th century, an outer layer of prayer spaces grew incrementally to accommodate larger congregations, its irregular plan fitting into the surrounding urban context (12.4). Traditionally, there was no need for the exterior of the mosque to conform to its interior, since the principal concern was preserving the purity of the central space and keeping it distinct from the secular world around it. The irregularity of the exterior was therefore acceptable. The contemporary plan consists of a set of varied and densely packed prayer halls connected by narrow interior passages, a pattern remarkably similar to the urban pattern of dense housing and shops connected by narrow alleys and cul-de-sacs surrounding the mosque (12.5, 12.6).

When the Fatimids conquered Egypt in the 10th century, they built a pair of large palaces on the west and the east sides of the main thoroughfare through their new capital city of al-Qahira, what is now the medieval quarter of Cairo. Their palace

280

plan type evolved from Persian precedents, with four deep iwans stretching out from a central court. The eastern palace disappeared, but the western one was later absorbed into a complex of buildings constructed by the Mamluk sultan al-Nasir Muhammad ibn Qala'un in 1285 (12.7). The Fatimid palace survived as a *maristan*, or hospital, including the first clinic for the empirical study of insanity. Its pattern is still clearly discernable, embedded among the 13th-century buildings (12.8).

A more recent example of metamorphosis is the Des Moines Art Center in Iowa (12.9). Eliel Saarinen designed the original building in 1948. Morphologically, it may be considered a split hollow square; the two halves were then pulled apart to create the two wings of the building, one for the art school and the other for the galleries, each of which, being U-shaped, partially enclosed a courtyard. The courtyard of the school held the parking lot and entrances, while the courtyard of the galleries looked south down a slope toward a distant view. In 1965, I. M. Pei constructed an addition to the galleries (12.10). In a bold move, he placed a new rectangular block in the gallery courtyard, shifting the south view to the interior of the addition, completely enclosing the courtyard, and closing a loop of interior circulation through the galleries. Richard Meier's 1984 addition did not attempt to extend either the original building or Pei's addition (12.11). Instead, Meier broke up the program into three kiosks—offices, a café, and a new gallery—that he attached to the older buildings in various ways. Pei had made a clear distinction between his addition and Saarinen's original both in form and in material, switching from the original limestone to hammered concrete. Likewise, Meier did not attempt to integrate his addition with the work of his predecessors, instead cladding his buildings with white enameled steel panels. The success of the entire composition is paradoxically not due to the complete integration of the work of three architects but is rather in the legibility of their differences. Each part is authentic to the vision of its creator without being either aggressive or submissive toward the others (12.12).

The previous examples have been cases where, within a limited architectural frame, individuals—clients and architects—have made incremental changes to the fabric of a building. Metamorphosis also occurs at a larger scale, both physically and sociologically. Venice emerged from a long process of synoecism, the gradual coalescence of separate physical and political entities into a single form (12.13). Its population grew from the retreat of mainland people to the safety of the Venetian lagoon in the face of a series of invasions from central Europe. Entire populations of villages and towns moved en masse to small islands in the lagoon, bringing with them their distinct local cultures and languages. Each island had its central church and well. These *campi* gradually grew closer, and in the 10th century they fused to become the Rialto. The canals of the Rialto are the vestiges of the lagoon that once separated the islands. Another example of a long historical metamorphosis is a sample of a street in Flensburg, Germany. We can discern major social, political, and economic changes in the city over four hundred years by tracing changes in the architecture of a few houses on a single street (12.14).

We live in an era of radical, unrelenting change. Architects can hold two equally reasonable yet diametrically opposed views with respect to this condition. One argument is that at a time of manic instability we need more than ever an architecture that imparts calm and continuity. Therefore, architecture should rely on stable, traditional forms, such as those offered by Classicism, that provide the comfort of familiar and durable images that are resistant to change. The other view holds that architects should enthusiastically embrace the instability of the present and should accurately reflect in their work the open, perpetually revolutionary spirit of contemporary culture. Metamorphic architecture can satisfy the latter goal, in the design of a building that transforms over time or implies a transformation. However, architects can also use it as a critical device to bring the dissolution of traditional values to people's attention, as Peter Salter did in his project in Japan (8.31).

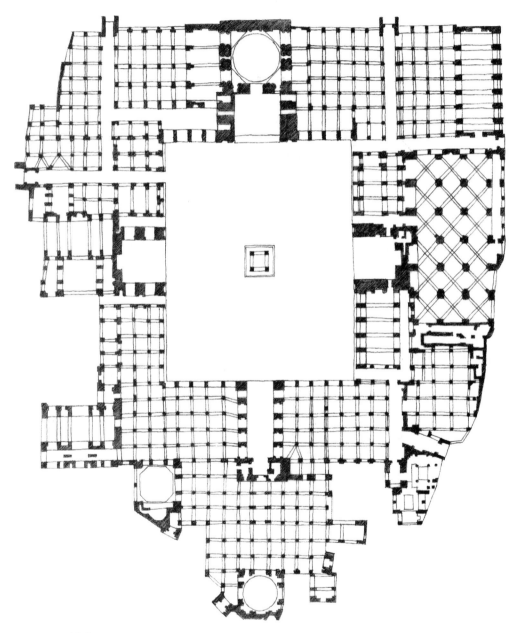

12.1

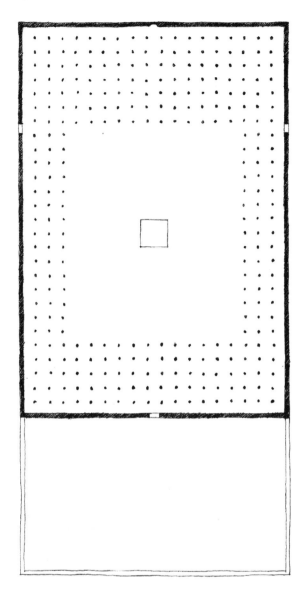

12.2

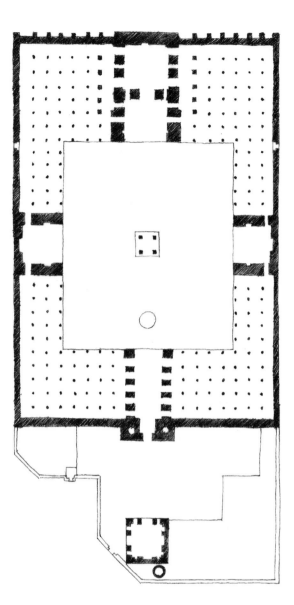

12.3

12.1
Great Mosque, Isfahan, Iran, 8th–17th centuries. 20th-century plan.

The Great Mosque is the principal congregational mosque of Isfahan. It has a typically Persian plan, with a central courtyard bracketed by four iwans. Numerous hypostyle halls that have accumulated over time surround this central space. There is an overall gradation of form, from a busy and highly irregular outer boundary largely determined by its secular urban context to a serene center appropriate to meditation and prayer. The courtyard is thus a quiet oasis in the city, its four-quartered form specifically derived from an ancient model of paradise.

12.2
Great Mosque, Isfahan. 8th-century plan.

Initially, the Mosque's plan followed an Arabic tradition, based on the model of Muhammad's house as a simple walled enclosure with a large courtyard surrounded by a columned portico or hypostyle hall, a plan that appears also at Samarra in Iraq, the Ibn Tulun Mosque in Cairo, and the Great Mosque of al-Qairawan in Tunisia.

12.3
Great Mosque, Isfahan. 12th-century plan.

By the 12th century, the four-iwan Persian model superseded the Arabic plan and the forecourt changed to accommodate a tomb. The Persian plan began to break the original homogeneity of the Arabic hypostyle hall into smaller halls within the enclosure.

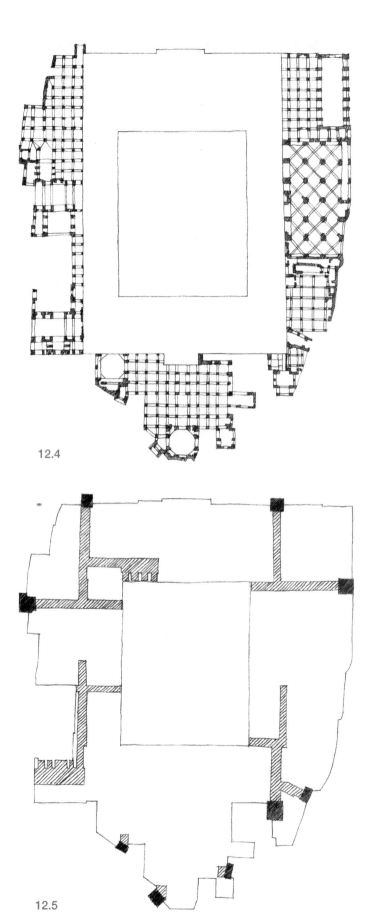

12.4

12.4
Great Mosque, Isfahan. 15th-century additions.

In following centuries, larger congregations required more halls for prayer, so the rectangular enclosing wall disappeared as halls accumulated in a new layer, and the character of the courtyard changed in response to a changing boundary condition. In the 12th century, the original central axis (from monumental entrance to mihrab) still dominated the plan, but this gave way to numerous entrances to the mosque from surrounding streets through the new hypostyle halls. Eventually its designers abandoned all correspondence between the exterior form of the mosque and its interior.

12.5
Great Mosque, Isfahan. Circulation pattern.

The original Arabic plan had one main entrance on axis with the mihrab and two symmetrically placed secondary entrances. As the mosque grew with the addition of new halls, the original formality of the plan disappeared in favor of convenient entrances from surrounding streets—nine by the 20th century. Most of these led to long passageways that terminated at the boundary of the central courtyard. The result is a spatial pattern consisting of narrow alleys penetrating a nearly uniform architectural matrix, familiar to the users of the building because it corresponds to the pattern of traditional residential development in Isfahan.

12.6
Great Mosque, Isfahan. Street pattern.

The pattern of the streets surrounding the mosque is similar to the pattern of passageways within the building: a branching form producing cul-de-sacs that lead eventually to the courtyards (depicted here as open rectangles) of private residences.

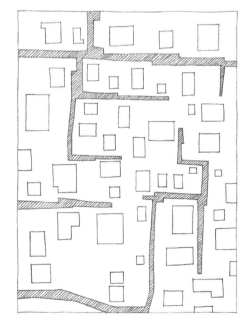

12.6

12.5

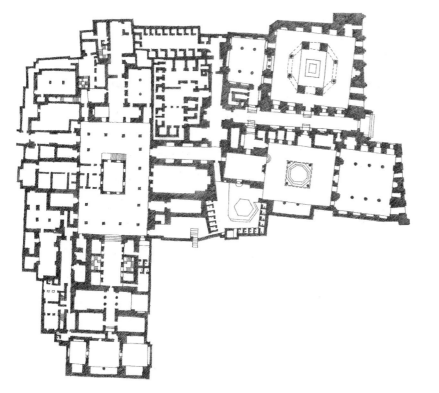

12.7

Complex of Sultan al-Nasir Muhammad ibn Qala'un Cairo, Egypt, 1285. Plan.

The complex includes a *maristan* (hospital), a madrassa (Koranic school), and a mausoleum. The composition appears somewhat chaotic until one realizes that it has two quite different halves. The *maristan* occupies a 10th-century Fatimid palace that once fronted upon a vast parade ground in the center of the medieval city of al-Qahira. Sultan Qala'un constructed his madrassa and mausoleum in front of the palace, orienting them toward Mecca. This project and others that followed reduced the parade ground to a street that continues to be the central spine of the medieval quarter of Cairo.

12.8

Complex of Sultan al-Nasir Muhammad ibn Qala'un. Composition.

The madrassa and mausoleum have two sets of paired entrances from an interior street that leads to the facade of the *maristan*, now buried in the center of the complex. The Fatimid palace originally centered on a large courtyard with long passages that extended outward in the cardinal directions. These are still discernable in the plan, as is the medieval mental hospital at its northeast corner. Note that there are two wards; the one for female inmates had standardized cells similar to a prison, while the ward for male inmates was a labyrinth.

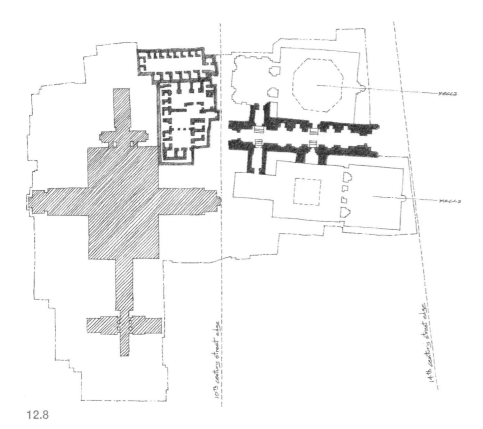

12.8

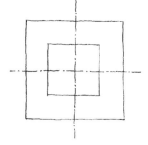

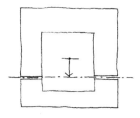

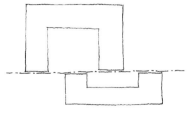

Des Moines Art Center, Iowa 1948–1984.
Eliel Saarinen, I.M. Pei, and Richard Meier.

The present form of the art center is the result of three building campaigns by three major architects of American Modernism, eventually producing an unusual amalgam of individual architectural styles. In 1948, Eliel Saarinen designed the original building to fit the graceful curve of its hilltop site by keeping it low and horizontal, and he used Lannon limestone in long horizontal courses to relate to the rural setting and its geology. Morphologically, his plan originates in a square with a central courtyard. He split it asymmetrically and allowed the two resulting U-shaped parts to slip past one another east and west to form two open courts. The shallow one to the east formed the entry into an art school, and a deeper one enclosed the principal view into the landscape to the south from the main western galleries. Minor deformations of the two displaced sections of the original square produced a Z-shaped plan with a simple circulation path from one end to the other.

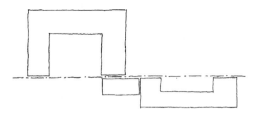

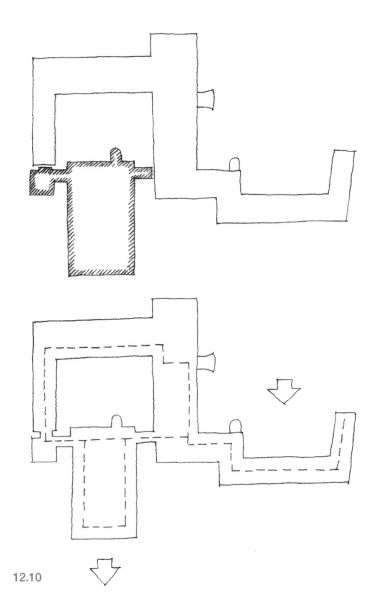

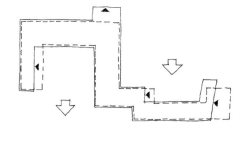

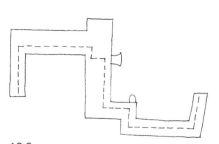

12.9

12.10

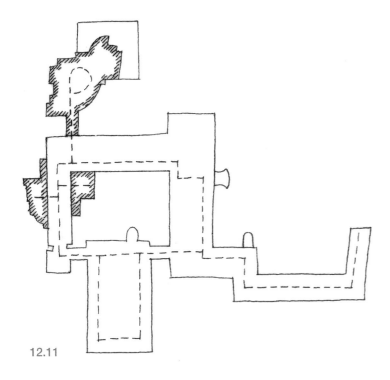

12.11

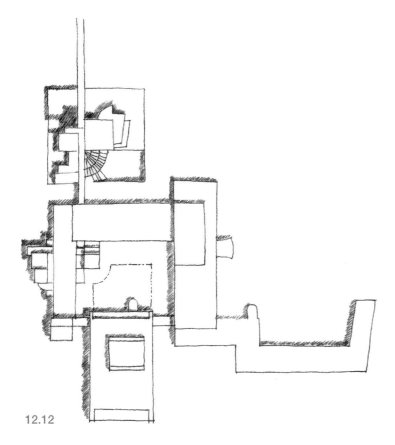

12.12

Des Moines Art Center. I. M. Pei addition, 1965.

I. M. Pei closed the view to the south from the original western galleries with his addition and created a fully enclosed courtyard with a reflecting pool. His building, in bush-hammered concrete, made a radical departure from Saarinen's sensitive treatment of the landscape. However, taking advantage of the side of the hill, Pei was able to construct a two-story gallery block while maintaining the approximate height of Saarinen's building in relation to the crest of the hill. Pei wanted to retain the view to the south from his new galleries, so he protected the interior from harsh sunlight with windows set deep within the south elevation while providing most of the interior daylighting through a large roof monitor. Circulation became a circuit around the new court.

12.11

Des Moines Art Center. Meier addition, 1984.

Richard Meier's program included offices, a café, and additional galleries. Instead of designing a single piece, he broke the program into three pavilions, attached the café to the inside of Saarinen's building facing into the court that Pei had created, attached the offices to the outside of the same wing, and placed the new galleries as a sculptural pavilion apart from the rest. Meier's gallery pavilion is a nine-square grid with a play of curves against cubic volumes in white porcelain enameled steel, and glass. It commands attention as one approaches the complex, but since it is slightly downhill from Saarinen's original building, it is not out of scale. Circulation then became a double circuit, and the court, with its serene reflecting pool, retained its role as the center of the composition.

12.12

Des Moines Art Center. Final form.

In its final form, the art center achieves a delicate balance between two identities. It has a unified plan combining the visual gravity of the central court with the centripetal force of peripheral extensions into the landscape (the original art school by Saarinen, the Pei gallery, and the Meier gallery pavilion). But the Art Center is also now clearly three buildings produced by three different visions of form, meanings of materials, and responses to the landscape.

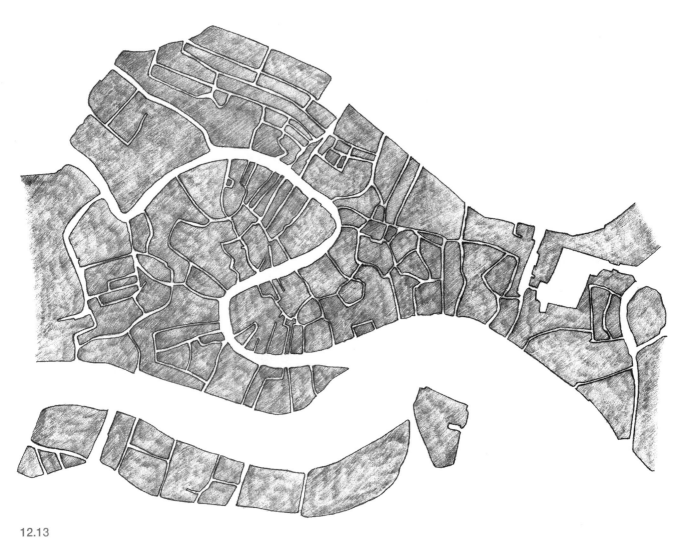

12.13

12.13

Venice, Italy. Synoecism.

From the beginning of the 5th century through the 9th century, Goths, Huns, Lombards, and Magyars invaded northern Italy and forced people from mainland towns and villages into the Venetian lagoon. Entire communities relocated en masse and established independent towns on islets, bringing with them their sacred relics, religious hierarchs, and languages. For example, the people of Altino settled on the islet of Torcello; those of Aquileia on Grado; Concordians on Caorle; Paduans on Malamocco; and those from Oderzo on Cittanova. In the early 10th century, an organized effort began to expand many of the islets and to consolidate them into the Rialto, which comprises the most densely built part of Venice today. The ancestral villages, or *campi*, each retained their own church and well at the center of a communal space that over time became a piazza. As one walks through the city today, it appears that the canals cut through a landmass, that is, they are subtractions from the land. However, the opposite is true. The canals are residual lagoon, what remained as the islets gradually grew together and the independent *campi* eventually united under a single political authority. This process is synoecism, an urban metamorphosis through which originally independent states aggregate into a single state. Identities of individual *campi* persist. They have retained their names, usually associated with their parish church, and at the center of each *campo* one still finds a piazza with a well, or a monument that has supplanted it. Even today, the identity of a native Venetian is primarily that of his or her ancestral *campo*, and secondarily that of Venice as a whole.

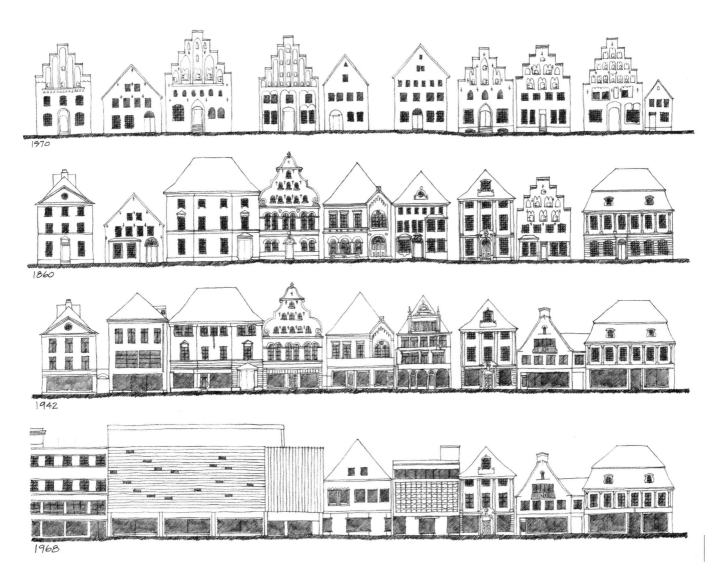

1570

1860

1942

1968

12.14

12.14
**Nos. 3 to 17, Abwicklungen der Ostseite des Holm,
Flensburg, Schleswig-Holstein, Germany.**

Elevations. These drawings document the development of nine properties over four hundred years, from 1570 to 1968. Flensburg is on the border of Denmark, and its 16th-century architecture was similar to much of the surviving late-medieval architecture one would have found along the south coast of the Baltic Sea from Denmark to Lithuania. Over time, we can trace a metamorphosis of Flensburg's architectural character, indicative of changes in urban culture, the economy, and building technology.

Architectural character and use. In the 16th century, merchants used the upper stories of their houses to store their goods. The six houses for merchants in this group had stepped gables with small wooden doors through which the merchant hoisted his goods. The other four houses in this group were residences, probably for artisans and their families. By the mid-19th century, the Renaissance and Baroque styles that originated in the south had become dominant. Only two of the 16th-century houses remained intact, while the owners of the others transformed them into upper-class townhouses. The street had become entirely residential as the scale of trade, manufacturing, and warehousing required larger, less expensive quarters elsewhere in the city. By 1942, another transformation had occurred: commercial activity dominated the street. All of the ground floors of the houses were devoted to retail stores, and the houses above became apartments and flats. Finally, by 1968 the street was entirely commercial, with retailing and offices occupying all of the buildings.

Pattern. Changing economic circumstances were the cause of changes in use on the street. In the 16th century, we find a street of compact buildings standing individually or in pairs. The affluence evident in the townhouses of the 19th century required larger buildings, so we find the building masses merging and squeezing out interstitial spaces. Owners compensated for greater density and scale by exaggerating the stylistic features of their houses. The pattern is, however, still a juxtaposition of highly individualistic buildings. By the early 20th century, the trend toward retailing on the ground level superimposed a new kind of uniformity on the older pattern by means of a continuous strip of large glass shop windows at the pedestrian level surmounted by a narrow zone of signage. By the late 20th century, the original pattern was lost, and any vestiges of the old pattern appeared anachronistic. The new commercial buildings were in the process of imposing a continuous, large-scale horizontal strip along the street that had no intrinsic pattern. Apparently, there was an effort on the part of the city planners to maintain a height restriction equivalent to that of the older houses, but the lack of any design integrity among the new buildings allowed them to destroy the architectural character of the street.

Scale. Though monumental for their time, the 16th-century houses were of a human scale. There was a shared vision of what was appropriate for a city street based on traditional building types: the street had an architectural culture. The closely spaced arrangements of doors, windows, and parapets tended toward the vertical, a pattern that produced a strong rhythm as one walked down the street. The ground-floor entrances with flanking windows associated with the life of the families within the houses offered a clear relation between the private and public realms. On the other hand, the introduction of Renaissance procedures for composing facades emphasized horizontal layering by means of cornices and string courses. There was also a shift of emphasis to the second floor, away from the street level, though each house remained an integrated compositional whole. The early 20th-century conversion to ground-floor retailing, with vast expanses of glass, disintegrated the building facades. The ground level produced two different scales to each building, one for the modern retail store and another for the residual traditional architecture above. Furthermore, the large shop windows seriously weakened the visual integrity of the buildings, as the glass at sidewalk level appeared to support the heavy brick walls above. By 1968, any sense of an integrated scale of the street had been lost with the introduction of large buildings that mixed horizontal and vertical elements haphazardly and arbitrarily and that failed to use architectural features such as windows and doors to provide a human scale.

Detail. The 16th-century buildings were austere and conformist, reflecting Calvinist ideas about what was proper when expressing one's identity architecturally within a community. Therefore, the only decorative features, the stepped gables and the ends of iron tensioning rods, were in fact strictly utilitarian. By the mid-19th century, the influence of Italian and Bavarian tastes permitted far greater personal expression and experimentation, with little concern for consistency along the entire street front, indicative of a more open society. The major loss by the mid-20th century was the architectural detail at the ground level, where most people would normally come into direct contact with it. By the second half of the 20th century, this trend had spread to the buildings as a whole. Rampant commercialism completely eliminated the facades or stripped them of their detail to make them "modern." The result was a disjunctive composition incapable of conveying any sense of a shared culture, either of the past or of the present.

12.

CHAPTER THIRTEEN
DEFORMATION

THE ESSENCE OF ART IS DEFORMATION. AS WIT AND humor rely on a surprising disruption of logic, so too are the visual arts dependent on an unexpected deviation from the norm. If we were to devote our creative energies to merely reiterating conventional ideas and reinforcing norms, life would be boring indeed. It is instructive to observe how tyrannies do exactly that. Deformation is essential in natural forms, also. Two fundamental properties of nature are helpful in understanding the importance of deformation in design. First, the force of evolution that produces the phenomenal diversity of species relies essentially on deviations from norms to allow organisms to adjust to changing environments and to take advantage of emerging opportunities. D'Arcy Thompson's comparative analysis of animal forms in *On Growth and Form* demonstrated that the forms among related species are not the result of distinctly different compositions but are rather deformations of one another (13.1). Second, expression is a basic survival technique that relies on a deformation of the body, whether it is a male peacock courting a potential mate on the lawn or a lounge lizard using body language to communicate more or less the same message in a hotel bar. Our response to art, and our need for it, may be an interpretation of our innate understanding of these two natural forces. Interpreted artistically, our fascination with form is largely due to how deformations inform us about conventional or normal expectations. The V-Girl, for example, (a small sculpture in someone's yard in San Antonio, Texas) draws upon several popular notions of feminine beauty, and by distorting these to an extreme degree, it allows us to observe them critically (13.2).

To understand the information a deformation conveys, one must have an appreciation for the norm as a basis for comparison. Two real houses serve to illustrate this. The normal house is in Massachusetts, and the distorted house is in Iowa (13.3). The normal house is almost as a child would draw an icon for a house: a door, a couple of windows, a symmetrical gable roof, a chimney, all where they should be in a proper composition. In comparison, the deformed house is intentionally perverse. Everything is wrong with it and that is the point. By virtue of its radical distortion of the norm, it instigates a heightened awareness of the norm, a reference to the expectation we all carry around in our minds. Like a good joke, it suddenly places that expectation and the values behind it in doubt.

The other examples of architectural deformation that follow are more sober than the last, but they all adhere to the same principle. Implicit in every one is a reference to a norm. The plan of the Yeşil Cami, or Green Mosque, in Bursa, Turkey, implies its derivation from a 2:√3 rectangle, deformed by the insertion of an entry block that pushes the main prayer space out of the original rectangle (13.4–13.7). A 19th-century house in Tunis, the El Daouletti, has a conventional orthogonal plan distorted to fit its site (13.8, 13.9). Similarly, the plan of the Church of Saint Aspais in Melun, France, has an orthogonal origin, its simple grid now stretched and contracted to fit the site (13.10, 13.11). Another small church in Greifensee, Switzerland, displays the flexibility of the Gothic system of vaulting by which seven slightly distorted cells supported by a single column could successfully enclose the entire interior space (13.12, 13.13).

A 2nd-century BCE stoa on the eastern quay of Leptis Magna in Libya (13.14) conformed to its site and function by becoming a deformation of an archetype exemplified by the stoa of Sikyon, Greece, built a hundred years earlier (13.15). Another deformation of a type is Jorge Cámera's Chapel in Tabasco, Mexico (13.16). Though at first glance it appears to be a radical departure from the plan of a Roman Catholic church, it is merely a distortion; the narthex, nave, altar, sanctuary, chapels, and vestry are where they would normally be. Just the rectangular frame deforms to experiment with a different quality of architectural space. The Jain Temple of Adinatha at Ranakpur, India, also refers to a norm, in this case a mandala from the Vriksharnava Shastra, a cosmological guide to design. The temple, however, extends subtly to the west to give that direction a slight emphasis over the other three cardinal directions (13.17, 13.18).

Erik Gunnar Asplund and Alvar Aalto experimented with ways to express the conceptual pliability of the skin of a building through deformation. Asplund's Villa Snellman of 1918 has a main building of two stories with an attached one-story guest wing in an L-plan (13.19). The one-story structure is, for no apparent reason, rotated slightly inward, out of the perpendicular; otherwise, everything appears normal on the entry court side of the building (except for a puzzling pair of entry doors). On the garden elevation, however, all of the ground-floor windows shift out of alignment with the norm, as indicated by the second-floor and attic windows. They shift to the right, toward the one-story guest wing, as if the rotation of that structure inward was pulling them, stretching the skin on the ground level (13.20). Thirty years later Aalto explored the same theme. Although Baker House on the campus of the Massachusetts Institute of Technology in Cambridge, Massachusetts, has its origin in a simple, four-layered bar form, Aalto took a cue from his work with bent plywood furniture and bent the building form, allowing the four layers to slip past one another (13.21, 13.22, 13.23). The process is particularly evident at the ends of the building, where one can see that the layers are unaligned. By deforming the bar, Aalto fit a larger program on the site than a straight bar would have permitted. In addition, the curved elevation of dormitory rooms created a variety of views up and down the Charles River. Windows of these rooms vary in width to accentuate the tension in the convex curve and compression in the two concave curves of the bent skin.

Asplund and Aalto also explored deformations in plan extensively in their work. In his design for the town hall at Saynatsalo, Finland, Aalto deformed a standard parti used in many town halls in northern Europe—a square frame around a courtyard (13.24, 13.25). Dramatizing the contest between the building and the forces of nature, he implies in the broken form a snapshot of the building torn apart by the upward pressure of the earth at its center. Though the impetus of the design may have been metaphorical, breaking the square provided several practical opportunities, such as two exterior entrances to the courtyard and a means to articulate the different components of a heterogeneous program. Asplund's design for the Lister County Courthouse differentiates the courtroom from the offices and residence above by suggesting that the cylindrical courtroom is forcing its way out of the center of its rectangular frame. The interior of the rectangular building deforms in response, and the resulting intermediate space is the entirety of the building's circulation (13.26). The compositional method by which one part of a building deforms another also occurs in the 16th-century Lala Mustafa Pasha complex in Ilgin, Turkey, a project by Mimar Sinan (13.27). The diminutive mosque is made prominent by virtue of its apparent ability to deform the much larger building that partially encloses it.

Deformations may be useful for allowing a building to accommodate the eccentricities of its site. In the late 16th-century design for the University of Würtzburg, Julius Echter broke the hollow square plan into its four sides to allow each side to shift independently in conformance with the surrounding streets (13.28). A more radical approach appeared in Vigevano, Italy, when, in the 17th century, a medieval market became a Renaissance piazza and a modification of the old church of Saint Ambrogio completed the new composition (13.29). The church stood oblique and off center to the new piazza; the solution to joining them was to create a new concave facade for the church that extended beyond the church and across an adjacent street. This made it appear that the church was symmetrical to the longitudinal axis of the piazza. At the Monastery of Hosios Loukas in Phocis, Greece, the larger of two churches, the center-domed Catholicon, rose a hundred years after the slightly skewed shrine of Theotokos (13.30). To connect the two, the Catholicon deformed at its northeast corner where it met the shrine. Then an extension of the central crossing of the Catholicon became a new porch across the front of the shrine. As a result, the two structures firmly fused together, and as one walks from one to the other, the transition is nearly imperceptible despite the shrine's distortion.

Interiors of buildings sometimes deform as well, either to fit the organization of their exteriors or to provide an entirely different orientation than that of their exteriors. A house in Dinkelsbühl, Germany, from the 18th century illustrates the first condition (13.31). It has facades on two parallel streets that are of different designs, so the central structural spine of the building shifts to fit two different fenestration schemes, slightly distorting the spaces to either side. An example of the second condition is the Pearl Mosque in the Red Fort of Delhi in India (13.32). It is a freestanding building on the palace grounds. The secular palace fit into a grid intentionally out of alignment with the orientation needed for prayer toward Mecca. Therefore, the private prayer space for the Mughal emperor within the Pearl Mosque shifts away from the secular grid, and the poché of the thick wall adjusts to the difference between the exterior and the interior. The plan of the 19th-century Rasoulian House in Isfahan, Iran, uses subtle interior deformations to adjust interior spaces to the irregular site, reserving regularity for the courtyard and the reception rooms around it (13.33–13.36). Finally, the architects of the Küçük Aya-sofya Camii in Istanbul, Turkey (originally the Byzantine Church of Saints Sergius and Bacchos) allowed the exterior shell of the building to deform to fit among existing buildings in a palace group while the core maintained a regular geometry and a proper alignment (13.37–13.40).

Deformation is more common in architecture than generally acknowledged. It is a critical device for examining norms and questioning their underlying values. Architects have used it metaphorically to imply change or to suggest contesting objectives in the design of a form. It can also mediate between two systems of order, as was the case in the Pearl Mosque and the Küçük Ayasofya Camii, and it can fuse two or more forms that are otherwise unrelated, as in the case of the piazza and church at Vigevano. In the work of Asplund and Aalto, we find the use of deformation as a way to examine a formal language, such as the meaning of a wall and the implications of movement in a static object.

13.1

Relations of Form, D'Arcy Thompson. Diagrams.

In his studies in *On Growth and Form* (1948), D'Arcy Thompson compared related species based on simple grids to suggest that differences could be explained by distortions and deformations. For example, mapping the silhouette of a human skull to those of a chimpanzee and a baboon suggests that differences in proportion are systematic through the curvature of a grid. The same applies to the relationship between two sets of genus of fish (*Diodon* and *Orthagoriscus*, and *Argyropelecus* and *Sternoptyx*). Deformation is a positive and controlling feature of variation in the evolution of related species.

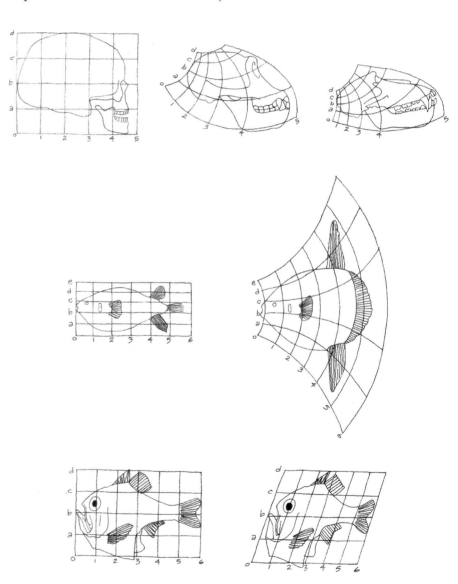

13.1

13.2
Folk Sculpture: "V-Girl," San Antonio, Texas, ca. 1986.

Deformation is an essential aspect of art. Normality is seldom interesting in its own right, while distortion and exaggeration of form bring out the essential qualities that express the character of a subject. In this small stone bas relief, each of the physical attributes of the woman is forced into high contrast with the others. Realism is not important. The extreme deviation from normality paradoxically brings attention to our cultural norms, or more precisely, the values and fantasies that shape those norms.

13.3
Normal House/Abnormal House. Views.

To appreciate what is abnormal, one must have a model of normality as a basis for comparison. The vernacular house on the left is in Massachusetts; its composition is entirely predictable and unremarkable, with each part exactly where we expect it to be, conforming comfortably to the image we carry in our minds of a proper house. The house on the right, in Iowa, has all of the same elements but in a delightfully distorted and unpredictable composition. The gable is skewed to the left and the front door has slid left also. Conventional windows defy conventional placement and scale. This composition is effective because of the underlying impression of what a normal house is. This house playfully resists the ordinariness we want to impose upon it.

13.2

13.3

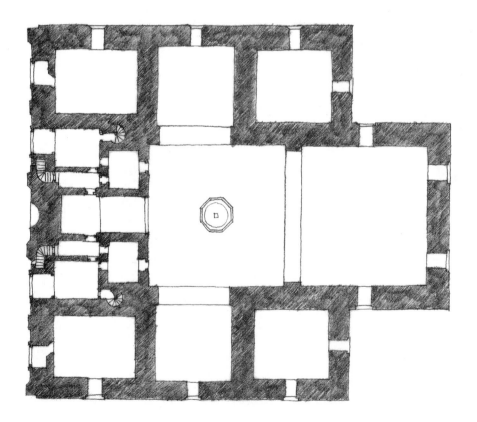

13.4

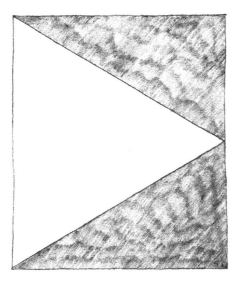

13.5

13.6

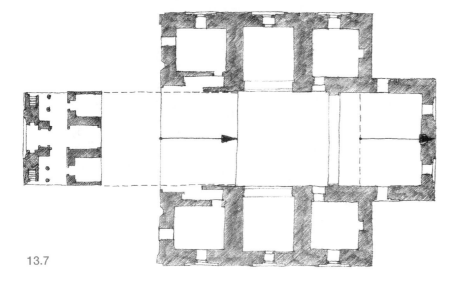

13.7

13.4
Yeşil Cami, Bursa, Turkey, 1420.
Plan and section.

Sultan Mehmet I founded the Yeşil Cami, or Green Mosque (due to the predominance of green and blue glazed hexagonal tiles in its cladding). Early Ottoman mosque designs, such as Yeşil Cami, relied on a Seljuk Turk model: a T-shaped plan with twin domes, one over a central hall and the other over the *qibla* hall. Smaller flanking rooms provided additional prayer and teaching space. Bursa had been the imperial capital since 1326 and remained the symbolic center of Ottoman rule and an important trading city in Anatolia long after the court moved to Edirne in Thrace in 1361. After the conquest of Constantinople in 1453, the focus of Ottoman mosque design shifted to the Byzantine model provided by the Hagia Sophia, a practice that culminated in the work of Mimar Sinan.

13.5
Yeşil Cami. Morphology.

The basis of the plan is a rectangle with the proportion of 2:√3, indicated by an inscribed equilateral triangle.

13.6
Yeşil Cami. Plan proportions.

The overall rectangle has eight spaces in a pattern comprised of squares and 2:√3 rectangles. The four corners and the central hall are squares, and the *qibla* hall and the two central rooms on the transverse axis are 2:√3 rectangles. Volumetrically, these spaces maintain their respective proportional systems, either cubic or 2:√3.

13.7
Yeşil Cami. Deformation.

The final stage in the morphology of the mosque is the insertion of the entry block that dislocates the two central spaces, producing the T-shaped plan. In addition to the monumental portal, the entry block includes a second-floor enclosure for the sultan on axis with the mihrab, or prayer niche, and overlooking the central prayer space. In earlier mosques, the sultan used a podium on the left side of the mihrab. The Yeşil Cami broke with this tradition. By linking the sultan's space with the mihrab, the architect indicated the twin roles of the sultan as a secular ruler and a religious leader.

13.8

House of El Daouletti, Tunis, 19th century. Plan.

The house has a labyrinthine plan at the ground level. A broad corridor leads from the street to the *salamlik*, or reception spaces, whereas a second, smaller corridor parallels the *haremlik*, or private quarters at the rear. Each of these standard Arabic features focuses on a small courtyard. More private household spaces are on a second level.

13.9

House of El Daouletti. Deformation.

To fit its trapezoidal site, the standard plan for a house of this type had to be deformed from an orthogonal arrangement of corridors and rooms. Otherwise, the plan is conventional for its time, with the formal entrance off the broad reception corridor and a second, rear entrance to serve the private family spaces of the *haremlik*.

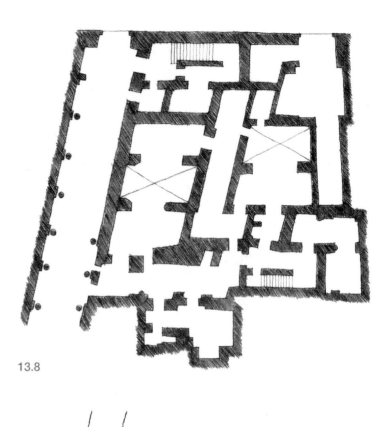

13.8

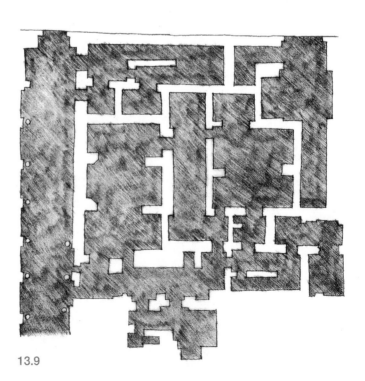

13.9

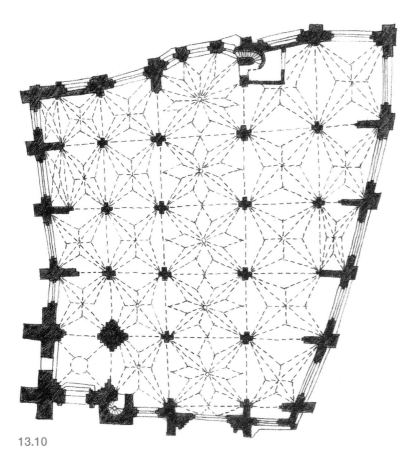

13.10

13.10

Church of Saint Aspais, Melun, France, 14th century. Plan.

This is an unusual plan for a medieval church, since it is essentially an open hypostyle hall with glazing on four sides. None of the standard features of western Christian church architecture appears in the plan. The entrance is at one corner, and slightly wider, more elaborately vaulted bays barely accentuate the centerline. All of the vaults are star vaults resting on composite piers.

13.11

Church of Saint Aspais. Composition.

The plan is a distorted five-by-five cellular grid. The most regular cell is at the entrance. The cells enlarge along the centerline, terminating in a nearly apsidal bay window and a tower. The entire grid shifts away from the entrance on a diagonal, opening to larger volumes and extensive glazing.

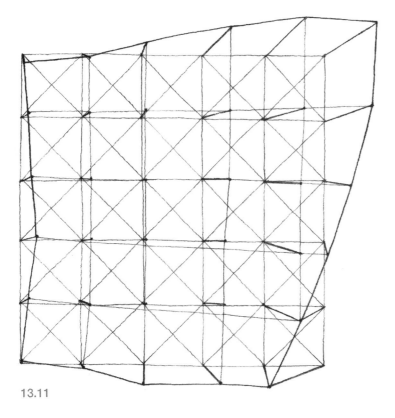

13.11

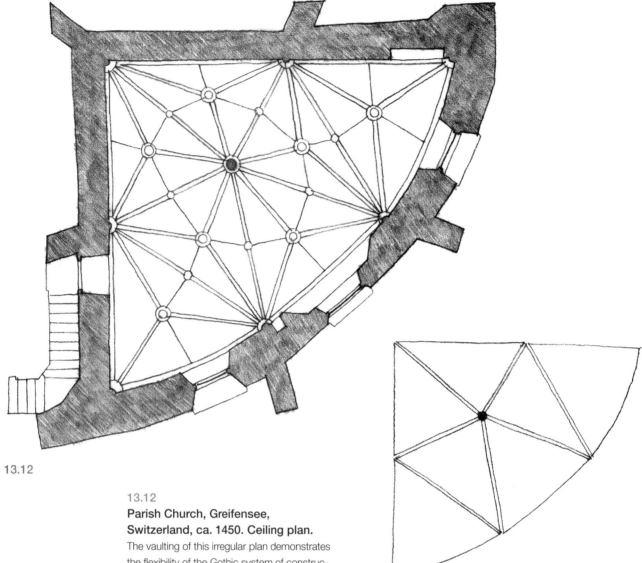

13.12

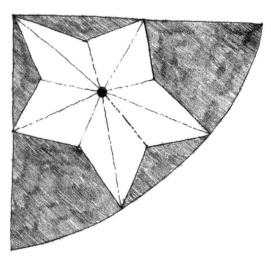

13.12
**Parish Church, Greifensee,
Switzerland, ca. 1450. Ceiling plan.**
The vaulting of this irregular plan demonstrates
the flexibility of the Gothic system of construction. Originally developed for orthogonal plans,
Gothic vaulting worked well for idiosyncratic
spaces too. In this case—a small church once
embedded in the town's fortifications—a system of three-ribbed vaults rests on a single central column and peripheral brackets. On the one
hand, the formal structure consists of seven triangular modules. On the other, it is a slightly
skewed star vault supported by the central column. This double reading of the space gives
the building a lively, surprising character.

13.13
Parish Church, Greifensee. Diagrams.
We can interpret the pattern of vaulting in two
ways. It is a set of seven isosceles triangles,
each varying slightly from the others to fill the
entire space. However, it is also a distorted pen-
tagram centered on the only interior column,
and all other parts of the vaulting then describe
spaces that are residual to the central figure.

13.13

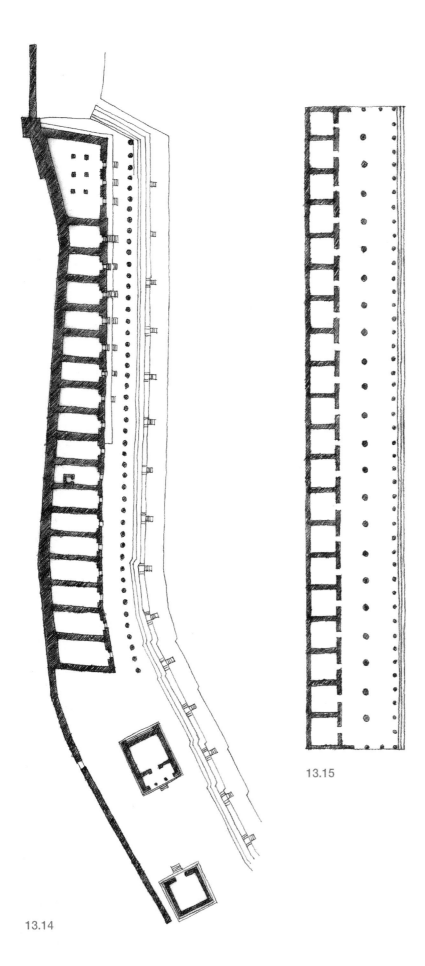

13.15

13.14

13.14

Stoa, Eastern Quay of Leptis Magna, Libya, ca. 200 CE. Plan.

This Roman stoa was part of an extensive construction campaign at Leptis Magna during the reign of the emperor Septimius Severus (193–211 CE), a native son of the city. It formed part of the harbor enclosure and functioned as a market building directly related to the quay. As such, it was a deformation of the classic Hellenistic design of the stoa, shaped to conform to its site, bending slightly, and varying considerably in width. The regularity of its colonnade, however, maintains its relation to its traditional building type.

13.15

Stoa at Sikyon, Greece, ca. 300 BCE.

According to Pausanias, Sikyon was the site of the earliest city-states in Greece, established by Ionian Achaeans about 1900 BCE. The stoa was a central feature of a new agora measuring 26 feet by 128 feet constructed in the Hellenistic period after the destruction of the old city. It is one of the purest examples of the stoa form, consisting of three layers of space: a row of twenty cubic shops, a row of twenty-two large interior Ionic columns, and an outer colonnade in the Doric order.

13.16
Chapel in Tabasco, Mexico, 1999. Jorge Cámera. Plan.

The plan is not as unconventional as it may first appear. It is essentially a curvilinear version of a standard organization of liturgical elements, albeit a design that produces a dynamic spatial experience. The basic parts of the church—narthex, nave, altar, vestry, and sanctuary—are all in their proper locations; only the chapels have migrated somewhat from their traditional locations flanking the nave. Therefore, this is not a radical departure from the traditional church plan; rather, it is a deformation of it.

13.17
Adinatha Temple, Ranakpur, Rajasthan, India, 15th century. Depaka. Plan.

This Jain temple, located about 50 miles from Udaipur, occupies a slightly distorted twenty-five-square diagram approximately 197 feet on each side. Constructed of white marble, it was designed in the Chaturmukha (four-faced) shrine form, and is therefore biaxially symmetrical. It has a central image of Adinatha facing in all four cardinal directions. In addition to the central shrine, there are four (two-faced) corner shrines and four other shrines that emphasize the north and south sides. Finally, there are eighty-six small peripheral shrines. Unlike most religions, Jainism does not subscribe to a single truth. Adinatha was the first of twenty-four Tirthankaras, or founders of the religion. However, Jainas do not worship the twenty-four Tirthankaras as distinctive personalities, so all representations of them look alike. They are all signs of the various truths of the universe, and the plan of the temple expresses this idea in its continuously flowing space dedicated not to a hierarchy of deities but to the repetition of the single sign of the Tirthankaras.

13.18
Adinatha Temple. Composition.

The architect, Depaka, followed the geometric formula of the Vriksharnava Shastra, a type of mandala, an expression of cosmic order. However, for reasons unknown, Depaka deviated from the strict bilateral symmetry of the mandala in the Adinatha Temple by slightly inflecting the plan to the west. The space in front of the central shrine on the west side extends by 7 feet, just enough to emphasize it with two additional rows of columns.

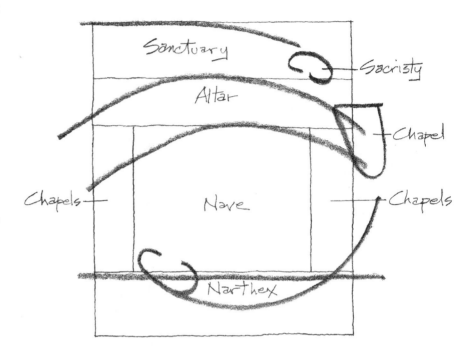

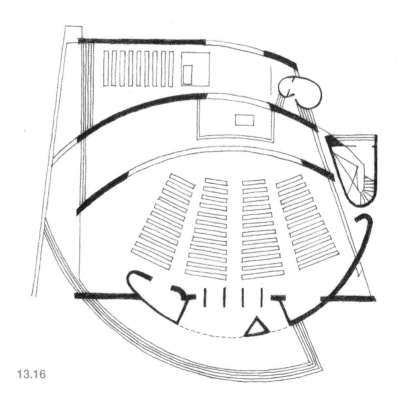

13.16

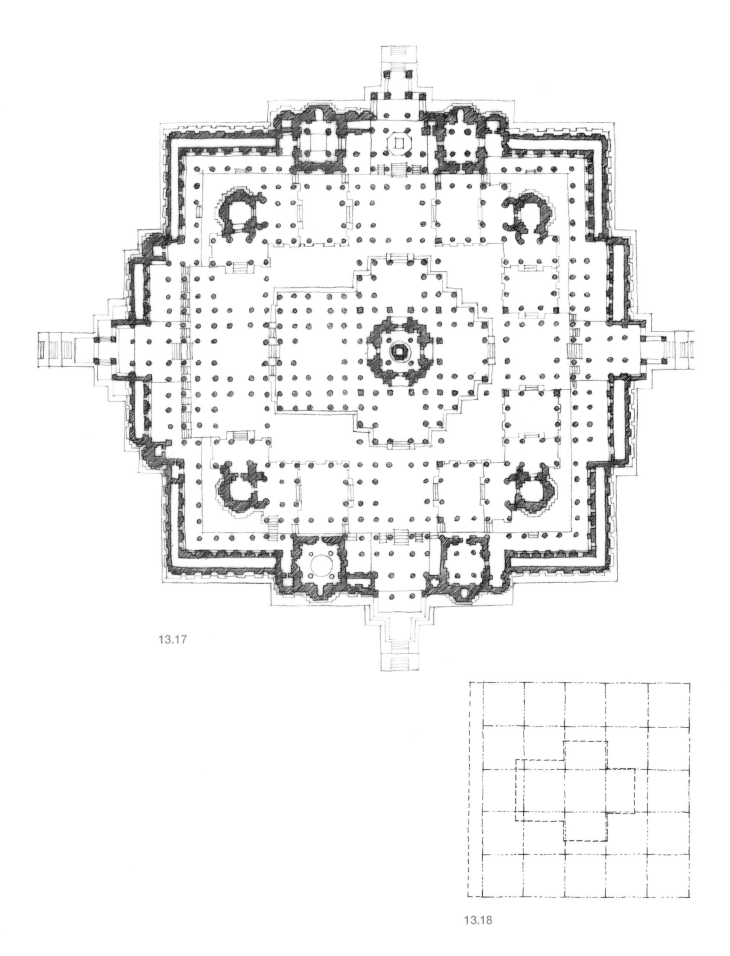

13.17

13.18

13.19

Villa Snellman, Djursholm, Sweden, 1918. Erik Gunnar Asplund. Plan.

In this small country house, an L-shaped plan separates an entry court from a garden. It is a two-story main building (with entry facade and garden elevation) with a one-story service wing. The service wing is rotated a few degrees inward for no apparent reason.

13.20

Villa Snellman. Elevations.

The only ornament on the elevations is a series of stucco swags, corresponding vertically with the windows of the entry facade and located between the windows on the garden elevation. Otherwise, the design of the exterior is austere. Asplund detailed the windows to appear to be virtually continuous with the outer surface of the walls, suggesting a smooth, uninterrupted skin on the building, a feature that is a key to recognizing Asplund's Mannerist deformation of the building. On the garden elevation (bottom drawing) the three windows of the first floor, second floor, and attic at the far left are aligned, thus establishing the norm. The next three are not; the first-floor window slips slightly to the right of the windows above. In each of the next three sets of windows, the first-floor window slips to an increasing degree. This progression of misalignments of windows on the first floor is in response to the slight inward rotation of the one-story service wing, as if it has stretched the skin of the first floor without disturbing the upper part of the elevation. The plan of the first floor reveals no reasons on the interior for the phenomenon.

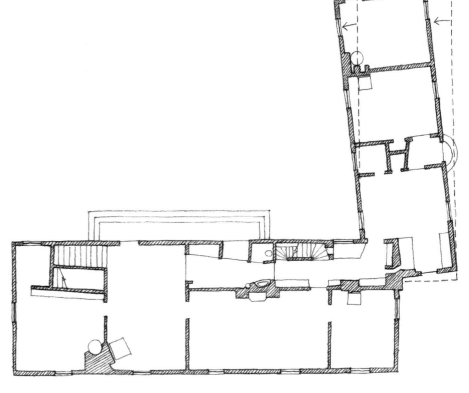

13.19

13.20

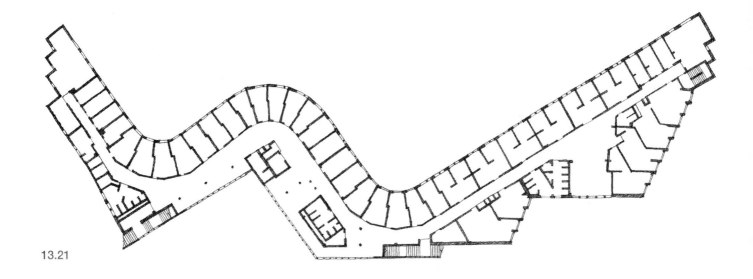

13.21

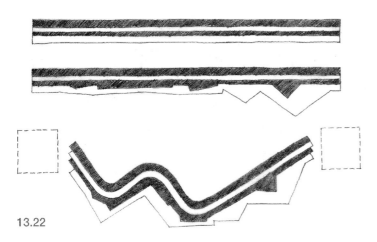

13.22

13.21
Baker House, Massachusetts Institute of Technology, Cambridge, 1949. Alvar Aalto. Plan.

One of only two projects by Aalto in the United States, Baker House was a successful solution to a difficult problem. The site was a narrow strip of land along the Charles River between two historic buildings. The program for 350 students would have required a much taller building than zoning permitted if it had been a simple Modernist slab. Instead, Aalto organized the building in layers, with the layer of private rooms facing the Charles, and then bent the form to fit the site. Thus, the length of the building is about 35 percent greater than the length of the site, and every room retains a view of the river, but obliquely. The overfired brick of its exterior gives it a rugged appearance yet relates it well to its two brick neighbors. The brick also appears within the interior to emphasize the impression of layers of walls.

13.22
Baker House. Composition.

The method Aalto used to shape Baker House was similar to what he used to form his bent plywood furniture. First, he assigned the parts of the program to four layers of a straight, linear scheme organized from the most private to the most public uses. Second, he allowed the more public spaces to deform in response to their requirements. Third, he bent this form to fit the site, bracketed by the two historic buildings. In this process, Aalto allowed the four layers of the plan to slide past one another, exposing their ends to emphasize the formal order of the building.

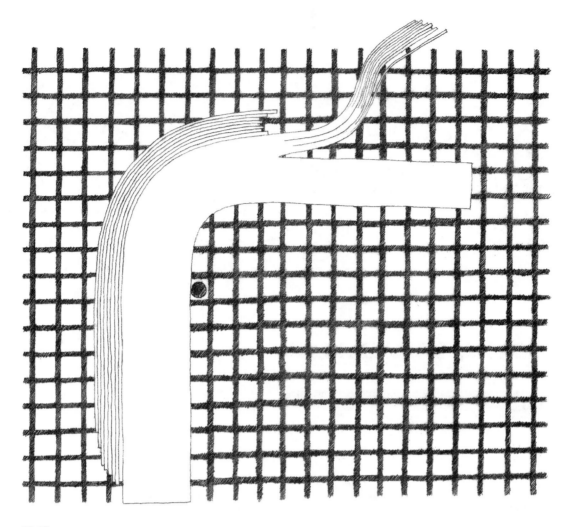

13.23

13.23
Bentwood Exhibit, Finnish Pavilion, Paris, 1937. Alvar Aalto.

Alvar and Aino Aalto began marketing their designs for bentwood furniture in 1935, and the Finnish pavilion at the Paris Exposition of 1937 displayed the use of wood for many products of modern design, including the work of the Aaltos. This exhibit illustrated the plastic qualities of thin laminations of birch, a technique that the Aaltos used in most of their furniture designs. In this example, note how the varying lengths of the laminations remained exposed, as Alvar Aalto also implied in the form of Baker House.

13.24
Town Hall, Saynatsalo, Finland, 1952. Alvar Aalto. Section and plan.

The Saynatsalo Town Hall is primarily a range of offices surrounding a courtyard on three sides with a library on the fourth. The principal meeting room, a tower form, dominates the silhouette. The section reveals that the building and its courtyard sit on an artificial hill slightly above the surrounding topography. Two stairs descend from the courtyard, one civilized and the other wild. The material palette is brick, wood, and glass. The courtyard plan produces a strong sense of enclosure and thus a focus for the community, yet the complex form of the building as a three-dimensional, composite figure in the landscape produces a sense of openness. The principal dimension of the building's character emerges from the tension between completeness and incompleteness.

13.25
Town Hall, Saynatsalo. Composition.

Throughout most of his career, Aalto was interested in the contest of two forces: the ordering force of civilization manifested primarily in architecture, and the entropic force of nature that inevitably tears humanity's works apart. He illustrated this view with many sketches in his travel notebooks of ruined Classical buildings in wild landscapes. The plan of the town hall type in northern Europe is a stable form that is virtually a sign for civilization—a square building with a courtyard. Starting with the traditional type, Aalto then broke off one side of the square for the library, since it is programmatically distinct from the operations of the town government. The break responds, metaphorically, to the force of the earth welling up beneath the building and pushing into the center opening, a vector that splits the building, forcing the library section away and spilling the earth out of the center to form the two staircases.

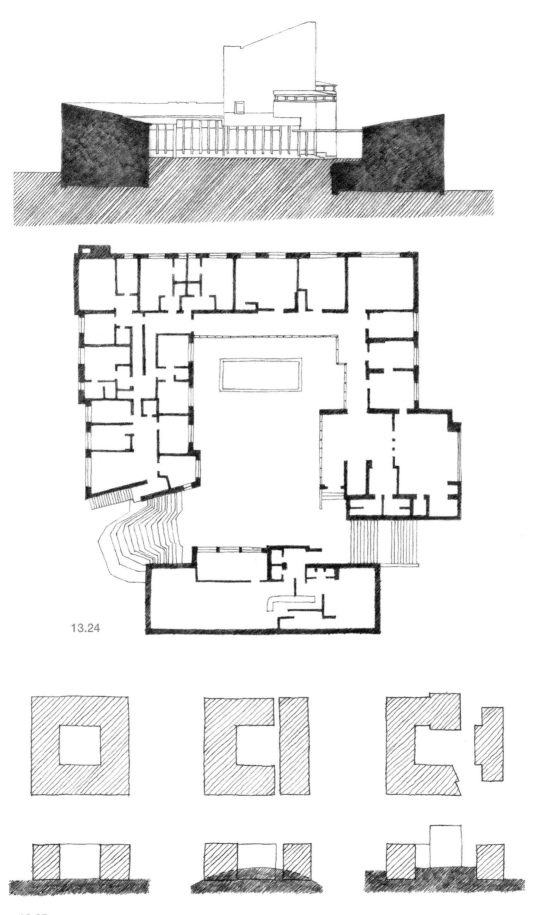

13.24

13.25

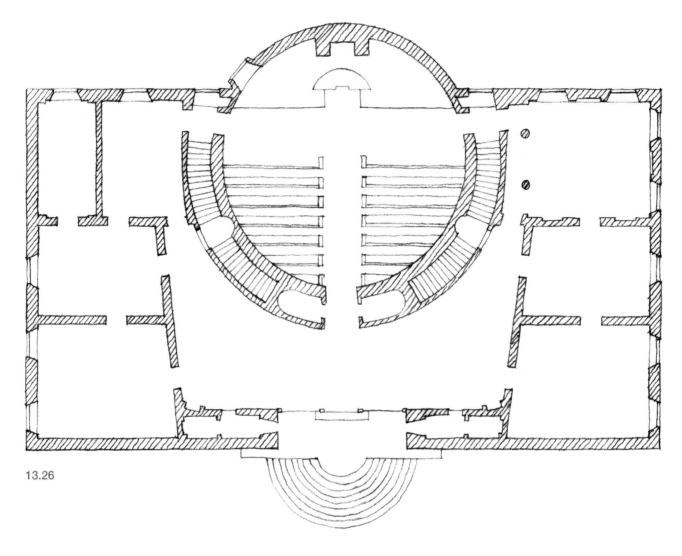

13.26

13.26
Courthouse, Lister County, Sweden, 1921. Erik Gunnar Asplund. Plan.

A recurring theme in Asplund's work is the insertion of a cylinder into a rectangular frame (the Stockholm Library, for example). In this small building, the courtroom is the cylindrical form that appears to reside tenuously within the rectangular body of the building as a whole, producing a deformation of the interior. The thick wall of the cylinder contains stairs that serve a residence for the magistrate on the second floor. The suggestion of a pregnant form is overt, a theme repeated in details, including bulbous balusters at the ends of the courtroom benches.

13.27

Lala Mustafa Pasha Complex, Ilgin, Turkey, 1567. Mimar Sinan. Plan.

Sinan was one of the most prolific architects in history, with hundreds of projects to his name. Many were composite programs such as this one: a madrassa, market, and mosque. Though the mosque is small, Sinan emphasized it by inserting it into a courtyard and deforming the flanking rows of cellular spaces, thus making it an object within a frame of surrounding buildings.

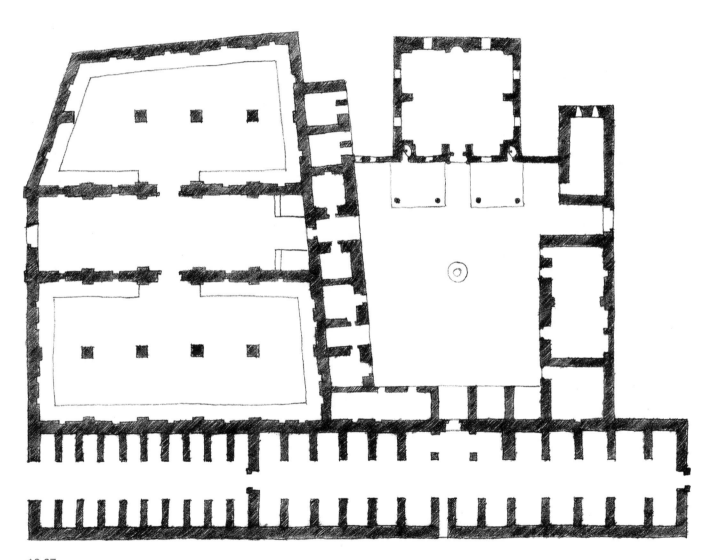

13.27

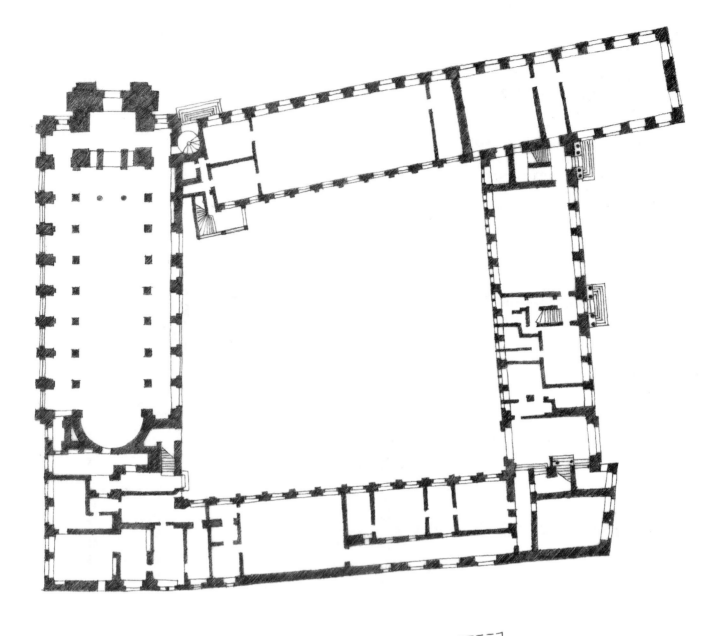

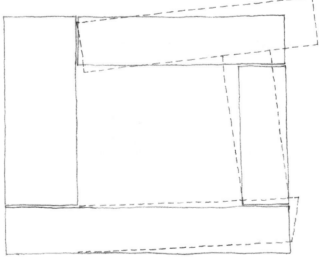

13.28

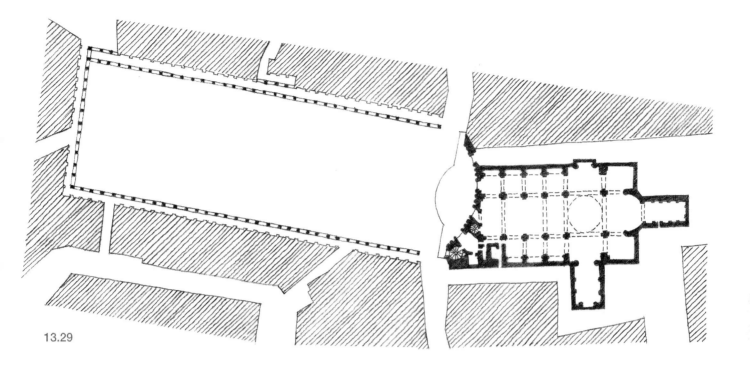

13.29

13.28
University of Würtzburg, 1582–91. Julius Echter. Plan.

The plan is a compromise between two design objectives: organizing the program rationally with respect to four functional rectangles surrounding a large central court and responding to the irregular geometry of the context. The architect took advantage of the context to accentuate the four separate components of the composition as disconnected sides of a rectangular frame.

13.29
Church and Piazza of Saint Ambrogio, Vigevano, Italy, 1684. Plan.

When the formal, Renaissance piazza emerged from a medieval market, there was a need to regularize all four sides of it, including one end occupied by a medieval church. However, the church facade was oblique and off-center with respect to the piazza. The solution was to eliminate the narthex of the church and construct a semicircular screen wall that terminated the longitudinal axis of the piazza symmetrically. The wall, though, does not correspond with the form of the church. Note that the principal church entrance is merely one of four openings in the screen wall. Thus, the church deformed to fit the new scenographic conception of the piazza.

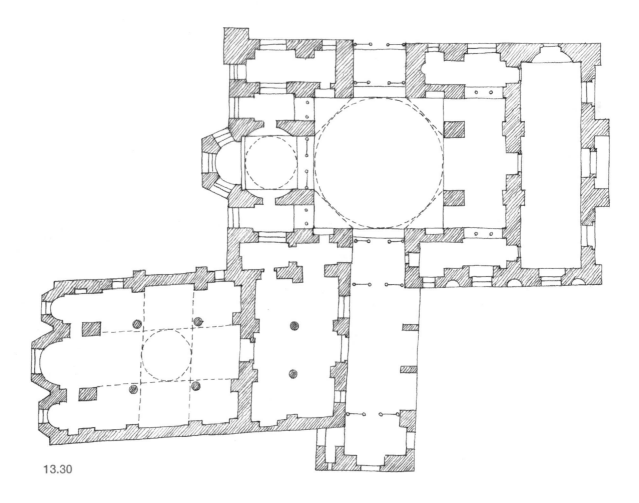

13.30

13.30
Monastery of Hosios Loukas, Phocis, Greece, 10th and 11th centuries. Plan.

The difference in the designs of these two conjoined buildings is striking, and it reveals a medieval revolution in thinking about architectural space. The 10th-century shrine of Theotokos (lower left) has a slightly skewed plan that follows the early and conservative Byzantine form of three barrel-vaulted aisles, each terminating in an apse. Construction of the larger Catholicon followed a hundred years later, connecting it to the older building in a graceful deformation of a corner chapel and a new porch that serves both buildings. The more ambitious Catholicon design, with its sizable central dome, used the Armenian and Persian method of squinches that converted the square plan to an intermediate octagon from which the dome could spring. The result is a greater emphasis on the central space as the intersection of the longitudinal and transverse axes.

13.31
House in Dinkelsbühl, Germany, 18th century. Ground-floor plan.

The organization of the interior of the house, otherwise typical of German merchants' houses of the period, reveals a deformation of interior spaces to accommodate differences between the facades on two parallel streets, one a four-bay design and the other an eight-bay design.

13.32
Pearl Mosque, Red Fort, Delhi, India, 1659.

In 1638 the Mughal emperor Shah Jahan transferred his capital from Agra to Delhi and laid the foundations of Shahjahanabad, the central feature of which was the Red Fort. His successor, Aurangzeb, constructed the Pearl Mosque, or Moti Masjid, for his personal use. It is a small white marble building, rectangular in plan, aligned on the exterior with the grid of the fort and its palaces. However, its interior shifts its orientation to align with Mecca. The difference in alignments is not noticeable as one enters the building through a crooked passage. This subtle deformation mediates between two orders—secular and religious.

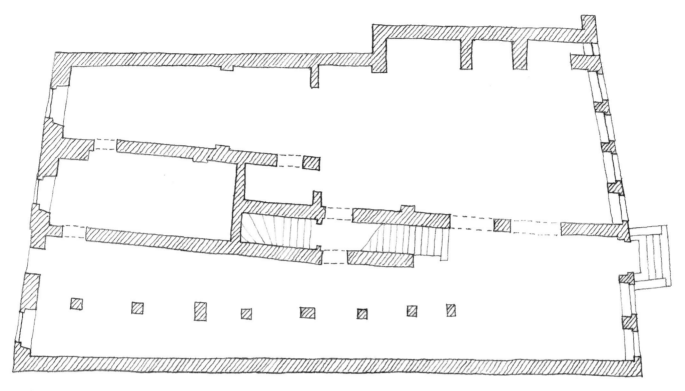

13.31

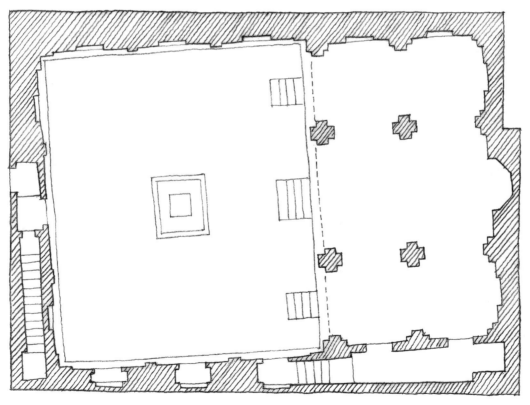

13.32

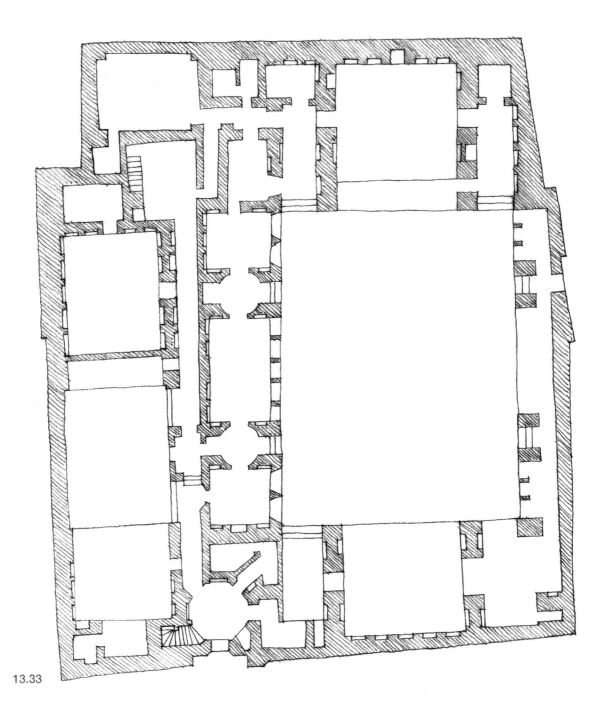

13.33

13.33
Rasoulian House, Isfahan, Iran, 19th century. Plan.
The plan of the Rasoulian House demonstrates the Persian genius for fitting a regular composition into an irregular frame by means of subtle distortions of forms and spaces. It is a courtyard house with two large iwans, rooms closed on three sides and open on the fourth side to the courtyard. These produce the communal living zone. The private zone has a separate system of circulation.

13.34
Rasoulian House. Entrance.
Typically, the entrance to a Persian house is a crooked passage that leads to one corner of the main courtyard. In this case, a subsidiary passage leads to the private quarters.

13.35
Rasoulian House. Formal adjustments.
Poché adjusts the regular order and orientation of spaces to the irregular shape of the lot. This adjustment is imperceptible as one walks through the house.

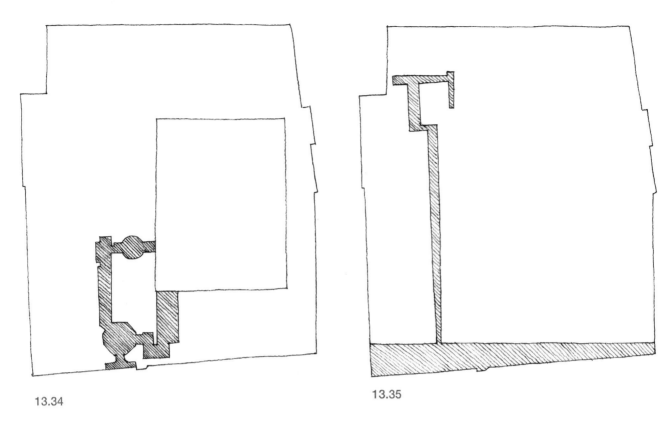

13.34

13.35

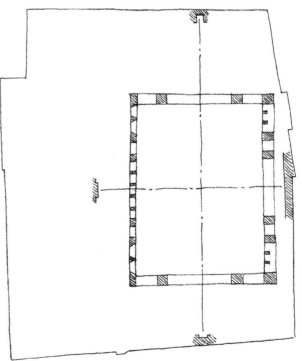

13.36

13.36
Rasoulian House. Symmetry.
The formal bilateral symmetry of the main
courtyard, with two axes relating to terminating
walls, creates an order for the house that over-
whelms all of the idiosyncrasies in the subsidiary patterns of the plan.

13.37
Küçük Ayasofya Camii, Istanbul, Turkey, 527–36 CE. Plan.

Converted into a mosque during the reign of the Ottoman sultan Bayezid II in the early 16th century, the building was originally the Byzantine Church of Saints Sergius and Bacchos constructed for the emperor Justinian within his palace. Its curiously distorted form probably resulted from the need to change the plan during construction to connect it to the Basilica of Saints Peter and Paul (later destroyed) as well as to a part of the palace wall. Spatially and structurally, it was a precursor of the Hagia Sophia and of San Vitale at Ravenna. It is an octagon within a square, a double-height octagonal space in the center composed of eight piers. Intermediate columns support a dome. Its four diagonal sides (facing the corners of the enclosing outer shell) form semicircular niches, or exedrae, crowned with semidomes above an upper gallery, a device that makes the interior seem considerably larger than its actual dimensions. Unlike the basilica type, the centrally focused Church of Saints Sergius and Bacchos did not employ a processional; instead, the emperor, as both secular ruler and high priest, occupied the center of the space, with his court surrounding him on the ground floor and in the gallery above.

13.38
Küçük Ayasofya Camii. Shifted plan.

The outer shell is a compound form resulting from the superimposition of two squares, most noticeable on the exterior at the double southeast corner and along the slightly bent north elevation. Each square has its own central axis, but the two axes converge at the center of the principal western entrance.

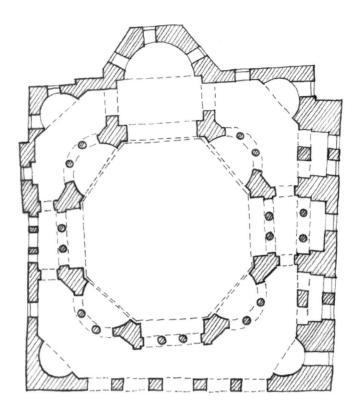

13.37

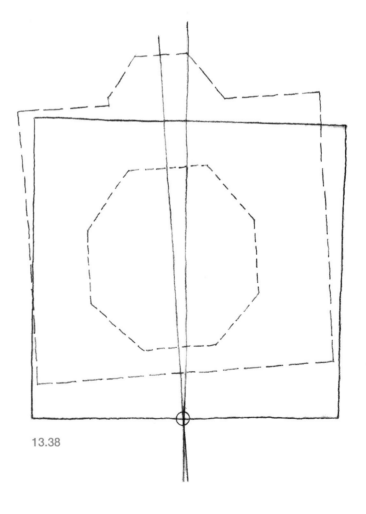

13.38

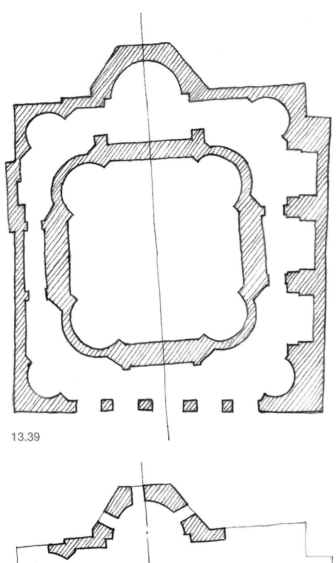

13.39

13.39
Küçük Ayasofya Camii. Ambulatory.

As one enters the building through the western portal on axis with the eastern apse, the deformation of the outer shell is not noticeable. The ambulatory visually absorbs the deformation of the shell and the shifted axes, and it is difficult to compare dimensions across the plan as one walks around the central domed space. The inner octagonal wall, alternating between flat and curved surfaces, acts as a gigantic screen that modifies the sunlight that pierces the outer rectangular shell.

13.40
Küçük Ayasofya Camii. Cross-axis.

A second entrance on the north elevation once led to a former palace garden. This was on axis with a chapel set into the south wall of the building shell, and narrow segments of the ambulatory at these two points accommodate the differences in orientation between shell and core.

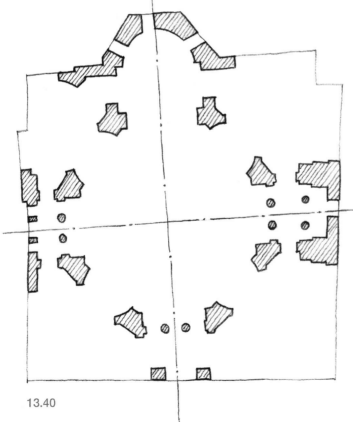

13.40

CONCLUSION

THE PURPOSE OF THIS BOOK HAS BEEN TO DEMONSTRATE a type of design research focused on underlying organizational strategies rather than on the appearances of buildings, their styles, or aesthetic qualities. The topics I have chosen are not by any means comprehensive, and I readily admit that this collection of examples is exploratory. Their purpose is to instigate a personal investigation of architectural design based on a particular assumption: without denying individual creativity and innovation, there is ample evidence of a canon of fundamental design strategies shared by architects worldwide; in fact, much of the process of design is devoted to discovering them and then producing variants of them appropriate for particular situations.

A close examination of the work of the greatest architects—Michelangelo and Le Corbusier, for example—reveals that much of their success was due to their ability to interpret these design strategies in fresh ways that made them seem new. As I have stated elsewhere in the book, embedding a new idea within a fundamental formal concept conveys a sense of familiarity, often at a subconscious level, that is the key to understanding and accepting the innovative aspects of the design. Michelangelo's design for the Basilica of Saint Peter was an imaginative and creative solution to a problem that many of the best architects of the time had failed to master. The brilliance of his solution lay largely in the clarity of the underlying order he imposed on the plan and the rigor with which he forced all other aspects of the design to submit to that concept. However, that order was not new. It was an ancient idea, derived from the Pantheon to be sure, but also virtually universal, as we find it as well in many projects in other cultures and other times. Similarly, Le Corbusier's design of the Villa Savoy was a distillation of his compelling theoretical ideas about architecture, and it established a new paradigm for the Modernist house. It was, however, not new at a fundamental level. It was essentially Classicist, and virtually identical in its basic tripartite organization with vernacular buildings such as the granary I show in Thailand.

As I warned at the beginning of this book, the categories I have used are simply to loosely organize the material, not to create a taxonomy of types. It will become obvious as one uses the book that most, if not all, of the buildings could be discussed under various headings. For example, it may be useful to study a building as a spinal plan, or as layered, or as a frame and object simultaneously. These are not contradictory, but rather conceptual dimensions of a complex form. Finally, I hope the book can contribute to a greater appreciation among students of architecture for the analysis of precedent by revealing its usefulness and practicality, and by demonstrating a technique by which we can discover the truly great and enduring ideas of our predecessors.

GLOSSARY

aedicule: a small temple structure in the form of a gable roof supported by columns.

atrium: the central hall of a Roman house; a central room of a building, open to the sky.

bastide: a medieval French town generally laid out in a grid.

cardo: the north-south street bisecting a Roman *castrum* (see *decumanus*).

castrum: a rectangular plan used for Roman military garrisons and provincial towns.

cloister: the central open courtyard, with a surrounding ambulatory, in a medieval monastery.

cortile: a central courtyard with an ambulatory embedded in the mass of the surrounding building.

decumanus: the east-west street bisecting a Roman *castrum* (see *cardo*).

domus: a Roman or medieval European house type with a central hearth and surrounding shell.

ecotone: the transition zone between two adjacent ecological communities.

en: Japanese term for the "in-between."

engawa: a veranda for a Japanese house that mediates between interior and exterior spaces.

fusuma: a system of sliding opaque and translucent partitions in a Japanese house.

gavit: a meeting hall in front of a medieval Armenian church.

geomorphic: of or relating to the form of the earth.

haremlik: the part of an Arabic or Persian house devoted to private family functions.

hierophany: a condition that separates sacred space from profane space.

hôtel particulaire: an upper-class French urban house, generally from the 17th to the 19th centuries.

iwan: a roofed or vaulted hall open at one end.

ken: a Japanese planning module in the proportion of 1:2.

kiva: a Pueblo Indian ceremonial structure that is partially underground.

lingam: a stylized phallic symbol associated with the Hindu god Shiva.

madrassa: an Islamic collegiate school often associated with a mosque.

maidan: a large open public space in Arabic and Persian towns and cities.

Mamluk: member of an Egyptian military class, originally Caucasian slave soldiers who converted to Islam.

mandala: a graphic geometric symbol used in Hinduism and Buddhism as an aid to meditation.

maristan: a hospital or infirmary in Arabic and Persian cultures.

martyrium: an early Christian building used as a burial chamber or to store the relics of martyrs.

mihrab: a niche in a mosque denoting the direction of Mecca.

Mughal: a lineage of Central Asian people who invaded northern India in the 16th century.

orthogonal: a pattern of lines intersecting at right angles.

palazzo: a large Italian residence.

pendentive: a triangular, spherical section of vaulting intermediary between a square plan and the circular base of a dome.

piloti: a slender column.

poché: solid masonry or compact secondary spaces used to shape major spaces in a building plan.

qibla: the wall in a mosque indicating the direction of prayer toward Mecca.

quincunx: a pattern of five parts in a nine-square grid consisting of the center and the four corners

ramada: a building type with a porch or terrace embedded into the body of the building.

raumplan: a type of plan espoused by Adolf Loos that organizes spaces independently, not by floor level.

rotunda: a building or building part that is round inside and out.

sabil: a public fountain in Arabic and Persian towns and cities.

salamlik: the part of an Arabic or Persian house dedicated to the reception of (generally male) guests.

salt box: a traditional house type of colonial New England with a simple gable roof sloping toward the front and the back.

squinch: a support across the corner of a rectangular room to carry a dome or vault above.

submedieval: a transitional period retaining some medieval characteristics.

syncretism: a coalescence of different, often conflicting, systems of belief.

synoecism: a joining together of several small communities into a single political union.

trabeation: a structure composed of columns and beams.

vesica: a geometric figure formed by the intersection of two identical circles, the circumference of each of which passes through the center of the other.

yoni: a Hindu symbol of a stylized vulva representing the god Shakti.

BIBLIOGRAPHY

Allen, Edward. *Stone Shelters*. Cambridge, MA: MIT Press, 1969.

Bachmann, Walter. *Kirchen und Moscheen in Armenien und Kurdistan*. Leipzig: J. C. Hinrichs, 1913.

Baker, Geoffrey H. *Le Corbusier, Analysis of Form*. New York: Van Nostrand Reinhold, 1984.

Baker, Philippa, ed. *Architecture and Polyphony*. London: Thames & Hudson, 2004. (Aga Khan Award for Architecture.)

Baldeweg, J. N. *Juan Navarro Baldeweg*. Corte Madera, CA: Gingko, 2001.

Bess, Phillip. *City Baseball Magic*. Minneapolis: Minneapolis Review of Baseball, 1989.

Binding, Günther. *Architektonische Formenlehre*. Darmstadt: Wissenschaftliche Buchgesellschaft, 1980.

Borie, Alain, Pierre Micheloni, and Pierre Pinon. *Forme et Déformation*. Paris: École Nationale Supérieure des Beaux Arts, 1984.

Borsi, Franco. *Leon Battista Alberti*. New York: Elektra/Rizzoli, 1989.

Büttner, H., and G. Meissner. *Town Houses of Europe*. New York: St. Martin's, 1982.

Correa, Charles. *Charles Correa*. Singapore: (Mimar) Concept Media, 1984.

Creswell, K. A. C. *The Muslim Architecture of Egypt*. Oxford: Clarendon, 1952.

Curtis, William. *Balkrishna Doshi: An Architecture for India*. New York: Rizzoli, 1988.

Davidson, C. ed. *Legacies for the Future: Contemporary Architecture in Islamic Societies*. London: Thames & Hudson, 1998 (Aga Khan Award for Architecture).

Dennis, Michael. *Court and Garden*. Cambridge, MA: MIT Press, 1986.

DiSalvo, Mario. *Churches of Ethiopia: The Monastery of Nārgā Sellasē*. Milan: Skira, 1999.

Eliade, Mercea. *The Sacred and the Profane*. New York: Harcourt Brace Jovanovitch, 1987.

Elbroch, Mark. *Animal Skulls: A Guide to North American Species*. Mechanicsburg, PA: Stackpole, 2006.

Eyck, Aldo van. *Aldo van Eyck, Works*. Basel: Birkhäuser Verlag, 1999.

Frampton, Kenneth, Charles Correa, and David Robson, eds. *Modernity and Community: Architecture in the Islamic World*. Geneva: Aga Khan Award for Architecture, 2002.

Garlake, Peter S. *Great Zimbabwe*. New York: Stein and Day, 1973.

Ginouvès, René, and Roland Martin. *Dictionnaire méthodique de l'architecture grecque et romaine*. Rome: École Française de Rome, 1985.

Gottfried, Herbert, and Jan Jennings. *American Vernacular Design, 1870–1940*. New York: Van Nostrand Reinhold, 1985.

Guidoni, Enrico. *Primitive Architecture*. New York: Harry N. Abrams, 1975.

Hallet, Stanley Ira, and Rafi Samizay. *Traditional Architecture of Afghanistan*. New York: Garland STPM, 1980.

Hoag, John D. *Western Islamic Architecture*. New York: Braziller, 1963.

Hubka, Thomas C. *Resplendent Synagogue*. Lebanon, NH: Brandeis University Press and University Press of New England, 2003.

Hughes, Robert. *Nothing if Not Critical: Selected Essays on Art and Artists*. New York: Knopf, 1990.

Koester, Helmut. *Pergamon, Citadel of the Gods*. Harrisburg, PA: Trinity, 1998.

Ladurie, Emmanuel Le Roy. *Montaillou*. New York: Penguin, 1980.

MacKay-Lyons, Brian. *Brian MacKay-Lyons*. Halifax, NS: TUNS, 1998.

Manoukian, Armen, and Agopik Manoukian, eds. *G(h)eghard*. Milan: Edizioni Ares, 1973.

_____. *Hakhpat*. Milan: Edizioni Ares, 1968.

_____. *Sanahin*. Milan: Edizioni Ares, 1970.

Martin, Roland. *L'Urbanisme dans la Grèce antique*. Paris: Editions Picard, 1974.

Mayer, Eugen, *Das Bürgerhaus zwischen Ostalb und oberer Tauber*. Tübingen: Wasmuth, 1978.

Mignot, Claude. *Architecture of the Nineteenth Century in Europe*. Tr. by D. Q. Stevenson. New York: Rizzoli, 1984.

Mitchell, George, ed. *Architecture of the Islamic World*. London: Thames and Hudson, 1978.

Morgan, William N. *Prehistoric Architecture in Micronesia*. Austin: University of Texas Press, 1988.

———. *Ancient Architecture of the Southwest.* Austin: University of Texas Press, 1994.

Morris, A. E. J. *History of Urban Form.* New York: John Wiley & Sons, 1974.

Netzer, Ehud. *Die Paläste der Hasmonäer und Herodes' des Grossen*. Mainz am Rhein: Verlag Philipp von Zabern, 1999.

Ojeda, Oscar Riera, ed. *Ten Houses: Christian De Groote*. Cincinnati: North Light, 1999.

———. *Ten Houses: Lacroze Miguens Prati*. Rockport, MA: Rockport, 1997.

Palmer, Sarah, ed. *Houses: The Architecture of Nagle, Hartray, Danker, Kagan, McKay, Penney.* New York: Edizioni, 2005.

Poleggi, Ennio. *Strada Nuova*. Genoa: Sayep Editrice, 1968.

Revault, Jacques, and Bernard Maury. *Palais et Maisons du Caire*. Cairo: Institut Français d'Archéologie Orientale, 1975-79.

Roller, Duane. *The Buiding Program of Herod the Great*. Berkeley: University of California Press, 1998.

Sachdev, Vibhuti, and Giles Tillotson. *Building Jaipur: The Making of an Indian City*. London: Reaktion, 2002.

Saint, Andrew. *Richard Norman Shaw*. New Haven: Yale University Press, 1977.

Schoenauer, Norbert. *6,000 Years of Housing*. New York: W. W. Norton, 2000.

Smith, Peter. *Houses of the Welsh Countryside*. London: H. M. S. O., 1975.

Strobel, Richard. *Das Bürgerhaus in Regensburg*. Tübingen: Wasmuth, 1976.

Tadgell, Christopher. *The History of Architecture in India*. London: Phaidon, 1990.

Thompson, D'Arcy W. *On Growth and Form*. Cambridge, UK: Cambridge University Press, 1961.

Thorne, Martha. *Rafael Moneo, Audrey Jones Beck Building, The Museum of Fine Arts, Houston*. Stuttgart, London: Edition Axel Menges, 2000.

Toman, Rolf, ed. *The Art of Gothic*. Königswinter: Könemann, 2004.

Upton, Dell, and John Michael Vlach. *Common Places: Readings in American Vernacular Architecture*. Athens: University of Georgia Press, 1986.

Villanueva, Paulina, and Macia Pinto. *Carlos Raúl Villanueva*. New York: Princeton Architectural Press, 2000.

Volwahsen, Andreas. *Cosmic Architecture in India: The Astronomical Monuments of Maharaja Jai Singh II*. Munich: Prestel-Verlag, 2001.

von Meiss, Pierre. *Elements of Architecture: From Form to Place*. New York: Van Nostrand Reinhold, 1990 .

Ward-Perkins, J. B. *Roman Imperial Architecture*. New York: Penguin, 1970.

Wrede, Stuart. *The Architecture of Erik Gunnar Asplund*. Cambridge, MA: MIT Press, 1983.

INDEX OF BUILDINGS

Abbey of Royaumont (France) 47

Abbey of St. Martin (Canigou, France) 48–49

Abbot's Residence (Villiers-Cotterets, France) 222

Acropolis of Pergamon (Greece) 239

Adinatha Temple (Ranakpur, India) 303

Adler House proposal (Philadelphia, Pennsylvania) 76

Ahmed Pasha Caramanli Mosque (Tripoli, Libya) 11

Al-Hakim Mosque (Isphahan, Iran) 264–266

Alkali Ridge Ruins (San Juan Valley, Utah) 138

Al-Razzāz House (Cairo, Egypt) 208–209

American Academy of Arts and Sciences (Cambridge, Massachusetts) 192–193

American Urban Baseball Parks (1909–1923) 43

Amin Hodja Mosque (Turpan, Xinjiang, China) 200–201

Amir Khayrbak Complex (Cairo, Egypt) 131

Andrew Melville Halls (St. Andrews, Scotland) 138

Apartment House "Martinelli," (Lugano, Switzerland) 255

Art Center (Des Moines, Iowa) 286–287

Art Tower (Mito, Japan) 237

Artists' Studios by F. & E. Barth (Stuttgart, Germany) 131

Asklepeion (Pergamon, Turkey) 160–161

Baensch House (Spandau, Germany) 109

Bagsværd Community Church (Bagsværd, Denmark) 155

Baker House, MIT (Cambridge, Massachussetts) 305

Baqeri House (Gorgân, Iran) 210–211

Baradari of Sikander Lodi (Uttar Pardesh, India) 67

Barthels Hof, No. 8 Markt (Leipzig, Germany) 118

Basilica of St Peter, Antonio da Sangallo (Rome, Italy) 70

Basilica of St. Peter, Donato Bramante (Rome, Italy) 70

Basilica of St. Peter, Michelangelo Buonarotti (Rome, Italy) 71–72

Bastides, France (Villeréal, Eymet, Domme, Lalinde, Beaumont, Villefranche-du-Périgord) 50–51

Bath House by Louis Kahn (Trenton, New Jersey) 75

Baths at Fatepur Sikri (Uttar Pradesh, India) 245

Bazaar (Kashan, Iran) 227

Beck Addition, Museum of Fine Arts (Houston, Texas) 195

Bernstein House (Great Neck, New York) 189

Bibliothèque Nationale (Paris, France) 64

Block and Ramada House Type 30–31

Brick Courtyard House proposal by Mies van der Rohe 18–20

Ca d'Oro (Venice, Italy) 268–269

Carcassonne (Languedoc, France) 52

Carruba Mosque (Tripoli, Libya) 11

Cathedral of Our Lady of the Angels (Los Angeles, California) 169

Cathedral of St. Gall (St. Gallen, Switzerland) 218

Cathedral of St. Michael (Hildesheim, Germany) 8

Centre Le Corbusier (Zurich, Switzerland) 153

Certosa del Galluzzo (Florence, Italy) 15–17

Chapel by Jorge Cámera (Tabasco, Mexico) 302

Chapel of the Burghof (Rheda, Germany) 150

Citrohan House proposal by Le Corbusier 152

Centre Le Corbusier (Zurich, Switzerland) 153

Church and Piazza of St. Ambrogio (Vigevano, Italy) 311

Church of Nārgā Sellasē Island, Ethiopia 97

Church of Santa Sophia (Benevento, Italy) 108

Church of S. Aspais (Melun, France) 299

Church of S. Maria in Campitelli (Rome, Italy) 82

Cistercian Monastery schematic plan 46

Classical Greek Temple schematic 144
Communication Tower 159
Comparison: house plans in Bergamo,
    Italy and Konya, Turkey 58
Comparison: two houses in Wales 63
Complex of Sultan al-Nasir
    Muhammad ibn Qal_'un (Cairo,
    Egypt) 285
Compound House (Kandahar,
    Afghanistan) 252
Concert Hall (Göteburg, Sweden) 167
Convention Center by Juan Navarro
    Baldweg (Salzburg, Germany) 168
Core and Colonnade house type
    30–31
Cottage by Nagle Hartray (Green
    Lake, Wisconsin) 86–87
Courthouse by E. G. Asplund (Lister
    County, Sweden) 308
Courtyard (Turpan, Xinjiang, China)
    217
Courtyard house type 38
Courtyard house (Cairo, Egypt) 39
Crescent Park (London, United
    Kingdom) 270
Crypt, Abbey of St. Germain (Auxerre,
    France) 150

Dana House (New Canaan,
    Connecticut) 189
Daniel Gin (Lubbock, Texas) 93
Datia Palace (Uttar Pradesh, India) 55
Der alte Bau (Geislingen, Germany)
    184
Diocletian's Palace (Split, Dalmatia) 57
Dome of the Rock (Jerusalem, Israel)
    100
Dominican Convent (Media,
    Pennsylvania) 175
Domus (Romania) 151
Double Shotgun cottage (New
    Orleans, Louisiana) 129
Dover Castle Keep (Kent, United
    Kingdom) 246–247

Église du Dôme, St. Louis des Invalides
    (Paris, France) 73

Farmhouse, Selva di Fasano
    (Alberobello, Italy) 206
First Unitarian Church and School
    (Rochester, New York) 253
Fletcher-Page House (New South
    Wales, Australia) 130
Franchetti House (Sardinia) 212–214
Freeman Residence (Grand Rapids,
    Michigan) 107
Free University (Berlin, Germany) 187

Gandhi Smarak Sangrahalayla
    (Ahmedabad, India) 188
General Chamber of Audit (The
    Hague, Netherlands) 140
Governor's Residence (Chandigarh,
    India) 165
Granary (Portugal) 92
Granary of the Fali People (Cameroon)
    151
Great Mosque (Isphahan, Iran) 262–
    264
Great Zimbabwe, Great Enclosure
    (Zimbabwe) 238
Great Zimbabwe, Hill Complex
    (Zimbabwe) 238
Greenham Lodge (Newbury, United
    Kingdom) 116
Gurgi Mosque (Tripoli, Libya) 11
Gurunsi house compound (Upper
    Volta) 234

Hagia Sophia (Istanbul, Turkey)
    145
Hajar Qin Temple (Malta) 202
Hill House (Helensburgh, Scotland)
    117
Hospital Ward (Antwerp, Belgium)
    132
Hostel, Sanctuary of Asklepios
    (Epidaurus, Greece) 54
Hôtel d'Amelot (Paris, France) 219
Hôtel de Beauvais (Paris, France) 220–
    221
House Compound (Cameroon) 204
House by Brian MacKay-Lyons (Upper
    Kingsbury, Nova Scotia) 62

House by Christian De Groote (El
    Pangue, Chile) 84
House by Christian De Groote
    (Villarica, Chile) 84
House in Gorriti Street (Buenos Aires,
    Argentina) 153
House of Mantegna (Mantua, Italy)
    164, 218
House of Rondane Bey (Tunis,
    Tunisia) 7
House in Dinkelsbühl (Germany)
    313
House of El Daouletti (Tunis, Tunisia)
    298
House in El Talar (Chascomus,
    Argentina) 88–89
House in Fez (Morocco) 104
House in San Isidro (Buenos Aires,
    Argentina) 256–257
House type (Yap Islands, Micronesia)
    36
House of Ibn Arafa (Tunis, Tunisia)
    12–14
House no. VI in al-Fustat (Cairo,
    Egypt) 103
House plan variations by Hiromi Fuji
    59
Hurva Synagogue proposal (Jerusalem,
    Israel) 254
Husain - Doshi Gufa (Ahmedabad,
    India) 206

Infants' School proposal by A. & P.
    Smithson (Wokingham, United
    Kingdom) 139

Jaipur (Rajasthan, India) 77
Jami Masjid (Gulbarga, India) 184
Jawahar Kala Kendra, Jaipur
    (Rajasthan, India) 78
Josef Eskers House (Krefeld, Germany)
    23–28

Kaedi Regional Hospital Addition
    (Kaedi, Mauritania) 137
Koto-in Temple (Kyoto, Japan) 133
Krak des Chevaliers (Syria) 262–263

Küçük Ayasofya Cami (Istanbul, Turkey) 316–317

Labbezanga (Mali) 205
Lala Mustafa Pasha Complex (Ilgin, Turkey) 309
Länderbank, (Vienna, Austria) 223
Latte House Type (Tinian, Micronesia) 37
Leicester University Engineering School (Leicester, United Kingdom) 226
Leper Colony (Chopta Taluka, India) 263
Lingaraja Temple (Bhubaneswar, India) 128–129

Madrasa and Mausoleum Group (Cairo, Egypt) 248–249
Magney House (New South Wales, Australia) 130
Mäntyniemi (Helsinki, Finland) 236
Masada (Israel) 261
Mausoleum of Santa Costanza (Rome, Italy) 101
Mercutt House (New South Wales, Australia) 86
Mobile Home (Colorado) 154
Monastery Church (Gračanica, Kosovo) 181
Monastery of Gheghard (Kotayk, Armenia) 244
Monastery of Hakhpat (Lori, Armenia) 224
Monastery of Hosios Lukas (Phocis, Greece) 312
Monastery of St. Catherine (Sinai, Egypt) 172
Morphology of Early Settler's Houses (Central Texas) 46
Mosque of Ibn Tulun (Cairo, Egypt) 146–147
Medieval Armenian Church Plan Types 245
Military Campaign Tent Compound of Emperor Akbar 124

Nagle House (Chicago, Illinois) 63
Nakayama House (Oita, Japan) 65
National School for Music (Havana, Cuba) 120
National School for the Plastic Arts (Havana, Cuba) 121
National School of Ballet (Havana, Cuba) 122
Necromanteion (Ephyra, Greece) 64
New Arabian House proposal (Riyadh, Saudi Arabia) 156
Ninomaru Palace, Nijo Castle (Kyoto, Japan) 134–135
Normal House/Deformed House 295
Nos. 3 to 17, Abwicklungen der Ostseite des Holm (Flensburg, Germany) 289–290
Notre Dame du Haut (Ronchamp, France) 278
Notre Dame-La-Grande (Poitiers, France) 163

Orphanage, Amstelveenseweg (Amsterdam, Netherlands) 186

Pantheon (Rome, Italy) 69
Palace at Jericho (Israel) 114–115
Palace of Albrechsburg (Germany) 236
Palazzo di Agostino Pallavicino (Genoa, Italy) 41
Palazzo di Baldassare (Genoa, Italy)
Palazzo Baldassarre (Genoa, Italy) 41
Palazzo di Giambattista Spinola (Genoa, Italy) 41
Palazzo di Luca Grimaldi (Genoa, Italy) 41
Palazzo di Tobia Pallavicino (Genoa, Italy) 41
Palazzo Rosso (Genoa, Italy) 41
Palazzo Rucellai (Florence, Italy) 267
Palestinian Redoubt 95
Parish Church (Greifensee, Switzerland) 300
Parochial Church (Attica, Greece) 162
Parson Capen House (Topsfield, Massachusetts) 152

Pearl Mosque, Red Fort (Delhi, India) 313
Phillips Exeter Academy Library (Exeter, New Hampshire) 74
Plan of Venice (Italy) 288

Raja Birbal Pavilion (Fatehpur Sikri, India) 182–183
Rasoulian House (Isphahan ,Iran) 196–197
Rasoulian House (Yazd, Iran) 314–315
Razvian House (Isphahan, Iran) 198–199
Reconstruction of the Souks proposal (Beirut, Lebanon) 173
Reliance Building (Chicago, Illinois) 271
Roman House (Volubilis, Morocco) 102
Rice Barn (Thailand) 92

Sabsiri House (Cairo, Egypt) 272
Sainsbury Wing of the National Gallery of Art (London, United Kingdom) 279
San Vitale (Ravenna, Italy) 98–99
Sanahin Monastery (Alaverdi, Armenia) 228–231
Sanctuary of Delphi (Greece) 240–241
São Bento Monastery (Rio de Janeiro, Brazil) 194
Schröder House (Utrecht, Netherlands) 9
Science Center proposal by Stirling and Wolford (Berlin, Germany) 176
Sculpture Pavilion (Arnheim, Netherlands) 85
Seigneurale (Segovia, Spain) 276–277
Semsi Ahmed Pasa Complex (Üsküdar, Turkey) 148
Serabit el-Khadim (Sinai, Egypt) 126
Shari el Mu'izz Li Din Illah (Cairo, Egypt) 123
Shed, Bin and Barn (Iowa) 217
Shoiken Teahouse (Katsura Villa, Kyoto, Japan) 23–28
Small Town Tavern (Iowa) 180

Souk el-Oued (Algeria) 185

Spanish Mission Churches (Upper Rio Grande, New Mexico) 42

Spinal Houses proposal 44–45

Step-well of Adalaj (Ahmedabad, India) 125

Stoa (Sikyon, Greece) 301

Stoa, eastern quay (Leptis Magna, Libya) 301

Stupa of Jiaohe (Xinjiang, China) 55

Süleymaniye (Istanbul, Turkey) 10

Sultan Hasan Mosque-Madrasa (Cairo, Egypt) 250–251

Taj Mahal, Agra (Uttar Pradesh, India) 68

Tayaba Compound (Burkina Faso) 202

Temple of Takeo (Angkor Wat, Cambodia) 149

Temple of Horus (Edfu, Egypt) 127

Thersileion Bouleuterion (Megalopolis, Arcadia, Greece) 106

Timgad (near Constantine, Algeria) 56

Tjibaou Cultural Center (Nouméa, New Caledonia) 83

Tomb of Ramses VI (Luxor, Egypt) 128

Tomb of Humayun (Delhi, India) 67

Town Hall (Saynatsalo, Finland) 22–23, 306–307

Tuwaiq Palace (Riyadh, Saudi Arabia) 119

Turpan street and house section (Xinjiang, China) 81

Tyuonyi (Frijoles Canyon, New Mexico) 96

Uffizi (Florence, Italy) 112

Unbuilt House by Hugo Häring 235

University of Caracas (Caracas, Venezuela) 113

University of Würtzburg (Germany) 310

Urban Infill House 02 (Milwaukee, Wisconsin) 170

Vidyadhar Nagar, Jaipur (Rajasthan, India) 78

Villa by Sverre Fehn (Norrköping, Sweden) 66

Villa Karma (Montreaux/Clarens, Switzerland) 105

Villa Lanza (Como, Italy) 90

Villa Savoye (Poissy-sur-Seine, France) 91

Villa Snellman (Djursholm, Sweden) 304

Village of Ramah (Ramah Valley, New Mexico) 190

Villa Henny (The Hague, Netherlands) 191

White House, Chelsea (London, (United Kingdom) 273–275

Williams-Wynn House (London, United Kingdom) 246

Winton Guest House (Wayzata, Minnesota) 234

Wolpa Synagogue (Poland) 155

Woodcarving Museum proposal (Inami, Japan) 177

Workers' Housing (Door County, Wisconsin) 130

Workshop Society Exhibition (Göteburg, Sweden) 112

Yale Center for British Art (New Haven Connecticut) 190

Yeşil Çami (Bursa, Turkey) 296–297

Zabel-Krüger-Damm Apartments (Berlin-Reinickendorf, Germany) 212

Ziegfeld Theater (New York, New York) 166